The Future
of American
Banking

The Future of American Banking

Managing for Change

David Rogers
Stern School of Business
New York University

McGraw-Hill, Inc.

New York   St. Louis   San Francisco   Auckland   Bogotá
Caracas   Lisbon   London   Madrid   Mexico   Milan
Montreal   New Delhi   Paris   San Juan   São Paulo
Singapore   Sydney   Tokyo   Toronto

Library of Congress Cataloging-in-Publication Data

Rogers, David, date.
    The future of American banking : managing for change / David Rogers.
        p.   cm.
    Includes index.
    ISBN 0-07-053538-8
    1. Banks and banking—United States.   2. Citicorp.   3. Chase
Manhattan Bank.   4. Bankers Trust Company (New York, N.Y.)
5. Morgan Guaranty Trust Company of New York.   6. Organizational
change.   I. Title.
HG2491.R62   1992
332.1´0973—dc20   92-17338
                                                                                           CIP

1 2 3 4 5 6 7 8 9 0   DOC/DOC   9 8 7 6 5 4 3 2

ISBN 0-07-053538-8

*The sponsoring editor for this book was Betsy N. Brown, the editing supervisor
was Marion B. Castellucci, and the production supervisor was Pamela A.
Pelton. This book was set in Palatino. It was composed by McGraw-Hill's
Professional Book Group composition unit.*

Printed and bound by R. R. Donnelley & Sons Company.

*For my three sons—Ed, Alex, and Paul—
each a long hitter in his own way*

Contents

Part 3. The Context Revisited

Preface

I undertook in the late 1980s to write this book on the U.S. banking industry because of my perception that it was experiencing many of the
same problems of competitive decline as were such other industries as
automobiles, steel, textiles, and semiconductors, as they all became
more globalized. U.S. banks, particularly the big ones, were either failing or suffering tremendous losses. Their industry was facing increasing competition, and many of their traditional businesses—such as corporate loans and deposit taking—were being taken over by other
financial service institutions. Fresh from the savings and loan (S&L) de-
bacle, which could cost taxpayers $500 billion or more, the country
seemed likely to face still another. By late 1991, the bank insurance
fund, which is administered by the Federal Deposit Insurance
Corporation (FDIC), had become completely depleted, much as its
counterpart for S&Ls had been depleted. In addition, commercial
banks, having been burned so badly in their many Latin American, commercial real estate, and leveraged buyout (LBO) loans, were putting a
damper on the economy's recovery from recession by being increasingly reluctant to grant loans to businesses that were seeking to expand
and modernize. A series of developments had thus conspired to create
a banking crisis in the United States—a crisis which merits closer
scrutiny.

I felt that, as an observer of how institutions manage change, I might
be able to provide further insight into the problems of the U.S. banking

industry and of particular banks, beyond what economists and banking scholars had written. As far as I could tell, the people who have traditionally written about banks have said little about how the banks are being managed and how this is affecting both the banks' performances and the performance of the industry as a whole. This became my starting point for the study.

I also decided to take advantage of my location. After all, here I was in New York, the site of the headquarters of some of the biggest and most significant banks in the country. Yes, some of them might well be in decline, or in the process of being displaced by competitors from other regions, other segments of financial services, or even other industries—and therefore no longer on the leading edge of U.S. commercial banking. Perhaps others among the New York banks were making it—and perhaps their stories were of wider relevance from that perspective.

It was with these thoughts in mind, then, that I began this book, hoping to find out more about an industry in deep trouble by looking at some of its biggest players. To find out what I wanted to know, I tried to get direct access to the people who had created the recent histories of these banks: their senior managers. I also sought out knowledgeable outsiders—people who had retired from the banks or who dealt with the insiders on a regular and sometimes intimate basis, such as bank analysts, management consultants, headhunters, regulators, and financial journalists. During the past 5 years I did a total of about 350 interviews, including many with senior managers of the banks and with highly informed outsiders. My story is about institutions that are struggling to adapt to many changes that they neither control nor always understand. As in other fields, there are winners and losers. Some banks have done very well in implementing strategies that enable them to compete effectively in increasingly global markets. Others have not. This book tells the story of both types. It focuses mainly on how management distinguishes between winners and losers.

The book has three parts. Part 1 provides a context for my case studies of particular New York banks. Chapter 1 gives a historical overview of the evolution of the U.S. banking industry, followed in Chapter 2 by discussions of why I chose the particular banks I did and the interpretive frameworks I used in analyzing them.

Part 2, the core of the book, contains four case studies that highlight differences in adaptation. The purpose of these studies is to provide an in-depth, historical interpretation of how four of the biggest players have adapted to the increased competition and turbulence which the industry has faced in recent decades. A major finding is that strategic focus is critical in contributing to effectiveness. There are benefits in diversification, and the histories of all four banks demonstrate how important it is, in terms of survival and effectiveness, for a bank to have high-revenue-producing businesses to carry the losing ones. Even so, diversification as a strategy seems to have clear limits. Because the competition in financial services is so intense in today's environment, it is no longer possible to maintain market leadership or profitability across a wide range of products. Bankers Trust and J.P. Morgan (two of my cases) illustrate the many benefits of having a strategic focus, while Chase and Citicorp (the other two) show the high costs of the diversification strategy.

A second finding relates to the importance of implementation. Just having vision (as Citicorp did in the 1960s and 1970s, with its early initiatives in international banking, technology, and consumer banking, or as Morgan and Bankers Trust did in the 1980s, with their emphasis on merchant and investment banking) is not enough. Just how these four banks have dealt with implementation is reported in the individual chapters.

The conclusion of the book, Part 3, discusses the findings at greater length and seeks to extrapolate from the four cases to larger issues associated with the future of commercial banking in the United States. I pursue these issues *at the firm level* in Chapters 14 and 15, relating them to what it will take to be a success in the financial services industry in the 1990s. Based on the experiences of these four banks and on what is known about others, I indicate what kinds of leadership, cultures, and strategies will be functional in this decade. As in other industries and institutional sectors, there is more than one way of being successful. At the same time, the range of success strategies is probably limited.

It is important also to look at the future on a *macroindustry level*. The issues covered in Chapter 16 are related to legislative and regulatory changes that would make U.S. commercial banks more competitive, after at least a decade in which they have fallen far behind. The discussion is focused on how the U.S. political, legal, and regulatory environments have hampered banks' ability to adapt, and on changes that would be appropriate. Particular emphasis is placed on how the industry can be helped to become more competitive globally and how it should be regulated in the future to facilitate this end. Chapter 17 forecasts changes that are likely to occur in the commercial banking industry in the 1990s.

Acknowledgments

So many people helped me in putting together this book that it is difficult to know where to begin. I'll start with my colleagues at the Stern School of Business of New York University. Though John Dutton probably doesn't remember, it was he who first encouraged me, in a casual conversation, to undertake this project about the banking industry. There has never been anything casual, however, about his intellectual judgments.

Ingo Walter and Roy Smith, who are founts of knowledge about banks of all kinds and in all parts of the world, shared much of their wisdom with me. Roy, in addition, made helpful comments on several chapters.

Larry Ritter and Dale Zand, each in his own good way, read chapters and provided comments on style and substance. Both are wise men, and I have been fortunate to be a recipient of their wisdom over the years.

Bob Lindsay sent me a steady stream of articles, references, and suggestions during the 5 years I worked on this project. People who know Bob will understand what I mean when I characterize him as not only an able economist but a caring person, whose sense of community almost stands alone.

Harvey Segal, another close friend and a former faculty member at New York University, spent hours prodding me to articulate more clearly what I was doing. Drawing on his considerable skills as an editor and economic historian and on his experience in banking, he read the entire manuscript and made numerous suggestions. I hope the book lives up to his high standards.

Both Bob and Harvey provided me with an informal education in the U.S. banking system. They also gave me the names of many knowledgeable observers and bankers whom I was able to contact. It is rare in my experience to receive this kind of continuing help from two such extraordinarily generous friends and colleagues.

Chet Borucki read an early draft of a chapter on Chase and made some helpful comments which I appreciate. Bernard Barber provided thoughtful suggestions, and I am grateful for his assistance.

I was fortunate to receive research grants from Banca Nationale del Lavoro, the Management Simulation Program, the Bank and Financial Analysts Association, and a General Electric fund for studies in strategic management. The last three were awarded through the Stern School. Thanks go to Sam Craig, Ingo Walter, and Bill Guth, who were responsible for managing these grant programs. The grant that really gave me the opportunity to get started came from Banca Nationale del Lavoro. I want to thank, in particular, Antonio Perrazzelli, Vice President of the bank, for his institution's support. One of the many bonuses I have received as a result of writing this book is development of a lasting friendship with Antonio, which I value highly.

Jim Murphy, a banker and formerly Executive Vice President of the New York State Bankers' Association, shared with me his many insights into the industry and into the politics of bank reform. His lifelong dedication to public service belies traditional stereotypes of bankers as being preoccupied with narrow self-interest.

I want also to thank Elisa Legg, Director of Education for the New York State Bankers' Association, for providing me with several years' worth of copies of *The American Banker*, the industry's daily newspaper. The time and inconvenience she saved me were considerable.

Rob Black gave me his wise counsel at a critical point. His professionalism and generosity are most appreciated.

Rick Rivere, Peter Humphrey, and Kevin Rockoff, all M.B.A. students at the Stern School of Business, were also helpful. Peter Humphrey made available his considerable knowledge of banking. For several months, Rick Rivere spent many hours—working beyond the call of duty, including late nights and weekends—helping me to complete the manuscript. His computer skills were of great help in the final stages of the project.

I have been blessed with a dedicated, highly competent secretarial staff. Karen Angelilo and Evelyn Davila-Gibson have been unfailingly helpful. Evelyn deserves many kudos for getting the manuscript on and off the computer with facility.

I want to pay particular tribute to Oscar Ornati, who was the chair of my department during the years I worked on this project. In countless ways, as friend, colleague, cheerleader, confidant, and boss, Oscar always let me know that my successful completion of the book was a high priority for him. He died in December 1991. I and countless others miss him deeply.

The vibrant intellectual climate of the Stern School of Business, and most of all, its Management Department and its Finance Department, provided a supportive setting for this study. The Stern School of Business, which has many distinguished scholars in banking, economics, management, and international business, contains one of the world's strongest concentrations of experts in the financial services industry. Many of these people contributed to my education and research.

My sons, Edward and Alex, each of whom is a scholar in his own right, also provided considerable assistance. Both possess keen analytical skills, and each helped me, in different ways. Ed pushed me to sharpen the main argument of the book, which appears in a more formal way in Appendix A. Alex read and critiqued various sections of the manuscript, particularly Chapter 16 on the politics of bank reform.

Mike Radway, a senior congressional aide, generously supplied me with copies of hearings, bills, and analyses. He also took the time to discuss some of the issues of bank reform with me.

I will not publicly thank by name the 350-odd people I interviewed, though many of them gave me much time and much information. I promised them all anonymity. The nonbankers among them probably wouldn't object strenuously to being listed here, but to list only those who wouldn't object would be unfair to those who might. Suffice it to say that they—the bank analysts, management consultants, academics, journalists, regulators, and bankers that I met—constitute collectively as knowledgeable a pool as one could ever find. Their knowledge encompasses both U.S. banking and the particular banks I have studied.

Betsy Brown, my editor, deserves special commendation, first, for her confidence in my ability to turn some rough drafts of chapters and a broad outline into a book, and, later, for her many suggestions for improving the book. Her professionalism and her perennial good disposition have made her a pleasure to work with.

Marion Castellucci, the editing supervisor, was unfailingly helpful in the final stages of the book's production. I would also like to thank John Rudi for his many kindnesses including his reading of the book in manuscript.

Finally, my patient and loving wife, Terry, endured the more than occasional hardships resulting from my time away from home and my obsession with completing the book. In addition, she provided astute comments on early drafts. She undoubtedly saved me from many embarrassments.

I hope the book lives up to the quality of assistance that all the aforementioned people provided. They should not be held responsible for any errors that may appear in the book.

David Rogers

Part 1

The Context

1

The Financial Services Industry Revolution

This is a book about an industry in very rapid transition. The industry is commercial banking, perhaps best analyzed as part of a larger financial services industry complex; and the story of the U.S. banking industry's rapid change (many writers refer to its experience since the early 1960s as a series of revolutions) is told here through the experiences of four of its biggest players. Those four are Citicorp, Chase, Morgan, and Bankers Trust, all New York City-based money center banks that have been hit hard by a series of *environmental jolts* over the past three decades. Deregulation, technological innovation, globalization, the decline of the corporate loan business, and increasing competition are among the most significant. Many of these jolts have hit other segments of the financial services industry as well—savings and loans (S&Ls), insurance companies, and investment banks. I have singled out commercial banks for special attention because of their unique problems, their asset size, and their strategic importance for the entire industry.

Even concentrating on this one segment of financial services is a monumental task. As of early 1990, there were roughly 12,600 commercial banks in the United States, two-thirds of them state chartered and one-third national. All are subject to multiple federal authorities—for example, the Federal Reserve, the Federal Deposit Insurance Corporation

(FDIC), and the Comptroller of the Currency.[1] Moreover, they appear in a variety of what industrial organization economists refer to as "strategic groups"—money centers, superregionals, regionals, community banks, full-service globals, niche globals, etc. The approach taken here has been to do an intensive analysis of four money centers as a way of shedding light on what is happening to commercial banks more generally.

A main argument of the book is that my focus on these four banks adds up to more than just a series of specific case studies. Rather, the experiences of these banks over the past few decades reflect broader trends in the entire U.S. banking industry. They constitute in that sense archetypes or flagship cases, struggling with problems of strategic and organizational change that other categories of commercial banks are beginning to face as well. The ones I look at are among the biggest commercial banks in the United States. As large money centers which are more global and diversified than other commercial banks and which have lost much of their traditional franchise in the corporate loan business, they have thus been hit earlier and harder by changes in their industry than have their competitors. Others—superregionals, regionals, and even small community banks—are now being hit with some of the same changes and forced to adapt. Lessons from these four banks' efforts to reposition themselves in an increasingly competitive industry may well be relevant to other, later comers.

In brief, one useful way to study strategic and organizational change in an industry is to examine in depth the firms in the industry that are furthest along in the change process. Such an examination may well tell us something about the experiences some of the rest are likely to have, when industry changes affect them. While the circumstances and impacts of the changes will not be exactly the same, there may nevertheless be enough commonality so that lessons can be learned from looking at firms going through the process earlier.

In particular, these four banks represent a range of types in terms of their strategies. Chase and Citicorp have pursued a highly diversified, supermarket-type strategy that encompasses retail and wholesale banking, including in the latter new investment banking activities as well. Bankers Trust and Morgan, by contrast, have focused much more on investment banking as the centerpieces of their strategies. Bankers Trust divested itself of retail banking in the late 1970s, while Morgan was never engaged in it.

The study on which this book is based looks intensively at these four banks, as they have repositioned themselves in recent decades, to ascertain:

1. Who is ahead and who is behind in terms of various measures of business success [e.g., return on equity (ROE), return on assets (ROA), market to book ratios, earnings per share, market share]
2. How the banks' cultures, strategies, leadership, and histories have shaped their performance
3. What lessons may be learned by other banks that will face similar competitive pressures in the very near future or are already facing them

It is a book, then, *about organizational adaptation to environmental change.* It looks at winning and losing strategies and extrapolates from them to suggest success strategies for the future.

The experiences of these four banks may also be relevant in suggesting directions that commercial banking as an industry, and not just individual banks, may well take in the future. Will there be a trend toward significant consolidation, resulting in fewer megabanks? Will those that survive tend to take on particular *forms* (in terms of strategy and underlying infrastructure), becoming, for example, universal banks or more strategically focused, niche banks? Will both of these types and perhaps others emerge in a new tiering of the industry? More generally, will U.S. commercial banks continue to suffer losses of market share in an increasingly competitive global arena, much as the automobile, semiconductor, steel, and machine tool industries have done?[2] Or do U.S. banks still have a chance to be major players in the year 2000? In addition, what regulatory reforms are required to increase the likelihood that U.S. banks will in fact be more competitive? It is ultimately to these larger questions of the competitiveness of U.S. commercial banking that this book is addressed.

In large part, this book focuses on a period of turbulence in which it is very difficult for banks to assess trends and reposition themselves accordingly. For example, there were three announced mergers of big commercial banks in the summer of 1991 that are likely to alter radically the size distribution and competitive conditions of the industry. Mergers of Manufacturers Hanover with Chemical, North Carolina National Bank (NCNB) with C&S/Sovran (Citizens and Southern), and BankAmerica with Security Pacific all created new megabanks that put others in their regions in even more serious jeopardy than they already were. While mergers were anticipated, the emergence of these three, with many more to come in the immediate future, has clearly escalated the industry's shakeout and consolidation. To study the banking industry is, in that sense, to look at a moving target and attempt to extrapolate from such an analysis what the future is likely to bring.

The Preturbulence Period

A useful starting point for gaining some perspective on such recent developments is one that describes both the environment and the nature of commercial banking for these money centers before the turbulence of the past few decades. The period I will be describing here includes the years from 1933 (when the Glass Steagall Act, separating commercial from investment banking, was enacted) to the early 1960s. Since then, the environment of banking has begun to change much faster and in more unpredictable ways than before, requiring some strategic response from the banks so as to maintain their market position and, for some, even to survive.

The financial environment ushered in by the New Deal reforms of the early 1930s was marked by protectionism, stability, and simplicity. Viewed in a larger context, each segment of the financial services industry performed its own specialized function, with little competition from the others or from nonbank or nonfinancial institutions. Management writers would refer to it as a *placid* environment that posed few threats for banks.[3] It led to a financial services industry that one economist observer has referred to as *turf and cartel,* or what might be called, more dramatically, *segmented sedation,* in which each segment exists in a quasi monopoly or has protected market status. Thus, commercial banks controlled much of the loan and credit business. S&Ls provided stable deposits in passbooks (on which checks could not be written) and channeled those funds into mortgage lending. Investment banks were the intermediaries for the underwriting and placement of securities, having a virtual monopoly in the United States in that business. Insurance companies managed risks with no reason to look over their shoulders at commercial bank competitors as they do now. It was, in brief, a protected world in which government had segmented the industry into secure and insulated compartments. An implicit *social contract* existed that perpetuated this condition. To indicate just how protected commercial banks were: In 1950, they held 51.2 percent of all U.S. financial assets, compared with 25.3 percent for insurance companies; 13.4 percent for S&Ls and mutual savings banks; and lesser amounts for credit unions, investment banks, and others. By 1989, that 51.2 percent had shrunk to 30.7 percent, with mutual funds and money-market mutual funds having increased from 1.1 percent to 5.3 percent and 0 to 4.1 percent respectively.[4]

The genesis of this social contract was the Great Depression, which some observers, including members of Congress, believed had been exacerbated if not brought on by underwriting and trading in securities by big banks, who did so using depositors' funds.[5] At least two bank chief executive officers (CEOs), Charles E. Mitchell of National City (predecessor to Citibank) and Albert H. Wiggin of Chase, reportedly used their banks' funds for their own speculations, and Mitchell was publicly disgraced in testimony before the Senate Banking Committee. His directors forced him to resign in early 1933, and *Time*'s report of the event included a caption under his photograph that read, "The U.S. Senators got their man."[6] Economist Eduard Balarin claims that there is now a general consensus that the commercial banks' speculation in securities was not a significant causal factor of the Great Depression, but that was not the prevalent view in the early 1930s, a time of frantic searching for scapegoats.[7]

The Glass Steagall Act of 1933, one of the important reforms, was designed to bar banks from the securities business. Other provisions of the social contract delineated what businesses commercial banks could or could not engage in and how, in return protecting those franchises from nonbank competitors. Commercial banks were thus positioned as the primary intermediaries between savers and borrowers and were in a position to make substantial, oligopolylike profits as a result.

During this era of high protection, banking was a relatively simple credit business and little else. As observers of banks noted, "American bankers for decades operated by the 3-6-3 rule: pay depositors 3% interest, lend money at 6%, and tee off at the golf course by 3 P.M. Profits were steady and certain."[8] Banks thus functioned in these years on "automatic pilot" rather than having to develop new products and aggressively market them. A staff economist for a money center recalled:

> If you took a snapshot of what banking was like in 1935 and then had a similar one in 1960, you would find that you could count the differences on the ten fingers of your hand. In 1960, a senior VP would deal with perhaps 5 loan-related products. Today, that same senior VP would deal with closer to 30 products. The diversification and skill-level requirements have increased exponentially from 1960 to the present.

Commercial banks in the earlier era of protection and stability were in many respects *public utilities* or *white-collar factories*. Commercial banking was essentially a credit business in which banks made money on the spreads between interest paid for deposits and that gained on loans. Banks performed in that sense an *intermediation* function between those providing deposits and those seeking loans. The product was a standardized, traditional one. It came in a small number of varieties, provided by a well-defined set of people. In addition, the production process was itself quite standardized, including an institutionalized credit management process.[9]

In brief, banking was a relatively simple and stable business. The technology for producing credit or loans was quite routine: there was little variety in end products, and what had to be done was well codified. It did not require much imagination or professional training to become a loan officer. Indeed, the skills and knowledge required—for example, knowing the industries and companies being serviced, being able to read a balance sheet and do credit checks, understanding covenants, and being able to establish and maintain personal relationships with large borrowers—were easily acquired. There was limited diversification and a long product life cycle. Banking was basically a relationship business, and many of the relationships banks had with their corporate clients went back several decades.

Not surprisingly, the *managements* of these banks, including their organizational structures, cultures, patterns of decision making, and human resources practices, followed directly from the banks' product and client relations. A bank was, in most respects, a stereotype of the hierarchical, bureaucratic form of organization. There were many layers in banks' chains of command, including a proliferation of different categories of vice presidents. There were clearly defined reporting lines and position-based authority. Communications were much more vertical than lateral, usually revolving around credit transactions, with much centralization and many committees that reviewed such transactions. The process of review was deliberate and, by contemporary standards, tediously slow.

The *cultures* of banks during this period also reflected the nature of the business. The emphasis was on following fixed procedures, maintaining long-term relationships with clients, minimizing risks and avoiding change, following rules and reaching consensus decisions through committees, and, finally, providing lifetime tenure for employees through civil service-type personnel practices. In brief, banks put great store upon passively servicing a captive group of clients and doing things as they had always been done. They functioned as static-style organizations.

Their *human resources practices*, in turn, reinforced this perspective. New, young recruits tended to be college graduates rather than people with M.B.A.s or other advanced degrees. At money center banks that served primarily blue-chip corporations and highly affluent individuals in long-term relationships, senior management emphasized the recruiting of people from social backgrounds similar to those of the clients: the recruits were expected to be upper-class; to hold degrees from Ivy

League and other elite colleges; and to be white, Anglo-Saxon, and Protestant. There were always exceptions, and some of the exceptions even moved to high positions within a bank, perhaps partly as a result of the bank's wish to signal to outsiders that it was a more open institution than they might have thought. But the exceptions were always, in fact, exceptions.

To illustrate: Morgan, until well into the 1980s, was widely known in banking circles for recruiting people from backgrounds that fit its mold as an aristocratic, British-founded, and British-oriented institution. As late as the 1980s, applicants were routinely asked on a personal history form to indicate the colleges their parents had attended. Chase, with a similar blue-chip corporate clientele to that of Morgan, was noted for its paternalistic, old-boy network of bankers tied to the Rockefeller and Aldrich families. Bankers Trust had, before 1974, a series of CEOs, all of whom had inherited wealth, were Episcopalians, and were Yale graduates.

The so-called best and brightest of the elite college graduates usually did not go into commercial banking, choosing the professions or a more challenging field of business such as investment banking. As Sanford Rose, an economist and an astute observer of banking, has commented, "Regulated industries tend not to attract fine minds."

Moreover, for those people who did go into banking, their compensation and career prospects fit well with the bureaucratic nature of the business and proceeded in lockstep fashion. Salary increments were based on seniority and rank. Pay for performance was not established policy, as people at the same level and with the same seniority were paid about the same. Further, there was an implicit understanding that one was hired at these money center banks in most instances "for life" and would likely make a slow but steady rise up the chain of command from loan officer to manager.

The result of these human resources practices was the development of a civil service mentality among bankers. Little emphasis was placed on developing new products or on the aggressive marketing of existing ones. The protected market of the commercial banks didn't require such an emphasis, and there were few rewards for it. Salaries were not high, because there was no need to attract the most talented people.

The Big Change

Beginning in the early 1960s, a series of cascading environmental changes took place, introducing a volatility and turbulence that have radically altered the financial services industry and have hit the large, money center banks particularly hard. Indeed these changes constitute a series of threats, though also opportunities, that have eroded the money centers' competitive position and performance. They have had to adapt by major *strategic repositioning*.

Observers of banking are in considerable agreement about the changes to which financial services has been subjected.[10] One such change is *macroeconomic trends*, particularly inflation, rising and highly volatile interest rates, and declining economic growth. These trends have had devastating effects on bank deposits, especially in what was known as *Regulation Q*, which (under the provisions of the Banking Act of 1933) imposed set ceilings on the interest rates commercial banks were allowed to pay on deposits. As open market rates went substantially above these ceilings, people took their money out of banks and put it into money-market mutual funds and other securities. Banks were thus bypassed as intermediaries. The Banking Act of 1980 eliminated those rate ceilings, and banks regained much of their deposits, but not before suffering a severe jolt.[11]

Globalization was a second major change in the industry; and while it increased opportunities for U.S. commercial banks abroad (e.g., they were able to open overseas branches and to service U.S. multinational corporations and indigenous groups with traditional credit and new investment banking products), it was also accompanied by the entry of foreign bank competitors into U.S. markets. Many foreign banks were able to undercut their U.S. competitors, in providing letters of credit, extending loans, and underwriting municipal bonds, partly because their governments imposed lower capital requirements on them. Japanese banks were particularly effective in this regard.

As with all the other changes in financial services since the 1960s, globalization posed opportunities as well as threats. U.S. banks went to Europe en masse, starting in the mid-1960s, and were very heavily involved in the huge Eurodollar market dollar-denominated deposits that are booked in banks outside the United States. Eurodollar operations allowed U.S. banks to escape the constraints of Regulation Q and to bid for funds on a more equal basis with their foreign competitors.[12] In the same way, many American banks began their investment banking-related businesses abroad (e.g., securities underwriting, distribution, and trading), where the constraints of the Glass Steagall Act of 1933, which act as the wall between commercial and investment banking in the United States, did not apply.

As the world became what Walter Wriston calls a *global village*, with the rapid growth of ever freer international transactions, flows of money and information, the financial services industry became not only more efficient but also more risky. The tremors of inflation, along with volatile interest rates and securities prices, were now more rapidly propagated to all parts of the world. Banks were compelled to develop a variety of new risk-management products to help customers hedge against foreign exchange rate volatility and other changes and were thus able to capitalize on the new developments. However, globalization brought with it many risks as well, and many U.S. commercial banks—for example, Chase and BankAmerica—have closed and/or consolidated their overseas branches, as they became overextended and suffered big losses on international loans and foreign exchange market transactions.

Still a third big change has been *deregulation,* which has proceeded unevenly throughout the financial services industry in the 1980s and 1990s. Banking is by far one of the most tightly regulated industries in our economy, and appropriately so, given its central roles in providing credit and as a conduit for the Federal Reserve's monetary policy. It has been regulated historically in terms of interest rate ceilings on deposits, limits on geographic expansion and product diversification, and capital and reserve requirements. In addition to Regulation Q, discussed earlier, the McFadden Act of 1927 prohibits banks from branching across state lines and requires that all banks, including those that are federally chartered, follow the branching laws of the state where they are headquartered.[13] The Glass Steagall Act of 1933 forbids banks from being involved in issuing, underwriting, selling, or distributing new stock and bond offerings of corporations or the revenue bonds of municipalities. These barriers to commercial bank expansion have been gradually lowered, through decisions by the courts and federal and state regulatory agencies, but the laws still stand. Moreover, many new competitors—including securities firms; foreign banks; and such nonbank banks as Sears, J.C. Penny, American Express, and finance companies—have had much more flexibility to diversify into commercial banks' markets. They have been able to use credit cards, cash management (depository) accounts, and automobile financing, whereas the banks have not had a corresponding freedom to diversify into the markets of their competitors. Thus, bank lobbyists have continually called attention to the absence of a "level playing field" when urging repeal of these old banking laws. It seems like a reasonable complaint.

Still another environmental change has been the development of computerized telecommunications and electronic *technology*. Many observers of this industry have argued that technological change may be an even more important driving force than the other forces we have discussed. (Sametz makes this point quite compellingly.) Contributing first to the rationalization of back-office operations through the automation of data processing and check clearing, the new technology has more recently been brought to front-office operations and customer services as well in the form of automated teller machines (ATMs), videotex systems, and many other new products (e.g., swaps; options; futures; and various custodial, trust, and cash management services).

The impacts of this new technology have been profound. It has integrated local, regional, national, and global financial markets by making information instantly available to many firms. As a result, it has generally increased the scale, scope, volume, and volatility of transactions. For individual banks, operating costs in an increasingly competitive industry have sometimes been reduced. Opportunities have increased to develop new products, enabling banks to differentiate themselves from competitors.

The challenge, and the potential downside, is that the new technology has required banks to make tremendous investments and to acquire new expertise. Some, like Citicorp, Morgan, Bankers Trust, and State Street Boston, have incorporated the technology with extraordinary foresight and success. Even so, technology remains a potentially high-risk aspect of the business that banks have had to commit themselves to, in which they may make many false starts and may lose a lot of money in building large infrastructures that raise overhead costs.

New competition confronting the big money center banks has been devastating. It embraces foreign banks, securities firms, S&Ls, newly merged superregional banks, and such nonbank banks as Sears, American Express, J.C. Penney, General Electric (GE), and automobile finance companies. These competitors engage in businesses that were once the exclusive preserve of commercial banks—for example, Merrill Lynch with cash management accounts, S&Ls with commercial loans, Sears and American Express with credit cards—while commercial banks under the provisions of Glass Steagall, are constrained from diversifying domestically into securities underwriting or insurance.

To fill out the picture, other environmental changes include *the rise of capital markets,* accompanied by a process of *disintermediation* whereby banks' big corporate customers floated their own IOUs as commercial paper and later as junk bonds, rather than go to the banks for loans; the movement toward *liquification* and *securitization* whereby loans could be packaged as securities and sold; the nonpayment on loans to less developed countries (*LDC loans*) that resulted from the recycling of petrodollars; and *new capital requirements,* imposed by the Federal Reserve and the Bank for International Settlements. Just as life for most bankers in the early post-New Deal years was relatively simple, it has become incredibly complex now.

A critical point about these environmental changes is that they took place in interaction with one another. New electronic communications technology, for example, was one of the prime change drivers. Along with other forces, it contributed substantially to the rise of capital markets and the banks' disintermediation, to the globalization of those markets, to the spawning of innovative securities products, and to securitization.[14] Organization theorists created the concept *turbulent environments* to describe situations where a multitude of forces, many of them remote and hard to read, interact to create unpredictable change. The concept certainly captures conditions facing commercial banks.[15]

Perhaps the biggest jolts of all for these money center banks were, first, the loss of the corporate loan business, their main franchise, and second, large losses on their LDC loans. When big corporations were able to raise money at lower costs by going directly to the capital markets—their credit ratings being often higher than those of the money center banks from which they used to borrow—money center banks faced new problems. They were going to have to scale down costs, find new sources of revenue, do much more strategic planning to analyze the changing environment, assess their strengths and weaknesses, and position themselves accordingly. One initiative many banks took in an attempt to recoup was to extend higher-risk loans, either down market to corporations with less than a triple A rating or to governments whose finances were extremely shaky. Thus, the crises for these banks in the 1970s and 1980s—real estate investment trust (REIT) losses and nonpayment on LDC loans—stem in large part from the banks' need for substitute revenue sources. Moreover, leveraged buyout (LBO) and real estate loan losses in the 1990s and the recession may well be the banking graveyard of this decade. Banks have, in these respects, often behaved like lemmings, following the fads of the times. They are not unique in this regard, but the results have been negative.

Indeed, the impact of environmental changes on money center banks since the 1960s has been devastating. Relative to other categories of commercial banks, the performance of the money centers has been way down. A study by researchers at the New York Federal Reserve, for example, indicates that the average ROE for all money center banks went from 11.0 percent in 1970 to 9.6 percent in 1985, compared with all other commercial banks, whose ROE went from 12.3 to 13.7 percent during that period.[16] The same pattern existed for the average ROA, which is a more revealing measure of profitability. ROA went from 0.64 to 0.45 percent for the money centers and from 0.74 to 0.77 percent for all others. The most profitable banks have a return on assets of 1 percent or more. More commercial banks (1037) failed in the 1980s than in the previous 48 years of the history of the Federal Deposit Insurance Corporation (FDIC).[17] Aggregate ROA for commercial banks had fallen by the end of 1986 to its lowest level since 1959, while ROE was the lowest since 1968. Again, the money centers led the way in this decline.

A lead article in *Business Week* further highlights these trends. It notes that the number of problem banks in the United States, though down from a high of over 1500 in 1988, was still at 1058 after the first quarter of 1990, or 8 percent of the nation's 12,588 commercial banks. Given the escalation of nonperforming real estate and LBO loans, the slowing of economic growth, and the possibility of a prolonged recession, the immediate future for U.S. banks is not promising, particularly because of unprecedented competition from foreign banks and domestic challengers. As Citicorp CEO John Reed said, "The whole banking industry is suffering from a rolling recession that's running across the country like a ball bearing." One result has been the rating agencies lowering the quality rating on many banks, including such money centers as Citicorp and Chase Manhattan.[18]

Some observers have even dubbed the years since 1985 (when a U.S. Supreme Court decision paved the way for many mergers among regional banks in adjacent states, while prohibiting money centers from doing so), as the *era of the superregionals*. Comparative financial performance data, as just reported, support this. Money centers were surpassed considerably by these newly emergent superregionals—for example, Banc One (Columbus, Ohio), First Wachovia (Winston-Salem, North Carolina), NCNB (Charlotte, North Carolina), and PNC Financial (Pittsburgh, Pennsylvania)—and by medium-sized and smaller regionals as well. These two groups of banks had not participated significantly in LDC loans and retained their protected oligopoly position in relation to middle-market (medium-sized companies) and smaller business customers. As one economist who has studied banking for several decades noted:

> The superregionals have [fewer] LDC loans [and] less big corporation lending, that being a business that has dried up, and exist in insular, sleepier competitive environments where they extract more economic rent from the consumer. Some of these banks are just 20 minutes outside New York City. They are convenient for customers, are on a first-name basis, and are seen as effective franchises. People leave their money there with little or no interest and see the cost of monitoring their money elsewhere as greater than that of leaving it there.

A 1988 report by the First Manhattan Consulting Group, which has done several well-regarded economic analyses of U.S. commercial and investment banking, summarizes these trends.[19] These analyses indicate that commercial banking in the United States has been undergoing a restructuring in the 1980s resulting from the environmental trends we have discussed. The conclusions are that the negative aspects of such trends have been greatest for the large corporate lenders and that *large-bank performance has suffered from a secular decline since 1970,* interrupted only by what they refer to as the *Volker boom* of the early 1980s. The recovery from the recession was precipitated by the Federal Reserve's successful effort to reduce inflation, at a time when Paul Volker was its chairman.

More specifically, the First Manhattan Consulting Group presents data from the Federal Reserve, the FDIC, and other such sources showing that top-quality corporate borrowers have been deserting the money centers, that bank loans as a percentage of business credit needs are way down, that there has been an upward trend in loan losses, that money-market mutual funds are way up while bank savings products are flat, and that money centers have the lowest ROE of all commercial banks. It also highlights how U.S. banks have lost loan market share to foreign banks and the commercial paper market. Such data all support the secular decline thesis.

Clearly, some money centers have done better than others, and available data indicate those differences. Taking ROE as one critical indicator, the high performers in recent years have been such superregionals as NCNB, First Wachovia, Banc One, PNC Financial, Fleet Norstar, and Wells Fargo, along with J.P. Morgan and Bankers Trust from among the money centers. They are followed by a middle group that includes Citicorp at the top (it has since declined significantly), followed by Chase (it has declined also) , with Chemical and Manufacturers Hanover even further down, and Bank of America (which since then has staged a comeback) and Mellon Bank among the lowest.[20]

Confronted by these changes, the money center banks have had to *reposition* themselves, sometimes quite radically, in order to compete or, in some cases, to simply survive. For some, despite the "too big to fail" policy of federal regulators, survival—or at least survival as independent entities has become quite problematic. Bank analysts are agreed, for example, on the significant overcapacity of New York money centers, asserting that at least one and maybe more will be bought up in the next few years and that some may merge, as dictated by economic conditions. Echoing the views of several colleagues, Mark Alpert, bank analyst from Bear Stearns, stated recently:

I think the case for intra-city mergers is so compelling that it will become more common. When revenues aren't growing, one of the only
ways to bring more earnings to the bottom line is to slap two stagnant
revenue streams together and cut one-third of the
expenses....Ultimately, I think that banks like Manny Hanny
[Manufacturers Hanover], Chase, and Chemical will have no alternative.[21]

Repositioning invariably involves several steps for these banks:

1. *Assessing industry changes* in terms of the new threats and opportunities they present

2. *Assessing the bank's internal strengths and weaknesses* in the context of
   those changes

3. *Developing a new mix of products, businesses, customers, and geographic
   markets* that align the bank better with the environment than had
   been the case before (e.g., finding profitable new market niches and
   exiting when new products become commoditized as spreads are
   driven down by competitors)

4. All the while *developing an infrastructure* (a culture, an organizational
   structure, a reward system, staffing capabilities) *to support the new
   strategic directions*

This book looks intensively at how four money center banks have
gone through such a repositioning process. It evaluates how well they
are doing and why, using the four case studies to explore the larger issues (mentioned above) in trying to understand better the directions in
which U.S. commercial banking is moving.

New Strategies: The Banks' Responses

As the environment of banking started changing in the 1960s, and as
the money centers' main franchise, the wholesale corporate loan business, started shrinking noticeably with the rise of commercial paper
and later junk bonds, the banks pursued several strategic options.
Many had very high levels of fixed costs, legacies of the 1950s and
1960s, such as big headquarters staffs and highly paid loan officers
whose special skills were no longer needed. They realized they were
going to have to do something about what had become serious expense
control problems. Many money center banks started selling off busi-

nesses to raise the capital needed under Federal Reserve capital guidelines requirements.

Beyond this, the banks have looked to new clients and businesses for additional sources of revenue. Some, including Citicorp and Chase, turned to consumer banking. All of them, but particularly Bankers Trust and Morgan, turned to investment banking or to a hybrid of investment and commercial banking that they call *merchant banking*—for example, acting as financial consultants, helping corporate clients in restructuring, and leveraging by providing loans. Still others turned to middle-market customers; to the information business; or to providing services in such technology-driven businesses as cash management, investment management, and other custodial and trust services. Some, like Citicorp and Chase, pursued most of these diversification options all at once, raising questions about the long-term viability of a conglomerate or supermarket bank strategy. Others, like Bankers Trust and Morgan, were much more focused, concentrating on merchant banking services and securities trading for corporate and other institutional customers. Some observers feel that none of these bank restructurings will reverse the decline, and one of the purposes of this book is to explore that issue in depth.

A particularly important strategic initiative has been that in investment and merchant banking. All money centers, including the ones discussed in this book, have pursued this initiative, either as a single strategy or in conjunction with others, such as consumer banking. Throughout the 1980s, banks lobbied aggressively for the repeal of Glass Steagall. While they haven't been successful in the U.S. Congress, they have secured many favorable rulings from the Federal Reserve, the FDIC, the Comptroller of the Currency, and various state banking departments for expanded powers in investment banking. Such powers have included opening discount broker businesses nationwide, underwriting and dealing in municipal bonds and commercial paper, and underwriting corporate debt and equities. These rulings seem to have steadily eroded Glass Steagall constraints.

Some bankers and their spokespeople see investment banking as "the promised land." They view potential profits in corporate finance, securities trading, and related businesses as an opportunity not only to recoup losses in traditional loan businesses but also to share at last in a seemingly lucrative and growing industry that throughout most of the 1980s had yielded inordinate profits and ROEs for investment banks in the 30 to 35 percent range. Others, particularly the banks' Wall Street competitors, fearful of losing their oligopolistic profits, suggest that investment banking might instead be a "valley of death" for commercial banks. They argue that these banks don't have the culture, the organizational structure, the people, or the backup product and trading capabilities to compete effectively.[22]

In many respects, developments since the stock market crash of October 1987 have borne out the pessimists' judgment. In an industry that has always been extremely cyclical, commercial banks entered it at one of the worst possible times, during a period of major cutbacks. Recent estimates suggest that between 30,000 and 35,000 people have been laid off by Wall Street firms since the crash, with many more layoffs to come. Meanwhile, commercial banks had made huge investments in infrastructures—technology, trading facilities all over the world, and high-paid product specialists and traders—as part of a gearing up for a major effort in the industry, only to have to cut back. Citicorp, for example, after having plunged into investment banking in the early 1980s in its usual aggressive fashion, has pulled way back in recent years.

It was going to be hard enough for the banks to change their cultures, organizational structures, and staff to support a big investment banking initiative, but to have the industry then go into such a decline put them once more in a difficult position in regard to overhead expenses. They are now reassessing what their commitments to various aspects of investment banking should be for the future.

The crucial questions about these repositioning initiatives that banks have taken since the 1960s concern winning and losing strategies. How do winning strategies best get implemented? What are their implications for other banks that will face similar changes and for the industry more generally? In brief, based on the experiences of four key players, what can be said about the future requirements for success in an industry so buffeted by turbulence? What can we learn about the future of these banks from analyses of their experiences over the past three decades? What about the future of commercial banking in general? These are the issues addressed in this book.

2
Different Banks, Different Models

This book attempts, by analyzing four banks, to explore some larger questions of organizational inertia and transformation. In a period of rapid change in the U.S. banking industry's environment, some banks have been more effective at adapting and transforming themselves than others. The four case studies analyze in depth what distinguishes effective from ineffective adaptation strategies. It does so through a study of the sociology of banks as institutions that explains how their cultures and leadership drive them to pursue particular strategies and develop infrastructures (organization designs, human resource practices, cultures) that affect those strategies' implementations.

A larger question in what students of management refer to as *organization theory* relates to the extent to which anything that senior managers do may make a difference in their firms' performance. One point of view held by a group of organization theorists interested in the rise and fall of organizations is that, over the long run (however that may be defined), managerial initiatives have little impact on organizational effectiveness or survival.[1] These people argue that changes in the macroenvironment of organizations select who will survive and what forms (strategies and structures) are required for survival. They go on to state that the environment, though it ultimately determines what firms will survive, is too complex and turbulent to be analyzable, and they conclude that luck and chance play a big role. The firms that select appropriate market niches will survive and prosper, argue this school of organization theorists, but given the complexity and unpredictability of changes in the environment, it is next to impossible to analyze them well enough to position the firm accordingly.

Other organization analysts disagree. They reject environmental determinism, asserting instead that intelligent decisions and timely managerial initiatives make a difference. Both camps accept the judgment that the banking environment is perilously turbulent, and that organizations are too constrained by inertia to transform themselves quickly.

This study is in part a test of these two views. Commercial banks are particularly apt subjects for testing, because as so many observers have noted, they have a strong, imitative, herdlike tendency. "They behave like lemmings," explained one consultant, "and it's amazing how much particular fads sweep through the industry—REITS, LDC loans, LBO loans, and so on." Just as most big banks couldn't help but be profitable in the protected environment of the 1940s and 1950s, so, too, has it been very difficult for them to perform well in the period since then.

Yet, as the environment became more competitive and turbulent, banks have had many more options in recent decades than they had before. The same bank analysts who saw banks as so imitative of one another acknowledge that in this new environment they have become much more differentiated. The range of bank strategies, reflecting, in turn, the differences in vision and values of their chief executive officers (CEOs), is much greater now than ever before. Most important, these differences provide a greater opportunity for comparisons than before.

Before taking the reader through the story of the four banks—Citicorp, Chase Manhattan, Bankers Trust, and Morgan—that are the centerpiece of this book, it is important to provide some background on (1) why they were selected and (2) the schema or interpretive framework I used to describe and analyze the repositioning of these banks since the 1960s. Two other critical issues, how I gained access to the banks and the specific kinds of data on which the analysis was based, are discussed in Appendixes A and B. I go through the first two issues in this chapter, not just as a matter of convention, but to provide the reader with an understanding of what it was like to peer in on four big institutions in the throes of rapid change and how I managed the task.

Why These Four Banks?

Four banks are obviously a small sample of an industry of over 12,000, which embraces several kinds of banks: small community banks, regionals, superregionals, money centers, and subgroups within each. But the four are important because they are archetypes or flagships, highly sensitive to larger industry forces to which they and many other banks have had to adapt through changes in strategy and organization. They have simply begun the process earlier than others, having been affected earlier and more markedly by industry changes. The problems these four banks face in managing change—deciding what types of new businesses to pursue and then adapting their internal infrastructures to support those strategic changes—also confront other categories of commercial banks. Thus their experiences may well tell us something about what is in store for others, when environmental changes affect them. While the changes will not be the same, there may nevertheless be enough commonality so that lessons can be learned from looking at what happened within New York's big four.

Moreover, these four banks represent a range of types within the industry in terms of the directions of their strategic and organizational repositioning. Chase and Citicorp have followed a highly diversified strategy and are perhaps best characterized as *full-service globals*. They have retained and, indeed, expanded their already large retail banking business, attempting to fit their wholesale, corporate, and investment banking activities into a larger, more diversified portfolio of financial services. Bankers Trust and Morgan, by contrast, have focused much more on merchant and investment banking as the core of their strategy. They are, in effect, *niche globals*. Both have a wide array of products and services for their wholesale clients and are diversified in that sense, but they are still niche banks in that they specialize almost exclusively in wholesale banking. Both provide private banking services—trust and estate management—for affluent individuals, but these services remain peripheral to their corporate, wholesale business.

These broad types clearly don't exhaust the range of strategies that commercial banks have adopted in response to change. There are newly emerging superregionals, for example, that concentrate on consumer and middle-market domestic banking, and they may soon surpass many money centers in size and market share, at least in the United States. They have been merging with local banks and buying up ailing savings and loans (S&Ls), and they may well become the most prominent segment of the industry. To take just one example, North Carolina National Bank (NCNB) acquired C&S (Citizens and Southern)/Sovran in 1991 and thus became one of the largest banking organizations in the United States, setting the stage for a decade of consolidation and establishing another major tier, namely, large, nationwide consumer and middle-market-oriented banks.

There are other strategic types as well—for example, small community banks that compose up to 75 percent of the population of the industry. The money centers, however, remain important. They are the most global banks in an industry that has moved far in the direction of global banking. They are still among the largest of global banks. In addition, other banks look to them for cues on what to do and what not to do, perhaps more of the latter in recent decades. The story of how four of the biggest managed during this time of such great turmoil therefore has broader relevance. It is particularly important because increasing numbers of scholars are agreed that the U.S. banking crisis of the 1990s is in large part a big-bank crisis.[2] The big banks are the ones with the most nonperforming loans and the least adequate capitalization. They are also the ones that appear in disproportionate numbers on the lists of problem banks. Though their mismanagement is not that of the entire industry, it could become so if others don't take a close look at how they adapted or failed to do so.

The Interpretive Framework

With the vast amount of information I accumulated on these four banks in the course of the study, it would have been easy to drown in the data without ever telling a coherent story. There were times when I felt as if I were drowning, but I was saved in large part because I had a consistent framework that guided both my data collection and analysis. It enabled me to delineate the *character* or *personality* of these banks as organizations in terms of a *configuration* of attributes. The most important attributes were the banks' histories, present cultures (which were often shaped in large part by their histories), CEOs and senior management groups (who did the shaping), strategies, structures, and staff.

The schema this comes closest to is one the organizational analysis group of the McKinsey organization developed, which is often referred to as the *7-S framework*. Purposely using an alliteration approach as an aid to memory, they suggest that one may best understand organizations in terms of the interaction of their structure, strategy, systems, style, skills, staff, and superordinate goals.[3]

Without going into detail in defining all these terms, it is important to indicate the basic ideas underlying the scheme. First, the seven factors listed above influence an organization's ability to adapt. Second, the factors interact with one another in such ways that a change in one (e.g., a new business strategy) will not contribute to effectiveness without a corresponding change in the others. They note, in that regard, that many new strategies that companies institute don't work mainly because of a failure in execution, that failure resulting from a neglect of the other Ss. Finally, no one of the factors will necessarily always be the driving force in helping an organization to adapt at a particular time. Instead, the driving force might conceivably be any one of them.[4]

Taking the 7-S framework into account, there is a complementary way of looking at organizations that I also used in doing interpretive histories of these four banks. The central theme of this complementary perspective is to look at how organizations adapt in terms of the concept of *fit* or *alignment*. There are two kinds of fit that an effective organization must maintain. One is its fit with external changes, which, as I indicated in Chapter 1, have been quite considerable in the banking and financial services industry. New competition, globalization, and deregulation, for example, have so fundamentally changed the nature of banking that banks have had to radically alter their product mix to survive. Some have done that more effectively than others, as the case studies clearly indicate. Others have been caught off guard, failing to acknowledge such external changes and the consequent requirement that an organization adapt its strategy to them.

A second kind of fit relates primarily to the internal workings of organizations. In order for a new strategy to work effectively, it must be executed or implemented well, and that requires simultaneous shifts in an organization's infrastructure—its culture, dominant coalition, structure, people, and controls. Unless these internal changes take place, even the most well-articulated strategy will not enable an organization to adapt. To cite just one example from banking, starting in the early 1980s, as senior managers in the money center banks were casting about for new revenue sources to compensate for the continued declines in their traditional corporate loan businesses, they moved into various investment banking businesses. To support that new strategy, however, it was necessary to change many other things. They had to change their cultures from an emphasis on the long-term relationships and slower-paced decision making associated with a credit business to an emphasis on short-term transactions and deals and much faster reaction times to fit the volatility and extreme competitiveness of capital markets. Likewise, they had to change their structures from the vertical, bureaucratic ones appropriate for providing standard products in less competitive and stable markets to the flat, more lateral, and flexible ones required to respond quickly to the fast-paced changes in investment banking. Other changes, in staffing, dominant coalitions, and management systems, were required as well. Some banks were slow in making these internal changes and were much less effective as a result.

As management experts Michael Tushman, William Newman, and Elaine Romanelli observed in a prize-winning article on organizational change, executive leadership plays a critical role in the process.[5] For that reason, we have emphasized the values and management styles of the banks' CEOs in effecting the adaptions. CEOs often take the lead in interpreting external changes and in changing the corporate culture and strategy to respond to such changes. The case studies to follow will illustrate how that worked out in the banks.

Still another factor that we examine as shaping the adaptation of these banks is what Frances Milliken and Theresa Lant refer to as banks' recent *performance history.* The conventional wisdom would suggest, as they point out, that past success would lead to a continuation of an organization's strategies and internal infrastructure, while past failure would lead to change.[6] There may be many exceptions, however, as they also point out. For example, past or even recent success may lead to complacency and a failure to sense and adapt to changing conditions. Likewise, failure may be rationalized by externalizing the blame to outside forces that are perceived as temporary and therefore as not requiring that the organization change in any basic way. The important point is that past and recent performance are critical factors in shaping senior management's propensity to change. They provide feedback on how the organization has been doing and may be interpreted in different ways and with different results.

Further insights into the dynamics of organizations and the larger implications of their efforts at repositioning that I have used in analyzing these four banks come from the configuration model of management writers Raymond Miles and Charles Snow.[7] They suggest that the adaptation styles of most organizations may be categorized as falling into one of four *strategic types,* as follows:

1. The *prospector* firm, which has as its main strategy the finding and exploiting of new product and market opportunities

2. The *defender,* which finds a stable market niche and attempts to protect its position against all comers

3. The *analyzer,* which represents a combination of the first two, pursuing many product markets that are stable as well as many that are new and changing

4. The *reactor* firm, which has no coherent direction or style

I have found these models very useful in telling the stories of the four banks that are the subject of this book. What all the frameworks indicate is that organizations are very complex entities that can only be understood in terms of the interaction of many internal and external forces. Most important, organizations are much more than just the personalities of their leaders, as critical as that is. While leaders do shape their companies, they are, in turn, shaped by them. Thus, the history of any organization, which includes its past CEOs, its culture, and its strategy, determines who will be tapped for present and future leadership and what the limits are within which such leaders may steer the organization.

With this background, we turn now to interpretive histories of the four banks. All contain important lessons for other banks that are going through similar changes. They also cast light on the larger issue of the future prospects of U.S. commercial banking in general.

Part 2

The Four Banks

3

Citicorp: From New York Bank to Global Giant

They are more anxious than other banks to leave no stones unturned and to commit resources to a multiplicity of promising financial activities. They are forced to be impatient by their driving cultural imperative of multiple ambition and opportunities. They want a lot. They would not be content to be a big merchant bank. Nor would they be content to be a North American retail bank. They want several things and always have. Maybe this is one of their Achilles heels. This attracts many talented people. But it also leads Citi to spitting them out a lot.

BANKING CONSULTANT

Our first case—a version of the universal bank strategy more common to Europe than to the United States—is Citicorp. The bank had many different names at various points in its history, as will be indicated below. It became Citicorp in 1974, the new name of its holding company, established in 1968 as First National City Corporation. While many students of U.S. banks see Citicorp as sui generis, and it clearly is that, it is also an important model or benchmark for other U.S. commercial banks. Indeed, its change from a primarily wholesale bank in the mid-1960s, with total assets of roughly $16 billion, some 20,000 employees, a single set of businesses, and a relatively unified corporate culture, to a highly diversified financial services institution in 1990, with assets of over $230 billion and 95,000 employees, contains many important lessons for other banks attempting to adapt to the environmental turbulence of recent decades.

If developing a highly diversified, full-service, supermarket strategy is one effective way of adapting, Citicorp is a premier example. Variously referred to as *the bank with the boardinghouse reach* and *the megaconglomerate of American banking,* Citicorp, though an extreme case, provides perhaps the most dramatic test of that strategy. Indeed, we often learn more from extreme cases, in which a particular strategy is enacted most forcefully, than from so-called average or ordinary ones. There is certainly nothing very ordinary about Citicorp. Moreover, its aggressive diversification strategy has come under particular stress in the late 1980s and early 1990s, when the entire U.S. commercial banking industry, including Citicorp, has been hit harder than at any time since the Great Depression by a series of economic jolts: a recession, declining real estate and leveraged transaction markets, and a depleted bank deposit insurance fund.

Senior managers in other U.S. banks should thus take note of Citicorp's successes and failures, as it has relentlessly pursued a strategy of growth and diversification. Unlike any other U.S. competitors, with the possible exception of Chase and BankAmerica, Citicorp resembles in that regard such other financial service giants as American Express and Merrill Lynch.

On the one hand, Citicorp has been widely acclaimed as one of the leading commercial banks in the United States and globally. It is first in total U.S. assets, with $217 billion as of July 1991, though recent megamergers and Citicorp's aggressive downsizing and cost cutting may soon change that. Its global consumer bank is by far the largest and most successful worldwide, having earned $979 million in 1990, and with tremendous strengths in credit card products, local branches, private banking, and management systems. In wholesale banking, it is a leading player in many markets: foreign exchange, risk-management products (swaps, futures, options), transaction processing (cash management, trust and custodial services) , U.S. government securities, and traditional banking services (with some investment banking) in developing nations.[1] It is the most global of all U.S. banks, operating in 92 countries from 3300 locations, with a huge array of retail and wholesale products. It has probably the most advanced electronic communications technology in the banking world, to support all these businesses and, in a variety of ways, to integrate its global strategy. It is understandably included in most lists of the financial services institutions likely to be among the leading players in the new Europe of the 1990s and in the year 2000 and beyond.[2] The Salomon Brothers Stock Research Group refers to it, for example, as "the only clearcut American bank winner in a Pan-European environment."[3] Stephen Davis, using a highly knowledgeable panel of bank watchers, included it in both 1984 and 1988 as one of the 16 best-managed banks in the world.[4]

At the same time, for all its strengths, Citicorp has gone through some very hard times in recent years that may well reflect deeper, systemic problems, rather than just temporary reactions to short-term economic decline. Indeed, Citicorp's performance since early 1990 may well call into question its entire mode of operations, including its strategy, culture, and leadership, past and present. Thus, Keefe, Bruyette, & Woods, an investment firm specializing in banks, ranked it forty-first in quality of loans, forty-third in profits, and fiftieth in risk-adjusted capital for 1990. Its performance has been spotty for some years. Salomon Brothers Stock Research Group ranked it thirty-second among the 35 largest U.S. bank holding companies in overall performance in 1989 and no higher than twenty-seventh since 1984.[5] On a series of performance measures [e.g., return on equity (ROE), return on assets (ROA), earnings per share, nonperforming assets as a percentage of total loans, loan loss reserves, and stock price] Citicorp's performance has been undistinguished. Reflecting all these problems, but particularly its nonperforming loans and limited reserves, Citicorp's stock price sagged from close to $34 a share in July 1989 to $11.25 in November 1990. It has come up some since then, along with other bank stocks, to $21 in May 1992, but it still faces serious problems.[6]

Citicorp's capital adequacy and creditworthiness have also declined seriously since 1989. As of June 30, 1991, for example, its equity/assets ratio was 4.08 percent, just over the threshold that regulators insist on and well below its New York money center peers. J.P. Morgan's ratio was 6.60 percent, Bankers Trust's was 5.75 percent, and even Chase, which had had hard times similar to those of Citicorp, was at 4.90 percent.[7] Nonperforming loans in commercial real estate and highly leveraged transactions, accompanied by low levels of capital and reserves, increasing mortgage and credit card delinquencies, and a continuation of such losing businesses as Quotron, its information firm (which had over $200 million in losses in 1990 and has been in the red every year since 1986, when Citicorp purchased it) have all contributed to serious problems. The same Salomon Brothers Stock Research group that has lauded Citicorp in the past nevertheless reported that as of early January 1991, Citicorp's reserve coverage for all nonperforming loans was only 33.2 percent, the lowest of the 35 biggest banks.[8] Some of the impacts of this decline have been quite devastating for the bank and its senior management. Moody's downgraded Citicorp preferred stock in January 1991 to the equivalent of a junk issue. Citicorp then faced increasing difficulty in its attempts to raise fresh capital. While it has boosted its equity capital in 1991, through intensified cost cutting, downsizing, and selling of "nonstrategic" businesses, it did much worse than it had hoped. It sold its municipal insurance business, AMBAC, in July 1991, for $350 million, instead of the $500 million it had wanted.[9]

For a while, the fallout even extended to John Reed, Citicorp's chief executor officer (CEO), as articles in the business and financial press intimated that he might be losing the support of his board. One such piece appeared in *Newsday* on July 7, 1991, suggesting that his grip on the bank was weakening and questioning whether he could remain as CEO. While some of this was journalistic hype, and while Reed's board did give him expressions of confidence, the fact that there were so many articles in 1991 that critically examined his management style throughout his tenure as CEO indicates that he and his bank had come under increased public scrutiny.[10] This press coverage contrasts sharply with the press's respectful treatment of him and Citicorp before 1991. Reed and his senior managers acknowledge the bank's many problems. They have also embarked on an austerity program of cost cutting, downsizing, and asset sales, and they express much optimism about the bank's long-term future prospects. Notwithstanding what they say and what they have begun to do, Citicorp, as a massive, diversified, and geographically dispersed organization, has serious management problems that will have to be tended to if the optimistic forecasts are to hold up.

This chapter looks at Citicorp's complexity, starting with a brief characterization of the bank and a summary of its history, and then highlighting its strategy, culture, human resource practices, organizational structure, style of operations, and weaknesses.

Citicorp, one of the true conglomerates of American banking, has pursued a consistent strategy since the late 1950s, reflecting in many respects an earlier strategy from the 1890s, when it evolved from being a personal and more specialized bank to being what its spokespeople often referred to as an *all-around bank*.[11] The strategy has been one of diversification, providing a comprehensive array of financial services ("If it is financial, we do it") and committing substantial resources to multiple promising activities. This strategy has been generally referred to as the *supermarket approach* of the all-purpose financial intermediary. It has been pursued in an aggressive, prospectorlike, innovative style ("on the cutting edge"), through a decentralized divisional structure with multiple profit centers, and supported by a corporate culture that stresses entrepreneurship. This has had many costs as well as benefits. Included among the costs are intense internal competition and conflict, as well as high turnover among talented managers.

Relentless, unconstrained growth, encompassing many products, clients, and geographic markets, has thus been a hallmark of the modern Citicorp strategy, and its roots that go back to the turn of the century. As a general rule, institutions often bear the imprint of their founders and early leaders, and Citicorp is no exception.[12] It is important, therefore, to put its recent experience in historical perspective, so as to understand better both what has driven it in recent years and what its future prospects may be.

History and Leadership

Citicorp's history may be seen in terms of several periods. The first, from its founding in 1812 through 1890, has been referred to as the *premodern stage* of the bank's development, when it served mainly the interests of New York City merchants and, later, emerging industrialists.[13] Its original name was the City Bank of New York. One historical-minded Citibanker claims that it was founded by New York City businessmen who had not been well served by Alexander Hamilton's central bank, The Bank of the United States, and that it has had an antiestablishment, anti-blue-blood orientation ever since.[14] Moses Taylor, a leading merchant, industrialist, and investor, dominated the bank in its early years. Taylor had been a director since 1837, was elected president in 1856, and remained in that position until 1882. The bank had a state charter initially and surrendered that for a federal one in 1864, when it became the National City Bank of New York.

The next stage, sometimes called the *Stillman era*, after James Stillman, its president from 1891 to 1909 and again from 1919 to 1921, was the period when "a small New York City bank became the country's leading financial institution."[15] It became, in 1894, the largest bank in the United States, already introducing in those early years the culture of innovation and entrepreneurship that were to be its hallmark in recent decades. Major developments during this period include the establishment of a foreign department in 1897; the setting up of an investment affiliate, National City Company, in 1911; the opening of the first foreign branch of any U.S. national bank, in Buenos Aires in 1914; and the purchase in 1915 of the International Banking Corporation with its Asian branches in 1918.

Still another important figure of this era was Frank Vanderlip, whom Stillman had hired. Vanderlip "would eventually influence the institution's development almost as much as Stillman himself," as the bank's president from 1909 to 1919.[16]

This stage was then followed in the 1920s through the early years of the Depression by much expansion into investment banking (particularly securities distribution), foreign banking (in Latin America, the Far East, and Europe), and the further development of a diversification strategy to become and remain a generalist bank, decentralized along product lines. All these initiatives are, of course, familiar refrains for contemporary Citicorp observers. The term *financial department store*, coined in the 1920s, reflected this strategy.[17] A key figure in these years was the bank's president, Charles Mitchell (1921–1929), who was chairman from 1929 to 1933. National City Bank of New York was singled out in congressional testimony leading to the enactment of the Glass Steagall Act in 1933 as one of the big national banks supposedly engaged in fraudulent securities transactions using depositors' funds. Mitchell became a symbolic figure in the national debates, as a leading culprit. The bank was hurt by the charges, and Mitchell was forced to resign.

There then followed a period of drift from the early 1930s through the 1950s, reflecting broader legislative and economic trends. Regulatory constraints, such as Glass Steagall and the McFadden Act, spelled a virtual end to the bank's investment banking operations and its expansion across state lines. It continued in a holding pattern until well into the 1950s. John Brooks, the financial journalist, referred to it as "a sleeping giant" during the 1950s.[18] As one investment banker who had followed Citicorp's history noted, "It was a sleepy bank in the 1940s and 50s, just like the other money centers."[19]

One exception to this pattern was the merger in 1955 with First National Bank; the new institution was named the First National City Bank of New York. This was one of a series of mergers in New York, creating diversified wholesale-retail banks.

A turning point in the newly merged bank's history came with the appointment in 1957 of two entrepreneurially oriented insiders, George Moore and Thomas Wilcox, to head the overseas and New York branch divisions. The modern history of the bank that is now Citicorp began at that time. It has been a history of tremendous expansion, first internationally, under the leadership of Moore and Walter Wriston, and then domestically, through the consumer bank which itself later became global.

George Moore, Activist: Waking the Sleeping Giant

Moore, who became president in 1959 and chairman in 1967 but was never CEO, started that expansion. He set the agenda for changes that were to shape the bank into its present form. Indeed, much of the strategy and many internal characteristics of Citicorp today began under his leadership. (Wilcox, meanwhile, lost out in a succession struggle to Wriston and subsequently became CEO at the Crocker Bank in San Francisco.)

Moore's priorities included:

1. Developing the overseas business

2. Recasting Citicorp's mission from banking (being in the loan and credit business) to financial services in a much broader sense

3. Revamping the personnel policies of the bank to recruit more MBAs and develop more of a meritocracy

4. Instituting a planning culture, with increased emphasis on heads of branches and businesses taking initiatives (bottom up) rather than just senior managers from headquarters (top down)

5. Most important, selecting Walter Wriston to head up the international operations and then take over as president and later as CEO.[20]

A man of boundless energy and with an irreverence toward rules that he felt were a constraint on the bank's restructuring, Moore was enormously successful in pushing these reforms. One of his first priorities, after he became president in 1959, was to develop the international bank. It was Citicorp's international expansion that transformed it into the colossus that it has become today. Moore became president at a time when U.S. multinationals, aided by an increasingly overvalued dollar, were establishing operations all over the world, and Citicorp became a leading bank in servicing them. Under Moore's leadership and later under Wriston's, Citicorp opened many new branches in Asia, Latin America, Europe, and the Middle East, and staffed them with a vastly improved caliber of personnel. It had already had an overseas presence in the 1950s and even earlier, but its older generation of branch managers had exercised little initiative in developing new business. As the historians Cleveland and Huertas write:

> Moore took over an organization badly in need of change. The overseas establishment had been eroded by long years of depression and war,

hot and cold. The overseas staff was competent and possessed a wealth of knowledge about foreign countries, but it was aging and morale was low. Moore moved promptly to put new life into the Overseas Division.[21]

Moore supported this overseas expansion with another big change, namely, the recruitment of a new, younger group of talented, high-achieving people, many with advanced degrees and a strong interest in international affairs. He shook up the personnel department, which had previously reflected an older bank culture, and he put a lot of energy into recruitment, working tirelessly to attract and then nurture and develop promising people with M.B.A.s and other advanced degrees. As John Brooks wrote, "Citicorp's director of personnel relations, Lewis Cuyler, persuaded people on campuses that banks weren't a place to go to die."[22] It was in the international operations that Moore instituted a meritocracy that was to spread later to the entire bank, giving it a depth of talent far surpassing that of most competitors. This new cadre of young, highly educated people became the core of the international business, and they had a sense of excitement about the frontier nature of their assignments. As one reported, "The 1960s was the beginning of the international business, and we had people who were almost pioneers, like special forces in the army. We even had some in the Middle East who all but lived out of tents. You might be the only bank person in a place like Australia."

Citibankers of that era recall well the many able people who started in the overseas branches and later moved up to senior management positions at headquarters. One of them, Tom Theobald, became head of the institutional and later the investment bank, was mentioned frequently as one of two or three candidates to succeed Wriston as CEO in 1984, and left Citicorp in 1987 to become CEO of Continental Illinois. There were many more from that cohort as well who moved up to prominent positions at Citicorp and elsewhere. It was a new generation of bankers that had been spawned by Moore's and later Wriston's leadership.

Still another change that Moore instituted to support the overseas division was decentralization, allowing for more local initiative for branch managers than before, and reflecting a style that was also to support Citicorp's later expansion in the 1970s and 1980s.[23] He reorganized the division to provide for both more decentralization and more centralization. On the one hand, he gave more local discretion to managers in the overseas branches, who were obviously closer to the markets they served than were headquarters staff. At the same time, he provided more central oversight, particularly on matters of credit control and personnel, both of them basic to Citicorp's later successes. Credit control had been a long-time priority in the bank, and Moore was simply reinforcing it.

More generally, decentralization fit the bank's new personnel policies in the sense that it was recruiting more talented managers who aspired much more than their predecessors to run businesses and develop new products. Providing opportunities to run decentralized overseas branches enabled the bank to attract such people.

The other big change under Moore's leadership was his redefinition of the bank's overall mission, from banking to financial services. The term *financial services* was more than just a slogan, and it became a vision that drove the bank's later expansion and diversification efforts. Those efforts included providing not just loans and credit, but rather a wide array of services—e.g., trusts, investment banking-related, information, and insurance. These services would be provided to customers (individual and institutional) all over the world. Walter Wriston was to embellish on it, but it was Moore who began movement in that direction. Referred to as an *activist* and a *builder*, "hell bent on doing things yesterday," Moore was the catalyst for Citicorp's vast expansion after the 1960s.

It wasn't always easy for Moore to play this leadership role, as he had to buck an older establishment in his change efforts. The manager who was the very embodiment of that old establishment was Stillman Rockefeller. Widely acknowledged as a professional banker, Rockefeller was reluctant to allow the bank to change too fast, and he kept a sharp eye on Moore, whom he never allowed to be CEO, guarding against Moore's excesses and enthusiasms. "George was a dynamic force. He was a great motivator and inspiration, one of the best phrase makers around, but a poor administrator," recalled a very senior Citicorp banker from that era. As Moore himself recalled:

> My accession to the chairman's post in June, 1967, had been accompanied by a change in the by-laws that left the bank without a chief executive officer—and a change in custom that left Rockefeller on the board after his retirement, presumably so he could continue to keep an eye on that Moore, who some thought was inclined to be a little brave. I noted in my diary that the action had been "ungracious, undeserved and unnecessary."[24]

One of the most important things that Moore did was to discover Walter Wriston, who started out as a manager in the shipping loan department. Moore made Wriston the head of the overseas division in 1959. Wriston became president in 1967 and CEO in 1970.

Walter Wriston: Citicorp's and American Banking's Visionary

The Wriston years were ones of unprecedented growth for Citicorp, and Walter Wriston was the person most responsible for the bank's vast expansion and diversification from the late 1960s to his retirement in 1984. His vision of Citicorp as a financial services conglomerate was critical in its growth. As a senior manager from those years said:

> Wriston saw even more than Moore that the world was really a global village, and I can remember the many times he said that. He used to come around the bank with his list of the top financial service institutions like Merrill Lynch, American Express, and Sears, and talk about all the products and services they provided which we could not. And he was furious that we would have been denied by legislation from competing in those fields. He was the one who then pushed so hard for deregulation.

Indeed, the very active role that Citicorp played under Wriston's leadership in pushing for geographic and product deregulation was just a further indication of its continuing style of being a "first mover" on many issues, often well ahead of its competitors. "Citicorp created the deregulation issue in banking," said one of its senior staff people, perhaps overstating the case, but not that much.

The number of strategic initiatives during Wriston's leadership involving decisions that positioned Citicorp well ahead of most competitors was impressive. It included: the further expansion of the overseas division; the early adoption of the bank holding company device as a means of product expansion (1967); the early investment in electronic communications technology (early 1970s); developing the negotiable certificate of deposit (CD) (1961) and the auction market for exchanging CDs; the consolidation of the consumer bank as a single division, and its subsequent expansion (1975); the further recruiting and developing of many talented people; and the establishment of an internal climate encouraging entrepreneurship, including the setting up of multiple profit centers to facilitate new business and product development.

A strong believer in the free market and in the benevolence of the multinational corporation, Wriston was the banking industry's visionary in its critical transitional years, which coincided with his term as Citicorp's CEO, 1967–1984. He saw the importance of diversifying away from traditional provision of credit and into more broadly conceived financial services. He saw more clearly than most that financial services had become increasingly an information business, and he made an early and huge investment in technology as a result. He later saw the importance of consumer banking to help deal with the bank's funding problems. He was the basic architect of Citicorp's famous "Five I's" strategy of pushing simultaneously into institutional banking, individual banking, and investment banking, as well as into the information and insurance businesses.

In implementing his vision, Wriston elaborated, but with his own stamp, upon many of the earlier initiatives of George Moore. He increasingly attracted talented people from the outside and encouraged them to develop new products, with the bank's financial and moral support. This meant setting up a highly decentralized, loose organization of multiple profit centers, reflecting his philosophy that good new ideas rise from the market level. "'Let a thousand flowers bloom' was his philosophy," recalled a retired Citibanker. "He thought it was an enriching experience for every manager to take total responsibility for a business."

Entrepreneurship and risk taking were thus highly valued, and Wriston announced early on that fame and fortune at Citicorp would be acquired by those who rocked the boat.[25] He was notorious, for example, for setting up several competing groups to work on the same product development problem, rewarding only the group that did the best job. The others often left the bank on their own volition or were fired. "Wriston didn't know how to deal with change and so he set up three or four groups to tell him what to do," explained a Citicorp staffer.

Internal competition soon became a way of life at the bank. Those who regarded this approach favorably often referred to it as "constructive tension." Others saw it as wasteful and as creating a negative internal climate, in which managers of redundant product groups were pitted against each other. Both views were right, but at some point, how to minimize the style's costs, both social and economic, became a serious question.

In Wriston's early years as CEO, Citibankers, particularly those in the institutional bank, which dealt with businesses, and in headquarters (HQ) staff positions, reported having much personal contact with him as a "hands-on" manager who circulated among the troops. One such banker reported:

> I remember when I first arrived at the bank, an old college friend introduced me to a tall gangly man, just outside the auditorium where all of us were to meet for an orientation session. There were a lot of people milling around, and I couldn't remember what she said his name was. He immediately started grilling me on what I thought of the bank, and I told him how screwed up I thought it was. Finally, I told him there was a meeting I had to go to. He said that it hadn't started yet and couldn't start without him. I asked him again what his name was and

he said: "Walt Wriston." He always had his ear to the ground and was a great listener.

Others had similar reports about Wriston coming to their office in shirt-sleeves or sitting down next to them in the cafeteria for lunch. Over time, as the bank got much bigger, there were fewer such reports.

The other characteristics of Wriston's style around which there was much consensus were his penchant for provocative showmanlike public statements to the media, often expressing iconoclastic views, and his somewhat feisty manner. Several Citibankers commented that his very strongly held views reflected a quality of arrogance that soon became an institutional trait. One staff person recalled, "At one point, I looked at his old performance appraisals through our personnel department. And they described him as very bright and talented, but then said that his arrogance would do him in as he made his way up in the bank." An investment banker highly critical of Citicorp's and other banks' forays into his industry said, "It was a loyal and happy group in the fifties and sixties, and was not a ruthless place at that time. Wriston changed it. He developed delusions of grandeur about what the bank should be."

For all his imperfections, Wriston was obviously a strong leader who had an enormous impact upon Citicorp and upon the banking industry. At the same time, leaders are also the products of their times and institutions. Would the bank have expanded the way it did had somebody else been at the helm? Perhaps not, except that George Moore had already set the culture and climate before Wriston became CEO. Wriston was both a product of the institution and a shaper of its style and performance. Had he not been available, there might have been another Wriston type, who would have had a different style but probably would have moved the bank in many of the same directions.

Strong leadership such as Wriston exercised often exacts a price, and his style had negative as well as positive impacts. On the positive side, the leadership that he exercised did in fact move the bank from the sleepy, public utility mode of the 1950s to a much more innovative and adaptive mode. Wriston was pushing a new strategy of expansion when the corporate wholesale business was declining markedly, when banks were being disintermediated and nonbank competitors were getting stronger, and when there was a need for more entrepreneurial types to develop new businesses to help banks to recover from the losses of the old. At various times and in various ways, Wriston may have oversold his message, and yet, perhaps some overkill may be necessary to move an organization from a past inertia to a new, more adaptive strategy and culture.

Turning to the downside, people who were at the bank during the Wriston years as well as knowledgeable outsiders agree that, notwithstanding all the benefits resulting from his style, there were some friction costs as well, particularly as a result of staged competitions among managers who were developing the same new products. These competitions created a highly turbulent internal environment, referred to by one financial journalist as "a series of barroom brawls." Many Citibankers who served under Wriston agree, and one reported:

> I remember a case that was typical, where two executive VPs were in Wriston's office, arguing over a turf issue. Each was saying to Wriston: "Look. You gave me this business and told me to develop it, and now this other guy claims you said the same thing to him." And do you know what Wriston reportedly said? He said: "It sure will be fun to see which one of you wins."[26]

Because of the infighting that resulted from Wriston's style, the bank lost many talented managers. The other fallouts were a high cost structure and a tendency to proliferate redundant product groups—for example, product teams unknowingly serving the same customers from many different parts of the bank. A now retired Citibanker tells a classic story about the Greek shipping magnate Stavros Niarchos, a long-time client of the bank and of Wriston:

> One day he went to Wriston and said he had three proposals from bankers to help him manage his finances and asked Wriston to give him some advice on what to do. Wriston reviewed the three of them, and when he was done, he said that Niarchos ought to go with the bank that offered him the best deal. Niarchos then replied that the proposals were all from Citicorp—I believe from London, Hong Kong, and Paris. You can imagine how Citicorp's competitors thrive on that. Wriston was furious and said he would end that kind of internal competition. But it kept going on.

In addition, customers were sometimes angered when jurisdictional disputes delayed responses to their requests.

The great albatross from the Wriston years was the overlay of bad loans that Citicorp, along with many other money centers, made to Latin American countries during the massive recycling of petrodollars in the late 1970s and early 1980s. For the banks, desperate to recover after losing much of their corporate loan business, this decision came back to haunt them. Pursuing a front-end returns strategy (getting the total fees paid out at the outset and worrying about the repayment later), the banks had put themselves in a precarious position. Wriston's oft-quoted comment, when he was questioned about the risks of less developed country (LDC) loans, that nations, unlike people and corporations, don't default, is frequently cited as evidence of his poor judgment.

Despite these very serious shortcomings, Wriston nevertheless emerges as the person most responsible for Citicorp's vast expansion and diversification, from the late 1960s to his retirement in 1984. Notwithstanding mistakes, he helped to make Citicorp one of the major players in global banking. As one bank analyst reported:

> The quality of Citicorp's talent, that Wriston following Moore was so responsible for, both those who stayed and those who left, is really something. I remember one meeting with the analysts that Larry Small (then head of Citicorp's institutional bank) orchestrated. The presentations of the senior managers and staff he brought with him were so good, one of us asked him how dependent the bank was on them and what it would do if they ever left. He replied that the bank was 14-deep in their positions, and we have found out since then that there was much to that.

John Reed: An Aloof Visionary

The last period in Citicorp's history, still unfolding, started in 1984, when John Reed became CEO. There was much publicity at the time about how Wriston was managing the succession.[27] Three senior managers were reportedly in line for the position, and nobody inside or outside Citicorp, with the exception of Wriston and whoever he confided in—if anyone—knew who the new CEO might be. Certainly, none of the three candidates reportedly knew. They included Hans Angermueller, an attorney, 58 years old, who had come to Citicorp in 1973 from Shearman and Sterling, a law firm that had serviced the bank. Widely regarded as a relaxed, caring, and effective conflict manager and problem solver, Angermueller had directed Citicorp's many lobbying efforts to push for more deregulation. Another was Tom Theobald, age 46, a graduate of Holy Cross and Harvard Business School, who joined the bank in the mid-1960s under Wriston, first ran a joint venture in Australia, and then returned to HQ and eventually became the head of the institutional bank. A corporate banker, Theobald was the choice of Citicorp insiders in his part of the bank, many of whom were sure he would be named as CEO. Instead, Wriston selected his long-time protege, John Reed, age 45, a Massachusetts Institute of Technology (MIT) graduate, who had developed a reputation as a maverick and technocrat. Brought in by Wriston and Citicorp's then president, William Spencer, in 1969, to streamline and modernize the back-office technology, Reed, after having served as an institutional bank loan officer, went on to do staff work in strategic planning and later to run the retail bank. A nonbanker for most of his early career at Citicorp, Reed ran the consumer bank from 1975 to 1984. During the first 6 years of his tenure, it suffered big losses.

He came under much criticism for decisions that he made and that insiders, particularly from the corporate bank that was subsidizing Reed's "losing" operation, felt were ill-advised. One such decision was to make mass mailings to phone lists in an attempt to enroll credit card subscribers, without checking on the financial status of the people on the lists. Losses resulting from these subscribers' nonpayment of their bills were substantial. Indeed, former Citicorp officials reported, perhaps wishfully, that Reed "came close to being fired for his nonchalant attitude toward years of mounting losses."[28] Throughout all this, Walter Wriston protected Reed, still regarding him as one of the bank's ablest managers. Reed's and the consumer bank's reported goal was to improve Citicorp's market share during a time when BankAmerica was changing the name of its credit cards and slowing the expansion of its consumer business.

Reed inherited formidable burdens: the internal competition, the proliferation of profit centers, the high cost structure, and the broken LDC loans. Also a visionary, and even more of an intellectual than Wriston, Reed was until very recently continuing Citicorp's expansionist course.[29] He committed the bank to a big investment in its new information business, marked by the purchase of Quotron in 1986. An even bigger commitment was made to develop a merchant and investment banking capability, including in that a worldwide infrastructure of product specialists, deal doers, securities trading and delivery systems, and supportive information systems. At the same time, Reed had little background or experience in wholesale banking, though he had been a loan officer for a short time in the institutional bank. Since the stock market crash of 1987 and the general decline of the mergers and acquisitions (M&A) and related businesses, Reed has reduced Citicorp's commitment to investment banking. Until 1991, it had been embarked on a big national and global expansion of its consumer bank.

The other big initiative Reed took was setting aside in 1987 some $3 billion in reserves for the bank's nonperforming LDCs.[30] Some of the other banks, particularly Morgan, were very angry about this, since they felt that Reed had not informed or consulted with them in advance, and yet forced their hand by his "Lone Ranger" action. In a counter-move, Lewis Preston at Morgan then proceeded to cover its LDC loans with 100 percent reserves, eventually putting Citicorp at a disadvantage since its reserves were only about 30 to 35 percent.

Given Citicorp's uneven profitability, its increases in nonperforming loans, its low reserves, and its consequent difficulties in raising capital for future planned expansions, Reed and his colleagues now have new priorities. These include: more strategic focus; controlled rather than unconstrained growth; expense control; internal consolidation to elimi-nate redundancy and turf struggles (e.g., the establishment of a global finance division, merging the investment and institutional banks); a more collaborative and collegial style for Citicorp's global bankers; and, perhaps most important, an increased emphasis on execution. Indeed, the term *execution* appears in numerous memos circulating around the world to Citicorp bankers from Reed's office. As he remarked in a press conference with bank analysts in August 1988, he expected the next year for Citicorp to be "contentedly boring," by which he meant that there would be no surprise acquisitions that might alter radically the bank's expenses. He also emphasized in many internal memos his strong com-mitment to nurturing the development of the bank's human resources, perhaps in part as a reaction to the past internal competition and high turnover under Wriston.

Reed's management style resembled Wriston's in some respects but differed in many more. While also a visionary, committed to continued growth and diversification, iconoclastic with regard to rules and tradi-tions, and having a large appetite for risk, Reed, unlike Wriston, was no-tably aloof from the bank's staff and its day-to-day operations, particu-larly those of the corporate bank. One Citibanker stated, "Reed is a very reflective person and is a longer-term thinker than Wriston. He looks at the big galactic picture. He is very academic and likes to play around with ideas and concepts, but the bank needs to be effectively managed as well."

Others noted his loose, nonbureaucratic style. One explained, "He is extremely informal and sets that tone in the senior management ranks. He paid little attention to managing, and little was ever written. The loose operation at that level did not help the bank."

In recent years, in an attempt to deal more effectively both with prob-lems he inherited and with such others as nonperforming loans in com-mercial real estate and leveraged transactions, high overhead, busi-nesses like Quotron that are doing poorly, and difficulties in raising capital, Reed has begun an aggressive program of cost cutting, placing more emphasis on short-term goals, selling off nonstrategic businesses, downsizing, and emphasizing collegiality and cooperation more than entrepreneurship. His priorities and style have thus finally been influenced by the bank's hard times. Some bank analysts have even commented that he has become a better manager in 1991 than at any time since joining the bank. At the same time, however, Reed was in deep trouble in 1991. Many articles in the business and financial press were highly critical of the way he had managed the bank and seemingly abandoned its credit culture with the vast accumulation of so many nonperforming loans. Their authors expressed amazement that Reed's board had not fired him. But Reed had always had remarkable staying power and was demonstrating it again.

Moreover, Reed announced in January 1992 a major shakeup of both his senior management group and the bank. He brought in H. Onno Ruding as vice chair. Ruding was a former Dutch finance minister and executive at ABN AMRO, the largest bank in The Netherlands. Ruding's assignments were to improve Citicorp's lending practices as its new chief credit officer, attract more foreign capital, and promote its role in financial transactions in Europe. In addition, Pei-Yuan Chia, head of Citi's Consumer Bank, was also added to the top management group, underscoring that division's importance to Citicorp's future. And new task forces of senior executives were established under Richard Braddock, the bank's president, to do monthly reviews of its various businesses. These changes and some successes in cost cutting have helped keep John Reed in office. How well he copes over the next months will determine his and Citicorp's long-term future. He seems to have maintained the confidence of his board as of this writing and has always been a survivor. That record, however, will be sorely tested in 1992.

In sum, these are some of the key stages and turning points in Citicorp's history, as it has evolved into a global, universal bank. As the analysis in Chapters 4 and 5 will indicate, it has been a most innovative bank, at the cutting edge in many areas, and in that sense a highly effective institution. At the same time, due both to its size and its style (which reflects its leadership, culture, and strategy), its performance has been uneven. Like the *prospector firms* in the writings of management theorists Raymond Miles and Charles Snow, it has been stronger on entrepreneurship and innovation than on execution. In brief, it has been more *effective* in finding new market niches and in moving into them early and aggressively with vast resources than it has been *efficient* in managing costs and attending to the details of implementation. The issues will be analyzed in Chapter 4.

4

Citicorp: Battlefields of Diversity

A Diversified Global Giant

Citicorp is by far the most diversified of all U.S. banks. It provides financial services in consumer banking (the individual bank), investment banking, and insurance and information services, in addition to its traditional franchise in institutional banking. The first four are very recent, the consumer bank having been established as a consolidated division in 1975, the investment bank in 1982, and the information and insurance businesses in the mid-1980s. A senior manager at Citicorp coined the term "Five I's" to characterize this diversity.

In point of fact, three of the "Five I's" account for literally all the bank's revenue: individual or consumer banking (retail) and institutional and investment banking (wholesale). The latter two are now combined in a single division called *Global Finance*—itself, in turn, broken down into a developing nations and an industrialized nations unit.[1] Viewed in what strategic management writers refer to as *portfolio terms*, the institutional bank had been the main revenue producer, through the mid-1980s. The consumer bank, meanwhile, was in the red its first 6 years, creating a big drain on the rest of the bank. Its purpose initially was to provide low-cost funding to the bank pool which fueled the loans made by the institutional and investment banks. The interest paid on retail deposits was less than that paid for wholesale funds bought in the money market.

Citicorp, like Chase and many other money centers, was traditionally a wholesale bank, and the institutional bank literally subsidized the consumer bank during those years, much to the consternation of many institutional bankers whose bonuses suffered accordingly. It was even said in the financial and business press during this time that Wriston was jeopardizing Citicorp's established franchise by making such a big commitment to a seemingly losing business. John Reed, as head of the consumer bank, came under much internal criticism from aggrieved institutional bankers, some of whom wanted him fired.

Ironically, the situation was reversed by 1990. The consumer bank has become the big revenue producer, subsidizing the institutional and investment banks, which have gone through a difficult period. Nonperforming or defaulted loans in commercial real estate and highly leveraged transactions, along with those to developing nations, are now the big drain. The high overhead and infrastructure expenses of the investment bank and some of its losing businesses also contributed. It experienced big losses on its equities and bond trading in Europe in the late 1980s. Thus, the consumer bank is now carrying much of the rest of the institution, having grown tremendously over the past several years. It has expanded from producing 33 percent of the bank's total revenues in 1986 to close to 60 percent in 1990, with John Reed predicting that it will probably go as high as 70 percent by the mid-1990s.[2]

It is a truism in the life of an institution that those who contribute most to its well-being, who help it deal best with its critical uncertainties, become the dominant coalition. Sociologists and organization theorists refer to this as the *strategic contingencies theory of power*. The critical uncertainty for Citicorp in 1991 is raising capital, as it has been forced to put earnings into reserves for nonperforming loans. This has depressed its stock price, which means that stock cannot be used to finance its acquisitions. One of the places to turn to for help has become the consumer bank, which is now producing a reliable and growing revenue for the bank as a whole. As the new golden rule goes regarding who gets the power, "He who has the gold makes the rules."[3] Consumer bankers have thus become increasingly prominent in senior management ranks. A reorganization in late 1989 put Richard Braddock, head of the consumer bank, into the presidency which had been vacant for several years. Braddock, a marketing man from General Foods, then began to make the rules, as he and his staff critically examined the bank, piece by piece, along with John Reed, to determine which businesses should be supported and which dropped or changed. (The fact that the presidency had been left vacant for several years attests to a serious weakness in the bank's management.)

This does not mean, however, that Citicorp will withdraw from wholesale banking. A Salomon Brothers report of 1988 referred to Citicorp's institutional investment (wholesale) bank as one of its "twin engines of growth," and it is committed to continuing in that direction.[4] It claimed quite rightly in its *1988 Annual Report* that it was the world's largest corporate and investment bank, in terms of earnings.[5] Despite some losing businesses and serious losses since then, requiring much restructuring, Citicorp is keeping its wholesale franchise.

In addition to high levels of diversification, Citicorp has pursued an intensively *global* strategy, again more than any other U.S. bank. It now provides both wholesale and retail financial services in 92 nations. At a time when such other big banks as Chase, Security Pacific, and BankAmerica have phased down or closed many of their global operations, Citicorp has maintained its presence around the world.[6] Its international banking and finance (IBF) sector, for example, does business in 62 developing nations; its industrialized nations sector, Japan, Europe, North America, and Australasia (JENA), serves 22 countries; and its consumer bank now has branches in 36. At a time when banking has become increasingly globalized, and when the needs of Citicorp's multinational, corporate customers are to do business on a global basis, this is an important competitive advantage.

It is no surprise, then, that the Salomon Brothers Stock Research Group sees Citicorp as the only U.S. financial services institution that is well positioned to embark on a Pan-European effort after 1992.[7] That effort will be mainly in consumer banking, as Citicorp has already elevated its European Consumer Bank to "group" status; moved its headquarters from London to Brussels, the designated center of the post-1992 European Economic Community (E.E.C.), and appointed a young, bright institutional banker as new group head.

Citicorp's strategy has still other important characteristics. One is its strong commitment to market leadership in many fields, supported by its emphasis on innovation and entrepreneurship. The examples, cited above, of the many strategic initiatives taken under George Moore and Walter Wriston attest to that.

Closely related to this strategic emphasis on market leadership and innovation was Citicorp's strong commitment to *expansion*. Walter Wriston's frequently enunciated goal of a 15 percent annual increase in earnings reflected this. Many outside observers characterize the bank as engaged in "uncontrolled growth," referring in that regard to a style of expansion without thinking through enough whether it is appropriate, how it will be implemented, or what its potential costs will be.

Another feature of the Citicorp strategy has been its heavy emphasis on *technology*.[8] Wriston saw clearly the extent to which financial services was a set of information-intensive businesses, requiring an advanced electronic communication technology capability. In selecting Reed as his successor, he was reinforcing that priority. Citicorp's automated teller machines (ATMs) have facilitated the successful expansion of its branches around the world. Its transaction-processing businesses—for example, cash management, and global custody and investment banking, including the development of many new products—and its strengths as a global securities trader have all been technology-driven. Its stated intention to "wire the world" undoubtedly drove it to develop its technological capability well beyond what most of its banking competitors had done. Citicorp may be the only bank with its own internal technology product development subsidiary. It designs and makes its own ATMs. This was a big marketing and technology project that differentiated Citi's consumer bank domestically.

In brief, Citicorp became a formidable competitor in the 1970s and 1980s, following a strategy of global consumer and merchant banking. It has many competitive advantages: a global outreach; technology; industry knowledge; a supportive culture; tremendous depth of talent; a visionary top management; and a flexible, decentralized organizational structure. Few other U.S. banks could lay claim to those strengths.

Moreover, Citicorp has a strong *strategic planning capability*. Several bank analysts report, for example, that they see Citicorp as having more of a long-term perspective than its competitors. While some view that perspective with mixed feelings, interpreting it as reflecting a style of delaying the "hard" choices about which businesses to continue or drop, most are agreed that the bank is engaged in extensive analyses of long-term trends in its markets. "They are very active in that and they have to be," explained one bank analyst. "Since they are so interested in acquisitions, they must look at a lot of things long-term." Sometimes, its long-term judgments have turned out very well, as in its consumer bank; but that has not always been the case, in part because environmental trends in this industry are so difficult to forecast.

Citicorp's Many Products

Another way of looking at strategy is in terms of *particular products.* Strategy is, in this sense, what organizations choose to do. Citicorp's products or businesses fall mainly under the rubric of either the consumer bank or the institutional investment bank. Until late 1991, when Reed and his senior management colleagues began a major restructuring to cut costs, consolidate internally, and gain more focus, the bank existed as a loosely coupled set of divisions or sectors, each with its own stand-alone businesses. There was some so-called cross-hatching, as different businesses collaborated (e.g., the securitization and sale of credit cards or mortgages, linking the consumer and investment bankers). The bank's main businesses, however, operated independently, and many still do.

Starting with the *consumer bank*, the biggest revenue producers are the *credit card* and *mortgage loan* businesses. Both have grown tremendously since the mid-1980s. Citicorp had roughly 15 percent of the U.S. market in credit cards in 1990, up from 7.8 percent in 1983, and second only to American Express, which had roughly 20 percent.[9] The next bank competitor, Chase, had only a fourth of Citicorp's market share. Citicorp has become a low-cost producer, having realized big-scale economies. A major shakeout is now going on, in which it is likely to emerge as a still bigger player than before, with smaller competitors exiting, as it buys up the card businesses of many of them. While none of the banks provide information on what each business contributes to their total revenue, bank analysts estimate that credit card earnings contributed roughly 20 to 25 percent to Citicorp's total revenues in 1988 and may now be contributing close to 30 percent.[10]

Mortgage loans are going through the same kind of shakeout and consolidation, through starting with a much more fragmented market. In 1988, Citicorp's servicing volume ranked second in the industry at 3 percent market share, and its originations were at 4.4 percent of the total market. It has emerged as a leader there as well, due largely to its favorable cost structure, which results from its having sharply reduced its back-office costs by building a national mortgage-processing "factory" in St. Louis.[11] Another 10 percent of the bank's total revenues is estimated to come from this business.

Other significant businesses within the consumer bank include the New York, U.S., and overseas branches; several savings and loans (S&L) acquisitions and their attempted turnaround; and private banking. Citicorp now has the biggest share of the metropolitan New York market, close to 12 percent. It has begun pursuing a one-bank national expansion strategy as an extension of its earlier purchase and attempted turnaround of S&Ls in Oakland, California; Key Biscayne, Florida; Chicago, Illinois; and Washington, D.C. These were very difficult experiences initially, and the bank had big losses as the turnaround problems were much more severe than it had anticipated. Over time, it has developed some expertise in repairing such troubled entities. The federal government may call on it to help bail out more S&Ls, as that part of the financial services industry appropriately begins to disappear, perhaps partly by being absorbed into commercial banking. Participating in the S&L industry restructuring may become an opportunity, then, if Citicorp is selective in which banks it takes on, and circumspect in how it does so.

Starting in 1989, Citicorp began developing its "One Bank, USA" national expansion strategy. This, along with its growing credit card and mortgage loan businesses, will make its consumer bank an increasing part of the total business. The strategy involves providing centralized support services in marketing and systems (utilizing common product lines, leveraging brand image and service capabilities, and combining back-office functions on a national basis), while at the same time decentralizing service delivery to local branches to ensure that products are tailored to customer needs. The strategy is now being worked out, both for the United States and globally, and it is likely to fuel tremendous revenue increases from this sector. Thus, late in 1990, the bank consolidated its U.S. branch and international consumer banking into a single sector, Global Consumer Banking, that should allow it "to gain greater advantage from our experience and expertise in branch banking, mortgages, and credit cards around the world."[12] This consolidation has proceeded so far that only U.S. card products and private banking remain distinct groups within the consumer bank. It represents both a big change from the previously "looser" collection of stand-alone businesses and, most would say, major progress in the way the consumer bank is structured.

An analysis of Citicorp's European prospects concludes that its consumer bank will be "the propellant for Citicorp's European profit growth."[13] The same methodology as in the U.S. expansion will be used again in Europe, namely, (1) consolidation of support activities in centralized locations (Brussels is the main one in Europe) and (2) decentralized service delivery. All the large branches, functioning as full-service centers, will provide a wide array of standard products: credit cards, mortgages, deposits, mutual funds, and private banking. Securities brokerage will also be provided. One bank analyst has even predicted that Citicorp might have up to $75 million in incremental earnings by 1991 in its European branches.

More generally, the consumer bank has been restructuring and fine tuning its operations in ways that will make it an even stronger competitor in the 1990s than it already is. Several products that had become a drag on earnings, though once very profitable, have been dropped, including mobile home lending and auto loans. Also, back-office expenses are being cut. The consumer bank has thus concentrated on expense control, while at the same time expanding in areas of strength, increasing the likelihood that it will become the mainstay of Citicorp's franchise in the early 1990s. It is already a big revenue producer. Its growth prospects are very good. It is also the business that chief executive officer (CEO) John Reed knows best of all, and to which he and his senior management have recruited many talented managers from outside.

These managers are nonbankers, by and large, who by definition have never made a loan. Many of them came from the sales and marketing segments of consumer goods industries. They bring in a new set of needed skills, adding to the bank's staff and subculture diversity, while at the same time contributing to conflicts with traditional bankers that have to be managed.

Meanwhile, the *wholesale business* within Citicorp will not disappear, though it, too, is being consolidated, after several years of very uneven performance. That consolidation strategy has involved focusing on selective growth in targeted product market segments where it has particular strengths [e.g., foreign exchange, derivative products (swaps, options, futures), LBOs, and transaction processing]. It has also included exiting from businesses in which the bank was not competing effectively; reducing infrastructure expenses sharply, where possible; and building a broad distribution capability.[14]

A restructuring in 1990 of the JENA sector of the wholesale bank provided an early indication of how that consolidation strategy may work. It involved eliminating two layers of management and reducing bureaucracy, with Reed and Braddock now paying close attention to all the businesses in that sector, and Michael Callen, its head, having every product head report directly to him. This was the first time that Reed had ever had such close surveillance over businesses in the wholesale bank, and while it may not be his favorite activity, given his big-picture orientation and past aloofness, losses there required direct intervention. Callen, meanwhile, had 53 operating executives reporting directly to him. They ran what are now called *activity centers* (ACs), sometimes referred to as *aches*. The not-so-humorous description of Callen's job was that he nursed 53 "headaches."[15] There were stars in the AC group as well, however, and Callen indicated in mid-1990 the bank's increasing emphasis on what he called its "seven towers of excellence": foreign exchange, risk-management products, real estate finance, transaction processing, highly leveraged transactions, securitization of assets, and loan syndications.[16]

By January 1992, however, Callen had resigned from the bank in a major shakeup "because there wasn't a major role for me in the reorganization."[17] Larry Small, head of the institutional bank, had departed in a similar way the year before, after having provided hundreds of millions of dollars in loans to Robert Campeau for his unsuccessful takeovers of several department store chains including Bloomingdale's, Abraham & Straus, and Federated.[18]

By contrast, the bank's emphasis in the early 1980s had been on broad-based growth, and the results had not always been good. In 1990, for example, while its developing nations businesses had an impressive net income of $430 million, its much larger industrialized nations group reported a net income loss of $299 million,[19] composed of losses in commercial real estate, leveraged finance, and Australian operations. Nevertheless, this part of the bank remains important, largely because of the areas of strength Callen referred to. In fact, two of those areas—foreign exchange and risk-management products—accounted for up to a third of the bank's total revenue in 1990.

Investment Banking

All the money center banks made big commitments to investment banking in the 1980s, pushing at the same time for the repeal of the Glass Steagall Act. Citicorp was no exception. Like its commercial banking competitors, Citicorp set up its investment bank initially as a separate entity, to achieve a critical mass and establish its own culture, compensation policies, and organization. The general philosophy at Citicorp, as elsewhere, was that, if the investment bank was a separate division, it was more likely to develop its own identity, expertise, and power base; to attract product specialists and traders; and to provide quality service for clients. It was less likely to be absorbed by the old culture and power structure of the institutional bank or to become embroiled in conflicts with traditional commercial bankers. There was merit in these arguments, though there were built-in structural problems. Both the institutional and the investment banks served the same corporate clients, and the relationship managers from the institutional bank who were the point of contact between Citicorp and those clients zealously guarded that relationship. It was clear, then, that the investment and institutional bankers had to coordinate. Sequestering the investment bank initially to build it up was all well and good, but a serious problem of integration would have to be managed.

Citicorp established a separate investment banking division in 1982.

It placed the bank's treasury functions in that new division, to give it some substance, along with other, securities-related businesses: corporate finance, mergers and acquisitions (M&A), and trading. From 1982 to late 1987, when the crash hit, Citicorp moved aggressively to establish itself as a premier investment bank, just as it had in so many other businesses. It recruited people from the top business schools and Wall Street. It set up training programs to familiarize commercial bankers with the workings of capital markets and their many products. It built trading facilities in New York and established a presence in securities trading in London, Tokyo, Hong Kong, and other exchanges around the world, helped immeasurably by its technological capability. It pioneered in developing such risk-management products as swaps, options, and futures, gaining early market leadership in those fields. In 1986, after only 4 years as a separate division, it accounted for roughly a third of the bank's total revenues. (The institutional and consumer banks also accounted for a third each.) Most important, Reed handed over the direction of the investment bank in 1985 to his former rival for CEO, Tom Theobald, who ran it for 2 years before taking the job of CEO at Continental Illinois. Theobald had a lot of experience in corporate banking, which Reed did not, and he could be expected to provide strong leadership. Many Citicorp managers noted that Reed essentially allowed Theobald to do his own thing in the investment bank, and that may well have been the reason that it remained separate for so long.

In perhaps typical Citicorp fashion, there were serious growing pains involved in this effort. For one thing, there was considerable reluctance among senior managers, including Theobald, to pay competitive Wall Street bonuses, and the bank treated many of its new investment bankers with ambivalence. As one senior manager explained, "Imagine if we said that the way for General Motors to do better was to escalate compensation costs. People would think [it was] crazy. That is a big question: How much to pay to attract people without falling into the abyss of an impossible cost structure." Another reported, "It sticks in our craw around here for these young punks at age 27 to be making $500,000. Yesterday, I saw a memo from one of our competitors on compensation for their investment bankers. These guys take it as a matter of right that they [should] be paid [at] Wall Street levels. We think it is stupid."

Many Citicorp managers reported on the bank's *cultural aversion* to providing such compensation, and for some time, it did not. One result was substantial defections of investment bankers from 1985 through 1987, sometimes in entire groups (e.g., a swaps group). A critical incident illustrates the problem. A senior staff person recalled:

> We had a trainee from Greece in the investment bank under Theobald. He went back to Greece for a vacation and then brought back a huge deal that would bring in a lot of revenue for the bank and go on for a long time. It was clearly the kid's deal, and people at the bank informed him he would get a big bonus. He thanked us but then said he was going to dictate that his bonus would be $1 million. Well, you can imagine what happened then. It caused a cultural crisis. We had tried for years to become an investment bank, and then we would not make the cultural adaptation on compensation.

Other money centers, but not Bankers Trust, also faced this problem; but it was particularly acute at Citicorp. Perhaps the fact that it had a strong consumer bank, in addition to its institutional bank, which had a compensation scale considerably below what the external market dictated for investment bankers, had a lot to do with it. Finally, in self-defense, Citicorp, which had always had a record of paying competitively, raised compensation levels for its investment bankers. It still struggles with the issue, however. (This was not a problem unique to Citicorp or to banks. American Express faced this problem when it acquired Lehman, as did Sears when it bought Dean Witter.)

Other transition problems that had a unique Citicorp flavor included duplication, severe turf struggles and infighting (within the investment bank and between it and the institutional bank), turnover (some unrelated to compensation), and constant reorganizations and reshuffling of personnel. One senior manager at the bank reported that he had to contact many colleagues at least weekly to see if they had been reorganized and moved to some other responsibility. His comment was made in the context of how difficult it was for him to stay current in an institution in which change was so constant.

Some of the most serious problems resulted from the buildup of resources, personnel, and trading facilities. The redundancy, sometimes referred to as *Citiswarm*, had particularly negative results. As a banker from a money center competitor reported,

> We were competing for a restructuring deal in an Asian country, and Citicorp sent three teams who didn't even know that others from their bank were involved. We arbitraged them right out of the picture and got the deal for ourselves. After a while, incidents like this from Citicorp, and there were many, became a standing joke. They were beating themselves.

Conflicts between investment bankers and commercial bankers were particularly severe. The commercial bankers regarded the new investment bankers as having poor judgment regarding credit risks, having little loyalty to the bank, and being motivated almost exclusively to make their deals and earn their bonuses, without much concern for anything else. One senior corporate banker reported, "For these new investment bankers, it is `My deal and the hell with everybody else.' I always referred to these investment bankers as having a kind of ontological blindness. Often their credit judgment was quite poor, and they were wild men, going too fast, not looking at risk; and that is bad." The uneasy fit between the new investment bankers and the bank's traditional culture made managing them very difficult. One top staff person in the wholesale bank explained,

> Managing these investment bankers is a pain. If you have ever been a parent of teenagers, that gives you good preparation for managing these people. Many are immature and very demanding. And who could ever believe that they could command compensation of over a million dollars for one year. We know that Bankers Trust paid whatever was necessary to get these people. We are not about to do that.

Another critical issue was that investment bankers often didn't perform well as general managers, and yet some were put in that role. The result in some instances was much lower performance than might otherwise have been the case.

After Theobald left in July 1987, Citicorp integrated the investment and institutional banks into a single division. It formalized what senior managers called a *pipeline* concept, in which the institutional bank was responsible for originating deals and the investment bank for distribution and trading. Michael Callen, who had previously headed Citicorp branches in the Middle East and in Asia, was appointed to succeed Theobald, and he and Larry Small, head of the institutional bank, both pledged that they would collaborate in making the newly integrated wholesale bank work well. A further restructuring in 1989 put Callen in charge of the industrialized nations segment of this division—the Organization for Economic Cooperation and Development (OECD)—and he had a reputation within the bank for his collegiality and interpersonal skills. Citicorp managers and outside observers note a decline in infighting over the past year or so among top people in the wholesale bank, though several have also said that it is not clear whether this integration at the top has yet had an impact at lower levels.

Investment banking, by whatever definition, has clearly not been the focus at Citicorp that it is, for example, at Bankers Trust and Morgan, two exclusively wholesale banks. It is part of a much larger portfolio of financial services at Citicorp, important but still secondary to consumer bank businesses. Nevertheless, the bank pursued it in the aggressive style in which it had pursued everything else. It followed the *broad-based expansion* approach that had become its hallmark, attempting to buy market share through acquisitions; making big investments in people, facilities, and technology; and constantly reshuffling personnel and reorganizing, even though this approach was not having the kinds of payoffs the bank had hoped for.

Starting in 1987, even before the crash, John Reed was acknowledging publicly that Citicorp had a serious expense control problem in its investment bank. It has begun to deal with that, as Callen's July 23, 1990, statement indicated, and with the exception of its seven products listed there, Citicorp doesn't have very many investment banking activities going on. It does some leveraged buyouts (LBOs), some cross-border M&A work, and some underwriting abroad, but investment banking seems not to be central to its efforts in the 1990s.

A Big Loser: The Information Business

The other important set of activities to which Citicorp has committed itself for the 1990s relates to the information business. In 1986, it bought Quotron, the largest securities information provider in the U.S. Thus far, Citicorp's information sector has been a drag on earnings, "due to the costs of acquiring Quotron and startup costs in a variety of new businesses." Quotron's losses have increased every year from $34 million in 1986 to $228 million in 1990.[20] Several problems contributed to the losses: the quality of Quotron's management, its failure to update and upgrade some of its systems, its lack of vision, and its loss of business to two main customers—Merrill Lynch and American Express—when Citicorp took it over. Both of those conglomerates saw Citicorp, understandably, as a prime competitor, and they weren't about to line its pockets. As a knowledgeable consultant in this field explained, "Big moneys were paid to Quotron for its services by Merrill Lynch and American Express. The prospect of putting that money into Citicorp profits turned them away."

Data on Quotron's market share, in relation to its biggest rivals, Reuters and Telerate, as measured by number of terminals installed, indicate that it has lost considerable ground since 1984.[21] Reuters did roughly twice the business that Quotron did in 1989, after being well behind in 1984, while Telerate narrowed the gap from one-third of Quotron's volume to close to three-quarters.

There are different views regarding what Citicorp should do in the information business. Some bank analysts have urged that it sell Quotron and cut its losses. They acknowledge the importance of the information services business but protest that Citicorp cannot continue to spread itself so thin and expect to turn in a strong financial performance and thereby inspire investor confidence. Citicorp's senior managers argue otherwise, claiming that they will make increasing profits in this business in the 1990s. Some cite Citicorp's new point-of-sale (POS) information management product, which provides manufacturers and retailers with an important service by recording data on buyers' demographic characteristics and buying decisions, as gathered at checkout counters. Another product provides travel-related services to business and is seen as a promising new business.

It remains to be seen whether Citicorp can make information services profitable. At least one analyst likens the Quotron trouble to Citicorp's struggle with consumer banking. "That was another business that people questioned," said Ron Mandle of Sanford Bernstein & Co. "Citicorp was tenacious in the past," he added. "I expect them to be so in the future."

5
Citicorp: Culture Shock

Many institutions develop distinctive characters that are reflected in the values and beliefs to which they are publicly committed. Social scientists and management writers refer to them as the *corporate cultures*.[1]

I have approached corporate culture by several routes: interviews with outsiders, mainly bank analysts, management consultants, regulatory agency staff, and journalists; interviews with bank staff people; and perusal of internal documents, including speeches and policy statements of senior management. There is a high degree of consensus on Citicorp. Because of its size and complexity, Citicorp has several different subcultures, in addition to a superordinate culture for the bank as a whole. Since success for an organization such as Citicorp requires that it be capable of managing not only its multiple businesses but its multiple subcultures as well, a balance must be maintained so that each subculture is accepted for what it is, while efforts are made to meld them together.

Citicorp came much closer to having a single, unified culture in the 1960s and early 1970s than it has now, in the 1990s. The predominant business was wholesale banking, and a large cohort of upper-middle-level and senior managers who had been recruited for the overseas division helped to set the tone of the bank. "Of the 20,000 employees in the early 1970s," recalled a Citibanker from that era, "there were no more than a couple of hundred at the very top. They were people who had been with the bank for a long time. And everybody knew everybody else. These were career people who got to know one another very well." They had a keen sense of excitement about the bank's growth during those years, a strong institutional loyalty, and an equally strong sense of camaraderie among themselves. This was so much the case, in fact, that the group still get together at least once a year to reaffirm old ties.

Three Subcultures

As Citicorp has moved first into consumer banking and later into investment banking, there has been much understandable disappointment among many in this cohort who saw the new cultures emerging. As one long-term consultant pointed out:

> The elite loan officer group from the institutional bank saw these new consumer bank people as the riffraff, polluting the bank. They were regarded as nonbankers who had never made a loan and did not have the social graces of the old-timers. Then along came the investment bankers, who were only out for themselves and their own deals and bonuses, and had no loyalty to the bank. They were seen as upstarts, another kind of riffraff. So you had a dominant culture of corporate bankers that was upset by two newcomer groups—both at about the same time.

Many in the George Moore and Walter Wriston cohort from the 1960s saw John Reed as surrounding himself with efficiency-minded, cost-conscious senior managers who, they felt, discouraged innovation. For these old-timers, the fulfillment they used to get from their jobs disappeared. Several bemoaned the fact that such strong headquarters (HQ) staff departments as the economic forecasting group were eliminated.

The institutional bank, in particular, underwent much belt tightening, as branches throughout the United States, and later in Europe, were closed, and as many of the Wriston generation left or were eased out. One corporate banker from the Wriston years noted:

> Loyalty and commitment to the bank are much less now. Also, taking chances and trying new things are no longer encouraged. Now, looking good is the name of the game, and that means keeping expenses down and not rocking the boat. The bank is not challenging people like it used to. It isn't that the bank shouldn't be demanding, but it is not challenging people to achieve the most that they should.

The three perhaps most significant subcultures are:

1. A mass-market, cost-control subculture associated with the consumer bank, referred to by one senior manager as the *MacDonald's culture*

2. A flexible, deal-doing, antibureaucratic subculture associated with investment banking

3. A long-term relationship subculture associated with institutional banking

Orchestrating all three within the same organization required tremendous resources and managerial skills, and some observers of banks and some senior bank managers felt that the costs outweighed the benefits. One such informant suggested, "Yes, it is possible to have these three sets of businesses, but they are incompatible, and it is a drag on performance to try to nurture all of them. They represent conflicting values and ways of doing things."

Briefly, the culture of the consumer bank is the most bureaucratic of the three. It represents, as one former Citicorp senior manager noted, "long-range, slowly crafted, predictable, and stable ways of doing things, mass marketing, controlling costs, and with standard products. I would call that the *Procter & Gamble culture*, just what you would expect in a consumer bank." John Reed, in the widely noted *Harvard Business Review* interview that outside critics have used both to praise and to criticize him, made a similar characterization:

> Consumer banking is a little like building cars. Success comes when you routinize things to a point where a group of people at the top build the strategy, drive the creative work, and push the new products, while execution takes place relatively effortlessly, through good blocking and tackling. That's what success transfer is all about. It's about implementing new ideas quickly and uniformly around the world.[2]

These are descriptions of a top-down, standardized structure and technology, similar in many respects to an assembly line, in which much of the creativity in product development and delivery comes from senior management. This is very close to what students of management generally mean by the term *bureaucratic*. It is used in this context in a purely descriptive sense and has no pejorative connotations.

At the opposite extreme is the investment banking culture, which, as indicated above, never had that favorable a reception in Citicorp, certainly not on the compensation issue. Ironically, one would have expected otherwise, given Citicorp's traditional culture of innovation and entrepreneurship. The investment banking culture tends to be short-term and ad hoc. It emphasizes a flexible organization, favors deals over relationships, and, in many instances, fosters unique products. As the same Citicorp manager described it, "There, in investment banking, you have to expand and contract quickly, do business and change overnight, pay huge bonuses and compensation one year and, if necessary, fire those same people the next year. That couldn't be more different from the stable consumer bank culture." John Reed's description captures the culture well:

> Corporate banking is more like delivering medicine. Your most expensive person, the doctor, is the guy who deals with the patients....In the corporate bank, we don't have common products that we design and sell. We have relationships and transactions that are specialized and unique. Moreover, our professional competence sits down low in the corporate bank, with the people on the front lines who deal with customers and devise the transactions. We can't develop new products at the center and push them out. Good corporate bankers are walking product development departments.[3]

Another senior manager summarized the differences between these two subcultures:

> I see the consumer bank culture as putting a big premium on loyalty, and less on intelligence. The investment bank, on the other hand, is a culture of little loyalty and of a lot of intelligence. There are also differences in attention span, with the retail bank culture one of a long span and the investment banking one [of] a short span.

Finally, there is the traditional culture of the institutional bank. It has much more in common with the culture of the consumer bank than with that of the investment bank, emphasizing as it does long-term relationships with corporate clients, more standard products, and a structured way of doing things. As the traditional corporate loan business got phased out, this culture became less critical for the bank's success, but it continued to exist to some degree. Moreover, as leveraged buyouts (LBOs) and the mergers and acquisitions (M&A) business decline, there may well be a return to relationship banking, whereby corporate clients will value once again a bank they feel they can "trust" over the long term, rather than just one with many new products.

There were conflicts among all three of Citibank's cultures, most intensely between the investment bankers and the other two. It took a while for consumer bankers to gain acceptance, but they finally did it, helped in part by the profits generated by their division. In contrast, the animosity of many institutional bankers toward the new investment bankers was particularly marked, as I indicated earlier. Some of this was a generational conflict, and much of it reflected a deep resentment of the perceived "greed" of the investment bankers, who were also seen as lacking both a sense of loyalty to the bank and the requisite managerial and banking skills. As one senior manager from the institutional bank observed, "They move too fast, without looking at risk. They don't care that much about the bank. And many of them are bad managers, as indicated by what happened when Citicorp bought up investment banks in Europe like Scrimmegour Vickers, where we got our clocks cleaned in securities trading and it ended up in a shambles."

A Bank of Entrepreneurs

In addition to these subcultural differences, Citicorp has a superordinate culture that clearly distinguishes it from other banks. That culture, reflecting Moore's and Wriston's values, has driven the bank's expansion strategy. The main values have included:

1. Entrepreneurship.
2. A high tolerance for mistakes.
3. A strong aversion to bureaucracy and centralization, encouraging managers to take initiatives on their own, through decentralized profit centers, without having to wait for higher-level approval and review.
4. A corresponding pattern of internal competition among highly individualistic managers, who were encouraged to vie with one another to develop new businesses.
5. A meritocracy, valuing talent and individual achievement.
6. An activist and confrontational approach to problem solving, in which little was swept under the rug and in which people were willing to confront differences and try to work them out.
7. An institutional flexibility and impatience, reflected in a tendency to constantly reorganize and reshuffle personnel.

One underlying theme that several Citicorp managers suggested might be driving some of this culture is the bank's traditional antiestablishment mentality. Throughout its history, it has been an aggressive, feisty institution that was competing with the so-called blue bloods. One headquarters staff person explained, "This was never really the establishment bank. It was founded in 1812 by businessmen who had not been well served by Hamilton's bank. And an outsider thread runs through its history." Another suggested, in the context of its past competition with Chase:

We had a competitive aggressiveness, and I do believe that part of it was just wanting to beat the blue bloods. Wriston, though the son of a university president, was never a member of the aristocracy. Spencer, our president, was from a ranch. Ed Palmer was from a middle class neighborhood in Brooklyn. And Costanza's father was a coal miner in Alabama. So that was a big thing: to beat the blue bloods at their own game.

At the same time, there were other values that reflected a more traditional orientation to fiscal prudence that all Citibankers were urged to follow.

8. One was an emphasis on careful *credit control* as a hallmark of the bank's operations. Senior bankers at Citicorp refer frequently to their strong credit culture.

9. The other was the bank's *integrity* in its dealings with clients. These values were reasserted in the 1980s, particularly with the hiring of many new investment bankers who were seen as a threat to the old culture.

Corporate cultures are not always followed to the letter, however; and the bank's abundant nonperforming real estate loans and shaky LBOs since the late 1980s have been a source of some embarrassment, even at Citicorp where arrogance is the rule. The bank is now being scrutinized more closely than ever by Federal Reserve examiners, and debt rating agencies like Moody's and Standard and Poor have downgraded its credit rating. Given Citicorp's strong cultural emphasis on credit control, these developments have to be a source of bank concern.

Remarking upon the entrepreneurial emphasis in the culture, observers have noted something unique about the Citicorp bankers who were recruited in the Moore-Wriston era. They were invariably talented and high-achieving people with extraordinary energy who were attracted and recruited precisely because of their good fit with the culture. Wriston, who has "a fanatical belief in free competition, with all its efficiency and all its cruelty,"[4] established an internal climate that both attracted such recruits and communicated to them the value Citicorp placed on people who liked to take risks. He indicated, for example, in his orientation speeches to new managers, that they would be penalized much more for errors of omission than for errors of commission, pointing out that he had made many mistakes in the course of his career within the bank, and asking why they shouldn't do the same. It was a sign, he went on, that they were at least out there in the trenches, working on new ideas. Using a baseball analogy, he suggested that batters who made 3 hits out of 10 or just a little better than that might well end up in the Hall of Fame.

As evidence of his strong commitment to these values, Wriston gave what appeared to be unwavering support to his protégé, John Reed, despite the latter's having made decisions while running the consumer bank that cost Citicorp an estimated hundreds of millions of dollars. His indiscriminate mailing of credit cards to uncreditworthy individuals, his mistaken bet on fixed-rate mortgages just before interest rates went way up, and his putting in place a very expensive computer system that worked poorly and had to be abandoned after a couple of years were expensive mistakes. Yet, they obviously did not hurt Reed's career. As one senior manager of that era recalled, "The bank lost a fortune on those decisions, but Wriston let him make mistakes like that without punishing him. He saw this all as a learning experience, and he would let you come out of it. And [he] judged the mettle of a manager by the extent [to which] and the way he did [come out of it]. John Reed always came out of these situations."

A big part of this culture, then, was the bank' s *high tolerance for mistakes*. (This is the exact opposite of Chase's approach, as I will discuss in Chapter 6.) Wriston reportedly preferred having daring managers who would generate and try out new product ideas rather than managers who were risk-averse. Another senior manager reported, "We are more tolerant of mistakes here than many Wall Street firms and are able to attract people from the street as a result. We are well enough capitalized to absorb such mistakes." That of course cannot be said today, and many capital problems the bank faces as of this writing result from the failure to recognize the new reality.

More specifically, the culture of the bank *supported managers functioning as their own idea champions*, providing them with lots of resources with which to work on new products. One senior manager who was a recipient of such largesse explained, "When I went to my boss with a new idea, he said, `If you think it's worthwhile, let's do it. Let's warm it up with $1 million and see what happens.' That's the attitude you see at Citicorp."

Carried to extremes, the value placed on innovation was associated, in turn, with the practice of *setting up several managers in a competitive situation*, to see which one might come up with the best product. It wasn't always clear what would happen to the losers, but in many instances, they were fired or they left voluntarily. One Citicorp manager described how it worked:

Just to give you an example, when Reed was starting up the credit card operation, he assigned three separate groups to try to develop it, knowing that one would eventually be chosen. After 18 months, they found that one group did it best. He then told the [heads] of the two losing groups that the next two in the hierarchy of the winning group would take each of them over, and eventually everybody in those two losing groups was fired.

The other key aspect of the culture that promoted entrepreneurship was the bank's *organizational looseness and flexibility*. Some observers referred to the bank's *idealization of disorder*, as it set up many profit centers and kept reorganizing and changing personnel within them to improve their performance. Others referred to its habitual *impatience* as contributing. Setting up multiple profit centers and fine-tuning them reflected the culture and supported a broader strategy of being a perpetual R&D hothouse, trying to preempt competitors by being a leader in many new products. The culture and the strategy it supported often worked, but they also often didn't work, at great cost to the bank.

Attracting Talent

Citicorp's human resources policies have been critical to its success. It went out of its way to recruit the most talented and aggressive people it could find, and its success in this regard was widely acknowledged in the industry. Consultants and executive searchers often commented that Citicorp bankers were among the best that they had seen. A Citicorp international banker recalled:

> When I returned from my overseas assignment, I tried as I had in the past to get at least an interview for graduates from my college. I could get them that but no more. I would hear back from one of the people in our human resources department that so and so was a nice young man but not aggressive enough for us at the bank. And not a single graduate from my college ever got a job here, even though many of them were bright.

Having recruited energetic, high-achieving people, the bank then provided them with abundant means to develop new products and businesses. Given its decentralized profit centers and its willingness to put money into new ideas, the bank thus provided a built-in opportunity for development. That, of course, became a double-edged sword, when these people were put in competition with one another, but the bank did provide them with much opportunity to grow.

Finally, much attention was paid, particularly in the Wriston years, to locating and nurturing the highest-achieving people, preparing them for possible later promotions. As a top staff person close to Wriston explained, "I remember that Wriston had one of his wall cabinets locked up with pictures of fast-track people that they had located, and he kept a watch on them." This was another way of developing talent, since these people, once identified, were often given more resources and opportunities.

A Decentralized, Loose Structure

As discussed briefly above, the Citicorp structure throughout its expansionist years fit its growth strategy. It tended to be highly decentralized, with product groups that functioned as profit centers. It was also unusually flexible (some would say too much so) in its tendency to reorganize constantly. The benefits were that the bank could mobilize quickly in response to market opportunities and could provide a setting that attracted talented people. The costs were the considerable internal competition, redundancy, consequent inefficiency, and failure to service customers with a unified set of products. It turned out that the large numbers of entrepreneurs that this structure attracted were often not collegial, discouraging the kinds of internal collaboration that were increasingly necessary.

As strategies change, so often do organizations' structures, and this reality may be reflected at Citicorp. Recent structural changes in the consumer bank are a case in point in what may be a harbinger of organizationwide changes. This may be so, notwithstanding the differences highlighted above between the consumer bank and the wholesale (institutional investment) one. As one consultant explained:

> The big change in the consumer bank has been centralization. Before, it was very decentralized, and there was a series of stand-alone businesses for different states. Now they have gone ahead with the "One Bank, USA" strategy. The central technical staff and management support group have increased tremendously, while the entrepreneurs in charge of product groups in the field have been stripped away. Before, they operated as a series of profit centers, but no more. The product heads are now called *marketplace managers*, but the middle line within the bureaucracy has been decreased, and they and these product heads have less discretion now. A new set of skills is required to succeed at the bank. They are collaboration, trust, and focus. This is so for the institutional bank as well. They and the entire bank are talking about the

importance of a centralized, collaborative mode. That requires overriding several decades of hiring practices, culture, and rewards. One
top person gave a presentation not long ago in which he talked about
how Citicorp over the next several years would lose some of its best
people. He suggested that the bank could not afford them, economically or psychically. It is wiping out entrepreneurship and is now creating uniform franchises with standard products.

Sources of Weakness and Vulnerability

It should be apparent by now that I see Citicorp as an institution with
both extraordinary strengths and serious weaknesses. It is going to
have to deal with the latter much more aggressively, if it is to maintain
its position as a major global player in the financial services industry.
The strengths are clear: a *global presence* far surpassing that of competitors; a *diversified income stream; an unsurpassed capability in technology;* a *tremendous depth in talent;* a *strong consumer bank,* along with a
strong market position in such other businesses as foreign exchange,
risk-management products, transaction-processing services, and local
currency exchanges throughout the world; and an *infrastructure* that
provides strong support for these activities (e.g., an entrepreneurial,
action-oriented culture; decentralized profit centers; and a meritocracy that helps the bank to maintain its talent pool). Some of these
qualities, however, are changing, as the bank attempts to recover from
the tremendous losses and nonperforming loans of the late 1980s and
early 1990s.

Since these are such basic strengths, how can one argue that Citicorp
has equally basic weaknesses as well? Until the bank's declining performance in 1990 and 1991, it had a very good press and many outsiders regarded it as one of the industry's stars. As one bank analyst
explained, "Citicorp has an aura for some people. There are big investors and institutions who are real fans of the bank. They are very
impressed with what it has done and don't see it as having major limitations."

My conclusion is different. I see Citicorp as having serious shortcomings that it must attend to immediately, and with the same aggressiveness and zeal that it has followed in its many external acquisitions and
expansionist forays.

A review of those weaknesses includes the following:

1. There is an overemphasis on long-term expenditures, supporting an aggressive acquisition strategy for broad-based growth.

2. There is a corresponding philosophy that "big is beautiful"—big in all major areas of financial services. To state it another way, the bank continues to try to be all things to all people more than it should.

3. In that sense, it has shown a continued reluctance to exit from bad businesses and an unwillingness to admit mistakes.

4. It has, in addition, not focused as much as it should have on the nuts and bolts of implementation, having instead done too much, too fast, without adequate preparation.

5. To compensate for these limitations, it has engaged in a constant reshuffling of personnel and restructuring of businesses, actions that have been poor substitutes for more careful strategic planning.

6. Finally, it continues to foster a competitive internal climate that has contributed at times to a ruthlessness in interpersonal relations among some middle and senior-level managers. This climate results in a high turnover.

While there is no precise way of validating these assertions, they do match the observations of a broad enough cross section of knowledge-able informants to take on face validity. Many reflect the general principle that even the most effective institutional practices may be very undermining, if carried to excess.

The first criticism, that Citicorp has been too long-term in its strategy, has a long history and has provoked an equally strong Citicorp response. Several observers have noted, for example, that Citicorp's "continual promise of returns and perennial disappointments" in the form of subpar performance [return on equity (ROE) and return on assets (ROA)] has been going on since the 1970s. They attribute it to the bank's perpetual R&D mode of operations, in which it keeps expanding by acquisitions without enough planning and preparation. Bank analyst Frank DeSantis refers to Citicorp as having become the ultimate "mañana" stock, with the payoff always promised and often not delivered.[5] Sarah Bartlett, financial writer on *The New York Times*, suggested that "Citi's future holds the possibility of both unparalleled growth and monumental mediocrity," unless it stops indiscriminately buying up new businesses.[6] In the late 1970s, *Fortune* carried an article arguing that Wriston's continued commitment to the consumer bank, with its big losses, was foolhardy. Bank analysts make the same argument now regarding its investment in Quotron. The general argument of the critics, then, is that Citicorp has invested in too many new and losing businesses, and for too long, to ever become that profitable an institution. As Carol Loomis wrote in *Fortune:*

> Citi...has displayed a continuing genius for getting into serious trouble. A few years back, the trouble was borrowings by less developed countries. These LDC loans remain a source of Citi migraines and possibly always will. The new troubles, also throbbers, are loans to finance leveraged buyouts and commercial real estate....The growing agility required and Citi's own stumbles make the company's expansive strategy of trying to be the one true global bank seem like hubris. Says a retired New York banker who competed against Citi for years: "The world has become so complex that it has outgrown the ability of bankers—Citi's very much among them—to manage all that's going on."[7]

Loomis and others argue that Citicorp should concentrate on doing well with what businesses it has now, including exiting from poor revenue-producing ones, rather than continually chasing after new ones.

The Citicorp response until recently has been that it was proud of its long-term perspective, pointing to the consumer bank as a perfect case in point. Its senior management pointed out that the bank was not deterred by 7 years of losses or by criticism, precisely because it had a long-term view that the business would turn around and become a big revenue producer. Think of what would have happened, they argued, if the bank had heeded the voices of the critics. They also argued that the bank's diverse income stream enabled it to absorb losses in businesses its managers felt would improve.

The same scenario is now taking place with regard to Quotron and the information business, as discussed above. It has lost money every year since Citicorp purchased it in 1986. The critics argue that it can't be turned around easily in the next few years, citing Citicorp's saying in 1986 that Quotron would be making money by 1990. Its spokespeople claimed until late 1991 that the turnaround would be in the early to mid-1990s and that they were fully committed to this important business. Finally, as Steven Lipin, staff reporter of *The Wall Street Journal,* wrote on October 18, 1991, "Five years and hundreds of millions of dollars in losses later, Citicorp has effectively thrown in the towel on Quotron."[8] One reason Quotron failed was that it was not as innovative as its competitors, being slow to develop new products. "They lost a lot of market share to Automatic Data Processing, Inc.," said Andrew Delaney, editor of an industry newsletter. "They sat around too long while others started using new operating systems. Many customers made the switch."[9] For an institution like Citicorp that had always prided itself on being so aggressive, it was ironic that it held on to a slow moving, weak performer like Quotron without either improving it or dropping it early. It was one thing to argue, as John Reed had done, that Quotron needed a long gestation period. It was quite another to have failed to upgrade it during that period. There is no question about the importance of information processing for many industries, not just financial services. The issue is whether Citicorp, with all its other commitments, can take on information processing as well.

Corollaries to this criticism are criticisms that Citicorp has not exited from low-performing businesses, that it still tries to be all things to all people, and that it needs more strategic focus than it has been willing to pursue. As one bank analyst observed, "The risk in the stock is that management continues to avoid making the tough decisions of cutting expenses and exiting [from] low return businesses, and operating efficiency stays put at the bottom of the barrel."[10] Another noted, "They are most reluctant to exit [from] losing businesses. When those businesses are mentioned, they point to all the good things they do and refuse to admit losses or defeats. Their general answer is that in the sweep of Citicorp's many activities, the losses will not show up, since it is so diversified."

John Reed acknowledged, in an interview for *Manhattan Inc.*, "that he sometimes dilly dallied in getting at problems. `Little ones?' asked the interviewer. `No, No, No,' he answered. `Big problems.' He admitted to being about five years late in addressing some manifest difficulties in Citi's commercial loan business."[11]

Citicorp's drive for market leadership and size is often cited as among the main reasons for its continuing in this aggressive acquisition mode. As a former Citicorp banker explained:

> We always seemed to proceed on the assumption that big is beautiful, when that turned out not to be the case. We put ourselves in situations where we bought small jewels and thought we could make them into larger ones and did poorly. The classic example is the two British securities firms, Vickers DaCosta and Scrimmegour Vickers. They were two small jewels. We merged them into a larger one and it was a disaster....We blew it up beyond the optimum size, and it became a big problem.

One Citicorp manager referred to what he called "profit centeritis" as a source of the bank's problem, suggesting that it encouraged too many managers to start too many new businesses, without sufficient results and controls. A bank analyst suggested, "One of our key gripes has been management's lack of distinction between profits and profitability, and it will continue to be one of our key gripes as the company points to size as a measure of success. How many times have we heard that the consumer bank will soon earn close to $1 billion. Who cares? Profitability is a ratio, not an absolute." Later, the same analyst said, "The simple fact is that banks like Wells Fargo have higher ROAs because they don't throw away profits from high return businesses like credit cards on low return investments like Quotron."[12]

In brief, wanting to have it all is seen as a fundamental weakness of Citicorp that keeps dragging down its overall financial performance. The bank is seen as having to learn to say no to what may look like new business opportunities, or, as a senior manager at Morgan was once quoted as saying, "We can't afford to dance with all the girls on the floor."

There is more to the criticism, however, than just that Citicorp has tried to do too many things at once. A common perception is that as oriented as the bank is to strategic planning and long-term thinking, it has frequently moved too fast and too broadly on new acquisitions and in new markets. As one Citicorp senior manager put it, "Part of our culture is to be willing to act before we have all the facts. Sticking your neck out forces you to pull it all together." While that view has much merit, as too much analysis may lead to delayed action and missed opportunities, the lack of preparation and needed implementation planning are widely regarded as serious shortcomings. One Citicorp staff person explained:

> One reason we have not executed as well in the past is that we have had a very fast-paced culture that has not allowed us the luxury of working though issues beforehand. We now recognize that we have rushed too quickly into various markets without thinking it through, and lost a lot. That was even so for our credit card business. We had a top-level executive in who had come here from American Express, and he told us that for every new product decision or marketing decision where we took 1 month to do it at Citicorp, it took him 3 months at American Express. All he was saying was that much more care was taken at American Express with the details of execution.

Another senior manager at Citicorp summarized this point well:

> We need to try to do less and wait longer to implement it than has been the case in the past. We have had a preoccupation with profit, and that accounts in part for the way we do things. And we have often over-budgeted and have had the feeling that it is not worth doing something if we don't do it big. But the main point is that we have had no tradition of good preparation. It requires time, and we have not taken it. Our European investment banking is an example. We suffered from "short-termism" and tried to do too many things too quickly.

Another, related style problem has been the bank's tendency in the past to constantly reorganize and change personnel to such a degree and on such a scale that it was difficult to get needed continuity and almost impossible to evaluate managers and products. This is seen as reflecting an institutional impatience that is part of the fast-moving, action culture of the bank. At first, it may seem to contradict the criticism that the bank is too long-term. In fact it is both, and in costly ways. On the one hand, it may stay with some losing businesses longer than it should. On the other, in the absence of enough preparatory planning, it often keeps changing managers and restructuring in ways that make it very difficult to figure out what is going on. A Citicorp staff person reported:

> This pattern of staff changes is constant. People develop new ideas for their marquee value, to give them high visibility, but there is no value added for the bank. The feedback to them disappears when they move and somebody else takes over their job who is not tuned in to the same new ideas. We change directions a dozen times in some businesses. And people and strategies and structures never last long enough to test any assumptions.

This constant change has been a poor substitute for effective strategic planning, particularly implementation planning. Having engaged in aggressive acquisitions before it had enough information, the bank would get saddled with a losing business and would then work feverishly to turn it around, but still without always doing the kind of careful analysis and implementation planning that would be required to succeed. The acquisitions of Scrimmegour Vickers, of several S&Ls, and of Quotron, and the investment in a computer system for the investment bank that was dropped in 1986, at a loss of more than $50 million, are all examples.

How do mistakes like this happen? In addition to the desire to be a market leader in so many different products, there is an institutional arrogance that many observers and Citibankers have acknowledged. Citicorp managers are extraordinarily talented people. If they survive the vigorous competition and get promoted to senior management positions, it becomes possible for some of them to develop an exaggerated confidence in their judgment. Then they push forward on new products or make acquisitions they have no business making. In brief, they get into areas in which they have too little expertise, and they don't have enough patience to develop it. This tendency shows up in their financial performance data.

A final set of weaknesses for which Citicorp has been criticized is its highly individualistic culture and the competitive atmosphere it fosters among managers. One management consultant described the bank's climate by saying, "They have a wealth of resources and good people. In fact, they have some terrific people, and they beat each others' brains out. And the numbers of top people who left is a shame for the bank. There is so much internal strife that could hurt them down the road and already has." Another commented, "Theirs is a high-turnover culture. They eat their children and thrive on it. The numbers of senior managers leaving Citicorp are astounding. They should do much more to rely on inside people for these top positions. Instead, they keep going outside, and they never give the recognition to insiders that they deserve." Finally, a former senior manager from Citicorp reported, somewhat sadly, "The inhuman qualities of the culture there are central. Being kind is not part of their operation. If one is to have a real meritocracy, a spirit of internal competition, a willingness to accept error, and an institution that encourages the taking of risk, then it is possible that some ruthlessness may creep in, and it does."

In conclusion, the very cultural values and institutional practices that have contributed to Citicorp's successes were pursued so aggressively that they have also contributed to serious problems. The institution's greatest strengths also became its greatest weaknesses. Thus, refusing to panic in the face of short-term losses in particular businesses had merit but, when taken to extremes, left Citicorp in an overextended position. Growth through aggressive acquisitions gave Citicorp strong market leadership, but pursuing this strategy too zealously moved it into businesses in which it had little expertise and dragged down earnings. Trying to be a leading firm in a vast range of products seemed like an admirable goal; but in the highly competitive financial services industry, no firm, not even Citicorp, had the expertise to be able to compete effectively across the board. Having the vision (which Moore, Wriston, and now Reed have had) of being a diversified financial services conglomerate has been an important competitive strength, but vision without effective implementation does not always pay off. Likewise, constantly reorganizing and changing personnel may well reflect pragmatic planning in which needed midterm adjustments are appropriately made; but chronic reorganizing and personnel changes lead to chaos and missed opportunities.

Finally, hiring aggressive, talented people and giving them the freedom and money to develop businesses had many benefits for them and for the organization; but encouraging too much competition by having several managers and their staffs working on the same products created too adversarial a climate. The adversarial climate in turn led to infighting, high turnover, politically inspired reorganizations (to soothe wounded egos), redundancy of functions and product groups, dissatisfied customers, loss of business to competitors who sometimes successfully arbitraged Citicorp groups, and high expenses.

Citicorp in the 1990s: A Problem of Institutional Balance

Citicorp has been one of the world's leading financial service institutions. It represents a model of one kind of adaptation to the increasing competitiveness, globality, and turbulence of its industry and the wider economies it services. Citicorp's approach to positioning itself under such conditions has been one of high diversification and innovation. Its performance indicates the strengths and weaknesses of that approach, with the particular embellishments that Citicorp, through its leadership, provided.

To overcome an institutional inertia and drift that Citicorp shared with other banks in the 1940s and 1950s, reflecting the economic and legislative environment of the times, Moore and Wriston undertook a number of assaults on the bank's past strategy and culture. Through an aggressive expansion strategy in several areas—international, consumer, and investment banking, as well as technology—they made Citicorp a leading global bank. Pursuing that strategy so aggressively, however, created some friction and other costs that Citicorp must deal with in the 1990s. Being on the cutting edge, as one banker commented, could also, at times, lead to being on the bleeding edge. Given the present environment of banking, it is better to assume such a change-oriented posture than to be more risk-averse. Sooner or later, one has to deal with the costs of such a posture, unless it is pursued with a careful prior assessment of how it is to be carried out.

What does that mean in terms of priorities for Citicorp in the 1990s? How aware are Citicorp's senior managers of these problems? Even if they are aware, how easy will it be to redirect an institution as large, diverse, and geographically spread as Citicorp?

What all this means in the most general sense is that Citicorp needs much more institutional balance than it has had since the late 1960s. Instead of just attracting talented entrepreneurs who develop new products and businesses, it must have more managers with collaborative skills and collegial commitments. Instead of just emphasizing new product development, it must complement development with implementation planning. Instead of pursuing growth and market leadership, it should also emphasize improving returns on businesses it already has and exiting from businesses in which returns have been very low for many years.

In conclusion, given the extreme competitiveness of its industry, Citicorp will not be successful in all the markets it may wish to enter. It needs more strategic focus and must learn to say no to things that, in its former mind-set, looked like new opportunities but that may not be wise directions, given Citicorp's levels of expertise relative to the levels of its competitors. It must manage strategy implementation more carefully than in the past, and it needs to control expenses that have pulled down its performance.

Finally, Citicorp needs a different human climate than it has had. While it attracted, rewarded, and developed many talented people, the costs of pitting them against one another were great. Management theorists refer in this regard to an *optimum level of conflict* within organizations. Some degree of diversity and dissonance, openly expressed, leads to high-quality decisions. Beyond a certain point, however, conflict can become quite costly. Battles get personalized, as beating the other party may become more important than performing the task. In the process, many able managers, repelled by the bad relationships that high-conflict situations generate, leave the firm, to the detriment of the organization. It may not be possible to quantify such a concept of optimum level, but judgments can be made, particularly in organizations like Citicorp, in which internal competition and conflict play such a major role in shaping performance.

These assertions about what is needed at Citicorp for the 1990s fit a larger view of organizations, suggesting that effective firms move in dialectical fashion and adapt by maintaining a balance between extreme styles of operation. Under Moore and Wriston, Citicorp effectively transformed itself from a relatively sleepy, static-style organization into a leading player in the industry. The aggressive expansion, the diversification, the meritocracy, and the freewheeling, entrepreneurial emphasis were all needed to overcome the previous style. At the same time, pursued as vigorously as they were, these strategies dragged down the bank's performance.

In brief, solutions to old problems create new ones. The predominant issues for Citicorp in the 1990s are no longer inertia and failure to adapt; rather, the predominant issue is handling the negative fallout (internal and external) that an aggressive posture toward change has created. If the bank can handle this fallout while still maintaining much of its past aggressiveness, it will remain a leader in its industry.

Little of this is new for Citicorp's senior managers. A review of speeches and memos of the past few years by John Reed and his colleagues indicates that these executives recognize virtually all these points. Reed is not only a manager who is versed in systems and technology. He is also a person who has a broad vision of how the financial services industry and the environment in which it functions are evolving. Moreover, by dint of having always attracted people of high intellectual caliber, Citicorp is an institution of abundant vision. Unfortunately, the strategies that emerge from visionaries don't always get implemented that well.

In the past, Citicorp has been a very aggressive institution. When it starts moving in a particular direction, it often does so in a kind of blitzkrieg fashion. As one consultant reported:

> If Citicorp is being bombarded in some important market by an enemy competitor, its first inclination is not, as banks like Chase do, [to] analyze the situation and make incremental changes to beat out competitors who are firing down from the hills. Its tendency is to bulldoze all those hills so there won't be any competitors left.

Citicorp now needs to evolve a way of dealing with the many problems that its past expansion strategy has produced. There is clearly an intellectual understanding of what those problems are. Whether the institutional will and capability to make needed changes exist among its top managers remains to be seen.

Several recent developments seem positive in that regard. The bank has exited from losing businesses, including mobile home lending, auto lending, and equity trading in England and Europe. It has begun to seriously reposition its wholesale business, focusing on selected growth in businesses in which it has its greatest competitive strength, exercising more caution in acquisitions, working to lower expenses, and building a broad-based distribution capability. It has rationalized its credit card and home mortgage products to become an increasingly low-cost producer. It is pressing to expand its consumer banking business while developing a centralized infrastructure of back-office operations, systems, standard products, and marketing. In brief, an administratively strong consumer business and an increasingly focused wholesale bank represent important initiatives in a positive direction.

Size and Citicorp's Future

Citicorp's size is critical to its future. Serious questions exist about whether it is possible to effectively manage a financial services organization of Citicorp's scale (roughly 87,000 employees), geographic scope (operating in over 92 countries and all the United States), and product diversity. Citicorp managers answer unequivocally that it is possible, citing the bank's combination of strong central controls and decentralized service delivery. Many mention its economies of scale and scope and the vast resources that are associated with its size. Others, including some former senior managers from the bank itself, have their doubts. One stated:

> Smaller is generally a hell of a lot easier to manage than bigger. It is extremely difficult to manage on the Citicorp scale. [Citicorp is] so big that you cannot easily get your arms around it to manage it. When many of us joined the bank in the early 1960s, it was very personal and informal. I remember going to Wriston's club and to his house for dinner. Over time, it became a large, faceless, and bureaucratic environment, and Wriston became extremely remote. In the 14-odd years that I reported to him, I was in charge of some major businesses of the bank. He never asked a question, and you could do whatever you wanted. But it was so big, it got impersonal.

Citicorp has done many of the things that successful, large corporations have done to overcome problems associated with its size: It has created smaller, decentralized business units and given their managers greater flexibility; it has eliminated management layers, pushed down decision making, and shortcut the approval process. One of its major weaknesses is well summarized in Peter Drucker's general comment: "A penalty of size is that you try to do everything, and no one can do everything well."[13] It seems clear that the conglomerate era of the 1960s and 1970s demonstrated how bigness and diversification can stifle either innovation or efficiency.

An ideally competitive firm may have the form that Jack Welch of General Electric (GE) referred to as the "big company–small hybrid." To be successful in keeping pace with strong global competitors may thus require a combination of the substantial resources and scale economies that bigness provides with the speed, agility, and ability to improvise and customize that a decentralized, profit center-oriented operation allows. Citicorp, in many respects, has both. If it can manage the problems that the last 30 years of expansion have created, it will, indeed, be one of the leading players in the industry in the year 2000.

Chase: A Case of Institutional Lag

Chase didn't have a clear enough sense of who or what it was. In the pursuit of elite banking, with blue-chip corporations, it copied Morgan in its customer base. In the pursuit of size and scope, it copied Citicorp. But it never quite defined who it was. It was bigger than Morgan and smaller than Citicorp, but it tried to be like both and never quite pulled it off. SENIOR STAFF PERSON

Not strictly a wholesale bank, as is the smaller Morgan Guaranty, not a financial department store, offering all services to all customers, as is Citicorp, not an investment bank like Bankers Trust, Chase chose to occupy a place in between. The result has been the failure of Chase to develop an identity. It became a bank with no singularity and no clear idea of what it wanted to be. SENIOR STAFF PERSON

Chase Manhattan Bank has traditionally had much the same portfolio of financial services as Citicorp. Both have pursued a highly diversified, universal bank strategy. Indeed, throughout most of their histories, the two banks have had an intense, cross-town rivalry, until the late 1970s and 1980s, when Citicorp's aggressive expansion had left Chase so far behind that Citicorp's senior managers rarely mention it any more as a significant competitor. Neither do their counterparts at Bankers Trust and Morgan.

Chase actually went from a position of being the largest New York City bank in 1967, second only in the United States to Bank of America,[1] to becoming less than half its rival's size in 1990. Though asset size is hardly a measure of performance, senior managers in both banks, pursuing a strategy of diversification and expansion, saw it as important. Asset size was a source of great concern to Chase management, for example, through the mid-1970s, when it became increasingly apparent that Chase would most likely never catch up again.

Moreover, Chase has also emerged on a number of other measures as the inferior performer of the two, and industry analysts widely regard it as such.[2] Taking return on common stockholders' equity as one such measure, Chase's average for the 1980s was 10.96 percent, compared with Citicorp's 11.76 percent. During the 5-year period 1983–1987, Chase's market value as a percent of book value was 60.4 percent, compared with Citicorp's 89.4 percent, reflecting its low stock price, which in 1990 fell to all-time lows for the period since 1980. Citicorp's did also, but Citicorp remained a much more aggressive competitor than did Chase. By September 1990, when both banks were experiencing major problems in raising capital, Chase's price/book ratio was 51.1, compared with Citicorp's 72. (Bankers Trust and Morgan, incidentally, had price/book ratios of 125.9 and 135.7, respectively.) Meanwhile, Chase's nonperforming loans as a percentage of total loans averaged 3.90 for that same 5-year period, as compared to 3.09 for Citicorp. In addition, Chase's market share on a wide range of products in consumer, institutional, and investment banking has lagged behind Citicorp's. Chase has been consistently later and less aggressive than Citicorp in moving into new markets and products, reflecting its more cautious style and its stronger interest in profitability and quality of products and services rather than simply in market share and size. It is widely referred to in the industry as a *scaled down version of Citicorp,* with serious doubts expressed about whether its goals of profitability and quality have been reached to any degree in the 1980s and 1990s.

Historically, in contrast to recent years, Chase had been widely acclaimed as one of America's leading wholesale banks. Founded in 1877, it soon developed an excellent national and international reputation as one of the premier wholesale banks in the world. Led by such distinguished chief executive officers (CEOs) as Winthrop Aldrich

(1935–1953), John McCloy (1953–1960), George Champion (1960–1969), and David Rockefeller (1960–1979), Chase became known both for its competitive strengths in banking—its correspondent banks, trust services, specialized industry expertise, real estate financing, global presence, and loan quality and judgment—and for its broader civic concerns, such as philanthropy and pro bono assistance to New York City as well as to developing nations. Indeed, until the late 1970s, it was known informally as *the bank of the Rockefellers* and sometimes as *David's bank*. It was identified with Rockefeller family interests, and it pursued a strategy of servicing blue-chip corporations, financial institutions, governments, and highly affluent individuals, while at the same time reflecting that family's long-time commitment to public service. In the 1970s, it was even referred to as a *shadow State Department,* so involved had David Rockefeller been, while president of the bank and then CEO, in having it play a public service role in its international operations. This was a banking franchise, then, which had panache and was regarded around the world as *the aristocrat of the money center banks.* It was much like Morgan, but it had a considerably more diversified portfolio.

Despite such auspicious beginnings, extending at least through the 1960s, Chase's performance since then has been uneven at best. It has experienced periodic declines and near catastrophes in particular businesses since the early 1970s, culminating in 1990 in a plummeting of its stock price and increasing rumors of a possible takeover. This chapter tells the story of that decline and explains what accounts for it.

How could a bank that many financial analysts regarded as number 1 as late as 1968 decline as precipitously as Chase? In trying to answer that question, I will look in particular at the traditional culture and the strategy that it spawned; at the bank's organizational structure and personnel practices; and, most important of all, at Chase's CEOs since the early 1960s.

Viewed in terms of our schema of strategic types, Chase emerges as a former *defender*-type firm that had secured strong positions in several wholesale banking markets—corporate, real estate finance, and correspondent banking—but that was slow to change with the times. It thus lost its preeminence in the 1970s, as the industry became much more competitive and turbulent. It has since become a *reactor*-type bank, lurching in many different directions. Though pursuing until quite recently much the same highly diversified, universal bank strategy as Citicorp pursued, Chase was a replica and a follower of Citicorp, not a leader. This model was reinforced by its traditional culture of risk aversion; its paternalism and inbreeding; its departmental and geographic fiefdoms; its senior managers' inability to develop a consensus around a unique strategy; its "gentlemanly" pattern of acceptable behavior, sometimes referred to as *bland conformism,* which was accompanied by a smoothing and avoidance style of dealing with internal conflict; and its inward rather than external market focus. The bank's centralized, hierarchical, and many-layered structure, slow-moving and top-heavy with headquarters (HQ) staff, further reinforced the reactor strategy, as did its poor internal (lateral and upward) communications. Chase managers reported often in the financial press in the 1970s and 1980s on the difficulty of getting departments to share information and to collaborate, as well as on the difficulty of moving critical information on problems requiring immediate attention up to senior managers.

One top-level insider suggested that, even in 1990, after many change efforts, Chase had a culture that was better suited to the stable, protected environment and public utility nature of banking in the 1940s and 1950s than to the competition and turbulence of the 1980s and 1990s. As he explained, "Our underlying core culture has not changed in being internally focused [and] risk-averse, and still emphasizing mediocrity. We are like a wealthy old family whose mansion on the outskirts of town is starting to decay, and we take umbrage at the fact that the local hardware store won't [give us] credit any more."

The story of Chase in recent decades shows it lurching from one crisis to another without evolving a coherent identity or strategic focus, notwithstanding its annual retreats and strategic planning statements to the contrary. As an old-line, senior manager reported, "It seemed that every 7 years or so we walked into a mud pile like our real estate investment trusts of the mid-1970s, our problems with Drysdale and Penn Square Bank in 1982, and [our] commercial real estate loans in 1989, and that set us back a lot."

There is another part of the Chase story, however—a much more positive one. This part involves domestic and international expansion of both the wholesale and the consumer banks, and it shows much market success in many businesses: credit cards, home mortgages, loan syndications, real estate finance, foreign exchange, and technology-driven service products (cash management, investment management, and pension fund and trust management). The bank still has an excellent international reputation, based in part on the many outstanding products just mentioned.

While Chase does have leading products and bankers, it has been hampered by systemic weaknesses that constitute residues from its past—cultural, strategic, and organizational—and that had not been eliminated in its many reform efforts prior to its recent changing of the guard in June 1990, with the move of insiders Tom Labrecque into the CEO position and

Art Ryan into the presidency. There have been many attempts at change since the 1960s—for example, Rockefeller's management reforms, new personnel practices and strategic planning initiatives, the shaking up of senior management ranks, numerous reorganizations, a culture change effort in 1985–1986, and major downsizing efforts since the mid-1980s. Despite these initiatives, much of the old culture persists, diluting their impact and making it difficult to restore the bank's reputation and performance to what they were in the 1950s and 1960s.

In brief, the environment and particularly the competition have changed much faster than has Chase. Its story is one of *institutional and cultural lag* relative to those forces, despite many efforts by able Chase senior managers, staff, and consultants to change the institution in fundamental ways. A senior staff person at Chase captured the debilitating aspects of the traditional culture and style very well when he recalled:

> One day, the elevator stopped at the wrong floor, and as I looked out, I saw a sign: Culture Change Department. I knew then that one more well-meaning change effort was doomed. As soon as we institutionalized it, which we do all the time, it became like all the other Chase units. It was absorbed into the old ways of doing things.

To understand how and why Chase has experienced its reverses of the past couple of decades, culminating in the crisis of 1990, when its earnings, capital, and stock price plummeted and it was mentioned as a strong takeover prospect, it is important to look back through its history. The record is limited for the years prior to World War II, but since then there has been much documentation of its operations. One source is John Wilson's *The Chase*. Wilson had been an economist at Chase from 1953 until his retirement in 1981, and he wrote his book as a very sympathetic company history. Notwithstanding his sympathies and a consensus among Chase old-timers that he was too far from the seats of power to acquire critical insights, Wilson provides abundant evidence of the flaws that contributed to Chase's decline.

Named for Salmon Chase, President Lincoln's Secretary of the Treasury, the bank has had a history since its founding in 1877 that may be characterized in terms of several patterns:

1. Its emergence as one of the premier wholesale banks in the world, growing mainly by acquisition and reaching its peak in the 1960s

2. Its tendency since then to go through cycles of expansion and retrenchment, the latter a result of major losses

3. An overall decline since the 1960s, due mainly to the traditional

Chase culture that it never quite eliminated through its continued efforts in recent years to reform

Chase's Emergence:
1877–1945

From its founding in 1877 to 1945, Chase developed as "the largest commercial bank in the country, and served as one of America's leading financial institutions."[3] It emerged as a primarily wholesale bank, having grown mainly through mergers and acquisitions (M&A). Prior to the Glass Steagall Act of 1933, it had been active in the securities business through its affiliate, The Chase Securities Corporation, established in 1917. It had set up a trust department in 1919, a business in which it became a major player. In 1929 and 1930, it had merged, first with American Express and then with Equitable Trust Company, both of which it later divested itself of. Equitable was represented in the original merger by Winthrop Aldrich, a lawyer, son of Senator Nelson Aldrich of Rhode Island, and brother-in-law of John D. Rockefeller, Jr. The Equitable merger made Chase the top bank in New York City, with assets of $2.69 billion. Aldrich became Chase's president in 1930 and its CEO in 1934.[4]

Many of Chase's traditional businesses, which were to become its trademarks during its recent history, thus date from those early years. These traditional businesses were its trust services, its worldwide correspondent banking relationships and branches, its underwriting and sale of government and general obligation municipal bonds, its commercial banking loan products to corporations, and its special industries groups. By virtue of its vast networks in the American corporate community, Chase became a leading banker in special industries, with strong expertise in such industries as petroleum, chemicals, railroads, public utilities, and real estate. A separate department for each industry reported directly to the president. Many of these businesses, particularly the corporate and special industries ones, were developed through extensive ties of the Rockefeller family.

Postwar Expansion and
Merger with Manhattan:
1946–1960

The next period in Chase's history was one of tremendous expansion, internationally and domestically, first under Winthrop Aldrich (through 1953) and then under John McCloy (1953–1960). In the final Aldrich years, Chase remained primarily a wholesale bank, "leading all others in loans to business and correspondent banking."[5] It also had an international department that, though it was growing, still played a secondary role in the bank's overall portfolio.

A turning point was Chase's merger in 1955 with the Bank of the Manhattan Company, which was a prestigious institution in its own right and had been founded in 1799. It had 96 branches, concentrated particularly in Queens, but also in the Bronx, Brooklyn, and Manhattan. It also had an excellent reputation for servicing both commercial and retail customers. This was one of several bank mergers that took place in New York City in the 1950s, including Manufacturers Trust with Hanover Bank, J.P. Morgan with Guaranty Trust, and Chemical with New York Trust Company.[6] The Justice Department and Congress initially viewed all these mergers as in possible violation of antitrust laws, but all were ultimately approved.

The merger made Chase the biggest bank in New York City and second only to Bank of America nationally, fueling a contest with Citicorp in which size was to become an end in itself. Despite taking on these branches, Chase remained a wholesale bank and would continue to be so up through the early 1980s.

By 1960, Chase had completed one of the most productive periods of its history. Its return on assets (ROA) peaked in 1960 at 0.80 and its return on equity (ROE) went from 8 percent in the mid-1950s to almost 11 percent.[7] In the postmerger years from 1955 to 1960, the line departments and internal organizational structure were consolidated into five groups: the United States, metropolitan, international, trust and investments, and financial planning departments. There was an emphasis on building up centralized staff functions at HQ, along with a middle-management cadre, as well as an emphasis on more delegation to the departments.

The 1960s: Continuing Expansion

The 1960s were years of still more expansion, both domestically, as Chase acquired branches in the New York suburbs, and internationally. It expanded its portfolio of loans to corporations, banks, and governments in many different countries; it invested in new projects in developing nations through the Chase International Investment Corporation; and it opened new foreign branches and correspondent banking relationships.

Aldrich, McCloy, and Rockefeller were all internationalists, and this was reflected in Chass's increasing presence around the world. All three were also public service-oriented, and this emphasis also was reflected in the bank's activities. The Chase International Investment Corporation, for example, which provided loans to new projects in developing nations, had a pro bono as well as a profit-oriented purpose. Victor Rockhill, a Chase senior manager and program director, explained, "We wanted to make money in the process, but it wasn't just to make money."[8]

By the late 1960s, Chase had become a leading global bank, with a distinguished reputation for the quality of its loan products, for its clients, for its professionalism, and for its public service orientation. At the same time, an institutional style had emerged that was to severely hamper Chase's capacity to adapt in the 1970s and 1980s, when the industry became much more turbulent and competitive. This style was one of caution in moving into new businesses, whether extending credit cards, expanding retail branches, opening foreign branches, entering the certificate of deposit (CD) and Eurodollar markets when loan funding became a problem, or adopting the bank holding company device as a way of supporting product diversification. On every front, Chase was consistently slower and later to react than were some of its competitors, particularly Citicorp. At Chase, manners, appearance, and appropriate form were emphasized, while Citicorp stressed performance. Style differences thus reflected the more gentlemanly culture of Chase as compared to the scrappier, more competence-oriented and entrepreneurial culture of Citicorp. A staff writer for the *Institutional Investor* summarized well the differences between the two banks:

> Walter Wriston, analysts say, [has] attracted a group of managers who, like himself, are tough, caustic, analytical, and "bottom line" oriented—and most important, encouraged to disagree with their boss. At Chase, on the other hand, the atmosphere is described as "clubby" and comfortable, with a premium placed on not rocking the boat. This reflects the personality of Rockefeller himself, who tends to be a less than "hard nosed" judge of people, to view events with a certain "equanimity" and to place a high premium on gentlemanliness.[9]

To be first wasn't necessarily to be best, as J. P. Morgan's tremendous success with its incremental style of strategic change was to indicate. Nevertheless, Chase was demonstrating by this style a more passive and reactive approach than did some competitors—an approach that was to contribute to its problems in later years.

Chase senior managers of that era would often argue, in their own defense, that they were much more interested in quality than in growth.

They watched Citicorp take big losses in some of its new businesses, such as credit cards, even while it was gaining a bigger market share. They maintained that their caution about plunging into whatever new product or opportunity suddenly appeared indicated strength rather than weakness.

Underlying the caution, however, was Chase's failure to develop a clear vision or strategic identity that would indicate what kind of a bank it wanted to become and what directions it wanted to pursue. David Rockefeller himself acknowledged in an interview for *The Bankers Magazine* that this had been a significant problem: "You could really say that until Bill Butcher became the president of the bank (1973), there was no unity of purpose within the top management. There's no question that all this had a very slowing-up effect so far as we were concerned at a very critical time."[10]

Stated another way, Chase was unable to develop any kind of consensus among its senior managers about strategy. Because of its many successes and excellent reputation from earlier years, its managers were not forced to even acknowledge this lack of a coherent strategy as a problem, or to see it as enough of one that it had to be confronted as soon as possible. Contrast that situation, for example, with the situation at Bankers Trust, where similarly poor performance and enormous real estate losses in the mid-1970s forced the bank to develop a more focused and coherent strategy, making it one of the highest-performing banks in the United States by the early 1990s.

Bankers Trust mobilized itself out of necessity. Chase was to face similarly big losses in the 1970s. For a combination of reasons that this chapter explores, while David Rockefeller and his colleagues may have had the same sense of collective urgency as their counterparts at Bankers Trust, they did not have the same capacity to coalesce and develop a shared vision of how banking was changing and to then implement that vision.

One of the prime examples of this institutional weakness was the deep conflict that existed in the 1960s between George Champion and David Rockefeller regarding Chase's international expansion. Chase's board saw both as such outstanding leaders that it was unable to choose between them for CEO, after McCloy retired in 1960. It therefore conferred the mantle on both, as co-CEOs, with Champion being appointed as board chairman and Rockefeller as president, until 1969, when Champion retired.

Though Rockefeller did not go public at that time about his unhappiness, he did recall much later the difficulties of the arrangement. In an interview with the editors of *Institutional Investor*, he stated:

To the best of my knowledge, there have been few—very few—situations in which this type of arrangement worked out well. Usually it only [works] when there are two people with a common vision but different, though complementary, interests and skills. In the case of Chase, however, I have to say that I don't think the arrangement worked particularly well. From 1960 until 1969, for almost a decade, we had two chief executives who had quite different visions as to where the bank should go. This caused us pretty much to stop dead in the water.[11]

The strategy in which this conflict became particularly acute concerned Chase's international expansion. Champion reportedly favored Chase's emphasizing domestic corporate loans and engaging in overseas business only through correspondent banks. He had grown up in the tradition of the Chase National Bank. Moreover, he was strongly committed to correspondent banking from his earlier days at Equitable and was concerned about undercutting correspondents by opening up competing Chase branches around the world. He was even reported, presciently, to have "abhorred the idea of lending money to foreign governments. If they refused to pay," he was quoted as saying, "how could we collect without an army?"[12]

Rockefeller, by contrast, was a strong internationalist who wanted Chase to open branches to service U.S. and foreign-based corporations all over the world. He was acutely aware that Citicorp had already gained a big head start in this arena and was by 1969 generating huge revenues from it.

Nevertheless, Champion ran the bank, and Rockefeller was unable to speed up overseas expansion until after Champion retired in 1969.[13] True to his style, which had become that of the bank as well, Rockefeller asserted that he did not come into open conflict with Champion. Said Rockefeller, "I don't want to put this in the form of confrontation, because it never became a confrontation."[14] These strategy differences between the two CEOs reflected different world views and social philosophies, with Champion being the more traditional of the two. Most important, they reflected deep-rooted divisions between "domestic" and "internationalist" camps that were to affect many strategic decisions of the bank.[15] Later, long after both Champion and Rockefeller had retired, the bank was to experience other divisions and a similar inability to develop a coherent strategic vision from the top and implement it through the ranks. That weakness, perhaps more than any other, may well account for Chase's decline in the 1970s and 1980s.

The 1970s: Troubled and Unsettled Years

Chase had a very difficult time in the early 1970s, as it began to experience a series of jolts that were a preview of things to come. Citicorp had passed it in size and was steadily widening the gap. In addition, it had even passed Chase in the latter's area of greatest comparative advantage: loans outstanding to domestic business. By the early 1970s, Chase's ROA was down below 0.50 for the first time in many years.[16]

Chase faced a new set of problems after Rockefeller became CEO. Rockefeller had selected Herbert Patterson in 1969 to succeed him as president. Patterson was the consensus choice of Champion and the board as well. Though he had done an outstanding job at the bank, Patterson wasn't assuming a position of strong leadership. Because Rockefeller was not a "hands-on," detail-oriented CEO and because he spent much time away from the bank, traveling around the world and visiting heads of state, there was a vacuum of leadership at the top. One financial journalist and critic of the bank suggested, "Two is one too many floaters" and commented, "When you have a geographic floater as chairman, you do not need a floater of any kind as president."[17]

Rockefeller finally realized what was going on, but Patterson had been in the position for 3 years (1969–1972) before he left. Rockefeller recalled:

> Herb was a highly competent credit officer who had run two or three important departments successfully….Unfortunately, Herb seemed unable or unwilling to assume the full responsibilities of the new position. I suppose it is not uncommon for someone who is very good in certain areas to be overwhelmed in others, but I had not expected this in Herb's case, and I probably waited too long to realize it and finally act on this realization.[18]

In addition to these problems at the senior management level, Chase faced still other difficulties that were to hurt both its economic performance and its reputation. One was its discovery in 1974 that its bond dealer account had been overvalued by $34 million and its earnings overstated as a result. While hardly qualifying as a catastrophe, this incident did cast some doubt on how well Chase was being managed, particularly on its controls and its information systems. Rockefeller had taken pride in his initiatives in instituting management controls, and the incident received wide publicity—for example, it was featured on the front page of *The New York Times* on October 3, 1974—which probably hurt the bank's image.

In 1975 and 1976, a much more serious problem emerged, in connection with Chase's real estate loans. Many banks, including Bankers Trust, experienced losses in these years, resulting from nonperforming real estate loans, but none were on the same scale as Chase. Chase had committed itself to its own REIT, the Chase Manhattan Mortgage and Realty Trust—a rare example of innovativeness. As New York City experienced devastating declines in its real estate market in 1975, Chase's trust moved toward bankruptcy, resulting in huge losses for the bank. Its earnings fell by 40 percent from 1974 to 1976, and 80 percent of its nonperforming loans were real estate loans. Indeed, Chase's ROA had fallen from 0.61 in 1970 to 0.24 in 1976, and its net operating profits sank to a low of $105 million in 1976, down more than 40 percent from what they had been during the previous 2 years.[19]

This was a tremendous blow to Chase, which had prided itself on the excellence of its real estate business. It had made a major strategic decision in the 1950s to get into commercial real estate lending in a big way. The business had become so successful that Rockefeller was quoted as recalling that the real estate department was put first on the agenda in senior management meetings because "it had no problems and no losses."[20] While Chase's real estate losses reflected an economic recession that would have been hard to predict, they also reflected poor bank management. The bank's rapid real estate loan expansion had been accompanied by an addition of inexperienced, untrained personnel; poor documentation of transactions; faulty communication between lending and administrative support staff; limited follow-up on construction projects; and "overly liberal" lending practices.[21] These losses pointed up systemic weaknesses within Chase that were to haunt it in the future.

In retrospect, Champion commented, regarding the bond and REIT debacles, "Nothing like that happened when I was chairman. When I was chairman, we knew what was going on in every department. I went through all the departments to see and observe for myself. If any loan was $5 million or over, I took it to the board after studying it personally."[22]

An immediate aftermath was a series of exposé-type articles in several newspapers, referring to Chase as a "problem" bank that had "inadequate" capital, "poor" management, and "horrendous" operating conditions. The *Washington Post* was the first newspaper to publish such articles, but they appeared in *The New York Times* also. Chase's reputation was damaged domestically and perhaps abroad as well.[23]

In brief, the period 1970–1976 was a time of much turmoil and decline for Chase. The bank was referred to in one *Fortune* article as "America's most renowned basket case."[24] Both its economic performance and its reputation had suffered so much that, by late 1976, a series of articles had appeared in the financial press, blaming Rockefeller and urging his retirement. One of the most critical, entitled "Why David Rockefeller Should Fire Himself," which appeared in *Financial World* on Jan. 1, 1977, concluded that "every month that passes reinforces the deeply held conviction in many quarters that the best thing for Chase, its stockholders, and…David Rockefeller himself, would be for him to relinquish the reins." Similar pieces appeared in *Fortune* and the *Institutional Investor*. The article in the latter concluded that Rockefeller's chairmanship had led to "poor management, lack of control, and a style of banking that is out of touch with the times."[25]

Equally remarkable, however, was the extraordinary recovery that began in 1977. It lasted through the end of Rockefeller's term in 1980 and extended for a couple of years into the term of his successor, Willard Butcher. Actually, Rockefeller had embarked upon efforts at reform beginning in 1974, when he brought in senior people in human resources and strategic planning, in an effort to upgrade the bank's staff and performance. These efforts were followed by much recovery and expansion, which seemed to constitute a turnaround. Rockefeller's board gave him a standing ovation when he retired at the end of 1979, pointing to the bank's remarkable performance since 1976.

The recovery years were a time of great excitement about recent achievements and much hope for the future. Besides the big improvements in the bank's financial performance, internal controls were tightened, credit quality was enhanced, strategic planning sessions among senior managers were initiated, and human resources policies were completely overhauled. In 1974, Rockefeller had brought in Alan Lafley from General Electric (GE), as the new head of corporate human resources. Lafley had drastically altered the bank's recruitment, training, and compensation practices, moving it away from its past paternalism. He placed more emphasis on compensation for performance, overhauled the training program, began bringing in many more midcareer outsiders to senior management positions, and pushed for early retirement of old-timers. A spirit of change was in the air. Chase was making such human resource policy reforms much later than Citicorp, but was making them nonetheless. Chase veterans refer to one of Lafley's early actions, which involved pushing out through early retirement many traditional Chase bankers and bringing in an entirely new group, as the *midnight massacre.* Lafley's actions reflected both his and David Rockefeller's strong conviction that the bank needed major personnel changes if it was to change the culture and improve significantly on its past performance.

In addition to Lafley, Rockefeller brought in Gerald Weiss from GE in 1975, as a strategic planner. Weiss was critical of the gentlemanly culture and began to play the roles of activist and lightning rod to force strategic decisions.[26]

Perhaps the most critical decision during this period was that of Rockefeller and his board to select Willard Butcher to succeed Rockefeller as CEO in 1980. Butcher had arrived at Chase in 1947, right out of college. Starting in the Manhattan branch operations, he rose through the ranks to become president in late 1972. Though at first he was reportedly in awe of Rockefeller, the two of them worked very closely together. By the late 1970s, Rockefeller saw Butcher as having driven many changes, making the bank more open, less turf-minded, and more entrepreneurial. Butcher was to run the bank throughout the 1980s, when it became known in some circles as *Butcher's bank*. He received many accolades during his first couple of years as CEO, when Chase continued its expansion of the late 1970s, and he was often described as quick-witted and incisive. Initially he was thought of as having managed Chase out of its decline, but later he came under strong criticism. The bank went through several years of lackluster profits in the 1980s, and Butcher's management style was singled out for special blame. He was described as having lost his zest for change and as having become an obstacle to continuation of the momentum of the late 1970s, rather than as the catalyst for change that Rockefeller and the board had judged him to be.

The 1980s: More Troubles and Decline

The dramatic improvements of the late 1970s and early 1980s were unfortunately not sustained. Chase went through an equally dramatic decline from 1982 to 1985. It experienced a series of losses unprecedented in its history, which turned its attention even more inward than before and prevented it from repositioning itself at a time when both the industry at large and Chase's competitors were changing in revolutionary ways. The particular episodes of the decline further reflected systemic weaknesses that Chase still had not corrected after its troubles of the 1970s and that were to hurt it even more in the late 1980s and early 1990s.

The first such episode involved Drysdale Government Securities, which defaulted in early 1982 on $160 million of interest payments owed to nearly 30 of the nation's top brokerage firms. Chase, as an intermediary, wound up paying $117 million of Drysdale's due interest, after first insisting that it had no obligation.

A few months later, just as Chase was recovering from that jolt, it was hit by still another. Penn Square Bank, N.A., of Oklahoma City, a Chase correspondent bank, collapsed in June 1982, after having sold more than $2.5 billion of participations in energy-related loans to other banks, including more than $275 million to Chase. A high proportion of those loans were in default, and by 1985, Chase ended up charging off $161 million from them.

As if that weren't enough, Lombard Wall, a thinly capitalized government securities firm that filed for bankruptcy in 1982, listed Chase as a creditor for $45 million. Fortunately for Chase, rather than lending directly to Lombard Wall it had issued letters of credit to the firm on a secured basis. Chase was able to close out the incident quickly and with little loss.[27]

These three episodes, taking place in such a short time, not only hurt Chase financially but damaged its reputation and contributed to many missed opportunities over the next few years. Chase projected an image of being badly managed, with inadequate controls.

Equally important, its senior managers became very cautious. They were understandably reluctant to expand existing businesses or move in new directions. Butcher removed or transferred the senior managers involved in the fiascoes and formed risk councils for each line of business. Meanwhile, the banking industry was changing very rapidly, because of increasing global competition, the disintermediation of banks, and the emergence of capital markets. Chase was not in a position to develop an appropriate strategy for adapting to these changes, given the damage control posture that it had adopted after these episodes. One top Chase staffer explained, "The senior management at that time acted like they were on a cross, and they became overly cost-conscious. You could understand why, but it hurt us." Another commented:

> Following those episodes, we had 2 years, from 1982 to 1984, of internal focus, [in which] we simply missed a rapidly shifting horizon. In those 2 years, commercial banking was changing totally, and we were nowhere in adapting to that. Citicorp, for example, was looking at the external market, as was Bankers Trust, and Chase was not. That series of events scared Chase and kept it in an internal focus for longer than the other banks. Labrecque was new as president, and Butcher was new as CEO; and they wanted to make sure that it would never happen again. They moved us toward what might be called a *command and control organization* long after it was effective. For us, the events shaped the culture to be more risk-averse and internally oriented than would otherwise have been the case.

In brief, Chase reverted to the reactive strategy that it seemed to have abandoned before.

It is important to reflect on the extent to which the 1982 episodes were idiosyncratic or a result of more systemic causes. The latter seemed much more the case. The unit most responsible for the problems was the domestic institutional banking department which was overseeing the accounts. It followed the old Chase culture, in neither collaborating with other departments nor reporting bad news. In the Penn Square Bank case, the issue was energy-related loans, about which the domestic institutional banking staff knew much less than they should have known, and certainly less than others at Chase knew. Wilson explained:

> Chase's loans to Penn Square were handled exclusively by officers in domestic institutional banking, even though energy specialists in the corporate bank were well known for their expertise in assessing the creditworthiness of complicated oil and gas credits. Cross-communication between the two departments was weak, and a sense of rivalry existed.[28]

The bank thus paid heavily for its political fragmentation, which constituted an unnecessary encumbrance in an increasingly complex and turbulent industry. Considerable expertise was required, as was much internal collaboration, to enable the expertise to be drawn on routinely and as needed. Such collaboration did not exist at Chase.

It took 2 to 3 years for Chase to recover from these mishaps, and by that time, it was considerably behind its competitors in many areas of wholesale and retail banking. Citicorp had moved aggressively, for example, since the early 1980s, in developing its investment bank, in corporate finance, and in capital markets-related products. It had also established a consolidated consumer bank in 1975. Chase didn't get going on any scale on either front until 1985, though it had the leadership to do so well before then.

One such leader, Fred Hammer in consumer banking, had been pushing aggressively since the late 1970s to expand his area of operation. He experienced continued frustration, as he ran up against the inertia of the institution. In particular, both the culture of the institution and its CEO, Willard Butcher, reflected the "old Chase," a wholesale bank lending to blue-chip corporations. The 1982 incidents reinforced that inertia.

By late 1984, however, Chase had recovered enough from these episodes to resume efforts at expansion and internal reform. Its main area of expansion was domestic banking, both corporate and consumer, and it initiated that thrust by acquiring Lincoln First Corporation of Rochester, New York, in 1984. It thereby took on 135 offices in upstate

New York and another 37 branches in Westchester County. Lincoln became the administrative arm of Chase's nationwide banking. It acquired six savings and loans (S&Ls), converted them to commercial banks, and pursued a middle-market corporate banking strategy, while also expanding its consumer bank. In addition, Chase established an investment banking department in 1985 and increased its commitment to various corporate finance and capital markets-related businesses.

What looked like a potential turning point was a series of related internal change efforts that Chase initiated in 1985. One was a reorganization of the bank into three main units: consumer banking, institutional banking, and investment banking. The head of each became a vice chairman within the bank and was the main strategist for his sector. All three were to collaborate in developing bankwide strategy and were to provide leadership for much more cooperation across sectors—to encourage more market- and customer-oriented cross-selling, bringing together in one place Chase's relevant expertise in meeting customer needs.

The other initiative was an internal change effort, led by an outside consultant, Daryll Conner of Atlanta, Georgia, who had already been working with Chase on executive development programs. His project was to bring together the bank's senior managers to work on developing strategy and changing the Chase culture so that it would better match the new banking environment of the 1980s. Conner worked with the bank for over a year on this project. He conducted many sessions with area and product managers around the world to help them change their strategies and cultures.

Conner's work went through two stages. The first involved his working with the bank's most senior managers—the CEO, the president, and the three vice chairmen—to help develop a corporate vision. This vision was based on an analysis of how the industry was changing and how Chase was performing, relative to its money center competitors. The decision was made to maintain the autonomy of each of the three new divisions, while at the same time having them follow some broad guidelines and participate in a bankwide corporate culture. This stage also involved aligning the next layer of managers, 100-odd people who were mostly heads of particular businesses, with the common goals and vision of their vice chairmen.

In the second stage, Conner worked intensively with many business heads, particularly those who were experiencing the biggest problems. Most of his efforts in that regard were with the investment bank, which was referred to in Chase as *global finance*, and he worked with such managers all over the world. While the consumer bank thrived over the next

several years, as it did at Citicorp, and while Chase had other high-performing businesses (its custodial, cash management, and investment
management services), the investment bank did not do as well. Rather,
it experienced big losses in securities trading. Moreover, the bank also
had big losses in its international wholesale operations, particularly in
corporate loan businesses.

By early 1989, it was clear that the reforms of 1985 had not turned
Chase around, at least not enough to enable it to improve its financial
performance significantly. Increasing volumes of nonperforming loans
in real estate and leveraged buyouts (LBOs), along with continuing less
developed country (LDC) loan problems and an impending recession,
all contributed to much lower earnings in the first quarter of 1990 than
Chase's senior management had forecast. By late spring, Chase was in
deep trouble financially, and its stock went down to record low levels.
Chase staff had issued a statement in the fall of 1989 to the effect that the
bank's total income was likely to be roughly $900 million for 1990, but
its experience of the first two quarters of that year indicated that $300
million would be a more accurate figure. A top staff person summarized
the situation:

> This year (1990), we are seeing the underlying erosion of our entire
> franchise. That process had been masked by the LBO spurt, but then
> the LBOs went into a steep decline. [With that decline and also] the bad
> real estate market, and the problem of having to build reserves for the
> third world debt and raise a billion in new equity...we were in deep
> trouble.

Into the 1990s

Starting in early 1990, the senior management and the board of Chase
moved quickly into a crisis-management mode. Willard Butcher, who
was not scheduled to retire as CEO until the end of 1991, was encouraged to take immediate retirement in June, so as to allow his designated
successor, Tom Labrecque, and a team Labrecque had assembled, to
deal with the emergency. One faction on the board reportedly wanted
to hire an outsider from investment banking as CEO, but Labrecque had
the strong support of the most powerful senior managers and a large
segment of the board. When Butcher retired, it was Labrecque who took
over.

Labrecque dissolved the bank's three divisions. He appointed Art
Ryan, who had been vice chair and head of the consumer bank, as

Chase's new president, and he gathered a small group of senior managers to work with him and Ryan to try to ensure the bank's survival. At this time the bank literally had no formal structure but was subject to whatever plans this small group developed for its future. Indeed, the entire bank was reporting to Ryan. As one top staff person facetiously reported, "We even have people with bumper stickers that say: `Honk if you are a direct report to Ryan.'"

Rumors escalated in the business and financial press about a possible takeover of Chase or a merger with some other institution. Chemical and Manufacturers Hanover were among the most frequently mentioned, such speculation having actually gone on for several years. (The two putative suitors announced their own union in July 1991.) Such rumors became more public and plausible as Chase's financial fortunes declined.

Many knowledgeable observers, however, had positive reactions to the choice of Labrecque and Ryan as CEO and president. Both men had gained considerable support inside Chase and in wider banking circles for their past achievements at the bank. Labrecque had distinguished himself as a troubleshooter and an able strategist, despite having had limited power while serving as president since 1980 under Butcher. Many of the positive changes in the 1980s—the expansion of the consumer bank, the hiring of able outsiders for senior management positions, and the continued pressure for more collaboration across various sectors of the bank to serve customer needs—were reforms that Labrecque had championed.

Ryan had a similarly positive reputation. An engineer by training, who had started at Chase in the operations sector, Ryan had demonstrated considerable skill in managing the orderly expansion of the consumer bank, which he had headed since 1985. He had successfully built up a series of product areas, finding economies of scale for each. "Ryan really built a consumer business for Chase," reported a top staff person.

Both Labrecque and Ryan are insiders, and some critical observers point out that significant strategic and cultural changes rarely take place in institutions without equally significant infusions of senior managers from the outside. Moreover, neither had distinguished himself in the past as a visionary or an aggressive change agent in the style of a Walter Wriston or a Charles Sanford. Nevertheless, both may now have the opportunity to demonstrate their leadership qualities. It won't be an easy task, and Chase may well have gone beyond the point where it can survive without a significant merger within the next few years. What is in the favor of Labrecque and Ryan is that neither is a product of the traditional Chase culture.

The immediate tasks for Labrecque and Ryan are to restore Chase to a viable financial state, to develop a vision of what kinds of financial services Chase may most profitably deliver, and to build an infrastructure to implement that vision. They have worked feverishly on those tasks since mid-1990, and Labrecque has distanced himself from Chase's past in his public statements. As he said shortly after becoming CEO, "We have nothing we can say about our performance over the past five years that is positive."[29]

The main directions of that activity include downsizing the bank, selling off the businesses that are not central to its survival, and developing criteria for determining which businesses should be sold by coming up with a vision and a strategic identity for the immediate future.[30] The two tasks—downsizing and developing a strategy—are obviously related, and the small management group under Labrecque and Ryan are working on both. They had already made several major decisions in this regard, including a shrinkage of 5000 employees, by the end of 1990. Chase's total head count was reduced from 48,000 in 1986 to 36,000 in 1991, by far the biggest staff reduction of any money center bank. It may well be that Chase's much more aggressive action in downsizing, relative to the actions of its competitors and particularly to those of Citicorp, will have a big payoff in the coming years.

In terms of future strategy, the most problematic issue for Chase is what elements of its wholesale business (which is where its biggest losses have occurred) it should retain. Chase's two strongest segments are consumer banking (which accounted in 1989 for roughly 50 percent of the bank's total revenue) and the cluster of technology-driven trust, cash management, investment management, and custodial services that have turned out to be a gold mine. As one top staff person explained, "There is nothing wrong with a MacDonald's-type service chain (the consumer bank) and these technology-driven products. We can have synergy with those, but what to do beyond that is not at all clear."

Chase's senior managers see many of its wholesale businesses as part of the bank's traditional legacy and identity. From that perspective alone, they are reluctant to sell off such businesses, even though Chase has suffered big losses in many of those businesses or, at best, has been a minor player. To become a bigger player, it would have to make a major outlay of capital, for technology, people, and products, and Chase does not have that capital available. As a top staff person explained:

> There is a prevailing mythology that we should do the glitzy things—like swaps, options, and futures—that Citicorp, Morgan, and Bankers Trust do. I'm afraid we are taking those banks as our model, even though the new investment banking products now sell like [commodi-

ties]. We could easily sell our foreign exchange and risk-management products businesses, as...separate [subsidiaries], and their linkages with Chase are not important. They are clearly separable. But when [selling them] is broached, the people at the top get very nervous. "That is close to our historic identity," they say. "It is part of our franchise." We remind them that the Japanese will pay more for these businesses than they can ever be worth to us, and...we [hope to] resolve these questions before too long.

By late 1990, then, Chase had reached a crossroads. It was struggling desperately to survive in a period of impending recession, when the future of U.S. commercial banking was in greater jeopardy than at any time since the Depression. For Chase, the problem was its legacy of having failed to establish a unique strategic identity and a supporting infrastructure, which would have enabled it to weather the economic downturn without a big struggle. Even if it mobilized itself strongly, there still remained serious questions about its survival, given its financial state at the beginning of the struggle. To provide a better understanding of Chase's future prospects, I will analyze in more depth in Chapter 7 the forces that brought Chase to the present crisis—that is, its culture, strategy, leadership, organizational structure, and human resources policies.

7
Chase: The Anatomy of a Flawed Culture

Cultures often drive institutions, and that has been very much the pattern at Chase. Chase's culture, or at least its traditional culture, has been in many respects the polar opposite of Citicorp's. Since the 1970s, when David Rockefeller and his colleagues saw the Chase culture as a serious impediment to the bank's effectiveness, there have been several attempts to change it. There are differing perspectives among Chase insiders as well as among knowledgeable outsiders about how much change has actually taken place and, indeed, about whether whatever changes have taken place are basic or more peripheral. The traditional culture has been variously characterized as *risk-averse, bureaucratic and hierarchical, inward- rather than market-oriented, paternalistic and inbred, gentlemanly, nonconfrontational in its management of conflict, turf-minded, accompanied by poor internal communications (upward, downward, and lateral), protective of senior management, and elitist with regard to the types of products and customers Chase would serve.* Table 7-1 compares the cultures of Chase and Citicorp.

Risk Aversion

A major point of disagreement regarding Chase's traditional culture relates to which of the characteristics listed in Table 7-1 represent the Chase of the past and which represent changes. My assessment is that some have changed but that the continued presence of others has con-

Table 1-1. Cultural Differences between Chase and Citicorp

Chase (traditional)	Citicorp
Risk-averse. Managers are fearful of making mistakes.	Entrepreneurial. Managers are punished more for caution than for errors of commission.
Paternalistic, inbreeding.	Meritocratic. There is much midcareer hiring.
Gentlemanly, polite, humanistic.	Internally competitive.
Bureaucratic, centralized.	Decentralized; more of a flexible "adhocracy"; profit centers.
Nonconfrontational. Managers avoid or smooth over conflicts.	Highly confrontational. Managers engage their differences. Meetings are like "a series of barroom brawls" among entrepreneurs.
Poor internal communications (vertical and lateral). No reporting of bad news to senior management. A "kill-the-messenger" style.	Much information flow.
Protective of senior management, who are insulated by staff from negative information and operational details.	Senior management more informed.
Elitist in products and customers. A wholesale bank, serving blue-chip corporations, governments, and highly affluent individuals.	Highly diverse products and customers. "All things to all people."

tributed considerably to Chase's present problems. Thus, though the many improvements in performance from 1975 to 1982 represented what looked like significant reforms and seemed driven by many cultural changes (as related, for example, to human resources policies), the bank regressed over the next few years and may never have recovered the impetus for change which it had generated before. In brief, the "old Chase" had begun to give way to the "new Chase," but in the face of the big losses of 1982, the "old Chase" reasserted itself, and its residues affected the remainder of the decade. The Salomon Brothers Stock Research Group's characterization of Chase in October 1989, for example, as "the sleeping giant" referred in part to the persistence of the old culture. The report concluded, "Historically, Chase has been very risk-averse and, therefore, somewhat slow to adapt to a changing environment."[1]

A style of caution and risk aversion was thus a cultural characteristic of many years' standing. It was reflected in the bank's inward orientation and bureaucratic style. One senior manager at Chase, who had come from another bank, explained:

> Chase had made many management mistakes and blunders over the years. In fact, it had a not-making-mistakes culture, and that was associated with its centralized style of decision making, its committees, [its] task forces, and [its] study groups, all of which slowed things down. Chase has historically been more control-driven and less entrepreneurial than, say,...Citicorp or Bankers Trust. We would always wait for 100 percent of the facts and then test them for their statistical accuracy before moving ahead on anything. I now tell the people here, "Lead, follow, or get out of the way."

The fear of making mistakes and having them reported up the chain of command was particularly pervasive. A top staff person explained:

> You got into deep [trouble] around here if you reported up any bad news. You might even get fired. So people didn't say much if things didn't go well, and they tried never to get themselves into situations where that was the case. As you can imagine, that bred a pretty conservative type [of] mentality and a lot of mediocrity in performance.

Contrast that with the culture Walter Wriston established at Citibank, in which people were told when they entered the bank that they should not be afraid to make mistakes and that they would be punished more for errors of omission than for those of commission.

The cautious mentality at Chase was associated with several aspects of its history, including its chief executive officers (CEOs). Serving blue-chip corporations, Chase had attained both a reputation and a level of performance in the 1950s and 1960s as one of the world's top wholesale banks. It had a strong concern for quality in its products and customers, and it was always reluctant to jump into new markets for purposes of growth alone. Chase senior managers preferred to let Citicorp be the first to move and run the risk of suffering big losses, confident that Chase could move in later, if a new product was successful. Like J.P. Morgan managers, they preferred to be right rather than first.

Moreover, having attained the stature of a top bank, Chase's top management saw no need to depart radically from what had got the institution there. George Champion, often referred to in the industry as *the bankers' banker*, seemed particularly committed to that position, supporting as he did Chase's traditional strengths—its U.S. corporate banking and its correspondent banking. Later, in the 1980s, Willard Butcher ended up in a similarly conservative posture, after having led the bank through a period of expansion. Both CEOs may well have illustrated the general phenomenon that *success generates inertia*. Indeed, one veteran staffer saw Chase as having sat on its laurels for too long, while its competitors were preempting new areas of opportunity. This person recalled:

> We had traditionally been very complacent. [Complacency] is less prominent now, but it still exists. We were that way with our credit policy, with many people at high levels in the bank saying, "We will not do interest rate swaps." The reason was that people were sitting back [and] remembering the old days, and they really thought that the market was not changing when in fact it was. We had senior management who became too sheltered from changes in the industry. They had the feeling that we were going to make it, based on our past successes. They felt they didn't have to hustle for the business or develop a lot of new products, and [this feeling] came back to haunt them.

This same staffer acknowledged, however, that the complacency and risk aversion began to fade by the mid-1980s. "That has started to change significantly since about 1984 or 1985," the staffer reported. "There was tremendous personnel turnover at all levels, and we now have a more systematic performance reward system. So the aversion to risk is less prominent now, but it still exists."

Perhaps the most vivid manifestation of that culture was Chase's continued lateness in moving into new markets. It was always a follower rather than a leader, and in some fields, such as investment banking, it was so late as to be considered almost a nonparticipant by its immediate competitors.

Given this culture, it is possible to understand how Citicorp could jump so far ahead of Chase, since the cultures of the two banks had such profound impacts on their strategies. Again, Citicorp, an aggressive competitor, was consistently the first mover, and Chase, a more slow-moving, passive competitor, was the follower. Going back to the early 1960s, it is possible to list a series of initiatives on which Citicorp acted and Chase delayed: global expansion; certificates of deposit (CDs); adoption of the bank holding company device; investment in technology; retail banking; and, later, investment banking. Wilson captured this culture and style well when he characterized Chase's early venture into the credit card business, the Chase Manhattan Charge Plan, as "established, only to be abandoned as unprofitable in the early 1960s, a somewhat cautious approach to innovation that typified Chase."[2]

This is not to say that first movers always win and latecomers always lose. Citicorp's significant decline in the 1990s belies the first proposition, and Morgan's strong performance during that time belies the second. Moreover, because Chase entered investment banking so late, it didn't get as deeply involved in the leveraged buyout (LBO) losses as its competitors did. On balance, however, its caution was a big handicap.

A dramatic example was Chase's lateness in opening wholesale branches around the world, in response to the emergence of U.S. multinational corporations and to the globalization of banking. Similar lost opportunities occurred in investment banking, a result of Chase's debacles in 1982 with Drysdale, Penn Square Bank, and Lombard Wall. The result of those unexpected losses, which reflected poor internal controls and communication, was that Chase turned inward and developed tighter control systems and more caution about expansion, just when opportunism and speed seemed most appropriate. Top staff and managers at Chase now acknowledge that the bank lost 2 to 3 years to such competitors as Citicorp, Bankers Trust, and Morgan, and that it was then difficult to catch up. In this instance, an institution already slow to adapt became even slower, and the negative impacts of its increased controls at a time of rapid change led to many lost opportunities. Consider the following comments by senior managers and staff:

> Drysdale and Penn Square involved incredible energy in damage control that clearly slowed us down in the years 1982 to 1985. And it hurt us psychologically—because we were reluctant to do risky things. The reason we lost our number 1 position was that we had become inwardly focused and the competition beat our pants off. We had become bureaucratic and risk-averse. We punished ourselves internally. In the period 1982–1984, after Drysdale and all those problems, our investment banking business really stopped. The senior managers concluded that we had really done ourselves in by the way we were running the place, and they turned down many deals. In their eyes, we were not in a position to take any risks. So we really lost those years. In 1984 and 1985, we started back and started to build. A few of us old corporate bankers found religion with the new corporate securities business.

Again, change has taken place since the mid-1980s. Chase brought many midcareer people into its investment bank, some at senior levels in corporate finance and trading. One was Michael Dacey, who came over from Bankers Trust to head up the corporate finance group at Chase, and who brought with him the Bankers Trust model of how to develop investment banking businesses in a traditionally commercial bank. Dacey was involved in continuous efforts at culture change, at least informally, as he tried to build a strong corporate finance capability at Chase.

Consumer banking suffered in the late 1970s and early 1980s from the same slow, risk-averse style. While Citicorp had put together its consumer bank in 1975, though admittedly experiencing big losses in its early efforts, Chase was very late in getting started in consumer banking. A senior manager in the consumer bank reported:

> In the late seventies, the whole focus of the bank was still to get out of real estate and cut costs. We never had a positive focus then, only the negative ones of cutting costs and avoiding losses. Our division was turned down at the top for a national mailing of credit cards. Citicorp made big mistakes there, but we didn't act at all. Then Chase was slow in doing consumer banking internationally, and Citicorp beat us to the punch there also. Then, as we pushed to grow home equity lines of credit, we were told that it was bank policy to be against second mortgages. It took us 8 months to get this policy changed. Meanwhile, Citicorp went way up in its home mortgage business, and Chase stagnated. Low risk was our outlook for everything.

Again, things have changed since the mid-1980s. Chase has built up a strong consumer banking business. It is now a major player in credit cards, home mortgages, and consumer branches. However, the culture did slow down these initiatives, and Chase would most likely have been in a better capital position to weather the recession and the nonperforming loan problems of the early 1990s had it built up its consumer bank earlier.

Paternalism and Inbreeding

Much of the paternalism and inbreeding that characterized the traditional Chase culture has been eliminated. These features were expressed in various forms. One form that has been eliminated was the provision of lifetime employment. David Rockefeller reported, "It was the rare exception for anyone to be fired unless [he or she] had committed some sort of crime. In one way, this engendered loyalty, but it also meant that less capable or energetic people were retained but were shunted off to areas [that were] then considered less important but that later were to prove very important."[3]

It wasn't just that Chase provided people with lifetime careers. Like so many other big competitors that were products of the post-Glass Steagall era in U.S. banking, it moved people up the traditional chain of command in somewhat lockstep fashion. Though some people moved up faster than others, there was no bankwide pay-for-performance arrangement that compensated people on the basis of a systematic assessment of their contributions. Again, Chase was no different from other big banks. It has changed in this regard in recent years, but it was much later in doing so than were some of its competitors, particularly Citicorp.

Another feature of Chase's paternalistic culture was the provision of a wide variety of perks. One old-timer recalled:

> In the sixties and seventies, this was like a country club. We had teams in chess, tennis, golf, bridge, all funded by Chase. We used to have an annual golf tournament, and the Chase funding was generous beyond belief: expenses at the pro shop, lavish meals, and so on. Today, there is none of that. [The change] was no big deal, but Butcher said: "Look, we are not in the country club business."

Indeed, the bank used to be referred to as *Mother Chase*, in recognition of how solicitous it was of its employees' well-being. Its solicitude was shown, in a particularly pronounced way, in the housing provided for branch managers abroad. Tales were legendary regarding these managers' quarters, furnishings, and other miscellaneous accoutrements, including artwork. These perks provided Chase managers in foreign lands with an affluent quality of life that was apparently in sharp contrast to that of the foreign managers of some competitors. For example, Citicorp managers marveled at the sumptuous homes of their Chase counterparts. Chase always did things with taste and style, unlike Citicorp, which some of Chase's old-line, senior managers regarded as uncouth and as an upstart institution.

The paternalistic Chase culture has not existed since the late 1970s to anywhere near the degree that it did before then. Changes in personnel policies initiated by David Rockefeller changed all that. After the huge losses of the early 1970s, he and his colleagues realized that the bank could no longer afford all those perks. In addition, he realized in particular the importance of bringing in new, midcareer people at senior management levels, encouraging early retirement for some of the old-timers, and instituting performance compensation. That was his impetus for bringing in Alan Lafley from General Electric (GE) in 1974, to head up the new human resources department and make such changes. In some respects, Rockefeller became a change agent for the bank, acting almost as a "traitor to his class." He made such moves later than did George Moore and Walter Wriston, his competitors at Citibank, but he nevertheless shook up the establishment at his institution. "David," one former Chase executive says acidly, "thought it was neat to single out disadvantaged bright young men and give them lots of chances."[4]

Thus, by the mid-1980s, Chase had a senior management group that was almost countercultural to the blue bloods of its past. Predominantly second-generation Catholic, they had grown up in places like Bayonne, New Jersey, and Brooklyn, New York, rather than in Greenwich, Connecticut, or Westchester County, New York. They had graduated from Holy Cross, Villanova, or Providence College rather than from an Ivy League school, and they were a completely different breed from their Chase counterparts of an earlier generation. Moreover, it wasn't just a small minority of the senior managers who came from these plebeian ethnic backgrounds. Two of the four most senior managers in the bank in 1987 were in this group: Vice Chairman Richard Boyle (a graduate of Holy Cross) of the global bank and Vice Chairman Art Ryan (from Brooklyn and a graduate of Providence College; formerly in operations) of the consumer bank. Ryan, of course, became the bank's president in 1990, accompanying Tom Labrecque (a graduate of Villanova), its new CEO, who was from the same sort of background as Ryan, though he has a more reserved and stereotypically patrician style than do most of the newer group.

A true archetype of the group was Anthony Terracciano (a graduate of Saint Peters College, Jersey City, New Jersey) who arrived at the bank in 1964 and was the head of Chase's global bank until he left in 1987 to become president of Mellon and later CEO of First Fidelity. Terraciano still lives a couple of blocks from where he grew up, in a modest stone house in Bayonne, New Jersey, a working-class town. His exit from Chase may have signaled that the guardians of the traditional Chase culture were not yet ready to accept one of the most intense and high-achieving people from this new ethnic cadre in a senior management position. A workaholic and a perfectionist, though not as gregarious as other bankers, partly because of his intensity, Terracciano was appointed head of the investment bank in 1984 and had greatly boosted its performance by 1986. He had begun the politically daunting task of melding the commercial and investment bankers before he left, to the consternation of people in both groups.[5] In 1986, Terraciano pointedly summed up Chase's problem with culture change as follows: "Part of the organization is living in the future, part is firmly rooted in the present, and...part wishes we could go back to what things were like in the 1950s."[6]

Thus, while there were big changes in the kinds of people Chase appointed, particularly to senior management positions, the old culture didn't automatically disappear. This created much stress for the new, more adventurous, and countercultural people, and they had difficulty in managing it if, indeed, they decided to stay. One high-level personnel staff member stated it well:

Since 1986, there [has been] a real effort to recruit more risk-taking people. I [have] heard it all the time, that we need to be a more risk-taking organization. It was very interesting to see what happened to [new people] when they came to the bank. They perceived the climate as much more negative than did others who had been here longer. We had tried to change the climate and culture by changing the players, and the risk-oriented people were literally bouncing off the walls. They diffused a lot of energy fighting internal battles, because the organization had not changed and yet we had all these new people in.

A Gentlemanly, Patrician Style

Underlying both the risk aversion and the paternalism was a perhaps even more basic feature of the traditional Chase culture, namely, its gentlemanly, patrician style. It shared the style with Morgan, which was also an aristocratic, British- and European-oriented bank, in contrast to Citicorp and Bankers Trust, which emerged in the 1970s and 1980s as much scrappier institutions. This aspect of Chase's culture, more than any other, constituted an institutional embodiment of the Rockefeller aura, even though David Rockefeller himself would not have wanted it to obstruct the bank's performance. Historically, there had always been a strong emphasis within the bank on appropriate manners and behavior, befitting an institution that serviced governments, the wealthy, and blue-chip corporations. Appropriate table manners, dress, speech, and other aspects of personal decorum took on enormous importance. One staff person explained:

> The patrician quality of the place still exists to some extent. We will never be the scrappy fighter that Citicorp is. People will always remember when Chase called on the kings and queens of the world. We had a grand and glorious past, and that is the hardest thing to say we won't have any more. So there is still some of that. We always had the perception that Citicorp was a gauche place and that we are an upper crust. We eat with the right fork, we dress right. Having good presentation skills is enormously important at Chase—making it look good, having the right polished slides, and so on. This was always part of the Chase culture, and we always contrasted it with Citicorp, where people were brilliant but…had their presentation on the back of an envelope. But being an upper-crust place, we were slower to change.

Another senior manager recalled, "We used to be royal, to the manner born, princely. And that all existed under David Rockefeller."

Conflict Avoidance

One of the ways in which this gentlemanly culture got played out to the detriment of the bank was in its frowning on direct confrontation between different points of view. Students of management and organizations often remind us that the ways in which companies and their managers handle conflict—that is, different interests and points of view—usually have a profound impact on their financial performance. The general consensus among academics and consultants is that more organizations are destroyed or seriously damaged by too little open expression of conflict than by too much. There is, to be sure, a level of such expression beyond which it is not desirable to go—a level at which the organization can get torn apart and the participants develop more interest in winning the battle and/or damaging the other party than in solving a business problem. Even so, up to a point, it is viewed as beneficial for a company to have a culture that encourages an open and vigorous expression of differences. Different specialized perspectives may be brought to bear on critical decisions, more information and expertise are thereby available, and the quality of the decisions that are ultimately made tends to be much higher than in institutions in which such open and free expression is not supported.[7]

The Chase culture has to be seen in this regard as an extreme case of conflict avoidance, in ways that have contributed over the years to the bank's many debacles and its overall decline. Consultants who worked with the bank often commented about it, as did some of the people inside. One such consultant had a vivid recollection of how Chase's senior management and staff responded to presentations and reports. This person worked with a firm that did surveys of the views of chief financial officers (CFOs) from big corporations about the strengths and weaknesses of their banks and reported the following:

> We visited banks regularly to report our findings. I remember when we went to Chase and Citicorp, the differences in their styles. This was in the midseventies, but my colleagues tell me it continued into the eighties. At Chase, we came into the room, sat down at a long, rectangular table with some 15 to 20 Chase senior managers and staff, and made our presentation. Chase people sat quietly, politely; and nobody interrupted or asked questions. When we were done, a person on our left politely raised his hand, indicated that the findings were interesting, and raised one question. There was a brief exchange, and then he stopped. That was followed by the person next to him making deferent comments about his colleague's question and about the report and asking another question. And they went around the table in that way, almost in lockstep fashion, giving their comments. When we went to

Citicorp, we all sat more informally around a large, circular table. One of us began summarizing our findings, and after a few minutes, all hell broke loose. Several Citicorp people aggressively challenged our methodology as well as our findings, and it soon became a free-for-all. Eventually, the dust cleared and we got through the meeting, pulling together our findings and their action implications for Citicorp. I can remember coming away from those meetings and saying to my colleague that the different styles of the two banks could make a big difference in how they would do in the changing world of banking. We both agreed, and in hindsight, it turned out that way.

Chase's accommodationist style probably has many sources. Several old-time Chase managers have suggested that the gentlemanly culture had a lot to do with it. Others indicate that the bank's extreme turf-mindedness also contributed, with managers and staff of various departments acting in protectionist ways, not wanting to share information. One of the most compelling explanations came from a Chase consultant who related this part of the culture to the concerns within the bank about protecting David Rockefeller. He explained:

> The underlings saw it as their responsibility to shield the Rockefellers from controversy and discomfort. The Rockefellers may not want this, but it keeps happening. The underlings see it as their responsibility to never make a mistake, because something disturbing will happen to a member of the family. So one should never have an argument. And people around the Rockefellers feel an absolute responsibility to cushion, filter, buffer, and avoid all unpleasantness. Related to this was the strong emphasis on managing appearances. Behavioral proprieties had to be observed: Were you seated at the right table? Did you eat the right food? Were you dressed appropriately? Those considerations were taken extremely seriously. And then it got transferred. Each member of senior management became a mini-Rockefeller: Butcher, Labrecque, Ryan. This [was] an institution [in which] people were very oriented to status deference. By contrast, Citicorp was very task- and competence-oriented.

A classic Chase story that one high-level staff person told indicated how far the filtering process could go, to prevent top management from having access to critical information that it was in the bank's interest to know and act on. The issue related to New York City's fiscal crisis in the mid-1970s, in which Chase had a deep involvement. This staff person recalled:

> I remember so vividly that I sat in on a big meeting of the senior people at the time of the city's fiscal crisis and I reported the sad state of the city's bonds and what it would mean to Chase. I so shocked the

room that one person there said, "We don't want to know those things." And I was never invited back to any more meetings. I realized that I had violated some unwritten code, particularly when I said, "You ought to find out more about the city's bond ratings." It later turned out that the SEC [Securities and Exchange Commission] investigations pointed to many of these things, and [then] later I was seen as a valued resource. But it was clear that I had not lived up to an important feature of the culture that [dictates,] "There are things we don't want to know."

Regardless of its origins, the existence of this cultural style is not disputed. It was a source of much frustration for one consultant who wanted to help the bank and its senior managers and felt that this aspect of the culture was a serious impediment to his doing so. He commented:

The Chase people are not stimulating as a client. In group meetings at Chase, nobody talks. It is as if they are a bunch of dummies, which they clearly are not. But there is no spirit of discussion. It is a closed-vest community. It seems as though they are afraid. There is clearly a lack of free expression. They do not have any of the creative tension of Citicorp. As a group, they are like a Russian version of a commercial bank. Citicorp managers are remarkably open in admitting fault. They see it right away and begin to talk about it. Chase people never admit fault. It is almost as if they won't trust you. Chase as a group is like a totalitarian state. The [people] are normal in a one-on-one exchange, but as a group, they don't react. They are like tight rubber bands when they are together in a group. That may change, but I still experience it. What they do as a result of our work I don't know. They don't want to talk about it. I don't learn anything from them. I'd like to help them, but I don't know how.

Cultural values often tend to hang together in a mutually reinforcing way, and the observations of this consultant indicate how this may work at Chase. What he saw as a lack of confrontation at Chase reflected several of its traditional values: the importance of not airing differences in public, the fear of making or exposing mistakes, and the turf-mindedness and consequent breakdown of communication among groups. An inability to collaborate was a problem that hurt the bank throughout its history, and it may have been evidenced in an indirect way in this consultant's experience. The appearance was one of complete unity, but in fact this appearance may well have simply covered over differences that weren't easily discussed among Chase managers, even when outsiders weren't around.

This point was highlighted in the comments of a staff person in regard to efforts of a different outside consultant to help Chase senior management to change the bank's culture. That consultant experienced the same sort of frustration as did his competitor (quoted above). He concluded that the bank's failure to follow up on his recommendations, which senior management seemingly agreed with at a closed meeting, reflected a lack of institutional integrity. The staff person commented, after talking with the consultant:

> When we had our culture studies here, one of the first things they told us was that though we had high professionalism and would not do anything unethical, we had a total lack of intellectual integrity. People would go to big meetings where they would commit themselves to a course of action, and all the while they knew they were never going to do it. So they would leave the meeting and not do anything. That is very common in our culture.

Turfs and Communications Breakdown

Much of this problem of nonconfrontation was related to Chase's long-term problem with departmental turfs. The firm was clearly not unique in this regard, but the problem was so severe for Chase that it had led to many breakdowns in communication. Chase had grown through numerous acquisitions that continued to function as separate entities. One alumnus referred to it as a very "political" place, which was inhabited by executives who were singularly uninterested in teamwork.[8] David Rockefeller himself acknowledged that the bank's history had contributed, though he saw the 1980s as a time when the different parts of the bank were finally coming together. He recalled:

> There is a sense of unity and teamwork within the bank that really didn't exist a number of years ago. For one thing, the bank is the product of a whole series of mergers; it took quite a long time to really absorb those mergers. There were different factions within the bank, and [those don't] exist to anything like the degree [they] did.[9]

While Rockefeller was right in his view of Chase's history, he was too optimistic about the extent of teamwork and collaboration that had developed by 1980, when he made these observations. Chase consultants and senior management spoke of this problem throughout the 1980s as one of the biggest facing the bank. Loyalties within Chase tended to be toward one's subunit and its managers. While many long-service managers expressed much abstract loyalty to the bank as such and to its distinguished history, their actual behavior often showed limited collegiality. That meant that customers would not be as well served as they should have been, in many instances, by the full scope of Chase's considerable expertise. It also meant that Chase was more vulnerable to unexpected losses through bad credit judgments, simply because one department had not called on the greater expertise of another in making credit decisions. The Penn Square Bank losses were an example of this.

Even as recently as late 1990, a top staff person commented on the continuing nature of these conflicts by saying:

> At Chase, there were always turf issues at the very top. As an illustration, in 1981, we had Frank Stankhart heading the international department and Jim Carey heading corporate banking. And the people in the Carey group would rather have given the business to an outside competitor like Citicorp than have [had] Stankhart take it over, so bitter were the rivalries there. It got better by 1986, when the bank was more desperate to maintain its position in relation to changes in the industry. But there were bitter turf struggles and we're still not out of it.

Poor Upward Communications: Rockefeller as the Isolated Monarch

As I mentioned in my original discussion of the fear of making mistakes at Chase, a lot of important information, particularly of a negative nature, never got passed up the line until it was too late. In brief, people were so afraid of reprisals for making mistakes that they preferred to cover up rather than to report problems. This style was perhaps accentuated during David Rockefeller's years as CEO, as Chase staff were reportedly in awe of him and didn't want to bother him with what they thought he would regard as trivial operations details. That he was away a lot and was not a detail-oriented manager only accentuated the problem.

When he would hear that his staff were protecting him from bad news, he would reportedly get angry and urge that it not happen again, but some of his staff regarded protecting him as one of their main tasks. This was particularly the case in view of the enormous load of activities he took on—both bank-related and nonbank-related. His staff felt that it was their job not only to keep him briefed and prepared for each meeting he attended around the world but also to keep so-called trivial bank operations issues and internal spats from coming to his attention. Many such issues probably should have been handled by the president or at lower levels, but Rockefeller needed to be better informed than he sometimes was. As I indicated earlier, this style of protecting the CEO continued when Butcher succeeded Rockefeller.

The irony was that Chase, the bank which had a culture that emphasized the importance of controls, bureaucracy, and centralization, in fact had perhaps more breakdowns and losses resulting from an absence of controls than did its competitors. One reason was that Chase's control culture bred a fear of mistakes that blocked the very communications and information flows on which its controls depended. The result was a bank that periodically ran out of control. This resulted in unnecessary losses, followed by a cycle of increased controls and bureaucracy that turned the bank inward, limited its flexibility to adapt, and set it back relative to its competitors. What seemed necessary in the face of this repeating scenario was a complete change in the corporate culture.

An Elitist, Wholesale Bank

A final aspect of the traditional culture that slowed Chase down in the 1980s was its strong attachment to the wholesale banking businesses that had brought it success in the past, to the exclusion of consumer banking. Butcher was particularly resistant to having Chase become involved in various consumer banking businesses, and in the late 1970s and early 1980s he became a major roadblock to such involvement. He played a role vis-à-vis consumer banking similar to the one that George Champion had played earlier in blocking international expansion through branches. Fred Hammer was the charismatic head of consumer banking from 1979 to 1983, and Tom Labrecque was also its advocate.

Butcher and Chase were working through an identity problem at the time regarding what they wanted the bank to be: either exclusively an elitist wholesale bank serving distinguished institutional and individual clients or an elitist bank plus a consumer bank. The message that consumer bank managers and advocates received from Butcher was that he was not prepared to have Chase serve the so-called riffraff—people on the low end of the income distribution. He finally gave in, but again, as in the case of international expansion, a lot of time was lost. One high-level manager in the consumer bank described that department's experience as follows: "I remember it took Butcher 2 years to develop a mission statement, and his first one left out the consumer bank. When we pointed it out to him, he said, oh, yes, add that on."

A Culture Change Agenda

In recognition of the negative impact of its traditional cultural values, Chase undertook a culture and strategic change effort in 1985, under the leadership of an outside consultant. As a top staff person associated with that effort recalled:

> We realized after the episodes of 1982, Drysdale and Penn Square, that there were problems within Chase that had contributed [to them]. Butcher asked for a plan on how to bring about change to prevent any future recurrences, and we did a study indicating that our strategies were not clear, that Labrecque had no control, and that we would fail if we continued on that course. So in 1983 and 1984, we concentrated on developing a strategy, and we finally, in 1985, set up three vice chairs, each responsible for one division. Now we had strategies and a structure and people at the top consistent with the strategies, and we moved on in 1985 to have a major study done leading the bank to culture change.

The cultural characteristics that the consultant and senior Chase managers and staff identified as still prevalent in 1985 and in need of radical change provide validation of the position taken in this chapter, that much of the "old Chase" reasserted itself in the 1980s, as the bank failed to build on the reforms of the last Rockefeller years of the 1970s. Six culture change issues were identified, including the needs:

1. To be more customer- and market-driven and less inward-focused
2. To push responsibility and accountability down
3. To have higher performance standards
4. To have strong senior management leadership
5. To have more collaboration and teamwork throughout the bank
6. To invest in Chase's human resources

A staff member working on the project explained that this was in large part the consultant's agenda, worked out in collaboration with senior staff. Commenting on the particular issues, that staff member explained:

1. The bank was not customer-oriented enough. "We did a survey of 9000 Chase officers around the globe and found that we were not listening to the customers as we should have been, driven as we were by our own internal processes. Before, a transaction had to go up and down the hierarchy for an approval process that took a very long

time. Now, we can process customer requests much faster, within a day or two. That is a revolutionary change for Chase."

2. It was too centralized. "We have made progress, but there remains a cadre of older managers who are uncomfortable with that."

3. Performance standards were too low. "Before, we defined our standards internally and never against the external market. Also, we had lower standards than we should have. Now, our standards are up, and we do use the external market."

4. There was weak leadership from senior management. "We have some way to go on that."

5. There was not enough collaboration and teamwork. "We have done a lot on that, as witness the integration of our investment bank into our global banking division, but we have a lot more to do."

6. There was not enough investment in personnel development. "We have always done a lot on that, and we are continuing, with everybody given a shot at our training programs."

By the late 1980s, this 18-month culture change effort seemed to have faded in importance. As social scientists continually remind us, culture change takes a long time, and even in 1992, Chase still has a long way to go to eliminate many aspects of the old culture that have hampered its ability to adapt to the increasingly competitive and changing environment of the past and coming decades. Consider the following comments of Chase staff: "It is still paternalistic, very risk-averse, still not enough market-focused, and still with no strategic image." "We like the new leadership in Labrecque and Ryan and are guardedly optimistic. But a lot of the old culture is still there: the secrecy; the caste system; the difficulty in assimilating outsiders; and the failure to develop a more collaborative, team organization."

A top staff person summarized what seemed a common view from within the ranks:

> The main features of our underlying core culture from the past—internal focus, risk-averse, and mediocrity—have not changed. Culture change programs never took hold here. Our human resources director here has said on any number of occasions that you can't change a culture from within. I believe that to be the case, and our experience illustrates that.

8

Chase: Culture, Strategy, and Survival

Another Financial Supermarket, with No Clear Direction

At Chase there has been no dearth of strategy statements, but strategy does not consist of what managers say they want. Rather, strategy is what the organization in fact does. For Chase, experience over the past three decades seems to suggest *no clear strategic identity or focus, a consequent tendency to move in many different directions at once, and a tendency to be a follower rather than a leader in the market. Underlying all these patterns there has been an inability to develop a consensus among the most senior managers as to goals.* A strongly voiced view from within the bank that reflects many of these points comes from a top staff person who is keenly disappointed with Chase's recent performance. He stated:

> We never had a vision or strategy, and that is what we are being forced to develop now. I remember so many times at directors' meetings, where Butcher would become very defensive about this, saying something to the effect that he was tired of hearing the criticism that Chase didn't have a strategy. "We have a strategy," he would say, "and it is to be the best in every business we decide to be in, and we have decided to be in them all."

This perception of Chase as not having a clear direction was seemingly widespread. Thus, another staff person reported in mid-1991:

> We now have these focus group sessions with people inside the bank and with customers, and they are asked to identify the styles of various banks. It is amazing how much consensus there is. Morgan [is] seen as prim, proper, and professional, Citicorp as very aggressive. All the others have recognized identities. And Chase is commonly seen as having no focus or identity.

Part of the problem may be semantics. Actually, Chase has been convening its senior managers on an annual basis since the late 1970s, to articulate strategy for all segments of the bank. Developing paper plans, however, is not the same as having a coherent strategy.

At the same time, it is possible to describe Chase's general directions. Historically, it was a predominantly *wholesale bank*, to such a degree that as late as 1979, according to Tom Labrecque in a speech he made in 1989, the consumer business was regarded as a "stepchild." He went on, "Our investments and staffing reflected this reality. We bought a good consumer franchise, and failed to capitalize on it."[1] Senior managers in the bank report that the retail area was, as one member of the retail staff said, "the dumping ground for people they didn't know what to do with." Since then, the bank's priorities about the relative positions of retail and wholesale banking have changed considerably, and the retail business now constitutes up to 50 percent of its total revenue.

Other general characterizations of Chase's traditional strategy were that it was a very *global* bank, reflecting the influence of Nelson Aldrich, John McCloy, and particularly David Rockefeller. It tended to service, in addition, many of the same blue-chip corporations, financial service institutions, governments, and highly affluent individuals, representing the *upper segment of the market,* as did Morgan, and perhaps more so than Citicorp. Like Citicorp, it pursued a *highly diversified* strategy, providing many products and servicing many different client groups in many countries around the world. In the late 1980s, the bank's businesses included consumer banking; corporate institutional banking; investment banking; middle-market-oriented banking; real estate financing; and technology-driven, custodial, trust, cash management, and investment management services.

Chase's diversity, like that of Citicorp, became part of its problem. Though diversification may limit risk, Chase suffered from diffuseness. As George Vojda, senior vice president and managing director at Bankers Trust, has noted, it is difficult in the increasingly competitive environment of banking to be a significant player in more than a few businesses, given the competitive strengths of so many other firms.[2] In addition, as new products and markets (new geographical areas and new clients) develop, strong, new competitors soon enter and drive down spreads. Unique new products soon become commonplace commodities.

From this perspective, a better strategy in the future for Chase, as for Citicorp, would be to become more selective, to move toward a more focused strategy by keeping only the businesses in which it has a comparative advantage and is generating significant revenues. That is, in fact, the direction in which Chase is moving as of early 1992, with some success. In this respect, the bank is now on target. It needs to continue to make the hard choices and in fact sell off those businesses that are not consistently profitable.

The best way to conclude this analysis of Chase's strategy is to analyze its main businesses in the late 1980s and indicate how it is transforming itself following the big losses of 1989 and 1990. With the 1985 reorganization, Chase essentially became three banks, loosely linked under a single banner.

The Global Bank: A Lackluster Performer

One of the three banks, called the *global bank,* included investment and merchant banking services, foreign exchange, risk-management products, and traditional, "plain vanilla" lending. The important features of this set of businesses were:

1. Chase, like its competitors, had increasingly emphasized corporate finance and capital markets services.

2. It consolidated, shrunk, or simply closed down many of its foreign branches, particularly those involved in traditional loan businesses that were declining.

3. It divested itself of many nonstrategic businesses, including Computer Power, Chase Econometrics, and Interactive Data Corporation.

4. It phased out much of its securities trading in England and Europe, where it, like Citicorp, had sustained big losses after 1985.

5. It pushed hard to reduce its less developed country (LDC) loan chargeoffs.

In the late 1980s, building on its historic strengths—a global network, long-standing corporate relationships, and specific industry knowledge—Chase had clearly changed the focus of its wholesale businesses from loans to merchant and investment banking. Though it made this conversion later than Citicorp, Bankers Trust, and Morgan, and was not seen by them as a significant player, Chase nevertheless did make the change. It also developed a new infrastructure to support these activities. It recruited aggressively from the outside (from Citicorp, Bankers Trust, and even some investment banks) to fill senior management positions. It made dramatic changes in compensation, providing Wall Street-style bonuses to investment bankers who made big deals. It instituted a new training program to recycle its commercial bankers into corporate finance generalists. It changed its traditional, tall, bureaucratic, staff-driven organizational structure to a flatter, more entrepreneurial, and line-driven one. It worked to change the corporate culture to an emphasis on more aggressive product development and marketing and a more collaborative team orientation. While those were serious, dedicated efforts, Chase was competing with commercial and investment banks who had begun similar efforts much earlier and with more resources. Many of them, including the three banks analyzed in this book, didn't even consider Chase a serious contender.

Just by virtue of its size and the traditional competitive advantages noted above, Chase was going to be some kind of player, but the question was what kind. Its estimated return on equity (ROE) of 8.4 percent and return on assets (ROA) of 0.51 for the global bank in 1988, not a very stellar performance, indicated that it was going to have to make some hard choices regarding its future in merchant and investment banking.[3] The strong businesses—for example, loan syndications, project finance, trade finance, leveraged leasing, employee stock option program (ESOP) lending, and trademark finance—were being buried under the many losing ones. An aggressive sorting-out process was going to be necessary.

The Old Chase at Its Best

The *institutional bank* was another segment that encompassed multiple businesses, in this case some of Chase's prize jewels. It included:

1. Infoserv International, a collection of highly profitable investment management, trust, and cash management services

2. Chase Investors Management Corporation, an institutional money management operation

3. Domestic institutional banking, servicing U.S. insurance companies and financial institutions

4. A series of other commercial banking businesses: real estate finance, national middle-market lending, and leasing

Unlike the global bank, this division did very well in the late 1980s, mainly because it housed a number of traditional commercial banking businesses that had been Chase's great strength. Overall, the division earned an estimated 1.23 percent return on average assets in 1988 and more than 20 percent ROE, a quite exemplary performance, and contributed roughly 25 percent of the bank's total earnings. Real estate finance, long a Chase strength, accounted for as much as half of that total, and a collection of technology-driven cash and investment management and global custody businesses, called *Infoserv*, accounted for another quarter.[4] In addition to those big revenue producers, the division in late 1989 housed the bank's correspondent banking services. Though this was an old division, it had a new corporate finance orientation, a leasing unit, a global money management business called *Chase Investors Management Corporation* (which it sold in 1991), and national middle-market lending (from which it has since withdrawn). This division, then, constituted a potpourri of businesses. It was distinguished by the fact that nearly all its businesses were in wholesale banking and were traditional commercial banking-type services.

Infoserv: A Chase Star

Now that the real estate business has experienced such declines, the Chase Investors Management Corporation has been sold off, and middle-market lending has been phased down, the remaining star in the division is Infoserv. It includes a cluster of technology- or information-based businesses: pension trust and securities services, global custody, international money transfer, and investment management. Before 1987, these services were scattered throughout the bank and were provided almost as afterthoughts or incidentals to various institutional clients. Michael Urkowitz, founder and present head of the unit, explained, "At one time these services, like cash management, were all add-ons and were all for free, to keep the lending relationship. As the lending business declined, we knew we had to find more income producers." In the 1980s, with the collapse of relationship banking, Urkowitz and his colleagues realized that they had become market leaders in products that could, in turn, be consolidated as stand-alone businesses with their own organization. They did the consolidation in 1987, and because of the limited capital the businesses require, Infoserv has an ROE of well over 30 percent.[5] Its net income increased 55 percent

from 1988 to 1989 and another 23 percent in 1990.[6] In a newly constituted Chase in the 1990s, if that proves possible, this cluster of businesses will stand high.

The success of Infoserv is so important, reflecting Chase's strengths
and possible future directions, that it merits further discussion. In addition to its autonomy, the division prospered because of Urkowitz's
management skills, the staff he recruited, the political leadership and
support the division has had at the most senior management levels, and
its use of traditional Chase resources. Urkowitz's background is in en-
gineering, and he has a strong interest in general management and operations. He reported:

> This business lives and dies with strong general management, and that
> is what we are practicing here. It requires meticulous attention to de-
> tail and managers from different functional backgrounds. For example,
> we need people with strong skills in customer services, sales, product
> management, operations management, and systems management. If I
> can find more people with those backgrounds and train them to "do it
> right" in our business, we will have even better results. We have al-
> ready found some managers like that, and we are looking for more.

Management skills are fine, as long as they relate to a larger vision and
to products that will make it in the marketplace. Urkowitz and his senior management colleagues evolved such a vision. "Several of us
talked a lot about these things, particularly Ryan and Labrecque," he reported. "These are people who [think] like I do, people with an operations perspective. We shared the dream for many years before we actually put it into practice."

Implicit in the above discussion is the presence in the division of powerful idea champions, who had an orientation similar to Urkowitz's and
who would promote it strongly. The coalition of Labrecque and Ryan,
along with people like Urkowitz, formed the core of the leadership that
was to work in late 1990 and thereafter to restructure Chase for its survival.

A final factor in the division's success was how it built on Chase's
competitive strengths. The bank's global presence, its reputation
throughout the world, and its cadre of sales-oriented relationship managers were all critical. Urkowitz concluded his comments by saying:

> We had branches all over the world, linked by telecom networks. Also,
> the Chase name is recognized and respected all around the world, as
> [standing for] an institution that is sound and has integrity. Chase's ro-
> bust presence with global systems helped a lot. And historically, Chase
> was strong on correspondent banking. I could take this correspondent

banking cadre and transform them into a global sales force. So there was a nifty infrastructure already in place.

Though this success has been somewhat atypical within Chase (as a rising star in a period of declining or, at best, mediocre performance for the bank as a whole), it could be a precursor of Chase's future revival. It has featured two senior managers, Labrecque and Ryan, who are a key to Chase's recovery, along with rising managers like Urkowitz. It has featured a strategy and a set of capabilities that capitalized on Chase's historic strengths while also utilizing contemporary management skills and technology. A big question, of course, is whether these leaders are willing to focus and thereby limit Chase's future direction to this style and set of capabilities or whether they will perpetuate the diffuseness that contributed to the bank's decline.

Another Star: The Individual Bank

There is ample precedent for the needed focus in the performance of still another set of businesses that Chase is involved in, namely, its *individual bank*. Late in the game relative to its peers, Chase's individual or retail bank was organized as a separate division only in 1985,[7] a full 10 years after Citicorp's. It now contributes close to 50 percent of the bank's total revenue, and that percentage will likely increase, as it did at Citicorp, in the near future.

Despite its lateness, the politics of which I reviewed earlier, Chase has nevertheless become a big player in consumer banking. It now ranks second among banks in the credit card business. This business, which continues to grow, earned $113 million in 1988 and made a 20 percent gain in 1989. The Chase Home Mortgage Corporation built up its servicing portfolio to $30 billion in just a few years. Thus, it advanced from being the forty-sixth largest mortgage servicer in 1987 to become one of the top five in 1990.[8] In 1989, its personal financial services business, which was targeted at consumers with annual incomes of more than $75,000, had 62 offices around the United States and a loan portfolio of more than $3.6 billion. Its private banking business, targeting the upper end of the market (e.g., clients with minimum household incomes of $250,000 annually, net worths of $1 million, or liquid assets of at least $500,000) has grown by 30 percent annually since 1982.[9]

Beyond these businesses, Chase has an international consumer group that attempts to capitalize on the bank's global outreach and reputation. As of 1989, that group contributed an estimated 15 to 20 percent of the

individual bank's earnings,[10] and there was a likelihood that the percentage would increase. Its profits in 1989 were an estimated $50 mil-
lion, half of which were from Latin America (where Chase had its
biggest international presence) and Asia. Chase consumer banking
around the world includes credit cards, mortgages, investment vehicles,
and savings instruments.

The important point about these successes in the individual bank is
that they resulted from the same general management and operations
skills as Infoserv. Art Ryan, the head of this division from its inception
in 1985 until he became president of Chase in 1990, was able to routinize
and realize economies of scale in each of a series of products. Together
with Infoserv, these products form a potent retail and wholesale bank
presence that could become the core of Chase's future. Such a presence
would represent a vastly scaled-down Chase, but it could at least be a
basis on which the bank could build.

The other part of Chase's business, which in many respects lies in between the individual and the institutional banks, is regional banking.
As part of an effort in the early 1980s to expand geographically to upstate New York, in 1984 Chase purchased Lincoln First Banks, Inc., of
Rochester, which included 113 branches.

The Lincoln acquisition, however, involved a lot more than just acquiring retail branches. Soon Chase made Lincoln part of a larger interstate expansion and middle-market strategy that it initiated by pur-
chasing nine troubled savings and loans (S&Ls) in Ohio and Maryland
and converting them into commercial banks. Also part of this strategy
was the purchase of commercial banks in Scottsdale, Arizona, and Saint
Petersburg, Florida.[11] Turning these banks around proved difficult, and
Chase asked Lincoln to do the job. Lincoln's mandate was to leverage its
skills as a large retail bank in managing and enhancing the profitability
of the acquisitions. A big part of the profitability goal was to reach many
middle-market corporate customers with a variety of wholesale products. Thus far, the strategy seems not to have paid off, and Chase has
backed off from it.

It did announce in 1991, however, a modified resumption of its earlier strategy for developing a national presence in retail banking.
Specifically, senior managers stated that they intended to acquire retail branches in New Jersey, Connecticut, and other states in the northeast. They followed up the announcement in August 1991 with the
purchase of two banks in Bridgeport, Connecticut. All this took place
in the wake of improvements in Chase's capital position and profits in
each of the first three quarters of 1991, suggesting that the bank's

many efforts to downsize and sell off nonstrategic business were starting to pay off.

Chase's retail bank, with the exception of its regional banking component, stands out as still another example of effective strategy that could contribute substantially to the bank's future recovery. Art Ryan, the head of that division, was largely responsible for its growth. Now the bank's president, Ryan came from an operations and general management background, as mentioned earlier. He used his skills to rationalize several key retail businesses, reach substantial economies of scale, and produce in the process big revenues for the bank. It is important to note that Ryan was not involved in the regional banking and branch components of the retail business, which were its most problematic aspects.

Chase may well need more than Infoserv and individual banking to survive, but these two businesses alone provide a huge annuitylike income and capitalize on many of the bank's traditional strengths. Its experiences in this area may contain important lessons for what it must do across the board to restore its financial health. There could probably be much worse fates for Chase than to become a selective generalist with a concentration on these two businesses. One would be the possibility of an outside takeover, which would end one of the premier banking franchises in the United States. Such an end, however, is not inevitable.

Strategic Changes Since 1990: A Struggle for Survival

When Chase's profits and stock price were declining markedly in 1989 and 1990, as a result of its huge losses in commercial real estate loans, it underwent the shakeup mentioned earlier. Willard Butcher took early retirement in the spring of 1990, Tom Labrecque moved from president to chief executive officer (CEO), and Art Ryan became president. The three divisions, including a layer of management, were eliminated, which placed senior management closer to the marketplace and clients. The workforce was reduced by more than 5000 employees, and the new team instituted a program of exiting from underperforming or nonstrategic businesses and selling nonessential assets. Enactment of this program was, of course, dependent upon development of a consensus about what the bank's core businesses should be.

As of late 1991, Chase's strategy was to build market leadership in six primary businesses: three retail and three wholesale. The retail busi-

nesses included such consumer products as credit cards, home mortgages, investment services, auto and education finance, regional branch
banking, and global private banking. The wholesale businesses provided global corporate finance services—underwriting corporate debt;
private placement; public finance; mergers and acquisitions (M&A),
and global risk management—(foreign exchange; swaps, options, and
other such new hedging products; and transaction and information services through Infoserv). This is still a wide array of products and services, but it is much less diffuse than what Chase had before.

The other critical aspect of the bank's strategy has been to exit from
nonstrategic and nonperforming businesses, and Chase has made much
headway on that front. In early 1991, it sold its money management
unit, the Chase Investors Management Corporation, to Union Bank of
Switzerland for $98 million.[12] Several months later, in August 1991, it
sold most of its leasing operation to Ford and General Electric (GE) and
reported other, smaller sales as well.[13] It was finally beginning to distinguish between core businesses and those that were not core, and to
sell off the nonstrategic ones. Robert Douglas, a Chase vice chairman,
said at the time of the sale of Chase Investors Management Corporation
that it had been "a consistent money maker, but it no longer fit into
Chase's core strategy."[14] Consumer banking and the Infoserv businesses have been mentioned frequently in the financial press as part of
the core strategy.

As a result of all these initiatives, Chase's performance in 1991 improved significantly over that of the previous year. Though it had a net
loss of $334 million in 1990, following a loss of $665 million in 1989, it
had a positive net income of $520 million in 1991. The sharpest
turnaround was in third-quarter earnings; the bank's net income was
$136 million, contrasted with a loss of $623 million a year earlier.

Meanwhile, Chase made its first foray into Connecticut in August
1991, by acquiring the deposits and branches of two insolvent banks
based in Bridgeport. Part of a larger northeast retail branch expansion
strategy, this acquisition included $2.5 billion in deposits and 67
branches, giving Chase entry to affluent Fairfield County, where most
of the branches are located. The move positioned Chase very well
against New York competitors that were also interested in expanding
consumer franchises in the Northeast. Citicorp is one, but it is too busy
struggling to raise capital to get involved in such acquisitions. Chemical
and Manufacturers Hanover, two others, are concentrating on working
out the complexities of their merger. "It's a minicoup for Chase," said
banking analyst George Salem.[15]

One year doesn't necessarily reverse the two decades that preceded it, particularly in an industry as volatile as banking. Faced with a major threat to its survival, however, Chase may well have responded to the challenge better than many competitors did. Cost cutting and downsizing were, after all, not alien to the traditional Chase culture, with its emphasis on caution and quality. Unlike Citicorp, Chase had been emphasizing these goals since the mid-1980s. In this respect, the traditional culture may have prepared it better than might have been imagined not long ago for the shocks of the past couple of years.

A Staff-Driven Bureaucracy Now Becoming Flatter

Throughout much of its history, Chase maintained a centralized, hierarchical bureaucracy, in sharp contrast to the structure of Citicorp, its more decentralized and agile competitor. In each instance, the bank's structure reflected its culture and strategy. Citicorp, with its entrepreneurial culture and its aggressive, first-mover-oriented strategy, could only implement its moves with a flexible, decentralized organization. Chase, which had a much greater concern for quality and profitability and a strategy of caution, required a more centralized, controlling structure.

Until the late 1950s, Chase's organizational structure, though centralized, was not complex. There were no staff functions, and the reporting structure was relatively short, with not many levels in the chain of command. George Champion reported, some years after he retired, "I went through all the departments to see and observe for myself."[16] In a word, the organization was smaller and much more informal than it was to become later on, and much of the management of the various departments was conducted through direct personal contact from the top.

The main basis of organization was along industry and geographic lines. Thus, in 1952, there were a U.S. department for domestic corporate banking; a metropolitan department; and a special industries department, which emphasized long-term corporate relationships that the Rockefellers and certain senior managers at Chase had cultivated over the years. Later, a trust department, an international department, and an investments and financial planning department were added.

In the 1960s, reflecting David Rockefeller's strong interest in management systems and planning, the bank took on many new staff functions and became staff-driven in a way very different from Citicorp's mode. Champion had reportedly resisted much of this, given his more informal, traditional style, but Rockefeller was deeply committed to professionalizing the management of the bank, and he eventually prevailed. After he became CEO in 1969, the change to more professionalized management and systems accelerated. Chase produced its first long-range plan in 1971, and a few years later Rockefeller brought in the bank's first strategic planning professional, in a staff position. Shortly before, he had brought in a human resource professional. Both became executive vice presidents, reporting directly to him. More important, they reflected a general trend toward building up the corporate staff, to give the bank an expertise in various management functions that it had not had before.

These changes had mixed results. While adding more expertise in critical functions, they also created more central bureaucracy, with additional layers of management. Much more paperwork was created than before, including endless reports and analyses that line managers had to review. The paperwork may have impeded Chase's efforts to encourage the innovative, entrepreneurial approach that managers at Citicorp embarked upon. There is nothing unusual about this. Many well-intentioned new management systems, introduced into organizations as a means to improve performance, become ends in themselves. Notwithstanding the able staff people Chase recruited, who made important contributions, this is reported to have happened at Chase.

Developments in the 1980s included the addition of such new departments as capital markets and consumer banking, increased decentralization along geographic lines, and a move toward consolidation and simplification of the structure. The three-division arrangement (global, national, and consumer banking) introduced in 1985 was one move in that direction. The subsequent elimination of these divisions, flattening the entire bank, was another. Management theorist Henry Mintzberg has hypothesized that organizations facing a crisis of survival in a hostile, threatening environment are likely to revert to a simpler, more centralized structure. This enables senior management to take charge and respond quickly in an emergency situation. It describes well Chase's experiences since 1990.[17]

There were two other structural issues that Chase faced in common with its commercial banking competitors. The first related to how it organized its global bank. Would it give more authority to geographic area managers around the world, emphasizing relationship banking? Or would the ultimate authority lie with product directors back at headquarters (HQ), with an emphasis on a transactional approach to the business? In the eyes of the managers who had to live through the crisis, none of the banks resolved this dilemma well. One solution was creation of a matrix, in which a banker in a particular locale was responsible to both geographic managers and HQ. Another was to keep moving back and forth between the two forms. Bankers in all the institutions I studied commented on the confusion and stress that resulted from how their banks managed this issue. One CEO wryly observed, "If you run a global organization, you need teamwork, some way of tying it all together. You need an accounts officer who has to say: `I need this and that at a particular time and place.' That is what got our matrix concept going, and it was what caused all the trouble. Nobody ever figured out how to do it."

The other key organizational issue was how to link the traditional relationship managers in the institutional bank with the new investment bankers. Anthony Terracciano, the first head of Chase's global banking, had tried in 1985 and 1986 to overhaul the wholesale bank by melding commercial and investment bankers into one seamless organization and retraining most of the staff. Both groups reacted poorly to his plan, and many left. As one financial journalist reported at the time:

> So far the transition has been turbulent. In March ten traders, angered by lower-than-expected bonuses and what they perceived to be a loss of autonomy, quit Chase's London merchant bank. And late last year numerous bankers, upset with the reorganization and the ensuing confusion, left the domestic corporate lending area, where, one insider says, "the headhunters were circling like vultures."[18]

After Terracciano left in 1987, it remained for his successor, Richard Boyle, to manage the reorganization. He did so in a forceful but seemingly fair way. Not surprisingly, there was still a lot of turbulence, though the consolidation he implemented has since worked out. It involved ending the autonomy of the investment bankers, many of whom were not effective managers, and having them report to senior corporate people, who had been recruited recently from outside. One such person, Michael Dacey from Bankers Trust, headed up the corporate finance group, and the other, Richard Huber from Citicorp, headed securities and trading. Both were accomplished, experienced managers, and many people inside Chase regarded it as a coup to have recruited them. The reaction from some investment bankers was particularly negative, and many left. They regarded Boyle as having given away most of the power to the commercial bankers and in that sense as having caved in to a group that was now out of step with new developments in the industry. Several of these disgruntled investment bankers then gave exclusive interviews to a *Wall Street Journal* reporter, who legitimated their view that the reorganization represented "the revenge of the nerds." They meant by this that the corporate loan officers inappropriately won the top jobs. One of the investment bankers was quoted as saying:

> Tony (Terracciano) stayed above the animosities and ran things rather well without being partisan. When he left, there was a vacuum. Boyle is a corporate lending guy, and when he came in all the good jobs went to corporate guys. These guys decided it was time to settle some old scores. People were fired without getting bonuses that they felt they were due. That's why there are such hard feelings over this.[19]

Chase officials never gave their version of what happened, though several did claim that the article was very biased and that there should be a follow-up piece to "set the record straight."

Chase's consolidation of the two groups made a lot of sense. In this area, Chase was well ahead of Citicorp, though Bankers Trust and Morgan had made the change some time before. While Chase did lose some high-performing investment bankers to Wall Street firms or its own boutiques, the general consensus within Chase and in the industry at large is that this consolidation has worked out reasonably well.

Chase has one additional structural issue, which is special to its own situation. This is the importance of linking together the various divisions and departments so that it can provide a more coherent, responsive package of services to clients than it has offered in the past. A problem that has plagued Chase throughout its history has been its failure to provide its wide array of products in one place and in an integrated fashion. Chase is not unique in this regard, but its difficulties in generating the needed collaboration are severe. Labrecque reportedly has informed many of his senior managers that this issue is high among his priorities. His, and his managers', use of such terms as *the seamless bank, teamwork,* and *cross selling* refers to a perceived need for more integration within the bank.

The issue is seen as being so important that it was highlighted through a Harvard Business School case in an executive development program for the bank's most senior managers, beginning in October 1989. Put together under the supervision of Prof. Benson Shapiro of Harvard Business School, the case, *Chase Manhattan Bank (A-F),* describes the lack of integration of the global, national, and consumer banks in servicing various clients in Spain. A staff person who was informed on the project explained:

> It was a real eye-opener for Labrecque, who assumed that in 1988 and 1989, things were a whole lot better on matters of internal integration. He thought that, after all the work on reorganization in 1985–1986,...somehow, there was more integration. What happened was that the three banks at Chase each had their separate reporting re-

lationships, and that made for great difficulty in delivering services fast and responsively. The case was used in an executive development session that included Huber, who reported to Boyle (vice chair of global banking); Urkowitz, who reported to Douglas (vice chair of national banking); and Holzer, who reported to Ryan (vice chair of consumer banking). This was October 1989, and then there was the annual January meeting of Labrecque with his senior managers, and he announced that we are not as seamless as we must be.

The Role of CEOs in Chase's Past and Future

While I referred in the historical account in Chapter 6 to Chase's various CEOs, I did relatively little assessment of their styles and impacts. The CEOs who have served since the early 1960s are the most important for our purposes. Before then, Chase had two distinguished leaders, Nelson Aldrich and John McCloy, who shared several characteristics that contributed to Chase's becoming such a preeminent bank. They were expansion-minded, they were internationalists, and they were dedicated to public service. There is little question but that their strong leadership, from Aldrich's arrival as CEO in 1934 to McCloy's retirement in 1960, enhanced Chase's reputation and performance. Both the merger with the Manhattan Bank in 1955 and the later completion of Chase Plaza (adjacent to Wall Street) as the bank's headquarters, were particularly critical in this regard, and both occurred under McCloy's leadership.

As in most organizations, CEO succession decisions were fateful in shaping Chase's performance. One was the decision in 1960 regarding McCloy's successor. There were two strong contenders. One was George Champion, who had an outstanding record as one of the nation's leading credit officers in Chase's domestic institutional bank, had built up its correspondent banking, and had been president under McCloy. The other was David Rockefeller, who was 11 years younger than Champion. Though Rockefeller was less experienced in traditional commercial banking than Champion, he was a person the board wanted very much to keep. Rockefeller had already done much to improve the bank's international operations and its internal management systems.

Champion and Rockefeller: A Co-CEO Stalemate?

Fearing that it would lose one of them if it made the other sole CEO, the board finally decided on the co-CEO arrangement discussed in Chapter

6, and that decision probably hurt Chase's performance a lot. The bank was still strong when Champion retired in 1969, but many initiatives were delayed during the 1960s because of major differences between the two on basic policy issues.[20] Rockefeller was particularly interested in management improvements, in addition to global expansion. For him, that meant modernizing the organizational structure and the human resource and management systems of the bank, introducing a new planning department to think through where the bank was going, and implementing a more aggressive marketing emphasis. Champion, by contrast, was much less committed to these initiatives. The result was long delays. Rockefeller described the situation as follows:

> Champion reluctantly went forward with overseas expansion, but each branch we opened was a battle. And because of his objections and our many differences, the process of global expansion was slowed up a lot. What would happen on many proposals I put forth was that he would sit on them and no action would be forthcoming for a long time.

Champion, as indicated earlier, represented a more traditional, credit officer view of what the bank should be doing. He was particularly reluctant to open foreign branches, lest they be poorly managed and undercut the global network of correspondent banks that he had established. His preferred strategy seemed driven mainly by a commitment to having Chase continue concentrating on domestic institutional banking, a business that he had built up, along with correspondent banking.

The contrast, then, was between two polar opposites. Champion was a traditional corporate banker, oriented toward domestic and correspondent banking, who had an informal management style involving direct contact and supervision and who was reluctant to move in new directions that might well be contrary to what had made the bank great. A prominent CEO of another bank summarized his perception of that style by saying, "Champion felt that two plus two is four every morning, and he was reluctant to have Chase become a world player." Rockefeller was much more oriented toward international expansion and toward professionalizing the strategic planning and internal management of the bank, including the development of a corporate staff and more delegation of authority. A Chase senior management person from the Champion era reported that as recently as 1990, Champion would regale old friends with tales about Chase's glory days of the 1950s and 1960s and note how ironic it was that Chase was now closing many of its branches around the world, after he had urged that it never open them in the first place. "He still holds forth in the Pan Am Building, at the Sky Top Restaurant," this staffer continued, "and he claims that many of the troubles that Chase and the money centers in general have had in the 1980s have been due to their expansion internationally."

Rockefeller as Sole CEO

After Champion retired in 1969, Rockefeller was the sole CEO for 10 years, and his management style had an enormous impact on the bank. There are various interpretations of the Rockefeller years, pro and con. On the positive side, his leadership in Chase's global expansion was critical, and he worked feverishly to make up for lost time. Old-time Chase bankers from that period noted that the revenue the international bank produced was critical in helping to bail the bank out after its big real estate losses in the 1970s.

Rockefeller was, in addition, a global statesman, having set up many organizations to improve international relations—for example, the Trilateral Commission. While his work with these organizations was peripheral to his role as Chase's CEO and to the bank's economic performance, he did establish branches throughout the world. He also did much to develop Chase's international reputation for integrity and professionalism. Often, one visit from him to a head of state or other top government or business official abroad would generate business for the bank, so great were his aura and his reputation as a public service-oriented person and not just a banker. An admiring old-time Chase banker recalled:

> Even though he had a negative reputation among some, that he spent too much time traveling all over the world and not tending enough to the bank's business, he helped spread Chase's reputation abroad. He only had to be with a client for just a short time, and they never forgot it. Even when our services were not quite as good as a competitor's, the fact that a client had seen David Rockefeller gave Chase the decided edge. The great amount of business we did abroad owed tremendously to him.

Improving the internal management of Chase was another of Rockefeller's priorities. He built a strong central staff in the bank (some would say too strong), to help guide its future directions. A top Chase staff person explained:

> We were much more staff-driven than Citicorp. There, they had Wriston and his line managers pushing ahead on new products and

businesses. Chase, by contrast, had its headquarters staff play a much stronger role. Staff people tend to be much more analytical and often end up with a more measured strategy, splitting the difference. People like Wriston are much more gung ho about what they come up with. And that may be another reason why Citicorp was ahead of us on so many things.

The positive side of this staff infusion, on the other hand, was Chase's increased professionalism and expertise in such areas as strategic planning, forecasting, and human resources management. Rockefeller was ultimately responsible for those changes.

He also played an important symbolic role, as an inspiring leader with whom people at all levels of the bank identified. Several Chase managers and staff recall with much nostalgia the Friday morning open sessions at which he would report on his many outside travels: meetings with foreign government officials or with members of a Senate Banking Committee. "We all felt [that we were] part of a larger purpose when we attended those meetings," reported a Chase banker, "and they were really cultural events for us. They made us proud to be here at Chase. There's been nothing like that since."

There were, in addition, numerous reports from Chase bankers of that era on Rockefeller's deeply humanistic and egalitarian style in dealing with employees. Though many of his staff continuously shielded him from outside intrusions and news from the ranks, his personal decorum and behavior toward Chase employees were anything but standoffish. He reportedly spent a considerable amount of time, for example, in informal interaction with the secretarial and management support staff. One senior manager recalled, "I remember one retirement party for a secretary who had been with the bank for some 35 years. It was in the big board room. I remember when I came into the room, there David was, talking, not with the many senior managers of the bank, but over in a corner with all the secretaries." Another related:

> I remember when we put our cardiovascular unit on the ground floor. It provided a stress test, aerobics, and all kinds of vascular related services. David wanted to use it and one of his associates called down and reserved time for an hour. He asked that the hour David had it, nobody else would be allowed to use it. David was furious when he heard, and he almost had a heart attack himself, before he began. That was the kind of person he was.

Finally, Rockefeller stamped Chase with his strong public service commitments. Its involvement in helping developing nations and in helping New York City deal responsibly with its fiscal crisis in the mid-1970s, and its many philanthropic contributions, were other hall-marks of his leadership. He had his own social causes that he pursued while CEO and later, and his private civic interests did identify Chase as a social-minded organization in New York City and in the world at large.

As one might expect, some of Rockefeller's competitors had their fa-vorite quips about his travels and social activities. A competitor from Citicorp remarked:

> George Moore, one of the best phrase makers around, once said: "Let David shake hands with the king and we'll do the business." God knows, George and his colleagues were shaking hands with the king, also. But David was looking for something else. He established an am-bience for his troops. He was never interested in the question "Now, how can I make a dollar?" That was always our only question.

A cruel joke among Wall Street analysts in the 1970s, when Chase was facing hard times, was, "At the end of a business day Walter Wriston knows how much money his bank made, and David Rockefeller knows how many minority employees his bank has hired."[21] Such humor prob-ably said more about the person who told the story than about Rockefeller, but the point is that he did become the butt of such jokes in the down days of Chase.

Despite the scapegoating, Rockefeller had a major positive impact on the bank while he was CEO, making it reflect his values and interests. He further internationalized it, he upgraded its internal management, and he broadened its dedication to include doing public services as well as improving its own financial performance.

There was, however, a downside to Rockefeller's impact on Chase, some of it his own doing and some resulting from factors that may have been outside his control. Obviously, as mentioned previously, he was not a hands-on CEO, traveling around the world as he did and spend-ing much time away from the bank. Furthermore, in view of the many internal political, management, and control problems that he inherited and that continued throughout his administration, he was not as atten-tive to detail as he should have been. One might well argue that a CEO's role is not to attend to operational detail but rather to develop a vision, a culture, and a style for the institution and to help set in motion some productive strategy directions—that the implementation of these ideals is best left to others. Rockefeller clearly did have a strong effect upon the goals and the culture of Chase, but to ensure the continued success of the bank, he then had to appoint a strong president and senior management team who would deal effectively with internal issues. He did not establish strategy for the bank in the sense that Walter Wriston had done it for Citicorp, nor in the ways that Alfred Brittain and later Charles Sanford had done it for Bankers Trust, nor as Lewis Preston had done it for Morgan.

In 1969 Rockefeller and Champion agreed on the appointment of Herb Patterson as president, to complement Rockefeller's role and to carry out internal functions. Patterson was a Chase insider who had had a distinguished career as the head of domestic and then international banking. As Rockefeller later acknowledged, however, the job was much too demanding for Patterson, and Rockefeller had to fire him after 3 years.[22] The decision was sound, but it came very late, after Chase had been drifting for much too long. Rockefeller, in his typically nondefensive and honorable fashion, has acknowledged that he should have acted earlier. "I let it go on for too long," he said, "and that was my mistake. It wasn't apparent at first that he was having such problems. Still, I have to take the blame for it. I should have done something before."

Rockefeller next, in late 1972, appointed Willard Butcher, a traditional wholesale banker with an excellent record as a manager, to the presidency. Variously characterized as strong on banking fundamentals, energetic, a good customers' man, and "a tiger on internal operations," Butcher worked well with Rockefeller throughout the rest of the decade. The bank's remarkable recovery and expansion in the late 1970s was due in part to the effectiveness of this senior management pair.

The Patterson incident reveals a management style that was characteristic of the Rockefeller era. Two things in particular stand out. One is that Rockefeller had been so out of touch that he was late in realizing that his president was having serious problems on the job. His being away from the bank so much undoubtedly contributed to that shortcoming.

Beyond that, the incident is an illustration of the effects of Rockefeller's being shielded and actively prevented from hearing so-called bad news. As already indicated, certain staff people felt that he should not be burdened with administrative details, and particularly not with internal problems. These staff members did him a great disservice. Unfortunately for Chase, their attitude became widely institutionalized. Many Chase managers and staff members were reportedly in such awe of Rockefeller that they were reluctant to burden him and his office with what might be seen as "trivial" operational details. The result of his extensive travels and of this restricted upward flow of negative information was to put both him and the bank in a weakened and vulnerable position. Serious internal problems were developing, and he didn't know enough about them and was therefore not managing them. Even Wilson, in his otherwise very supportive treatment of Chase and Rockefeller, commented, "Most troublesome was upward communication, especially the reluctance of subordinates to bring bad news to their superiors. Outsiders had criticized this in senior management, holding Rockefeller to be too isolated and not informed of problems, and there was some merit in this allegation."[23] One troubled insider who had enormous affection and respect for Rockefeller nevertheless referred in disappointment to him as having become a kind of *isolated monarch*, not at all through personal choice but rather as a victim of people inside the bank who were trying to protect him.

The difference between Rockefeller and Champion was particularly pronounced in this regard. One top-level staff person recalls having several private meetings with Champion when he was CEO, but he recalls no meetings with Rockefeller that didn't include at least one other staff person in the room, and often there were several others present. The only exception was when he traveled with Rockefeller, as the staff member responsible for briefing him on details of the trip. This person recalled:

> You never saw David one on one, or very rarely, because there were always many people in the room. And nobody ever said much in that room, when we were talking about strategy issues. With Champion, it was very different. I remember one day I got a call from his secretary saying that the chairman wanted to talk with me. It was on some issue related to the welfare system in New York City, and it was just the two of us. That would never happen with David Rockefeller, who was always surrounded by a large retinue who protected him.

The consensus among many informed Chase staff and managers is that Rockefeller's strengths—his vision; his internationalist perspective; his charisma; and his extraordinary integrity, human concerns, and public service orientation—would have had to be complemented by two others for the bank to have been effective while he was CEO. One of these strengths would have been an attention to internal administrative matters, in the broadest sense: improving communications and managing the turf conflicts that had hurt the bank so much. The other strength would have been development of strategy in a more explicit and action-oriented way. While Chase had some able senior managers during the later Rockefeller years, and while these managers did contribute significantly to the bank's turnaround, there was no systematic process whereby they could discuss their ideas and come to a consensus among themselves about where the bank should be going and how it should get there. Instead, each manager did effective things on his own initiative, and the strategic planning that did exist was much more staff- than line-driven.

The decision about Rockefeller's successor in 1979 was, if anything, even more critical than such decisions had been previously. The future of money center banks was increasingly threatened by accelerating changes in the industry, and Chase was going to require extraordinary leadership in order to perform effectively.

The board faced a difficult decision on whether to select an insider or an outsider. The strongest inside candidate was Willard Butcher, and he was the one finally chosen. As a top Chase staff person close to the decision recalled:

> The board felt it was easier to go along with an internal person than an outside one. To go outside could be controversial, and they didn't want that. The outside list was pretty short, and the concerns around the outsiders were that they were well known and people had strong opinions either way about them. It was easier to take somebody from inside, and Butcher was the strongest of that group.

The bank's ultimate judgment on Butcher's 11 years was not favorable, notwithstanding the enormity of the job. In 1990, when Chase's financial performance dipped to new lows, he was encouraged to take early retirement. Following David Rockefeller in the CEO position would have been difficult for anyone, and this difficulty may well have been a factor in Butcher's performance. Several observers commented on the amount of time Butcher spent outside the bank, trying to emulate Rockefeller's style in cultivating public officials, business leaders, and other distinguished clients.

More important, many Chase insiders characterized Butcher as a centralist, who was dedicated to the old wholesale culture and who consistently either vetoed or moved much too slowly on badly needed reforms. They also characterized him as being unduly defensive when critics questioned Chase's lack of any clear strategy. One top staff person explained:

> Butcher was very bright and could be strong when the bank needed it, but he was dedicated to the old wholesale culture. Only if things were going well would he be effective, and then he would start to shift the culture back, which is what happened. It started to shift back after he became CEO, and that was just when we needed more rather than less change. He had a nervousness about risk that reinforced just what we

didn't need. He became somewhat of a damper on how far Chase could move to expand and adapt. And his approach throughout was to go back to the old corporate banking culture, highly centralized and with strong audit and controls.

The earlier discussion on how Butcher responded to efforts to build the consumer bank illustrates the problems well. He reportedly sat on proposals for months on end—for example, proposals to expand the credit card business interstate, to develop the home equity loan business, and to expand the consumer bank globally—stating that they were in violation of established bank policy. The same pattern was repeated in many other strategic decisions. One result was that the reform impetus of the later 1970s was curbed. External pressures also had an effect upon Butcher's record as CEO. In the Drysdale and Penn Square incidents of 1982, for instance, he responded decisively and fairly. The overall posture of the bank in the 1980s, however, was one of delay and caution in many strategic areas. Much responsibility for that posture belongs to Butcher.

Labrecque: Will He Make It?

The other major figure of the 1980s was Tom Labrecque, Butcher's president throughout his term. Labrecque was chosen over several strong candidates, including Barry Sullivan, who went on to become CEO of First National Bank of Chicago, and Bill Ogden, who became CEO of Continental Illinois. Labrecque was one of the first senior managers who had not come up through the traditional, corporate wholesale business, and he was highly regarded in many sectors of the bank. He had gained much visibility and received much praise for his work as Rockefeller's representative in helping the city to manage its fiscal crisis and later in championing the development of the retail bank and the trust business.

Labrecque's style was very different from Butcher's. While Butcher had a top-down, centralist approach, Labrecque was much more participative and team-oriented. He was also much more open to new people and ideas, and many of the innovations of the 1980s, including the expansion of the retail bank and later the investment bank, were instituted as a result of Labrecque's strong support. One top staff person reported, "Labrecque was much more of an initiator and active in recruiting key executives, and that was against Butcher's will. Those that came in immediately bumped into a whole old culture. They were very uncomfortable in this environment, and it was Butcher's environment."

Chase was clearly Butcher's bank during his term as CEO, and Labrecque was limited in terms of what he could accomplish. When he first became president, he had an organization but no power to make it work. There were two vice presidents, Bill Ogden, who ran finance, and John Hooper, who ran credit. They essentially controlled both the assets and the liabilities of Chase, and they reported to Butcher.

In time, Labrecque became able to use his initiative more. He developed the reputation of being an effective troubleshooter and strategist. In late 1990 he was effective in assembling a coalition to restructure the bank. Also, his recent championing of the "seamless bank" concept suggests that he has made an excellent diagnosis of one of the bank's key internal problems.

A remaining issue, which has been a problem since Rockefeller became CEO in 1969, is the continued isolation of Chase's most senior management from the rest of the organization. Rockefeller's isolation was attributed to his travels, his limited attention to detail, and the efforts of the people around him to protect him. Unfortunately for Chase, the same condition continued when Butcher was CEO. His strongly centralist style may have encouraged continuation of the protective attitude that isolated Rockefeller. Labrecque's more participative and team-oriented style may contribute to a lessening of the problem. Consider, however, the following comment from a staff person who is very supportive of Labrecque and anxious to see him succeed: "Labrecque is not into the organization. He is removed from what is happening. And he often takes information too uncritically and doesn't know it has been filtered. " On the other hand, he has spent more time mingling with lower-level people, and he did choose, as his president, Art Ryan, an operations person.

In brief, Chase has had CEOs with markedly different styles since the 1960s. The one thing they have all had in common was an isolation from the wider organization, as a result of poor upward communication. The isolated condition of the CEO, to the extent that it still exists, must be managed much better in the immediate future in order for Chase to be able to restructure itself effectively before it is forced to merge with another institution or is taken over.

Viewing Chase in comparative perspective, it had been until 1991, when Citicorp took a big dip, the poorest performing of the four banks considered here. The main reasons seem abundantly clear: a culture much more suited to the protected and stable environment of the 1950s and the early 1960s than to the changing environment of the 1980s and the 1990s, the absence of a coherent strategy, a bureaucratic structure that was slow to change, fragmented politics that prevented senior managers from coalescing, and CEOs who were unable to provide enough vision and leadership to overcome those weaknesses. Citicorp was much more aggressive and entrepreneurial than Chase, under the strong leadership of George Moore, Walter Wriston, and John Reed. Morgan, the leader in wholesale banking, was much more effective than Chase at maintaining internal consensus and collegiality. Bankers Trust transformed itself in the late 1970s, also under strong leadership, in ways that Chase was unable to do.

In many respects, Chase had a culture and a style that most resembled those at Chemical and Manufacturers Hanover, two second tier money center competitors that had the same difficulty in overcoming the inertia of their public utility cultures fast enough to become high performers in the more competitive and turbulent environment of the 1980s and the early 1990s. Chase has by far the most distinguished history of the three, and it continues to have many strengths that may carry it through the 1990s. In order to survive, however, it will have to make radical changes in its culture, strategy, and senior management. The extent to which it can do these things remains to be seen. It may well merge with another bank in the near future, and rumors to that effect have been rampant for several years. In the meantime, it has made significant strides since mid-1990, under a new top management team, toward downsizing, gaining more strategic focus, and otherwise preparing itself for the competitive struggles of the 1990s.

As of February 1992, Chase's senior managers had begun to restore its profitability in ways that were winning over the bank's many skeptics. They had produced five consecutive quarters of strong earnings, with a sixth announced in late April.[24] Net income for 1991 was $520 million, compared with a net loss in 1990 of $334 million. This was a result in large part of their doing what they and the bank's outside critics knew they had to do: Identify some core businesses where they had competitive strengths, sell or leave businesses that did not fit the strategic focus that those core businesses represented, and work to keep improving products and responsiveness to customers in the core, all the while zealously controlling expenses. Labrecque and Ryan thus concluded in their letter to stockholders of February 4, 1992: "In summary, we know what we are, what we do well and where we are headed."[25] One doesn't undo in a year and a half the results of several decades of mismanagement. At the same time, the bank has clearly begun a comeback, an impressive performance in light of a depressed economy.

9

Bankers Trust: The Great Transformation

Since 1978 Bankers Trust has transformed itself from a second-rate, ill-focused, near-insolvent commercial bank into a dynamic, well-capitalized, highly profitable merchant bank. Its senior management stands apart in a business in which conformity of thinking and failure to live up to grandiose visions have been all too common. In the 1980s it was able to demonstrate insight and originality in anticipating the squeeze on commercial banking....Bankers Trust was the success story of the 1980s. By turning itself into a transaction-driven merchant bank, it became more profitable than any of its rivals.[1]

Having analyzed how the diversification—wholesale and retail—strategy worked out for Citicorp and Chase, we turn now to a very different adaptation style, one marked by a singularly sharp strategic focus. Bankers Trust was a struggling, full-service bank in the mid-1970s, but in 10 years it transformed itself into a highly successful merchant bank.[2] The term *merchant bank*, which in the United States differs markedly from the original British model, refers to a kind of hybrid bank that provides both traditional commercial banking products (loans and trust services) and products associated with investment banking (underwriting, trading, and distribution), and a range of activities loosely grouped under the rubric *corporate finance*—for example, financial counseling related to capitalizations.

Bankers Trust is particularly important in that it represents what has become *the* classic case of successful transformation. Since the mid-1970s, it has undergone a radical change in culture, strategy, leadership, structure, human resource practices, and most of all, performance. Its annualized growth in earnings had been 19 percent since 1978, and that growth had taken place in new merchant and investment banking businesses. Thus, noninterest revenue accounted in 1990 for 75 percent of total revenue, as compared to 27 percent in 1979. The bank's trading revenue alone was over $1 billion that year.[3]

Referred to as "the most sophisticated U.S. merchant bank" in a Salomon report,[4] Bankers Trust is the very model of what that transformation involves, how it may best be managed, and what kinds of problems accompany the change. Other banks attempting to move in this direction can learn a lot from Bankers Trust's experiences, and in doing so, they may perhaps avoid or at least minimize some of the problems it faced. Indeed, no institution undergoes radical change without experiencing significant stresses, no matter how well managed the change may be. Bankers Trust was no exception.

From Mediocrity to Success

In the early and mid-1970s, Bankers Trust was staggering under the weight of huge losses from its real estate loans [through real estate investment trusts (REITs)] and its limited retail branch and credit card businesses. One bank analyst aptly characterized it in retrospect as "a lemming that nearly drowned." By its own admission, Bankers Trust was fifth or sixth in the retail business of the New York metropolitan area, well behind Citicorp, Chase, Chemical, Manufacturers Hanover, and one or two others. A senior manager from the bank recalled that when he would appear at social functions attended by his New York City banking competitors and by other business leaders, he was embarrassed to identify himself as from Bankers Trust. A management consultant, called on in the mid-1970s to advise the bank about a possible exit from the retail business, prefaced his remarks on its senior managers' deliberations by indicating that one of the first observations he wanted to make was to mention their inferiority complex about the present status of the bank and to ask where they thought it should go.

By contrast, the Salomon group ranked Bankers Trust in 1988 as number 1 among 35 of the largest U.S. bank holding companies. Included in that ranking was a composite of some 70-odd measures of profitability, liquidity, productivity, efficiency.[5] It was only the second time in the history of that annual survey of bank performance of the 35 largest commercial banks that a money center institution had finished first. Morgan was the other.

The financial performance data confirm this ranking. Bankers Trust's return on equity (ROE), for example, moved from between 8 and 9 percent in the late 1970s to 27 percent in 1990.[6] Its return on assets (ROA) during that time moved from 0.35 to 1.04. Viewed in terms of banking industry statistics that highlight market share, a similarly positive picture emerges. In 1988, Bankers Trust ranked first among banks in the mergers and acquisitions (M&A) advisory business (thirteenth overall), second in the world in swaps, third in loan sales (one of its specialties), fifth as a dealer in commercial paper, seventh as a private placement agent, seventh in foreign exchange, and fifth in government securities dealing.[7] (Morgan passed Bankers Trust in M&A standings in 1989 and has stayed ahead.) In view of Bankers Trust's brief experience in investment banking, and the intensity of competition in that business, this is an impressive performance.

Another Entrepreneurial, Prospector Firm

To characterize Bankers Trust very briefly in terms of the schema followed in this study, it is like Citicorp in being a highly aggressive, prospector firm, though it has its own unique history and style. Modeled in many respects upon investment banks, with strong emphases on a partnership culture and on maintaining a flat, informal, and decentralized organization of entrepreneurially oriented professionals, Bankers Trust evolved a three-pronged strategy that served it well in the 1980s. That strategy, reflecting its hybrid, merchant banking emphasis, includes:

1. A set of technology-driven, trust, custodial, and investment management businesses, along with a private banking business for highly affluent individuals. These businesses are grouped together in a separate division called *PROFITCO*. (With the exception of the private banking, Banker's Trust's PROFITCO is similar to Chase's Infoserv.) Two other clusters are loosely combined under a larger financial services unit.

2. A series of trading businesses called *global markets*.

3. A corporate finance division.

There is a strong emphasis on maintaining a *strategic focus* on the global wholesale business while providing a *diversified*, complementary series of merchant and investment banking products. This strategy is driven by chief executive officer (CEO) Charles Sanford, who, as head of that unit, rekindled the bank's securities trading capability in the 1970s and early 1980s. He later transferred the culture, strategy, organization, and human resource and management practices he had developed in the unit to the rest of the bank. He is now seen as a visionary regarding the evolution of financial services over the past decade.

Indeed, bankers and analysts of the industry often refer to Sanford as providing the same kind of leadership for his bank in the 1980s and 1990s as Walter Wriston had done previously for Citicorp, based on a similarly perceptive analysis of trends in the industry. Just as Wriston prodded his institution to become more of a diversified financial services conglomerate, so did Sanford do likewise to make Bankers Trust into a merchant and investment bank. "One such prodding," explained a bank analyst, "[occurred] when he would ask his people, `How come KKR [Kohlborg Kravis Roberts & Co.] makes so much money with so few staff? Why can't we do that?'"

Sanford is an accomplished trader and a leader of the securitization and liquification strategies for packaging and selling loans. He and his senior management colleagues have developed an organizational style and supportive infrastructure that greatly facilitate the effective implementation of their strategy. The style has been what Morgan Stanley bank analyst, Art Soter, has referred to as *executional intensity*. The infrastructure includes a high-performance, antibureaucratic, partnership culture; a decentralized, flat, informal structure; a human resources strategy that involves aggressive recruiting of staff members of other investment banks as well as talented MBAs and that is coupled with an equally aggressive and competitive compensation policy; a highly developed risk-management system that provides a much-needed set of controls in Bankers Trust's volatile trading businesses and a useful methodology for evaluating individuals and businesses; and a well-conceived technology that effectively links the bank's global businesses.[8]

These are all recent developments that reflect Bankers Trust's effectiveness in adapting to major changes in the industry and in reversing its past decline. They may be best understood in the context of the bank's history.

History of Bankers Trust: Challenge and Response

A Trust Company

Founded in 1903, Bankers Trust started off as the bankers' bank—"as a trust company for the existing commercial banks...an area of finance which was not open to commercial banks at that time."[9] It was in that sense not a competitor but an adjunct of the commercial banks, serving an unfilled demand in the banking industry. The leadership at the time included Henry Pomeroy Davison, a 35-year-old vice president of the First National Bank, who originally conceived of the idea, and a young, enthusiastic group of banking colleagues, most of them in their early or middle thirties. They included such notables as Edmund Converse, former president of the Liberty National Bank; Thomas Lamont, who was later to be chairman of the board of J.P. Morgan; and Benjamin Strong, who went on to become the first president of the Federal Reserve Bank of New York. As a Bankers Trust manager explained, "It was founded by blue bloods from the turn of the century."

A critical practice that contributed to the bank's early success was the weekly dinner at which Davison and his colleagues reviewed how the bank was progressing and developed plans for its future growth.[10] It was also important that Bankers Trust's board consisted primarily of people from the commercial and investment banks it was servicing. They functioned as a very active body, rather than deferring to senior management. "We have a picture of all those bank CEOs, from that time, sitting around the table, as our board of directors," explained an old-line Bankers Trust staff person.

The first stage in the bank's development lasted from its founding until the establishment of the Federal Reserve in 1914, when commercial banks were first granted trust powers. Thereafter, Bankers Trust no longer filled a need in the marketplace. Thus its future appeared destined to become increasingly tenuous unless it broadened its strategy, which in fact it did.

A Full-Service Commercial Bank and Junior Morgan

The next stage, marked by tremendous growth and diversification, lasted from 1914 through 1928, when the bank completed its transition from a special-purpose trust company with limited goals to a full-service commercial bank. The businesses Bankers Trust moved into were the same ones its competitors took on at that time: foreign banking and investment banking. It established a foreign department in 1908 to conduct overseas transactions, particularly with correspondent banks. For example, it opened a large branch in Paris in 1920 and another in London in 1922. It set up a securities department in 1916, for underwriting and distribution, and it became a substantial underwriter during the period 1916–1928. It was known within banking and business circles as a *wholesale commercial bank* and was sometimes referred to as a *mini-Morgan*. It was on a tier below that of its distinguished competitor, but it was highly successful nevertheless.

Depression-Era Retrenchment

A third stage began in the Depression years and ended with the onset of World War II. It was a time of retrenchment in every business except the trust department, which by contrast expanded significantly. The reason for its expansion was the instability of securities and real estate values during the Depression, which had the effect of requiring "extraordinary efforts to protect the interests of the beneficiaries of trusts and estates."[11]

International and Retail Banking Expansion

The next period, from World War II through 1958, was one of tremendous expansion once again, mirroring the wider national and international economies. One development was in retail banking, which got started in 1949, with the establishment of a metropolitan division. The postwar suburban expansion, accompanied by the need for "housing, appliances, automobiles and other `high ticket' consumer items[,] created a new demand for credit by American householders."[12] Bankers Trust, like its competitors, made many acquisitions, establishing branches in every borough except Staten Island. By the end of this period, it had become the ninth largest commercial bank in the United States. As a Bankers Trust manager recalled, "Just after World War II, our chairman and other senior managers here saw the emergence of the suburbs and the building over the old potato fields in Long Island, and we decided to get into retail banking. Frances Bear was one of the leading lights in that, having come over from Bank of America."

Still more expansion was yet to come, and the period from 1955 to

1978 reflected that strategy. Retail branches were opened in the five boroughs as well as in Westchester and Nassau counties, in response to suburban growth. After the New York State legislature passed an omnibus banking bill in 1960, opening the way for statewide banking, Bankers Trust also acquired branches in such upstate cities as Albany and Poughkeepsie.

On a different front, with the growth of U.S. multinationals, the number of overseas branches and affiliates also increased. By the 1970s, the international banking department had branches in more than 30 countries and a correspondent network of more than 1200 banks.[13] Indeed, in the middle and late 1970s, the overseas division helped the bank to bail itself out from huge losses in its real estate loans.

Still other initiatives were made in corporate banking. Specialist groups were formed to service particular industries (e.g., petroleum and natural gas, construction, and public utilities). Also, Bankers Trust was one of the first banks to install computerized back-office systems, which were completed in 1962. It set up a management services division in 1961, staffed with management scientists, who used operations analysis techniques in evaluating the bank's various businesses, in improving the efficiency of operations, and in strategic decision making.

By the early 1960s, then, Bankers Trust had both wholesale and retail businesses. However, though it had expanded its retail operations, the corporate banking group had resisted this expansion, much as had their counterparts at Chase. One old-time Bankers Trust staffer recalled:

> By the early 1960s, Bankers Trust was schizophrenic. We were wholesale and retail. I argued strongly that we needed more of the latter. But the retail bank never got to be more than 10 percent of our total business, and there was a lot of resistance to it. That was the cultural bias of our traditional wholesale bank. At the same time, we were only a second-class corporate bank, and nobody was pushing that hard there, either.

The Transformation

The period of perhaps most dramatic change has been the present one, from 1978, when Bankers Trust finally decided to exit from the retail business, to the early 1990s. During this period it transformed itself into a merchant bank. The transformation took place in two stages. The first stage began in 1978, when the decision was made that the bank would divest itself of the retail business and become an exclusively wholesale bank, "moving back to our roots," as several Bankers Trust managers explained. The second stage began in 1982, when the merchant banking strategy was adopted. Since these two changes represented a major repositioning of the bank, the circumstances surrounding them and the processes by which they were arrived at merit particular consideration.

The Exit from Retailing

The 1970s was a tumultuous period for Bankers Trust, as for its competitors. It faced two crises that forced it to radically change its strategy. The first crisis related to real estate loans, while the other had to do with the mediocre performance of the retail bank. An old-line manager recalls:

> In the fifties and sixties, we had one of the best ROEs in the banking business, but by the late sixties, we were on a downhill trend. We had some questionable real estate loan commitments, and [we] made a series of other bad judgments that hurt us so much that by the early 1970s, a key thing was survival, even though we may not have completely realized it at the time.

Another reported, "The real crisis was our lack of identity, and we finally began to solve it by the end of the decade."

Two decisions were made in the early 1970s that were precursors of changes to come. The first, which one staff member referred to as *our redundancy program*, was a workforce reduction of 800 in 1971. The action was unprecedented in any U. S. bank, so accustomed were banks to providing virtually guaranteed, lifetime employment. As a Bankers Trust management memo indicated at the time:

> It is very unusual for a company with a tradition of lifetime service and a management which grew up in that tradition to undertake such a program at all....The scope of the action taken represents a major shift in the...bank's culture—away from the current emphasis on personal affiliation tenure and avoidance of conflict in the officer group, toward relatively more emphasis on competence and performance.

All levels were affected, and the decision sent shock waves throughout the bank, signaling the onset of new cultural values—namely, indicating that higher performance standards were to become a standard feature of employment and that profitability counted. At that time, the action was understandably a major trauma within the bank. By today's standards, as Bankers Trust has become more like an investment bank, even though a similar action would be traumatic for the people who were pushed out, it would nevertheless be defined within the bank and the industry at large as more common practice.

This workforce reduction program was followed in 1972 by a decision to exit from the corporate agency business, the bank's shareholder processing and stock transfer operation. A service for corporate customers that was started in 1916, it had become labor-intensive and unprofitable.[14] It set a clear precedent for the later exit from the retail business. As one senior manager commented, "This was the first time the company said, in effect, `Just because we have been in this business from day one doesn't mean that we have to remain in it forever.'"

Divesting itself of the agency business probably made it easier for the bank to exit from retail banking later, although it seemed to be a unique situation at the time. A key aspect of this exit decision was that it marked the beginnings of the bank's long-range strategic framework for sorting out its businesses and their prospects. It was in sharp contrast to how Bankers Trust and its competitors had made decisions in the past.

Shortly thereafter, the bank confronted two crises. The first was in real estate, and it was to take up much of senior managers' time in the mid-1970s. It resulted from the bank's having made large loans to REITs, which were "groups of real estate lenders organized as mutual funds to support construction and real estate development."[15] Bankers Trust made loans directly to developers and to REITs through its construction lending business. It was also involved in the trusts through Bankers Trust Mortgage Investors, a REIT advised by a subsidiary of the bank. When the real estate market in New York City collapsed in the mid-1970s, accompanying both a national recession and a municipal fiscal crisis, Bankers Trust had $681 million of loans outstanding and took a heavy loss as a result.

The other problem area, which was rapidly becoming a concern in its own right, was the retail banking sector. Though Bankers Trust's retail banking grew considerably from 1949 to 1974, with acquisitions and new branches throughout the New York metropolitan area and with expansion upstate, it had not kept up with its five or six money center bank competitors. A critical event that forced the bank to do something about its commitment to retail banking was Citicorp's announced intention to invest up to $100 million in automated teller machines (ATMs) for its retail bank. A Bankers Trust staffer recalled:

> We saw Citicorp saying it would invest $100 million in ATMs. At that time, $100 million was all our revenues for 1 year, so we knew we had problems. Besides that, depositors' funds were leaving us for money-market funds and jumbo CDs, with "Reg Q" [Regulation Q of the Banking Act of 1933] limiting how much interest we could give, while

inflation raised interest rates to double digits. We also decided [that] we couldn't be all things to all people, and that we were stretched too thin.

Though the retail bank had a very able manager in Bill Knowles, a combination of inflation, the high cost of ATMs, and the disproportionate amount of senior management time retail banking consumed in relation to its contribution to the overall bank (it made up only 10 percent of total revenues) made investment in ATMs increasingly problematic for Bankers Trust.

The bank then did a series of studies and convened a strategic planning committee in 1975 and 1976 that raised, for the first time, the question of why it was in the retail business at all. "We saw that [retail] was a big overhead and people-intensive business and that we didn't need it for funding," reported a member of one of the planning groups, "and we concluded that it was not a good business for us to be in, since we didn't know how to make it profitable."

At first, several options were proposed: (1) that the bank increase its commitment to consumer banking, invest in ATMs, and work on ways to expand interstate; (2) that it cut back, perhaps by selling off some branches and shrinking the size of others, but remain in the retail business; and (3) that it simply exit from the retail business. There were many debates inside the bank regarding these options, which often ended in turf battles across divisions about which business should be cut back. "The people in the retail business defended staying with it, saying that wholesale spreads were coming down a lot, and that was where we should cut back," recalled one active participant in these debates. "Meanwhile, the people in wholesale were saying that retail wasn't making it and that it should be eliminated."

The planning groups, originally commissioned to assess the feasibility of interstate expansion, urged instead the view that the big issue was not how and where Bankers Trust might expand but rather whether it should be in the retail business at all. They did not get a lot of senior management attention at first, but they did soon thereafter. "Brittain [the CEO] didn't want to listen at this time," reported a participant, "because of the press of other emergencies, particularly the REIT problem and the bank's big losses there. But when that was resolved, he finally did get our message, and the bank went on from there."

A couple of other critical incidents helped to turn the tide. One was a rejection by the Federal Reserve of Bankers Trust's attempted purchase of a bank in upstate Mexico, New York. "They told us not to throw away our limited capital on such a chancy purchase," reported a senior manager. "This woke a lot of us up." The other was the statesmanlike acknowledgment by Bill Knowles, who was then head of the retail bank, that his division should be cut back or eliminated. He took such a position, knowing that it would upset his constituency within the retail bank and might well cost him as well as them their jobs. That he was arguing for the exit in the face of those costs got senior management's attention.

Top management then held two conferences, in 1976 and 1977, at which it assessed the retail bank's profitability. It separated out retail and wholesale corporate business conducted in the branches, to get a financial performance picture of each, and it also did an analysis of branch costs. Booz, Allen, the management consultant, was brought in to do a separate study, and it essentially confirmed the recommendation to exit. The decision was finally made in 1978, and the branches were sold off piecemeal over the next several years. Bankers Trust also sold its credit card business, at a profit, in 1982. That business had struggled since its inception in the 1960s. "We were not controlling receivables properly, and we had problems in managing through the rapid growth stage," reported a staff person.

While Bankers Trust was getting out of the retail business, many of its money center competitors, particularly Citicorp and Chase, were moving in the opposite direction. Some senior managers from these banks, including Walter Wriston, were quoted as being very critical of Bankers Trust for its decision to exit from such a potentially profitable sector. As it turned out, these managers had the right opinion for their banks but not for Bankers Trust. This indicates that there is no one best strategy for success in banking, just as there is no one best strategy in other industries.

A critical question relates to the role of consultants in this exit decision. Bankers Trust called on two main consultants, each of which was given roughly half the job. Booz Allen was called in first, to do an early analysis on whether the bank should exit. Its staff and senior management were reportedly hoping they would be asked to finish the job, but instead, McKinsey was commissioned to help the bank work on implementation. Consultants generally tend to legitimate decisions that have already been made by top management. They may take the flak from inside groups who feel dispossessed by changes, and they may provide further data and fact-gathering services to help in the decision and its implementation.[16]

These were essentially the roles played by the two consultants in this instance. As a senior manager at Bankers Trust recalled,

> What I learned from all this is that the consultant just says yes to please the client who is paying for it, and they were ready to agree on anything. But they also made an organized effort to gather data that would

be relevant for us, and that was helpful. They were looking at how we could restructure, and they provided us with a model.

Basically, then, the bank made the decision on its own.

While the exit decision was bound to be traumatic or at the least disruptive for Bankers Trust employees at all levels in the retail bank, it was made easier bankwide by cultural considerations. As in several of the money centers, retail banking had a much lower status than corporate banking. Money centers started as wholesale banks, and their corporate and international bankers saw the retail businesses that were added on, after World War II, as secondary to the businesses in their domains. A senior manager at Bankers Trust explained:

> We were an Ivy League bunch, and retail banking had always been seen as strange, foreign, and unpleasant. The traditional bank people at Bankers Trust had always looked on retail banking as a place of giveaways of toasters to the rabble, and of petty thievery in the branches. They were a more elitist group, and our retail banking had never quite taken psychologically. So the fact that our retail business was not really prospering and was a stepchild within the bank helped in gaining acceptance of the decision.

Also, knowing that Citicorp had invested so heavily in ATMs and that Bankers Trust didn't have the capital to follow suit made the decision even more acceptable. As a participant in the decision explained, "When Citicorp invested all that money in ATMS, we said to ourselves: 'Wow! This is big money. Are we prepared to commit that level of resources to such a task?' The answer was we weren't."

This unprecedented exit from retailing was a bold decision, made ultimately by Alfred Brittain, who had become CEO in 1975. He has been appropriately praised within the industry for taking the action. He showed equal decisiveness at the implementation stage. In 1978, Bankers Trust located a potential buyer, Bank of Montreal. The CEO of that bank was a tough negotiator, and he kept lowering his offering price. Brittain finally pulled out of the negotiations and sold off the branches piecemeal. A senior manager at the bank recalled: "We ended up making much more selling it off, branch by branch, than we would have, even with a more decent price by the Bank of Montreal. Sometimes, it's better to be lucky than to be smart, but we kept in touch with the market, and we knew what we were doing."

The sale of the credit card business to First National Bank of Chicago was much easier. "The business had hemorrhaged badly for a number of years," recalled a Bankers Trust senior manager, "but we had brought it back to profitable status, and when we sold it, it was making money."

Becoming a Global Wholesaler and Then a Merchant Bank

The exit from retail banking was one of the first instances of strategic planning for the bank. Line managers as well as staff were involved. Managers from the retail division, and particularly its head, Bill Knowles, recommended divestment, in an unprecedented example of transcendence of turf loyalties for what these managers saw as the broader well-being of the bank. Bankers Trust did preliminary analyses in 1977 and 1978 of all its other businesses and proceeded over the next several years to make two major strategic decisions.

First, in 1978, Bankers Trust decided to become an exclusively wholesale bank. Senior management and staff worked during the next 2 years to define a new structure for wholesale banking. It was announced in September 1979 and included *four core businesses: wholesale banking*, encompassing the traditional corporate loan business; *fiduciary*, which included the bank's old trust, custodial, and investment management, along with private banking; *capital markets*, which included government and municipal securities trading; and *corporate finance*, which reached into new restructuring and M&A businesses (as well as several others, which will be discussed below). Capital markets and corporate finance, representing a new investment and merchant banking focus, were expanded significantly.[17] However, there was no explicit strategy at this stage to become a merchant bank. Rather, the term *wholesale banking* was generally used when senior managers described the bank's direction.

This restructuring coalesced older functional departments into new product- and customer-based divisions. It also began to deal with what Bankers Trust managers and their consultants saw as the weaknesses of the old structure: overcompartmentalization, internal competition, poor communication, and inadequate information systems. The *World Corporate Department* was established to coordinate relationships with multinational corporations. The *United States Department*, which was already in existence, was given a clearer identity as the center of domestic commercial banking.

The next significant redefinition of strategy came in 1983, when senior managers announced that Bankers Trust was not just a wholesale bank but a merchant bank as well. It had been moving in that direction since 1978, and this announcement simply put a label on what the bank had already been doing. By this time, the world corporate department, which had been a bank within the bank, was broken up, with new investment banking divisions having taken on much of its activity, in corporate finance and trading. I turn now to discussion of these changes, which involved a radical transformation to merchant banking.

Managing Change
Effectively: A Model

Bankers Trust's transformation from a full-service bank to a merchant bank was a success. An analysis of the ingredients of this success indicates, in more formal terms, what it takes to transform a poorly performing institution such as Bankers Trust was in the mid-1970s into the effective one that it has become in the early 1990s. Senior managers in other banks, which are facing many of the same problems in the 1990s that Bankers Trust faced in the 1970s, may thus learn from its effective management of change, even though their circumstances will obviously differ in some respects.

This is not to say that Bankers Trust's successful transformation was primarily the result of rational planning. Its senior managers and staff didn't sit down at some point in the late 1970s and decree that, based on an analysis of the bank's strengths and weaknesses and of changes in the industry, they were going to make it into a more focused merchant bank. Many of the key players in this transformation are quick to acknowledge that they had no clear intention in 1979, when they began selling off their retail businesses, of becoming a merchant and investment bank. "We had no clear vision at that time of what we wanted to become," explains a top staff member. "There were the big real estate losses, the retail business wasn't doing that well, and we felt we had to do something. Selling the branches and credit card business became symbolic, indicating that in fact we were doing something."

Moreover, as the analysis below will indicate, chance and luck also played a role in the successful transformation. Such forces are usually involved in such situations, as senior managers at Bankers Trust are quick to acknowledge. A combination, then, of managerial initiatives and favorable circumstances over which the bank had minimal or no control contributed to the positive outcome.

Perhaps the first major precondition for effective change was that the bank faced a *crisis* in which its future was in doubt. Given the size of its nonperforming real estate loans, its mediocre performance in retail banking, and the likelihood that its poor competitive position in retailing would erode further if it remained in that sector (which, as stated above, provided only 10 percent of the bank's total revenue), senior managers felt that they had to take drastic steps to ensure the bank's survival. "We were a second-tier money center bank," recalled one Bankers Trust manager. "Morgan and part of Citicorp [were] top tier, and we wanted to get there."

For some time, there may not have been a *recognition* of the enormity of the bank's problems, but by 1976 and 1977, top management was very much aware of them. An objective crisis, then, combined with a recognition by senior management of the scope and intensity of that crisis, precipitated the bank's initiation of an interrelated series of changes— based on cultural, strategic, structural, political, and human resources factors—that were to move it, in about 10 years, to an effective transformation.[18]

A second condition for success was *strong leadership*. Alfred Brittain had just been appointed to the position of CEO in 1975, having entered the bank after World War II and later headed the national and then the international banking departments. Not known primarily as a charismatic, entrepreneurial manager, Brittain surprised many in the bank and the wider industry by the decisiveness with which he handled the change. When the time came to make such critical decisions as the exit from retailing and to cut off relations with the prospective buyer who kept lowering the price, he didn't hesitate. He soon developed a reputation as a strong leader who would confront the bank's difficulties directly. This reputation probably enhanced his ability to continue making effective decisions.

Brittain did not act alone, however; two other senior managers joined him in this effort. They were John Hannon, whose career in the bank paralleled Brittain's and who became president in 1975 when Brittain was appointed as CEO, and Carl Mueller, who had returned to the bank in 1977 as vice chairman, after a 17-year absence. Mueller had worked as an investment banker at Loeb Rhodes during that 17-year period and might well have remained there, except for its impending merger in 1977. He preferred not to remain with the firm under its new management, and Brittain was able to talk him into returning to Bankers Trust. The personal friendship and mutual respect among these three men were so strong that they became an effective top management team. Brittain clearly led the bank, but his two colleagues played critical roles as well.

Mueller was particularly important, because he brought to the bank much expertise and experience in investment banking, the direction Bankers Trust was to pursue. During the time he was at Loeb Rhodes, Mueller had served as president of the Securities Industry Association, the lobbying arm of investment banks, and his networks within the industry were extensive. Moreover, his management style was one of strong implementation, and he played an important role during the transformation. To illustrate, he helped to swing critical decisions in the selling of the retail bank. A Bankers Trust staffer explained:

> Mueller was a man of action. When Mulholland of Bank of Montreal was giving us all that trouble, playing games on the price, Mueller wrote a note to Al Brittain, saying he would have none of it and would pull out himself if Al did not vote for cutting off negotiations and for exit. He came [to Bankers Trust] in November 1977, at a time when the retail exit had been studied to death, and [there were] many vetoes below the top of the bank. Brittain and Hannon were too busy at the time with other things like getting out of the REIT fix, and Mueller got it to gel.

Relying on his investment banking network, Mueller brought in Morgan Stanley to assist in the sale of the retail bank. Later, he brought in McKinsey to help in implementing the exit decision and formulating a new strategy. Though I do not wish to detract in any way from Brittain's critical role, I do recognize Mueller as an important senior management participant in his own right.

One of Mueller's most significant contributions was the recruiting of a brilliant young investment banker, David Beim, from First Boston. A Phi Beta Kappa graduate from Stanford University, Beim was appointed as head of the corporate finance group. He was given almost unlimited resources to use in recruiting a staff of investment bankers and developing a set of new businesses and products, which he proceeded to do. There was much friction along the way. The commercial bankers deeply resented the bonuses which Beim's new staff received. They regarded the first cadres of this staff as second-rate or maybe worse. A Bankers Trust commercial banker from that era recalled:

> [Beim] was brilliant, and he was actually a nice guy, but somehow he came across as above most people in the bank. He hired his own group and made a tribe out of [them], having all of them relate exclusively to him. We, the bankers, didn't like that at all. We felt he had hired a second-rate group doing transactions like [the ones] we were doing, only they got paid twice as much as we [did]. "Why have this cowboy from corporate finance screwing up our long-time relationship with a particular client?" was how some of the commercial bankers reacted to him. Some of them really hated Beim, but regardless of their feelings, he was a catalyst for the development of investment banking.

Beim built five separate product-oriented groups, including M&A,

public finance, private placements, LBO equity financing, and leasing. He had the revenue from these group's transactions flow directly through them, rather than through the commercial bankers. He also maintained a sharp separation between his corporate finance group and the commercial bankers, for reasons similar to the reasons that prevailed among Bankers Trust's competitors. He felt that it would be easier to build a new investment banking culture, a new compensation system, and a new power base if his group was separate. Again, some commercial bankers considered him arrogant and thought that he saw himself and his new group as above them in expertise and value to the bank.

Throughout much of the period in which he built up and ran the corporate finance group, in the face of much early opposition from the commercial bankers, Beim had strong support from two powerful senior managers: Charles Sanford, who ran the bank's trading operation and became president in 1983, preparatory to becoming CEO in 1987, and Carl Mueller, who protected Beim at various times when commercial bankers tried to gang up on him. As one senior manager recalled with regard to Sanford's support, "Charlie Sanford kept telling him: `Whatever you need to make it, I will provide.' They were very supportive in the bank for this."

As for Mueller, a senior manager explained:

> The commercial bankers hated Beim. But he was a catalyst for the development of investment banking. He would have been out of there a long time before he left in 1987, but Mueller liked and protected him and kept the rest of the bank off Beim's back. But then, when Mueller retired, the rest of the bank got Beim, and it was only a matter of time before he would leave.

The other key figure in the change, in addition to Brittain, was Charles Sanford, who was to emerge in the 1980s as the visionary and architect of Bankers Trust's merchant banking strategy. Head of the liability management and securities trading department, which was called *resources management*, Sanford ran his shop like an investment bank. His operation included worldwide foreign exchange and trading in bank, government, and municipal bonds. The term *liability management* refers to the fund-raising function of the bank, and fund raising was essentially what Sanford did. His trading activities essentially bought money to fund the bank on a daily basis.

Sanford's trading group was located in the Wall Street area, away from the rest of the bank. He was able to recruit and train professional traders, compensate them at competitive Wall Street rates, institute a risk-control system, and essentially have an operation almost indistinguishable from that of a Wall Street trading house. The grandson of the former chancellor of the University of Georgia and himself a former academic, Sanford emerged in the late 1970s and early 1980s as an increasingly powerful voice within the bank. He began to favor a major conversion to merchant and investment banking after it became apparent to him and others that the bank had no future in wholesale corporate banking, in the traditional sense.

Bankers Trust managers report that Sanford urged Brittain for a long time, with much persistence and persuasiveness, to move the bank toward investment banking. As one recalled, "Brittain would often say to him: `Charlie. If it was up to you, you would turn this place into an investment bank.' `That's right,' Charlie would respond. And then it actually happened."

In sum, two critical preconditions for the transformation were the *crisis* of the 1970s, which threatened the bank's future, and the gradual emergence of a *strong and highly cohesive senior management group* (which was headed by Brittain in the early years and increasingly by Sanford, after he was appointed president in 1983). As one Bankers Trust manager explained, "After 1983 and 1984, nobody but Charlie ran the bank."

Related to these preconditions was Brittain's effective *succession management strategy*. He had decided in the early 1980s that Sanford would follow him as CEO, and he paved the way for an orderly transition by building internal support and by providing Sanford with a prolonged period of apprenticeship and training, particularly after he appointed Sanford president.[19] Again, with very few exceptions, the chemistry among members of this group was so good, with personal friendship and career ties bonding several of them, that they were able to give a unified leadership and direction to the change efforts.

One of the last power struggles inside the bank, before the merchant banking strategy coalesced, occurred between Sanford and Carlos Canal. The struggle was about who would be Brittain's likely successor. Canal, a swashbuckling international banker and bon vivant, was one of Bankers Trust's leading bankers in the late 1970s, when he was head of the international banking department. He was a traditional commercial banker, and he preferred a structured and centralized approach. It was his department that had generated the revenues to help bail the bank out after its huge REIT losses. As one staff person explained, "In 1978, Brittain spent an enormous amount of time on the Canal and Sanford fight. He kept getting still another 80-page memo from one side or the other, and he hadn't made up his mind."

By 1979, however, Brittain did choose between them. As another staff person reported:

> In 1979, Carlos lost his power. The international department started slipping, was stripped down and restructured; and he was demoted to an administrative officer and later left the bank. It was Sanford who had the vision that banking was changing very fast and that we had to go further into the securities business to survive. Though Canal [had] helped the bank [to recover] from the big losses of the seventies, he was forced out [because] his views were out of date with the new vision. Brittain, despite being personally uncomfortable with Sanford, had the maturity to select him. He was by far the most creative and knowledgeable [of the candidates]. It became clear that Sanford led the next wave, under our second transformation, in 1983.

Other components of Bankers Trust's successful transformation included a series of interrelated actions its top management took to change the *culture, structure, human resource policies,* and *management systems* of the bank. In the early stages, from 1978 to 1983, it was Brittain who led the change. Increasingly since then, Sanford has been the major figure, even though he didn't become the CEO until 1987. He is now, without question, the dominant person in Bankers Trust, and the bank's direction throughout most of the 1980s has been driven by his vision, values, and management style. It is anticipated that his dominance will continue well into the 1990s.

10
Bankers Trust: The Benefits of Culture Shock

Back to the Roots

As indicated in Chapter 9, following Bankers Trust's exit from retail banking and its decision to focus on its roots in the wholesale business, its strategy became one of coalescing four core businesses: wholesale banking (the traditional loan business), the fiduciary business, capital markets, and corporate finance (which served four customer segments: corporations, financial institutions, governments, and affluent individuals). The capital markets group under Charles Sanford and corporate finance under David Beim, the two main legs of a merchant banking strategy, were provided with the most resources, and both grew tremendously after 1977. Sanford's capital markets group, in particular, began to fund the domestic banking business and expanded it into a global trading operation after taking it over in 1979.

In time, Bankers Trust's wholesale banking division (which had contained its traditional commercial banking businesses) was eliminated. The bank has settled into a three-legged strategy, though reorganizing and fine tuning continue. The three legs include: (1) merchant and investment banking, which are housed in a division called *financial services*, (2) Sanford's old capital markets group, which is now called *global markets*, and Beim's old corporate finance group; and (3) a group of nonbanking service businesses, which coexist with private banking and investment management in a division called *PROFITCO*.

The important point about this strategy is that its implementation involved a fundamental restructuring of the bank, in the course of which a series of stand-alone businesses was established. PROFITCO has four such businesses, which are run as separate enterprises; corporate finance has five; and global markets has seven divisions (with roughly 60 individual profit centers), representing market-based products. Bankers Trust is constantly reorganizing, and anything written about its structure is soon rendered obsolete. Most of the changes in recent years have been in the nature of fine tuning, however, with the basic strategy remaining intact. The one exception is a turn to more relationship banking.

The general contributions which the segments make to the company's profits are about 20 percent for PROFITCO, 30 percent for corporate finance, and 50 percent for global markets, though corporate finance and trading are highly cyclical businesses and change a lot from year to year.[1] The global markets division, which houses the trading businesses, has been particularly prominent over the past few years. "It got over 50 percent of our total revenue in 1990," noted a staff person, "fueling our rocket ship for the nineties. Over a billion dollars in 1 year, with swaps, options, and such New Age products. Wow!" Global markets had already earned over $1 billion in the first three quarters of 1991, which promises to be still another record year.[2]

PROFITCO, by contrast, provides a stable annuity income for the bank and appears to be growing at a rate of more than 20 percent annually.[3] At one time, the bank considered selling it off, but its consistent performance has earned it a strong place, seemingly permanent for now, in the bank's stable of businesses.

Bankers Trust was the first money center to do such a fundamental restructuring and shift in strategy. The main features of that restructuring involved putting together in these three clusters a series of horizontally aligned but vertically integrated businesses, each of which has a stand-alone status. In the past, Bankers Trust had a single, shared resource pool in a central bureaucracy that serviced the entire bank. Since the restructuring, it has had a series of autonomous businesses and/or business clusters, each with its own resources. McKinsey helped to move it in this direction, in line with its decentralized model of how banks should be restructured. As one bank analyst recalled, "[McKinsey] may well have used Bankers Trust as a test case, almost as a guinea pig, but it was done, and it worked. It was somewhat like the Citicorp model with profit centers, but Bankers Trust stressed coordination more."

To summarize the Bankers Trust strategy briefly: it is a *full-service investment bank*, with competitive advantages that investment banks generally don't have—namely, foreign exchange trading, credit expertise, more capital, and a bigger global position. These are some of its commercial banking strengths. It aspires to have the *trading capability* of Salomon and the *mergers and acquisitions (M&A) capability* of Goldman Sachs, along with the ability to initiate and syndicate large loans. It also prides itself on its agility in moving in and out of product markets quickly. As the Salomon report comments:

> Generally, two or three new profit centers are added each year. In 1985, the top five businesses within this segment earned two thirds of the total revenues. By 1988, this proportion declined to slightly under 50%, illustrating the declining reliance upon any given product to carry earnings. In addition, in each of the past four years, the list of top five businesses [has] been different.[4]

An academic who has studied banks observed:

> They [Bankers Trust managers] are moving directly into the most competitive end of every market. They have to be fast on their feet and [move] in and out of markets before the competition [gets] there. Their earnings are extremely volatile, and the whole bank strategy depends on volatility for their income. They bank everything on prices moving up and down.

Some bank analysts have been skeptical in the past about Bankers Trust's strategy, expressing great concern about what they saw as the volatility of its earnings. They have become less skeptical in recent years, because Bankers Trust's performance has been so strong.

An Investment Banking, Partnership Culture

None of these changes in strategy and structure would have been possible without equally fundamental changes in Bankers Trust's culture. Indeed, the culture changes drove the others, as they do in most organizations. Culture changes as radical as those at Bankers Trust usually take a long time, for obvious reasons. Individual people, as well as the departments and divisions they work in, develop strong attachments to old beliefs and values. They also form equally strong coalitions for the purpose of resisting changes in their beliefs and values. Yet, Bankers Trust has been able to effect radical changes in its culture in less than a decade. As a senior manager leading the change effort noted, "You cannot move fast enough on such a transition, if you don't have a new culture and structure. I thought it would take 10 years, and it took a lot less." To be sure, the transition was not easily or smoothly accomplished, but that was not because Bankers Trust necessarily managed it poorly, though there were probably some mistakes made along the way. Rather, the task itself was a difficult one.

The themes described below emerged in the 1980s as central features of the new Bankers Trust culture: (1) There was a strong emphasis on *performance*, accompanied by (2) an equally strong emphasis on *entrepreneurship* and *individual ownership* of particular products and businesses. (3) The bank was explicitly defined as a *partnership*, much like a Wall Street investment bank. Accompanying these themes and supporting the partnership culture were (4) an *antibureaucratic and antistructure* approach to organizing, in which a flat, informal, decentralized, and lateral emphasis was valued, and (5) an *aggressive, scrappy* style, through which Bankers Trust, as an outsider and the "new kid on the block" in investment banking, was working feverishly to position itself in its chosen segment of financial services. It was doing all these things while also (6) *valuing employees from diverse backgrounds* (educational, ethnic, religious, and racial), as long as they were competent. In addition, there was much stress on (7) *organizational flexibility and agility.* The trader strategy of moving in and out of product markets very quickly was supported, and Sanford's strategy of *liquifying* assets and getting them off the balance sheet was matched.

Two other culture values that were stressed in early stages of the change but that no longer get much mention were (8) *common purpose,* a critical theme that helped to keep the bank from flying apart in the first several years of the transition to investment banking, and (9) *work at Bankers Trust as fun.* This idea did not take hold among middle and lower-level staff, many of whom never regarded their careers at the bank in that light. Rather, they saw the bank as a place that made tremendously high performance demands on people, with a "What have you done for us lately?" message that often created considerable stress. All these themes bear further scrutiny.

The most significant cultural theme in the early stages of the transition was *common purpose.* Alfred Brittain was the person responsible for it, and it communicated his strong concern about managing the conflicts between investment and commercial bankers. He was a very effective transition chairman. In particular, he was keenly aware of how the investment bankers, with their individualistic culture, oriented toward earning their bonuses and making short-term deals and transactions, would clash with the commercial bankers, whose bonuses were much lower and who were oriented more toward long-term relationships. A senior manager recalled:

It was hard at first for the investment bankers to accept this culture of common purpose. But Brittain made a public announcement and said [that] we insisted on people working together, and that we rewarded people if that was practiced, and [that] if it was not, we issued one warning. Then if it was not [practiced] again, people would be out.

Through a clearly communicated set of rewards and punishments, then, the bank emphasized collaboration and collegiality. Several senior managers reported that the common purpose theme did help during the transition. They indicated that even though the theme didn't always control the conflicts, the bank would almost certainly have become an armed camp without it. As one senior manager recalled:

Common purpose was to keep the bank from flying apart. After all, we had set up systems to encourage individuals. Common purpose kept the conflict down in the bank, so if people were too overt in grabbing for business, they were told to cut it out, and, if necessary, they would be sent away.

At the same time, however, the culture also emphasized entrepreneurship and rewarded people for developing new products and businesses, and for doing deals. It was often difficult for investment bankers to reconcile this emphasis with common purpose, however, and in time, the individualistic ethic seemed to prevail. "Whopping bonuses made it hard to maintain a common purpose culture," explained a former Bankers Trust staff person. After a while, people inside the bank grew cynical about common purpose. The cultural emphasis on defining the bank as a collection of entrepreneurs made more sense to Bankers Trust employees, despite the bank's many attempts to link bonuses to investment bankers' collegiality. A senior manager in human resources reported, for example, "We have resisted any temptation to pay on a commission basis. We have rewarded people by their team contribution, as do Goldman Sachs and Morgan Stanley."

That same manager, however, acknowledged that collegiality and common purpose had become subordinated to a more individualistic ethic. He explained, "The winners among banks in the nineties will not be like those of the eighties, which was a decade of `me-ism' and narcissism. We have to move back to a more collegial and institution-oriented person."

Cultural emphases in organizations often reflect the values of their chief executive officers (CEOs), and that was certainly the case with common purpose and entrepreneurship. As indicated, Brittain emphasized the former, and Sanford, the latter. Common purpose's gradual decline, then, coincided with Sanford's rise to power. As one senior manager explained:

> There were basic differences between Sanford and Brittain. Brittain wanted teamwork. Sanford said he did, but he paid for individual performance, and he had a much more aggressive approach to things. Salomon, the aggressive trader, was his model, while Morgan Stanley, the old-style, corporate finance oriented firm, was more Brittain's. Brittain was very client-oriented, while Sanford was much more transaction-oriented, and they just had different values and styles.

There is an obvious incompatibility between these cultural themes. They reflect not only the values of these two Bankers Trust CEOs but also a tension within the bank that it shares with other investment banks. Actually, the bank needs both sets of values, and its performance in the 1990s will depend in part on its effectiveness in having both.

As mentioned above, though the cultural theme of *work at Bankers Trust as fun* was emphasized briefly in the mid-1980s, it was dropped after its lack of compatibility with the actual present climate or the likely future climate at the bank became apparent. Many middle- and lower-level employees regarded it as a cruel hoax and were not hesitant to say so. As one reported:

> I have done a lot of MBA recruiting and we are given the party line to use with prospective employees. Besides common purpose, which you rarely hear around here any more [late 1988], [another theme] is the quality of our work life and how much fun it is to work here. I have to bite my tongue and catch hold of myself when I talk about it, because that's not the way life is around here. We function as 12,000 little individual banks. And we have become a warehouse of producers. But to say it is fun or that we are encouraged to be collegial is not the way it is.

A top staff person commented, "Sanford says he wants people to have fun here and also have a family life, but he does not act that way."

One reason common purpose and quality of work life have been downgraded in the culture and don't reflect the actual operations of the bank is that Bankers Trust puts so much emphasis on *individual performance*. Indeed, the bank is an extreme example of a *high-performance culture*, and the expectation of high performance outweighs everything else. A senior staff person reported:

> We see ourselves as being successful competitors by remaining lean and focused. We have a high vision of what we would like to achieve, and we have an intense drive to make it happen. You can see and feel

that intensity here. This place is driven to perform. We are beyond a meritocracy. We are a "performance-ocracy."

A lower-level staff associate agreed:

> This is not a fun place. There is an understanding that it will be very hard and demanding work, and [that] people will be paid well for their efforts. If their performance isn't good enough, they will be out. That is the tradeoff. There are many who feel the pay is not worth the stress, and they leave here for very good jobs. Many choose to stay. But this is a stressed place, the way it is set up now.

Another staff person explained, "The bank does aggressive hiring from the street, and it is understood that if those people don't succeed, we will ask them to leave. They are paid big bucks and expected to produce. Here at Bankers Trust, you live and die by the sword."

The bank further supports this high-performance culture through other values, particularly those that stress its partnership quality and its strong opposition to structures or practices remotely resembling anything that might be characterized as bureaucratic. It has established, in brief, an antibureaucratic culture, reflecting Sanford's basic philosophy, and this culture is reflected in many different ways. Several layers within the organization have been eliminated in the investment and merchant banking sectors. Status and authority differences, in turn, are downplayed in the levels that remain. Thus, low-level associates and vice presidents are encouraged to call on anybody in the bank, regardless of rank, if that person is seen as a valued resource for a deal they are working on. Beyond that, Sanford and his senior colleagues go out of their way to play down any trappings of bureaucracy. There are no organization charts. The phone book no longer contains any reference to the ranks or functional specialties of the employees listed. Sanford has also made clear his aversion to meetings. This is an action culture, and formalized structures and procedures are generally defined as constraints against getting things done.

Instead, what is valued is a loose, informal, decentralized type of organization that is considered necessary to support the bank's fast-moving, transactional strategy. In addition, the kinds of people who are valued are those who are seen as energetic, aggressive, high-achieving, and competent—qualities senior management values much more highly than whether people come from upper-middle-class or upper-class backgrounds and whether they graduated from elite universities. In that sense, Bankers Trust has become a kind of populist institution, with a much more diverse group of employees than many banks—certainly more diverse than that of Morgan, one of its prime competitors. As one Bankers Trust staff person explained, "Charlie Sanford would much prefer the bright, aggressive, and hungry person who finished high in [his or her] class at San Francisco State [to] the one who graduated from Harvard or Yale and was bright, but didn't have the other qualities."

In sum, Bankers Trust now has a Wall Street-type investment banking culture. This culture is not without strains and internal contradictions, but it does nevertheless support the bank's aggressive trading and corporate finance strategy.

At the same time, there are subcultures in Bankers Trust. The most important is the one that exists in PROFITCO, which provides standard products in its many businesses. Despite being, as one former senior manager described it, "a high-tech business that has PhDs and engineers by the quart," PROFITCO has been structured and managed in a much more traditional, bureaucratic way than the rest of the bank. Edward Lesser—director of PROFITCO, a member of Bankers Trust's top management group, and at one time a possible candidate for CEO— preferred to retain the traditional hierarchical structure rather than to adopt the partnershiplike culture and organization of the rest of the bank. "They kept the old titles and lower bonuses," reported a senior manager. That makes a lot of sense, given PROFITCO's tasks, goals, and environment. Its tasks are much more routine, its products more standardized, and its environment more stable than those of the trading and corporate finance segments of the bank. Cash management, investment management, pension fund and trust management, and private banking services for affluent individuals all come in predictable, established packages and don't require a lot of creativity in how they are put together and delivered. As a result, the culture and management of this segment of the bank are more like those of a mass-marketing, MacDonald's type of business than those of a free-wheeling investment bank.

A Flexible, Antibureaucratic Structure

Sociologists Tom Burns and G. M. Stalker have coined the terms *mechanistic bureaucracy* and *organic bureaucracy* to characterize polar types of organizations that fit the Bankers Trust experience well.[5] The mechanistic bureaucracy is characterized by rules, procedures, a clear hierarchy of authority, and centralization. Most decisions are made at the top; tasks are rigidly defined; there is tight, top-down control; and communication tends to be mainly vertical and is accompanied by many written memorandums. Formalization, centralization, standardization, and specialization are the main characteristics of the mechanistic bureaucracy. By contrast, in the organic bureaucracy, rules are often not written down, or if they are written, people ignore them. There is less hierarchy of authority and control. Tasks are continually adjusted and redefined through employee interactions. Knowledge and control of tasks are located anywhere in the organization, and communication is primarily horizontal and informal. These two types of bureaucracies appear in different situations. The mechanistic bureaucracy is more prevalent in stable environments and in organizations that utilize routine technology, provide standard products, and can concentrate on current operational problems and day-to-day efficiency. By contrast, the organic bureaucracy appears in rapidly changing environments, in which a looser, more free-flowing, and more adaptive style is required.

Money center banks are a prime example of organizations that have moved from the stable, protected environments in which they once provided standard products to changing environments in which constant product innovation and adaptation to changing client demands are required. Bankers Trust is *the classic case* of such organizational transformation, and its CEO, Charles Sanford, has established a culture and organizational forms that fit the model to an unusual degree. His philosophy of playing down titles, levels, organization charts, rules and procedures, meetings, written communications, and other such formalities precisely fits the organic bureaucracy that Burns and Stalker describe.

Thus, as Bankers Trust evolved, it went from seven or eight levels in the chain of command to no more than five. The present structure in the merchant banking segments includes analysts at the bottom, followed up the chain of command by associates, vice presidents, managing directors, partners (some of them managing directors), and the bank's management committee, its senior management policy-making group of five people, at the very top. The managing director level is the main new level in this nontraditional hierarchy. It is composed of the people who head up Bankers Trust's 100-odd businesses and is similar to a level that exists in investment banks. In fact, the entire structure resembles that of investment banks.

Another characterization of the bank is that it has no clear structure but rather is constituted as a series of separate businesses, grouped under broad segments of the bank, with each headed by a management director. Some within the management director group are the equivalent of the old executive vice presidents, while others are like the old senior vice presidents. In addition, some of them have been made partners. There are now some 60 partners who have special rights to stocks in the bank and are defined as an elite group who help to set strategy. Many at this level disagree with such a characterization, seeing the bank as much more centralized and themselves as not having power.

In addition to being flatter, the bank has few positions with solely administrative responsibilities. Such remaining positions are mainly in budgeting, systems, and personnel. As a Bankers Trust staffer explained, "In the past, officers existed who had managerial tasks. All our people now are transactional people, doing deals."

A related change was to reduce central staff functions. A bank analyst who had studied Bankers Trust pointed out, "The word 'staff' was anathema to Sanford, and one of the early things he did was to cut out such positions."

Beyond that, there are fewer of the kinds of traditional, hierarchical reporting relationships that used to exist. "Our associates deal with anybody," continued this staff person. "They may call people from the management committee or whoever, and it happens all the time here. The entire organization is one big *project team*."

In brief, Bankers Trust is close to providing a *textbook* confirmation of organization theory that indicates the structural changes required to be effective in a changing and uncertain environment. CEO Charles Sanford was a visionary, not only in the new strategies he formulated but in the culture and organizational structure he put in place to support the implementation of those strategies. As a keen observer of the bank explained, "Sanford's philosophy drove most of the changes that took place, including these organizational ones."

Fueling the Rocket Ship: A New Cadre of High Performers

One of Sanford's favorite themes in his many talks and articles is the importance of people to Bankers Trust's success. The bank is in many respects what management writers would refer to as a *highly professional bureaucracy*, and its human resources policies have been a critical part of its effective transformation. They have included an aggressive approach to both recruitment and compensation. Before making the change to merchant banking, Bankers Trust, by its own admission, recruited BAs and average but probably few high-achieving MBAs, mainly because the bank did not have an especially good reputation. "We lost MBAs who were the really fast-track people, because this was not the culture for them," explained a personnel chief.

Because of its new merchant banking strategy, Bankers Trust developed a systematic recruiting program that targeted fast-track people. That program involved singling out eight top business schools—the ones at Stanford University, the University of Chicago, the University of Virginia, Northwestern University, Columbia University, and Harvard University, as well as the Wharton School of Business at the University of Pennsylvania and Tuck at Dartmouth College—as primary feeder institutions. For each school, the bank assigned a senior-level manager, along with representatives from the particular bank function that was doing the recruiting as well as younger staff members (often alumni from that business school), who had been at the bank for at least a couple of years. "Roughly 40 to 50 percent of our new investment banking staff came from that MBA group," reported a top human resources department manager. "Over time, as we got enhanced credibility as a merchant bank, we attracted more and more excellent people. Citicorp was 15 years ahead of us on that."

Approximately another 30 percent, this staff person continued, came from Wall Street firms. Again, Bankers Trust was able to attract these recruits as it became more respected for its investment banking. Wall Street's cutbacks after the crash of 1987 were also a factor. The bank appointed several people from these firms to senior positions in the late 1980s, with the help of executive search consultants.

The other part of Bankers Trust's human resources initiative was its compensation practices, which were reported to be more competitive with the pay offered by Wall Street firms than were those of other commercial banks. "We went from being next to lowest in the sixties and seventies to...the highest," reported a top staff person. Sanford had set a precedent in the late 1970s in his securities trading (resources management) group. He lobbied successfully to set up a bonus system that matched the ones offered by investment banks. Over time, incentive compensation was spread to all parts of the bank, particularly to corporate finance and securities trading.

Though precise compensation data are not easily obtainable, there is a consensus within the industry that Bankers Trust provided consistently higher total compensation for its investment bankers than did any of the other money centers. Citicorp, as already discussed, was initially reluctant to give big bonuses and lost a number of investment bankers as a result. Chase was late in moving into investment banking and also was said to be slow in changing its compensation practices. Morgan, hesitant to give up its traditional culture and compensation practices, also lagged behind Bankers Trust in this regard, though it seems eventually to have caught up. Its senior managers argued that the psychic rewards of working at Morgan, with its collegial climate, more than made up for higher compensation at other commercial or investment banks. Morgan thus defined compensation in broad terms and justified its practices accordingly.

Bankers Trust's other human resources policy was to stay as lean as possible in total staff, trying through financial incentives to make people increasingly productive. In 1980, it employed 12,970 people. Despite all its expansion and diversification in the 1980s, it still had only 13,522 employees in 1990.[6] Though the count for year-end 1991 is not yet in, there have been enough layoffs to indicate that it will be down from 1990. Some of that stable head count was, to be sure, a result of Bankers Trust's exit from retailing, but much of it was simply a reflection of the bank's efforts to become and remain a low-cost producer. While other money centers were struggling in the late 1980s and early 1990s to cut staff and to downsize, Bankers Trust had already taken such steps, several years earlier. A top staff person explained that the years 1980 to 1986 were "our years of pruning, so we have not had these cutback pressures to the same extent as other banks."

The human resources policy that Bankers Trust followed as it went about its downsizing in the transition to merchant banking was both effective and humane. It also reflected the traditional culture. Senior management required, in its exit from retail banking, that the purchasers of its branches retain all the employees and their pension plans. "I am so proud of Bankers Trust for doing that," stated one of its most senior managers. In the phasing out of its traditional, wholesale banking, senior management recycled as many commercial bankers as it could, encouraging them to become corporate finance generalists. There were many who could not be recycled, and they were generally provided with generous severance and relocation assistance.

Final elements in the successful transformation were Bankers Trust's *risk-management system* and its recent initiatives in building a strong *technology* capability. Sanford had developed in his trading division a methodology for managing risk that he called *risk-adjusted return on capital (RAROC)*. It provided a framework for measuring risk levels of all operations and assigning capital based on the ranking of risk-adjusted returns and losses. That Bankers Trust has generated profits from its volatile securities trading activities for some 22 consecutive years attests to the many benefits of using this control system.

Actually, the use of RAROC has been broadened, and it has become a major management tool throughout the bank. It is also used for performance measurement, to assess various businesses and groups; in portfolio management, to determine where the bank should invest or cut back; and as a framework for decisions on investment position taking.[7] Like most other Bankers Trust initiatives of the 1980s, this was a technique that Sanford created.

Important though technology is, Bankers Trust didn't initially have anything like the early technological capability of Citicorp. By 1990, however, it had caught up, having developed a bankwide and global technology architecture strategy that integrated "virtually all its operations, by both product and location."[8] The purpose of Bankers Trust's technological improvements was to develop more consolidation and compatibility, as well as to make the deals it could offer to clients less costly, more timely, and of higher quality. As a senior staff person in technology explained:

> We launched our strategy for the nineties in 1985. We concluded early that there was too much duplication, in our bank, of hardware, software, networks, and data-based management, and that we were reinventing the wheel for all the different product groups. Considerations of cost and timeliness led us to consolidate. Otherwise, we would have incompatible technologies that would slow us down a lot. So we developed what we call our *integrated communications architecture*. We can do cross-product transactions, where, for example, we can buy a foreign exchange product in London and then engage in the necessary hedging and have instant, split-second, cross collaboration where one person can do it all. This allows for a holistic, integrated view in which a single manager can draw up a full picture of what he or she has done.

As a result of these many changes, Bankers Trust now has one of the strongest technological capabilities in the banking industry.

Managing Change: Senior Management's Role

Presiding over this series of changes since 1979 has been Bankers Trust's *management committee*, a small group of senior managers who have made virtually all the bank's strategic decisions. As presently constituted, that committee includes Charles Sanford; Eugene Shanks, president and head of global markets; Edward Lesser, vice chairman in charge of PROFITCO; and George Vojda, vice chairman and director of headquarters management support services and of emerging nations businesses. With the exception of Sanford, these senior managers all wear two hats. They participate as a group in formulating strategy for the bank as a whole. At the same time, each is responsible for line operations in one major segment.

The management committee is clearly a very powerful body. It runs the bank, meeting on a regular basis (at least once a week), and reviewing everything of consequence to the bank's well-being. In that sense, Bankers Trust is a highly centralized institution, seeming to contradict my prior characterization of it as flat and decentralized. In truth, it is both centralized and flat. Managing directors, who are perhaps the key group because they preside over the bank's many products and businesses, function along with their associates as free-wheeling professionals. They do so, however, only within the framework of the strategy, culture, organization, and human resources practices established by top management. This framework is unlike the one at Citicorp, for example, where strategy developed as a result of many decisions made by profit center managers. (Since its recent decline, however, Citicorp has become much more centralized.) Bankers Trust is much more centrally managed, by a small group of senior people who run the bank. Even so, people at lower levels have a considerable degree of flexibility to engage in their various transactions.

A brief description of each management committee member is in order.[9] Eugene Shanks, at age 44, is the youngest. He has a Ph.D. in economics from Stanford and is a protégé of Sanford. He has been in charge of global markets, having succeeded Sanford there, since 1986. Shanks was named president of the bank in late January 1992, after his division accounted for almost two-thirds of the bank's record 1991 earnings. Until Shanks was named president, another prominent member of the management committee was Ralph MacDonald, age 50, a former commercial banker at Bankers Trust, who had been in charge of corporate finance since 1987. He had played an important role in the transition, helping to integrate the commercial bankers into the new strategy. MacDonald, whose division's profits plunged in 1991, reportedly lost out in a duel for the presidency to Shanks.

Ed Lesser, age 58, heads PROFITCO and was at one time seen as a possible successor to Brittain. He is widely regarded as an excellent manager of his division. Finally, George Vojda, age 56, is in charge of development and administration and emerging markets. The newest member of the bank, having joined in 1984, Vojda is one of the most highly regarded conceptualizers and strategists in U.S. banking. Before joining Bankers Trust, he was at Citicorp, where he developed some of its strategic plans and at Phibro. Sanford, an intellectual in his own right, is said to develop the bank's vision and strategies himself, but Vojda is one of his prime resources in that activity.

As in many organizations, Bankers Trust thus has some tension in maintaining a balance between centralization and decentralization. Some high-level staff people in the bank are critical of the present structure from that perspective. They seem to be in the minority, but their argument is that the bank has too few people making its major decisions. "I am of the view," explained one such person, "that we have to keep proliferating brains and new products and should have more strategic planning at lower levels, among the management directors who are close to the action, and not just in the management committee. I don't think this is a widely shared view, however."

The Change Model

To summarize the change model implicit in the above discussion, there were several ingredients in Bankers Trust's successful transformation. The first were its *crisis* and the *recognition by top management* both that the crisis existed and that radical changes had to be made if the bank were to survive or to become a top-tier money center. Another was the emergence of a *small senior management group* with both the vision and the implementation capability to act on that recognition. It was of critical importance that this senior management team was *highly cohesive*, with close interpersonal bonds among several of its members, and that it included *some newcomers* (Beim and Mueller) and several people with the investment banking *expertise* most relevant to its new strategy (Beim, Mueller, and Sanford).

The *interrelated series of actions* that top management took with regard to *strategic change* (the exit from retailing, becoming an exclusively wholesale bank, and building the corporate finance and global trading capability of a merchant bank) were supported, in turn, by *changes in the bank's culture, organizational structure, human resource practices, control systems, and technology*. All these factors contributed. That the actions were taken in an integrated, holistic way was important to the success. The combination of a *strategic focus* and an *implementation intensity* was also important.

These were, with few exceptions, what might be labeled, in organization theory, *voluntaristic factors*. They were initiatives taken by management to change organizational characteristics that were largely under its control. But what about *luck* and *chance*? What roles did these factors play in the causal chain?

It is clear that luck and chance did play important roles, in interaction with management initiatives. There was, first of all, Mueller's returning to Bankers Trust after his 17-odd years on Wall Street. He would likely not have returned if his firm, Loeb Rhodes, had not merged at that time. He became a major figure in the senior management group. He brought in Beim to develop the corporate finance division; he provided encouragement and expertise to Brittain in many key decisions; and he helped, in particular, in the implementation of many new strategies.

Beyond that, Bankers Trust was fortunate that investment banking as an industry thrived as well as it did in the 1980s. Its senior managers are the first to acknowledge that their original intent, after exiting from the retail business, was to become *not* a merchant or an investment bank but simply a wholesale bank. To be sure, the bank had at least two senior managers, Sanford and Beim, who were pushing hard in investment banking, but there was no clear initial organizational vision, based on an analysis of the changing industry, which dictated that underwriting, distribution, trading in securities, and corporate restructurings were the way to go. Sanford himself did have much of this vision, but there were many other powerful voices at the bank in the late 1970s. The strategy emerged only gradually.

Still another favorable factor involving chance was the state of the economy. Bankers Trust was particularly fortunate to be making all these major changes in a prolonged bull market. As one bank analyst noted, "Charlie Sanford had told me that he didn't think he could necessarily pull off all these culture changes if the economy turned sour the first year or two he was trying to do it." In this respect, Bankers Trust was again lucky that it had such favorable conditions in which to continue its vigorous change efforts. Many able change agents don't have that luxury.

It was also fortunate that Bankers Trust had fewer entrenched competitors among the commercial banks than would a bank trying to move in this direction in the 1990s. Morgan did have an established franchise among the Fortune 500, which had been built up over the previous century, but it moved more slowly than did Bankers Trust in making the strategic and infrastructure-related changes necessary to make it a competitive force in merchant and investment banking. Citicorp, one of the few other formidable competitors, had its own cultural problems, which were associated with compensating investment bankers and which made it less threatening than it might have been. In addition, Citicorp was committed to expanding its consumer bank and had begun cutting back on investment banking in the late 1980s. Thus, Bankers Trust was probably the first commercial bank to move into these businesses in the single-minded and forceful way that it did. Much of its success resulted from management vision, judgment, and good timing, but the limited number of immediate competitors also helped.

Even the investment banks, obviously the strongest competitors, did not take Bankers Trust seriously when it first ventured onto their turf. As a senior manager at Bankers Trust recalled,

> We had expected the investment banks to squash us, but that only happened in the securities markets. Otherwise, because of our small size and poor past performance in the 1970s, we sneaked up on everyone. Also, at the time, Morgan Stanley was under a lot of strain itself, and they were reorganizing, so we were able to become competitive.

Now, any commercial bank that moves into investment banking will find that Bankers Trust, Morgan, Citicorp, and selected others are there already, and that will make it harder.

One last factor that should be given consideration was Bankers Trust's size. It was small enough to be able to make the changes without more inertia and internal friction than it had. The management committee could oversee the entire bank. A performance culture could be established across the board. While there was much scepticism and active resistance to change from various "old-guard" interests—corporate bankers and consumer bankers—the bank was small enough so that their resistance was visible and could be managed. Sabotage is more effective in larger organizations where it is much more difficult for the change agents to keep track of the resisters. In this sense as well, a chance factor contributed to Bankers Trust's success. Bankers Trust's small size may well be as related to its success as Citicorp's large size is to its decline.

11
Bankers Trust: Its Future of a Vision

The Role of the CEO

I see the chief executive officer (CEO) as a significant force in a business organization: the person responsible for the strategic vision or its absence, the culture, and the general style of the institution. Bankers Trust is more leader-dominated than almost any bank I have studied. Citicorp under Walter Wriston would probably be the closest comparison. The background and values of a CEO are best understood in the context of the organization's history and culture.

Historically, Bankers Trust was an upper-class, white Anglo-Saxon Protestant (WASP), establishment bank, much like Morgan and, up to the early 1970s, Chase. As a staff person at the bank explained, "This was a class-conscious, preppy, skull-and-bones, Yale and Princeton tiger type of place. We were like a small Yale Club bank in the late 1940s. We were sometimes even referred to as *Big Blue*. At that time, $25,000 was the minimum checking account we would take." One person who held a high-ranking staff position in the 1960s but who was not from this social station, described his culture shock upon arriving at the bank:

> I came in at the tail end of the old-boy network that had operated for so long there. The people who worked at Bankers Trust were very wealthy, owned [apartments] in Manhattan, and had big money trusts

themselves. They used such terms as *remainderment* that were beyond anything I had ever experienced, and they were members of country clubs.

The bank's CEOs reflected and reinforced this culture. One person with a high-ranking staff position explained:

> They had real ethnic history. Before Brittain, all the CEOs were independently wealthy Yalies and Episcopalians. Brittain and Sanford broke the mold. Brittain was a Yalie and [an] Episcopalian but did not have independent wealth. Now, Sanford is independently wealthy and an Episcopalian but not a Yalie. As it happens, Brittain opened the bank more to other groups, from other backgrounds, and Sanford tore it open.

Continuity in leadership has been an important characteristic of Bankers Trust throughout most of its history. Its CEOs not only came from similar upper-class backgrounds but also served for unusually long periods of time. S. Sloan Colt, for example, from the old Colt family, served from 1931 to 1957.[1] He presided over much of the bank's growth and diversification into international, corporate, and retail banking. William Moore, his successor, was CEO from 1957 to 1974.[2] Also from an old family (his mother was a Hanna), he led the bank first through a period of growth and then through a marked decline. Though he was well liked within the bank, he lost control in the later years of his reign, which were a time of economic recession. "He was fabulously wealthy," explained a staffer who was at the bank during those years, "and was definitely a class act. But he was not an effective CEO. He was not a forceful or forward-looking enough leader, and he refused to make the hard decisions when the bank came on hard times."

A more sympathetic assessment came from a Bankers Trust old-timer: "Moore was a patrician. He was not an outstanding CEO, but he was a good leader within the limitations of his class and breeding. He did lose control over our asset portfolio, our real estate loans. But we were not a hungry bank in those days."

Brittain and Sanford: Collegiality and Entrepreneurship

By far the two most significant CEOs for my purposes are Alfred Brittain and Charles Sanford. When Brittain became CEO, he was not thought to be a charismatic, aggressive, change-oriented leader, but his later actions clearly belied that impression. "He was a gutsy, ballsy guy," reported a senior manager, who echoed the consensus within the bank and the industry with regard to Brittain's leadership role in Bankers Trust's great transformation.

Brittain's role went beyond simply making the difficult strategic change decisions. He turned out to be an extremely effective transition manager. Though he broke radically with tradition, he also had the requisite management skills to keep the bank on an even keel and to effectively blunt the resistance of the old guard. As one top staff person recalled, "Brittain and Sanford played different roles. They had different qualities, and we needed both. Brittain was much more tolerant of the old-timers. If Sanford had been CEO at the beginning of the changeover and had called the shots without Brittain, it would have all blown up. Brittain had more empathy."

Indeed, Brittain's insistence on collaboration between the commercial and investment bankers, in line with his constant emphasis on the *common purpose* theme, was a reflection of his approach to managing the transition. There was still much old-guard resistance and much conflict, but he was both mindful of the importance of managing the resistance and conflict and aware of how these qualities might get out of hand. Brittain combined at least two characteristics that helped in the transition. First, he was decisive when he needed to be, as in his moves to exit from retailing and to select Sanford as his successor. Second, he was very skilled at managing people and politics. He showed empathy for the members of the old guard even while he was eliminating their businesses and culture, and even while he was managing the conflicts between them and the new investment bankers.

Sanford has a very different style. Much more of an intellectual and a visionary than Brittain, and a faster-moving, transaction-oriented trader, he doesn't have Brittain's conflict management skills or tact. "He was very rough in the beginning," reported one knowledgeable outsider who had many contacts with senior managers at the bank, "and there was some mentoring done by Brittain." A senior manager reported, "He was a kicker and screamer, impatient, demanding; and he could alienate many people. He did prove that a different kind of strategy and system would work, and to his credit, he developed [them] and helped Brittain's confidence. But if he had been the CEO at the start, we could have failed, because he could be abrasive." Still a third senior manager recalled:

Charlie put us on a rampage to wipe out the past culture, and after a while, there was clearly not the gentility and collegiality of the past. He has a tub-thumper style, but often you can have strengths that are taken to excess. Charlie was strong, and his ideas were great. But some people ask, "Where is the soul of the bank?" and they are not just the people who want to turn the clock back.

These descriptions of Sanford's style, while critical, portray him accurately as a great visionary who was impatient with a status quo that he felt would continue to drag down the bank. Brittain provided a humanizing, leavening effect. He eased the transition and attempted to soften Sanford's intolerance of people or operations that he felt were not performing up to his high standards of excellence. Sanford is a brilliant conceptualizer and innovator, who has needed assistance in the human and political aspects of managing such radical changes. Brittain provided that assistance, as did Phillip Hampton, a commercial banker at Bankers Trust who became vice chairman in the mid-1980s and had a management style similar to Brittain's.

Both Brittain's and Sanford's qualities are needed to manage change effectively. Without the vision, ideas, entrepreneurial drive, and energy of a Sanford, there would be no impetus or direction for change. Without the initial decisiveness and the interpersonal skills and sensitivities of a Brittain, the vision might well founder for lack of an effective implementation strategy. Brittain stayed as CEO from 1975 to 1987. During his later years, he handed over the reins to Sanford and acted as mentor, to help temper Sanford's impatience with the traditional culture. Sanford, a brilliant conceptualizer, has no problem in intellectually understanding the human and political side of managing change. By temperament and by personal style, however, he was not comfortable with the slower pace of change that the Brittain approach seemed to entail.

The differences between Brittain and Sanford are particularly reflected in their ways of running the management committee. Brittain was a consensus manager, who tended not to impose his will when he was outvoted by the group. Sanford, by contrast, is described as running the committee in accord with his vision of what is right, and allowing only a minimum of dissent. Some senior managers argue otherwise, claiming that the committee is a collective body, all of whose members may and do exercise independent voices. That seems not to be the case, however, from the reports of several senior managers close to the situation. One explained:

Brittain used the management committee to lead a bank discussion about where we were going. Sanford [runs] it to impose his views and [leaves] no doubt where he [stands] on everything. If everybody disagreed with Brittain, he would grudgingly give in, but not so with Sanford. What Sanford has bred is a system [in which] the younger people are afraid to challenge him. He agrees, in theory, when you point this out to him, but he then keeps running it unilaterally. People used to speak out more, but then they found out it was hopeless, and they have stopped. It is much more centralized now.

Another senior manager, from a different background and career experience, agreed. "The bank and the management committee are doing great things," he said, "and Sanford runs the show in every respect. I have never seen such a CEO-driven institution as ours. He is the big boss. The management committee [members] are all under his thumb. He runs this place with an iron hand."

Contrast these views with the following, from still another senior manager: "We have the policy that everything can be debated, and in that sense, we have an open style. In any major decisions, we deliberately put ourselves through a challenge and debate the issues intensively. That is part of our openness and informality."

Since management committee meetings are closed to outsiders, I had to reconstruct what happened from the reports and perceptions of people directly involved. When these reports and perceptions were diametrically opposed, I had to try to make sense of them. By fitting together all the information I was able to glean, I developed a sense that the claim of openness is not as valid as is the charge of dominance by Sanford.

What are the larger organizational change implications of this discussion of the management styles of CEOs Brittain and Sanford? As already indicated, effective change requires both the vision, the will to succeed, and the intellectual substance of a Sanford and the skills of a Brittain in managing conflict and resistance. Bankers Trust was fortunate when it had both, in that each reinforced the other. Sanford gave Brittain the ideas and the confidence to move ahead, while Brittain mentored Sanford to help him be more mindful of the human and political dimensions involved in effective implementation of change.

One other such question relates to the dangers of what social psychologist Irving Janis called *groupthink*.[3] Citing numerous examples of organizations in which the quality of strategic decisions was undermined when there was a limited acceptance of diverse points of view and information sources [e.g., the United States under President John F. Kennedy (1961–1963) in the "Bay of Pigs" incident, and again under President Lyndon B. Johnson (1963–1969) in the Vietnam war]. Janis called attention to a common condition in organizations that fail. Bankers Trust seems not to have reached the degree of *coerced conformity* to the leader's views that is reflected in Janis's examples. To the extent that the bank shows tendencies in that direction, however, its future prospects are less bright.

A critical question is whether the possible flaws in Sanford's management style are serious enough to hurt the bank's performance in the future. Because his flaws do contribute to staff alienation (particularly among senior executives) and lead to a high turnover, they could become a problem. One financial journalist, Thomas Bancroft, argued that this might happen. Writing in *Forbes*, he listed several executives who had left Bankers Trust since the late 1980s, some of whom had taken their staffs with them. He concluded that between 50 and 60 of the bank's top performers had left from 1988 to 1990. He referred to "dozens of interviews with former and current Bankers Trust executives and employees," providing "a litany of complaints" whose common thread related to Sanford's "abrasiveness and failure to develop teamwork."[4]

Brittain and Ralph MacDonald dismissed the turnover as no different from what happens in most Wall Street firms. Thus far, Bankers Trust's performance has stayed very high, and it remains to be seen whether Sanford's management style will become a detriment.

Weaknesses, Strains, and Contradictions

Overall, Bankers Trust has been highly successful. Other banks that seek to transform themselves would probably do well to emulate many of its actions. Nevertheless, it has weaknesses and internal strains that may have to be managed better in the 1990s, if it is to fulfill its aspirations to become a major global merchant bank. Some of its problems relate to its strategy, others to the infrastructures it established to implement the strategy.

One issue in regard to the latter is the bank's *human resources* practices. People are a critical resource in an industry that has become so much more professionalized in recent years. Indeed, Charles Sanford has said on numerous occasions that the quality of his people is a major competitive strength. Yet his bank may well have significant people problems, as the previous discussion indicates.

Bankers Trust's high performance standards and the long hours of work it requires have made it into a demanding institution. It resembles in these respects the investment banks with which it competes. As at the investment banks, people are compensated well. As a staff person explained, "There is an understanding that it will be very hard work here, and [that] people will be paid well for their efforts. If it doesn't work in terms of their performance, they will be out. That is the tradeoff."

At the same time, Bankers Trust employees experience considerable job stress, meaning that high levels of anxiety and strain are associated with their work at the bank. It is difficult, in the absence of survey data, to make judgments about just how widespread the stress may be and among which ranks and specialties it is more prevalent. However, on the basis of many personal interviews, I concluded that stress is so prevalent as to be a salient problem. One staff person, for example, told the following story:

> There is a lot of stress here. We may well be able to do it in the market, but at what human cost? We recently provided stress help services through our human resources department to any employees at the bank who felt they needed assistance. [The services were provided by] a private company whose staff reported that our bank was off the scale in terms of the massive numbers of requests. We had that many people dialing for help. What does that say about the climate here?

Another staff person had a similar tale:

> There is a feeling of stress and strain among the ranks. This is not a fun place. We have had more amicable separations of people from here than most places. We do not have a big exodus, but there are many here who feel the pay is not worth the stress, and they leave here for very good jobs. So this is a stressed place. That is just the way it is set up.

If the main source of the perceived stress were just the high performance demands and the long hours, that would hardly make it a critical, organizationwide problem, particularly in light of the high pay. There may well be some systemic causes, however, that affect different categories of employees in different ways. High levels of internal competition may be one cause. Feelings of unfairness regarding compensation may be another. These feelings were most pronounced among some people in PROFITCO, whose compensation is considerably lower than that of investment bankers, and among management support staff, particularly an old-line group who entered the bank in the 1950s and 1960s and sustained it through the difficult transition years.

Consider the following quotes from PROFITCO staff members, all of whom spoke favorably of their division head, Edward Lesser, even as they expressed their alienation from the bank. One reported, "The management style here is one of lean and mean, to get the best out of everybody and not reward them. That is why we have such a rapid turnover." Another reported, "Ninety percent of our MBAs at

`FASTCO' leave, overworked and overwhelmed." Still another complained:

> The small bonus I get in my 40-person group is a real demotivator. The result is that people leave, or they become bitter and disillusioned if they stay. We have been undergoing a big reorganization under a new manager, but we are never told what it is or who will be kept or let go. What that communicates to us is that we have no value for the bank, and that we are seen as interchangeable pawns in a chess game. You feel you are always out on a limb that is about to be sawed off. It works like a sweat shop.

Bankers Trust employees also cite the "unfair" treatment of management support staff. A former Bankers Trust senior manager reported:

> In the 1950s and 1960s, we had a very good group of lower-middle-level management people. They were what carried us through this change period. And they have not been given the pay and recognition that they deserve. I feel that our support groups who had been here for years and were the last generation of people who helped bring us through our big changes should have been treated better. They did excellent work and were not properly rewarded.

This group and others (in PROFITCO, for example) described many issues of fairness in the bank's compensation practices. The senior manager whom I quoted above continued, "When these people complained, Sanford replied that only a few people were the real rainmakers and the others, troops down in the trenches, the support people, could leave and he would find others to replace them. There was a lot of anger among the troops about that. We had many big fights over it."

Still another compensation action that some Bankers Trust staff cite as an example of unfairness was the bank's decision in 1990 to cut pensions. One former senior manager reported:

> Pensions were cut 10 percent, without any notice. The bank changed it at the last minute. For a bank making $600 to $700 million a year, I think it is unfair and cheap. Just to give you an example of how it worked out in one case, we had a guy who was the head of one of our upstate branches who sold his house in Darien to go up there and he later came back in operations. His $45,000 house in Darien cost close to $400,000 when he returned, and he had a hard time finding housing. Anyway, he was probably making around $85,000, but not much more than that, and he suddenly found 10 percent sliced off his pension. He sees the members of the management committee all making over $1 million, and it seems unfair. This guy had given a lot of service to the bank and was so loyal. You can imagine how he feels about the way the bank treated him.

There are at least two results of these human resources practices that the bank will have to manage more effectively in the future. One is the possibility of employee burnout, which would ultimately affect productivity. The other is the issue of loyalty to the bank, which might conceivably have a later impact on its ability to remain a strong competitor. "It is not clear that we are generating a lot of loyalty here," reported a staff person, "given the high performance standards, long hours of work, and feelings of injustice in different parts of the bank. If that is so, it could come back to haunt us."

How could such practices have evolved, if in fact they do exist on a wide scale? The perception among those in the bank who feel that they are widespread is that Sanford moved too fast and too zealously in wiping out the old culture and in trying to attract able investment bankers through attractive bonuses. Somehow, in the process, argue these people, as the bank became leaner and meaner, it "lost much of its soul." It treated some people less fairly than it might have, by refusing to acknowledge that they were making important contributions and to reward them accordingly. One former senior manager summarized this view:

> There is not the gentility and collegiality there was before, and that is not all to the good. We got on a wild rampage to wipe out the past, but often you can make changes that are taken to excess. Bankers Trust has done very well in the marketplace. It is productive and profitable. But where is the soul of the bank? And is the bank's policy fair to all the little people, the "NCOs" out there who make an important contribution but are not sharing in the returns? So it became lean and mean, but with very high compensation for an elite group of investment bankers, and not much fair treatment for the workers in the trenches. Does this bode well for the bank's future? It's not at all clear to me that it does. If I had stayed, I would have tried to be a counterbalance wheel, but I probably wouldn't have been that effective.

One interpretation of these views is that they reflect the disappointments of old-guard members who are nostalgic for a past order that is no longer relevant and would be dysfunctional in the present highly competitive environment of banking. Another interpretation is that these views correctly point to excesses that could come back to haunt the bank in the 1990s. The practices they highlight may well reflect a common sociological phenomenon in which converts to a new culture (investment banking, in this case) are sometimes more zealous in pursuing it than those who have been in it for a long time and take it more for granted.

A related human resources issue, which Bankers Trust may share with its investment banking competitors, has to do with the extent to which the bank is developing a cadre of senior managers to run the bank in the future. This may well be a serious problem. As one former senior manager explained, "The transaction business has not produced good general managers. They can be great specialists, and they may be good specialty managers, but there is not a good general management development process....There are exceptions, but by and large, we are not training such people, and that is a serious limitation of the bank."

The failure to develop senior managers and the issue of organizational loyalty may well constitute related problems, to the extent that they reflect a sharp break from the past that has hurt the bank. A former senior manager explained:

> We have had cohorts in the past. There was one very good group, now probably in their late forties, with Ralph MacDonald, our head of corporate finance. Then there was another such group, now in their late fifties,...Lesser, Hampton, Knowles, and several others, and they made many contributions to the bank. The very young people now are not a cohort. The bank cannot count on their loyalty, and they don't have a broad managerial perspective. We discussed it a lot and have not made the necessary changes.

In sum, there may well remain some critical human resources issues that the bank must address, given the importance of people to its success. If it fails to do so, it might lose its place as a top competitor, particularly in view of industry and market changes that are making it much harder to compete effectively.

Managing the continuing tension between entrepreneurship and collegiality is a related issue. One of the bank's human resources staff summarized it well:

> A big problem for us in the nineties is balance. Charlie Sanford has a style of presenting the antithesis to whatever anybody else has presented, or if he is trying to move away from an old culture, he will go to extremes. Now, we have to emphasize collaboration and collegiality, after emphasizing individual entrepreneurship in the past. The latter is an unintended consequence of necessary changes from a time when we weren't nearly aggressive enough. Now we have to move back to the middle and have a more institution-oriented and collegial person.

As Eccles and Crane have indicated in their study of investment banks, developing collaborative lateral linkages among specialists (e.g., bankers, salespeople, and traders) is critical to success.[5] Bankers Trust has done a lot of this through its reward and incentive systems. "We have resisted any temptation to pay on a commission basis," reported a human resources department manager. "Instead, we have rewarded people [according to] their team contribution [and]…their contribution to the total institution, as do Goldman Sachs and Morgan Stanley. And ones who have not done that, like Drexel, Shearson, and Salomon, have all had postcrash trouble." The bank has also conducted many cross-function performance appraisals (e.g., of investment bankers by commercial bankers and vice versa) that have helped in developing lateral linkages. At the same time, it probably ought to do more in the future to encourage collegiality, particularly if the reports of its internal competition and limited institutional loyalty are valid.

Another problem the bank faces, resulting in part from its radical transformation, has been the lag between its reputation among bank analysts and regulators and its actual performance. Some of that reflects a lack of understanding by these outsiders of the bank's strategy and particularly of the risks inherent in it. Examiners from the Federal Reserve, for example, may well judge Bankers Trust's risks from a commercial banking perspective, even though it no longer resembles a commercial bank in most important respects.

Though both groups of outsiders, the bank analysts and the regulators, have become more positive about the bank's capabilities and performance over the past couple of years, because it has done so well, it continues to face the problem of having to manage its reputation. A widespread image of Bankers Trust among these groups is that its dependence on volatile income streams, particularly in its role as a trader but also in terms of its deep involvement in leveraged buyouts (LBOs), makes it a risky investment. This image of Bankers Trust's trading operations has persisted despite the bank's 22 consecutive years of profits in those businesses. One commonly expressed view is that just as Bankers Trust might make big profits in trading businesses in one period, so it might suffer big losses in another.

Two related incidents in 1988 reinforced that view. One was the extensive publicity given to Andrew Kreiger's career at Bankers Trust and then to his resignation.[6] A foreign currency trader, Kreiger made $338 million for the bank in 1 year and then resigned. His resignation was attributed in part to his dissatisfaction with his bonus. An issue for the bank analysts and regulators was how free Kreiger had been to "bet the bank's money" in various transactions. They asked to what degree he was a "loose cannon," and what his activities reflected about the adequacy of controls within the bank in its securities trading.

Later, in a related incident, the bank restated its earnings in foreign currency trading for 1 year, after being questioned by Federal Reserve examiners on the matter. The restatement was for $80 million and was apparently related to Kreiger's activities. The restatement posed further "appearance" problems, notwithstanding Sanford's and his colleagues' explanations. An insider attempted to explain the restatement as follows:

> The restatement of currency trading income arose out of Kreiger's transactions. He had found an inefficiency in the New Zealand currency market, and in the good Bankers Trust style, he went for broke. We were on a roll and made $388-odd million in one quarter. He was a workaholic and a crazy genius. Shanks and Sanford decided they had to find a way to cut back and control him. They closed the books in an acceptable way. In December 1988, they met with auditors and announced that we were making more profit than we thought we had. The Federal Reserve decided they didn't like it at all. It was like an $80 million restatement, and we said we would take the money out of a kitty of rainy-day funds and write it down. It was painful and tarnished our image. Kreiger had become ungovernable, taking new risks. Our senior attorney finally told Kreiger that he had exceeded his bounds. He was a product of the Bankers Trust system and had to leave when Bankers Trust could not control him. The New York Fed covered their rear in the case.

In actual fact, Sanford's risk-control system, risk-adjusted return on capital (RAROC), which he had developed in the 1970s in the securities trading department and which later spread throughout the bank, protected the bank from the risks that outside critics kept raising. It sometimes takes a long time, however, for reputations to catch up with reality.

Another argument the critics commonly use is that Bankers Trust's new strategy has never been tested in a recession. The bank will be subjected to such a test in the 1990s and will have a chance to improve its reputation at that time.

Finally, there are issues of the adequacy of Banker's Trust's strategy. I described it in Chapter 10 as a three-legged one that includes (1) the technology-driven, custodial, trust, cash management, investment management, and private banking businesses of PROFITCO; (2) a series of corporate finance businesses; and (3) a series of securities trading businesses. At least two questions may be raised about the bank's strategy. One is whether it is comprehensive enough to enable Bankers Trust to remain a major global competitor, even if it has the personnel, technology, products, and agility to move in and out of markets quickly, as products become commoditized and spreads decrease. While PROFITCO-related businesses provide a strong, annuitylike income, the other two segments are volatile and highly competitive, and may represent shrinking areas of opportunity. This may require that Bankers Trust develop a fourth set of businesses. A former Bankers Trust manager suggests that they might be "an international collection of corporate finance businesses,...to give us an additional earnings dimension."

A second question about strategy relates to the relative emphasis Bankers Trust will give in the 1990s to relationship banking as opposed to transactional banking. It has opted more for the latter since the early 1980s. This is not an either-or choice, but the bank's senior managers have had many debates on the matter. One senior manager recalled:

> That has been a long battle, as between a more client [and a more] transaction orientation. Brittain was very client-oriented, while Sanford was more of the other, and the bank vacillated back and forth on it. I feel it is important to develop stronger client relations, because now that the business has flattened out, corporations will select [the] bank they feel most comfortable with. We had this issue before the management committee on many occasions, and we never resolved it.

Apparently, it has now been resolved. The bank is putting much more emphasis on relationships than ever before.

Some Conclusions: A Need for Institutional Balance

If a single theme could encompass many of the developmental issues Bankers Trust will face in the 1990s, it would be the need for institutional balance. The bank's historical development has many parallels to that of Citicorp. Facing a crisis in the 1970s that threatened its survival as a significant player in its industry, Bankers Trust transformed itself from a mediocre full-service bank to a high-performing merchant bank. It developed an excellent vision, implemented that vision well in many respects, and managed a difficult transition with a minimum of disruption and upset. The bank was tough but fair with the many people whose skills and values did not fit the new strategy. It assisted humanely in their exit and relocation.

An important factor was that Bankers Trust had a complementarity of strategic priorities and management styles among its senior managers. Brittain placed strong emphasis on some of the best aspects of the old order: relationship banking, collegiality, rewarding loyal employees, treating people humanely, and moving ahead incrementally in transforming the bank's strategy and infrastructure. Sanford, by contrast, emphasized the new order: transactional banking; entrepreneurship;

and as rapid a change in personnel, strategy, and infrastructure as possible. From Brittain's perspective, though Sanford was a brilliant visionary, conceptualizer, and investment banker, he needed some tempering of his style to adapt it to the Bankers Trust setting.

From Sanford's perspective, Brittain's approach involved moving too slowly with the changes, based on an unnecessary paternalism and attachment to older ways of doing things. He acknowledged the importance of being humane and fair, but he was sensitive to the need for fast action, based on his reading of trends in the industry, and was by style and temperament attuned to that approach. His impatience and his vision for the future were also a source of great strength for the bank.

That Bankers Trust did so well in the 1980s is a reflection both of Sanford's many strengths and of the balancing or tempering of his style, first by Brittain and later by Phillip Hampton, a commercial banker who stayed with the bank, converted to the new merchant banking strategy, and became vice chairman and a member of the management committee. Even though Sanford often prevailed while Brittain and Hampton were around and active, they at least provided a different view. Now that both have left the bank (even though Brittain remains on the board), Sanford has fewer countervailing pressures than before. He has many able senior managers, both on the management committee and among the bank's partners and management directors, but they seem not to be questioning the bank's overall strategy and style.

One change that would enhance Bankers Trust's competitive position in the 1990s would be a return to the emphasis on collegiality and team that characterized the Brittain era. Many Bankers Trust staff at all levels referred to the internal competition and infighting as most undesirable and as contributing in particular to the bank's high turnover of senior managers. As one rising star at the bank explained:

> We will soon be in deep trouble if we don't stop the backstabbing that goes on throughout this place. It has to come from a tone that is set from the top. Gene Shanks, our new president, has started to use the word *trust* as a goal for us, and if he can make that part of our culture again, it will bode well for our future. Otherwise, we may face some serious problems down the road. It's not a pleasant place to work, when people treat each other that way, and that's one reason why we have so many people leaving.

The future for Bankers Trust may thus be contingent in part upon its achieving a better balance between its old and new strategies, cultures, and management styles, while at the same time continuing to emphasize its primary focus on merchant banking. It may generate more loyalty among clients and staff by achieving such a balance and may thus end up a stronger competitor than it already is. Its present CEO, Charles Sanford, has clearly emerged as a major figure, both at Bankers Trust and in the industry at large. He is the person most responsible for its many successes. Like all strong leaders, he needs a cadre around him who not only work well with him in implementing his ideas and strategies but also serve as an independent voice that continually questions and helps to modify his visions.

12

The Morgan: "Doing First Class Business in First Class Ways"

There is an incredible quality, style, strength, and class to those people and to that place. They are a little like the old continental armies. You shoot one person and another soon emerges to take his place. They have an international presence, and they have been willing to commit to new investment banking products and activities. The bank is not flashy, but in its own quiet and classy way it has become the front-runner. They [sic] are a worthy organization and deserve the accolades they get. MANAGEMENT CONSULTANT

Their internal cooperativeness is stunning. There is that much collegiality. They are also very patrician. They constitute rich people dealing with rich institutions. And they are also as anonymous and faceless as one can get. There is powerful modeling that works internally. People there have always been selected [for] their character and manners. Civility is highly valued. Also, hard work and tremendous professionalism. And service is

critical, not only to clients, but to the wider
community [the service they render] by being
on boards and doing good works. I have
known them since the late 1950s, and they
have always been that way.

BANK ANALYST AND CONSULTANT

Morgan is a class act. They [sic] have never
made headlines for dramatic change, but they
have excellent managers and products.
Bankers Trust is more of the alley-cat, street-
fighter style. They would be like the Ferrari of
banks. Morgan would be the Rolls Royce.
They are smart, effective, nice people who
work incredibly hard.

BANK EXECUTIVE HEADHUNTER

If one were forced to name a single commercial bank as the consistently best-managed, best-capitalized, and highest-performing in the industry, it might well be J.P. Morgan. It has been the only big bank to keep its triple A debt rating from Standard and Poor's in 1990. Often referred to as "The Morgan," this bank has been a top performer throughout its long history. Its history can be traced back to a merchant banking business founded in London in 1838, in which the eldest Morgan, Junius, was a partner. The U.S. bank actually began as J.P. Morgan & Co. in New York in 1860.[1]

The Noble Hustlers of Wall Street

By far the most elite bank in the United States in terms of its corporate clients and employees, and fiercely proud of its history, Morgan has evolved in the 1990s into a global merchant bank, while maintaining much continuity with its past. Its client list of Fortune 500 companies, many of whom it helped to found and has served for decades, is the corporate equivalent of the social register. Also on its client list are financial institutions, highly affluent individuals, and governments that further reflect the bank's blue-chip clientele. Referred to frequently as U.S. banking's *class act*, Morgan more than any of its competitors has maintained a relationship style of banking, even in the "casino age" of the 1980s, when a more transactional and deal-oriented culture pervaded the financial services industry.[2]

Morgan has not been exempt, however, from the many changes in banking since the early 1960s. Like its competitors, it has had to adapt to the jolts they all faced, particularly the decline of the corporate loan business and the globalization of financial services. Indeed, despite its many competitive strengths, including long-term relationships with clients, Morgan's primary corporate loan business has been in permanent decline since the 1960s, just as those of the other money center banks have been.[3]

This chapter tells how Morgan repositioned itself in the face of the decline, by evolving from a commercial bank into a merchant and investment bank. In the process, it took on much the same portfolio as Bankers Trust—corporate finance-related businesses, mergers and acquisitions (M&A), securities trading and distribution, investment management, and private banking. The two banks have often been mentioned together as exemplars of a new merchant banking strategy. Morgan made the change, however, with a markedly different style and history. First of all, Morgan had been around much longer than Bankers Trust, having managed a highly successful merchant banking business from the 1860s until 1933, when the Glass Steagall Act compelled it to separate this part of its operation from commercial banking. Bankers Trust, formed in 1903, had been in merchant banking for only two decades when Glass Steagall was passed. A senior manager in Bankers Trust's investment banking division, when asked to explain the difference between his bank and J.P. Morgan, replied "Bankers Trust began its investment banking thrust in 1976; J.P. Morgan began in 1876!"[4]

Beyond that, Bankers Trust's move into merchant banking was made out of desperation and crisis, as a turnaround effort to reverse its poor performance of the 1970s. Its style was thus very entrepreneurial, as the "aggressive upstart" or "new kid on the block." It was seeking desperately to find a viable wholesale market niche, after experiencing much mediocrity in the years leading up to the change. For a while, it was referred to in the banking industry as a *junior varsity (JV) Morgan*, since it professed to want the distinguished corporate client base that Morgan had never lost.

Morgan, by contrast, followed a much more balanced approach. Once referred to as the *noble hustlers of Wall Street*, Morgan has melded its traditional conservatism with innovation.[5] It is in that respect a prototype of what Miles and Snow refer to as an *analyzer firm*, moving aggressively into new businesses. Only rarely has it been the "leading edge," the first player, and then only after much agonizing over how it could effectively balance innovation with its past culture and style. Thus, it was cautious about getting into new investment banking products, waiting until it was confident it had developed the needed understanding and expertise. There were some businesses—leveraged buyouts (LBOs), junk bonds, and other highly leveraged transactions—that its senior managers regarded as so "un-Morganlike" in their promise of quick profits that it largely passed them by. It was also initially reluctant to bring in too many outside investment bankers (traders, product specialists), for fear that they would disrupt its traditional emphasis on collegiality and its discouragement of "stars." Moreover, it had serious early problems in changing its traditional compensation policies to attract and retain such people, through bonuses that were competitive with those on Wall Street or at such banks as Bankers Trust. Chief executive officer (CEO) Lewis Preston (1980–1990) summarized the Morgan style quite well in this regard when he said, "We aren't likely to deviate radically from the clear strategic path we have been on since the days of the first Morgan partners."[6]

Continuity, then, has been critical for Morgan, even in the face of radical changes in the financial services industry to which it was compelled to adapt. Morgan has thus changed in its own evolutionary and incremental way in the 1980s, from a commercial bank to what has been called a "British-style merchant bank." As the authors of a recent company report on J.P. Morgan note, "It would not be incorrect to say that there is a large-sized Wall Street securities firm inside JPM's corporate body." It was much easier for Morgan to make the change than it was for competitors like Bankers Trust, because Morgan began with a much less diverse set of businesses. It wasn't involved, for example, in any retail or middle-market banking that it had to manage or divest itself of during the changeover.

Morgan is in many respects, then, a pure case of evolution from commercial to merchant and investment banking, in that it has stayed in the wholesale business and maintained many of its past relationships. Indeed, it was largely to keep those relationships that Morgan had to make the change. It always had a strategic focus on international wholesale banking for the upper end of the market, and its move into investment banking simply involved, as Morgan spokespeople so often said, following its clients to the capital markets with new products and services, so that it could continue to meet their needs.

Moreover, as Morgan's performance in the 1980s indicated, it has made the change in a way that generally surpassed its competitors' ways, not in every respect but certainly in most. Consider the following: In June 1991, Morgan's market/book value was 193 percent, as compared to 176 percent for Bankers Trust, 64 percent for Citicorp, and 66 percent for Chase. Its average return on equity (ROE) for the 1980s was 14.84 percent, contrasted with 16.47 percent for Bankers Trust, 13.42 percent for Citicorp, and 11.69 percent for Chase. Its average return on assets (ROA) was 0.93 percent, as compared to 0.76 percent for Bankers Trust, 0.55 percent for Citicorp, and 0.51 percent for Chase.[7] Moreover, it stayed away from bad loans much more than did its money center competitors. Its ratio of nonperforming/total assets for the decade, for example, was only 1.22 percent, compared with 1.90 percent for Bankers Trust, 2.18 percent for Citicorp, and 3.00 percent for Chase. Thus, while Morgan also pursued what Ron Chernow refers to as "the lemming-like rush into Latin American lending,"[8] it still had considerably less exposure than did such competitors as Citicorp and Chase. Its conservative loan policies kept it away from the real estate loan problems and LBOs that were to plague the other banks.[9]

This is not to say, however, that Morgan has managed the transition without serious problems. All banks have found the change difficult, and Morgan has been no exception. The main reason for the difficulty is that changes in strategy such as those the banks have had to make require corresponding changes in culture, organizational structure, and human resource practices. The corresponding changes don't take place easily, even in the best of circumstances. Culture change, in particular, is a slow, agonizing process for most organizations. For a bank like Morgan, with its century-old traditions, changing the culture was particularly difficult.

Moreover, all money center banks, including Morgan, are managing the transition in an industry and an international economy that are much more turbulent and harder to predict than any that banking has experienced before. Market opportunities come and go so fast that keeping up is hard. For example, in the 1980s, investment banking looked for a while like a set of businesses that could not help but enable money center banks to recover significantly from past losses. Securities trading, underwriting, M&A, and other corporate finance-related activities seemed very promising. Many are still promising, and new ones are emerging, but the 1987 crash did drive down spreads and commoditize many products. Future earning prospects aren't nearly as good as it appeared that they might be, even for a bank with the client relationships and other competitive advantages that Morgan had. What I want to do in this chapter is to show what lessons other banks and the industry more generally may learn from an analysis of Morgan's adaptation.

In many respects, Morgan provides a positive role model for other banks and for the industry at large. At the same time, the problems of managing this transition are so complex, and the environment is so un-predictable, that even Morgan is groping.

A History Never to Be Forgotten

No other bank and maybe even no other U.S. corporation has ever had more of a sense of its history than has J.P. Morgan, a point of great significance in understanding how the firm has adapted in recent years. New recruits, for example, get an extensive exposure to Morgan's history when they arrive, with particular emphasis on the character, values, and banking strategies of the two J. P. Morgans and of the bank. Even today, senior managers at Morgan take a training course that presents the basic values and strategy of the company in a historical perspective.

The genealogy of the firm is complicated. Its roots go back to Junius Morgan, the founder of the family dynasty.[10] He was a partner in the merchant banking firm of George Peabody & Co., which was established in London in 1838. That firm became J.S. Morgan & Co. in 1864 when Junius Morgan took it over after Peabody's death. Meanwhile, his son, J. Pierpont Morgan, established his own bank, J.P. Morgan & Co., in New York City in 1860, at the age of 23, after having worked at Peabody under his father's supervision.

Junius Morgan was the dominant figure in all these firms until his death in 1890. He endlessly tutored his son Pierpont and appointed mentors to tame his fiery temper.[11] The businesses went through several stages. Thus, in 1871, J.P. Morgan merged with Drexel & Co. of Philadelphia, an investment bank, to form Drexel Morgan, which still has headquarters (HQ) in New York City. In 1895, the firm was renamed J.P. Morgan & Co., with a separate and reconstituted Drexel & Co. set up in Philadelphia.

Meanwhile, J.S. Morgan & Co. of London was succeeded in 1910 by Morgan Grenfell & Co., which, in turn, was incorporated many years later. E. C. Grenfell came into the firm in 1900 and was made a full partner after 4 years. When Morgan Grenfell was incorporated, Morgan Guaranty, a successor to J.P. Morgan, held a one-third stock ownership.

The two J. P. Morgans were the bank's only CEOs from 1860 through 1943. *The elder Pierpont*, as J. P. Morgan, Sr., was called, ran it, until his death in 1913, with a minimum of delegation and an inordinate attention to details. His son, the younger Pierpont, who was usually referred to in the bank as *Jack*, had a much more delegative style and managed it as a team of strong, independent partners who made decisions by consensus. A bank that had two CEOs in 80 years may rightfully be said to have had continuity.

Morgan partners and senior managers have told legendary stories about these two men since their deaths, and many of the stories involve ways to preserve the values and strategies of the two J. P. Morgans. J. P. Morgan, Sr., was a major figure in U.S. and international finance. Indeed, the Morgan funeral in 1913 was a world event, with many heads of state as well as business leaders in attendance. Though he was such a world figure, Morgan was not nearly as wealthy as his robber baron contemporaries John D. Rockefeller, Andrew Carnegie, and Edward H. Harriman.[12] At one point in Morgan's funeral service, Carnegie leaned over to Rockefeller and said, with some amazement and perhaps jealousy at the turnout, "And to think that he wasn't even rich." Vincent Carosso, a historian and a leading authority on the Morgan family, reports that J. P. Morgan, Sr., had a distaste for his contemporaries' conspicuous consumption and garish displays of wealth. "His home, the Morgan House, was on Thirty-Sixth and Madison, not uptown on Fifth Avenue like the others," explained Carosso. "This was a form of inverse snobbery. Morgan felt that you did not need an address to give you position. Also, he was a very private man."

To help maintain the continuity that he valued so much, Morgan indicated that his will, along with his testimony in the Pujo hearings of 1912 investigating the "money trusts," the articles of partnership, and the form used for letters of credit that reflected the nature of Morgan as a merchant bank, should be placed inside a cornerstone in the new Morgan building at the corner of Wall Street and Broad Street. He also designated his son, J. P. Morgan, Jr., as his successor, having groomed him for the position for many years.[13]

Until the enactment of the Glass Steagall Act in 1933, Morgan was primarily a nineteenth-century-type merchant bank. It did much underwriting and securities trading, gave advice on corporate and industry restructuring, and provided loan and trust services. In that sense, its intensified efforts since 1980 in new corporate finance and securities trading markets were simply a return to its past, as was the case with Bankers Trust. Morgan's strategy had been that of a global bank. It served a select clientele of governments, large U.S. and European corporations, central banks, and wealthy individuals, offering depository, loan, underwriting, brokerage, and trust services.

Morgan's traditional organization and human resource policies fit its strategy, and in that respect, the bank's changes since 1980 have been simply a return to its roots, again somewhat as Bankers Trust did. Historically, Morgan had operated as a loosely organized partnership.

The selection of partners who would match the elite nature of its clientele was one of its most serious and time-consuming tasks. The bank was both a meritocracy and a closed, class-bound group.[14] Partners were recruited disproportionately from among family, friends, and well-known business associates. As Carosso reports, Morgan, like the big international banks with which it competed and cooperated, always included members of the senior partners' families. It also sought people with experience that matched the particular businesses in which it was engaged.[15] When traditional merchant banking was Morgan's main business, it looked for partners with broad mercantile experience. When government and corporate loans and securities trading became important, it looked for partners with more specialized investment banking skills. Lawyers and former government officials were also well represented. Indeed, up to 1940, lawyers constituted the next-largest group, second only to bankers, among Morgan partners. No other private bank had so many lawyers as partners.

Not surprisingly, the Morgan partners of these years maintained close relationships with one another.[16] Business and personal lives overlapped at many points in this highly homogeneous, upper-class group, who shared many basic business and social values.

The values that were emphasized were the ones that might be expected to prevail among a group of traditional bankers: prudence, thrift, political and economic conservatism, quality service and integrity in dealings with clients, and privacy and confidentiality. Vincent Carosso quotes a *Tribune* reporter after the senior Pierpont Morgan's death in 1913: "The men of the house of Morgan keep in the background as far as possible. They shun the limelight as they would a plague."[17] Chernow refers to Morgan in the prologue to *House of Morgan* as "the world's most secretive bank."[18] The passion for privacy that the Morgan family maintained and that both J. P. Morgans perpetuated was imprinted on the bank from its inception. As we will discuss shortly, these cultural values were to remain with the bank through the 1980s and early 1990s in modified form, shaping in important ways its style of adapting to the turbulence of that era.

From Family Firm to Corporate Bureaucracy

Two critical events in Morgan's history since the 1930s have been its incorporation in 1940 and its merger with Guaranty Trust in 1959. The decision to incorporate was driven by the partners' fear of capital depletion as well as by their desires to provide a strong base for the future; to ease the impact of estate taxes; and, most important, to enter the trust business, which was closed to partnerships.[19] That just three partners— Morgan, Thomas Lamont, and Charles Steele—held substantially all the firm's equity probably also helped to precipitate the decision, as did Steele's death in 1940 and the advanced age of J. P. Morgan, Jr.

Immediately after incorporating, Morgan formed a new trust department. The bank was fortunate in that its start in this business coincided with the boom in trusteed pension plans. By 1950, it had become a trustee for about 21 plans, with a combined value of $200 million. It also took on investment advisory accounts worth another $600 million. The bank has further expanded its trust business since then.[20]

Its most dramatic action in this regard was the merger with Guaranty Trust in 1959, the last of a series of mergers of big New York City banks. Unlike the others, each of which brought together a wholesale bank and a retail bank, this merger involved two wholesale banks and resulted in the formation of the nation's biggest trust. A big impetus for the merger was Morgan's tremendous need for increased capital. It had become increasingly difficult for the bank to match the big money center banks with their retail deposit business.[21]

Guaranty had become one of the largest fiduciary banks in the nation in the 1920s and 1930s, as a leader in the administration of corporate trusts, estates, and testamentary and other personal trusts. It was, in addition, a major underwriter and distributor of corporate and tax-exempt securities, as one of the largest bank dealers in U.S. government bonds. It had a strong international business and was a leader among American banks in developing the commercial letter of credit and the foreign collection business. Unlike Morgan, it was very long on capital. If this was not a marriage made in heaven, the complementarity of the two banks was at least substantial.[22]

One reason the merger went as smoothly as it did was that officers and directors of the two banks had had close ties since the 1870s, when J. P. Morgan became a vice president and director of the National Bank of Commerce, which was later to merge with Guaranty.[23]

Thus, Guaranty was no stranger. As Chernow points out, however, there was much resistance within Morgan to such a merger. The bank had existed for 100 years as a small, paternalistic institution, and there was great concern that it would become the junior partner, since Guaranty was four times its size.[24] As he notes, the press likened Morgan in the merger to Jonah swallowing the whale.

Instead, Morgan assumed the ascendancy, and its culture prevailed. Guaranty employees who had suffered under the coercive rule of their

CEO, J. Luther Cleveland, felt liberated by joining Morgan and having a different senior management. Most important, the newly merged Morgan Guaranty Trust became one of the world's largest and most powerful wholesale banks, with an unmatched clientele of Fortune 500 corporations.

Over the next couple of decades, Morgan gradually transformed itself from the informal, clan-like partnership that it had been since the mid-nineteenth century to a more rationalized, bureaucratic organization. "We used to be a paternalistic, clubby place, even after the merger," explained a senior manager. "At one time in the late 1950s, we only had some 800 people." It developed a strong national banking division (NBD) and an equally strong international banking division (IBD). In 1966, it started continuing-education seminars that eventually became the equivalent of a miniuniversity through which all bank employees passed, as they became "Morganized."

At the same time, Morgan made a big investment in establishing systems, controls, and procedures to handle the massive increase in volume that had resulted from the merger. It paid particular attention to rationalizing the back-office operations, so that it could continue to serve its long-standing customers in a responsive manner. Reflecting this increasing commitment, the number of staff in Morgan's methods and systems department increased from 12 at the end of 1959 to 266 at the close of 1978, and there were another 225 people in overseas offices.[25]

Since Morgan did not have consumer deposits as a basis for funding its loans, it had to develop substitutes. Making a virtue out of necessity, it soon became a pioneer in what has come to be called *liability management* or fund raising. This includes using certificates of deposit (CDs), the federal funds market, the growing Eurodollar market, and government bond dealer activities.

A final development of lasting significance was the formation of a holding company (JP Morgan & Co. Incorporated) in 1968 to enable the bank to broaden its wholesale activities. It did diversify in the 1970s and 1980s, with considerable success. Below, I will discuss the bank's establishment of various subsidiaries during those years, in anticipation of a broadening of opportunities to move into various new investment banking activities.

Getting Morganized: An Old-World, Clan Culture

Culture drives many institutions, and it does so with particular force at Morgan. As already indicated, there is more emphasis at Morgan than at most other institutions on transmitting traditional values and beliefs. An inordinate amount of attention is given to symbolism in this regard. How many other firms, for example, have anything like a cornerstone containing the will and other papers of the founder? How many have preserved as many other artifacts from their pasts? These symbols and artifacts are reflected in the distinctive old-world, upper-class, British tone of the bank, which one can only sense by being there. Thickly carpeted floors produce a quiet hush, tasteful art adorns the offices, and the floors where many people work together behind large wooden desks create more the impression of a library reading room than of a bank.[26]

There is thus a clear Morgan style that continues to pervade the institution and shape employees' actions, despite the many changes that the bank has undergone in recent years. The culture includes the following core values and beliefs:

1. Relationship banking and service to clients

2. High standards of professionalism and integrity

3. A strong emphasis on teamwork and collegiality, as opposed to rewarding individual "stars"

4. Civility and nonconfrontation in internal relationships

5. Decision making by consensus, associated with an incremental and evolutionary approach to strategic change

6. A Japanese-style, clan-type relationship between the bank and its employees, reflected in practices such as lifetime employment, extensive welfarelike services and perks, unparalleled management training, job rotation, and a prolonged "Morganizing" process in which people are socialized to the firm's values

7. Maintenance of a predominantly home-grown staff in senior management positions, rather than recruitment of outsiders

8. A meticulous attention to detail in both strategic and mundane administrative decisions

9. Continued allegiance to the firm's history, to keep reinforcing its traditional values

10. Community service, reflecting an upper-class sense of noblesse oblige, much like that of David Rockefeller at Chase

Virtually every one of these cultural values may be traced back to both J. P. Morgans, and particularly to J. P. Morgan, Sr., the bank's founder. A close reading of Chernow's and Carosso's definitive histories indicates just how closely the bank has followed the traditional values of the two J.

P. Morgans. That it was privately held until 1940 and that the two Morgans were its only CEOs during the first 83 years of its existence further suggests the influence they had on its culture and style.

Relationship banking was the cornerstone on which the Morgan franchise was built. The bank now lists 97 of the top 100 U.S. corporations as clients, and the relationships go back many decades. Carosso and Chernow also describe the close relationships that both Morgans and their partners established with corporations and sovereign states. The bank not only provided loans and underwriting services but also became a much trusted financial advisor.

Coupling these traditions with a similar pattern at Guaranty Trust before its merger with Morgan in 1959 gives one a sense of the extensive corporate and governmental networks that the bank had built up over the years. "The French government still remembers how J.P. Morgan helped finance its army in the Franco-Prussian War over 100 years ago," recalls a senior Morgan banker. To bring such a resource into the increasingly competitive financial services industry of the 1980s and 1990s was, indeed, to make Morgan a formidable player. It has thus emerged in recent years as, once more, a leading firm in the industry. Not that Morgan had ever been anything else; but in the 1950s, after Glass Steagall had forced the bank to divest its securities-related businesses, it was in danger of becoming somewhat eclipsed by expanding and newly merged money centers. "The small J.P. Morgan before 1959 had to live by its wits," explained a Morgan senior manager, "because of its need for capital."

The Client Comes First

Relationship banking has meant for Morgan a strong emphasis on service in dealings with clients. In the "casino age" of the 1980s, with the rise of takeover deals and transactional banking, Morgan went to great lengths to differentiate itself in this regard from its competitors. Its institutional advertisements often featured an empty tombstone, symbolizing an M&A deal that Morgan did not complete, because it decided, in consultation with the client, that the deal would not meet the latter's needs—even though it would have meant substantial profits for Morgan. Many Morgan publications refer to how much the bank values its long-term relationships with corporate clients, which are based in large part on its commitment to serve their needs. Service and "principled conduct" are frequently mentioned. Thus, in its letter to stockholders in the *1990 Annual Report*, the bank's senior management proclaimed,

"We are proudest of the advisory relationships built on the premise that, unless the client's strategic needs are met, the best deal is no deal at all."[27] The same letter continues, "[We are] always emphasizing our desire to build relationships, not simply do deals."[28] The bank has thus traditionally forgone pursuit of what it has referred to as *the fast dollar*.

Indeed, building long-term relationships with select clients has always been a top priority for the bank. One of its main arguments in justifying the repeal of Glass Steagall, for which it has lobbied vigorously, is that it wants to follow these clients to the capital markets by providing them with a wide variety of investment banking services, rather than lose out to investment banking competitors. Relationship banking for Morgan has meant in recent years returning to the advisory and underwriting services that the J. P. Morgans and their partners had traditionally provided for their clients. Customizing products to meet particular client needs was certainly a part of that early service, as was Morgan's emphasis on being "above profits." That is what its oft-repeated slogans "Doing first class business in first class ways" and "Not the fast dollar" meant.

Services of the Highest Professional Quality

Maintaining high standards of professionalism and integrity is a further extension of the Morgan service culture. As one talks with Morgan employees and with the many knowledgeable outsiders who have dealt with them, a theme that is often mentioned is the high quality of the Morgan staff and their work. When Morgan is referred to by outsiders as a *class act*, they are often commenting on its people and the quality of services they provide.

One of the first things that bank analysts and management consultants who have dealt with Morgan mention is its extreme professionalism. The epigraphs at the beginning of this chapter provide a sample. The bank's professionalism is related to its original culture, with its emphasis on "Doing first class business in first class ways."

Collegiality and Team: No Stars

A big part of Morgan's professionalism and quality is that it has always tried to provide services in a collective way, and the emphasis within the bank on collegiality and on functioning as a team is another central feature of the Morgan culture. People have been traditionally discouraged from being individualists or stars, from doing their own thing, and from being concerned mainly about their own earnings and achievements. Instead, they have been urged to subordinate such personal goals to the well-being of the firm as a whole. As a former Morgan manager, who had been in the bank for many years, recalled, "I remember so vividly a speech that Preston gave at one Christmas party where he talked about how we were all part of one team, and the implication was that we all had to coordinate almost like cogs in a wheel." Morgan managers and staff often use the slogan "One bank" to describe this aspect of the culture. Like the cultures of many other firms, J. P. Morgan's culture has a long history, reflecting the partners' emphasis on working for the benefit of the institution rather than for their own personal benefit.

Interviews with Morgan staff at all levels and functions indicate the salience of this aspect of the culture throughout the bank. A top staff person explained, "We are proudest of the team effort here, as opposed to any one guy who does it all. Mendoza [who was then head of the M&A group] is the only person around here in that sense and who appears to the outside world as such. Otherwise, Morgan is a group." A senior manager reported, "People who are individualists don't do well at Morgan." Still another senior manager explained, "We haven't liked people who wanted to be headliners. We are not headliners as a bank. We want people who want to do something, rather than to be somebody."

The team-oriented culture has both an upside and a downside. It does give Morgan a competitive advantage in merchant banking, where an effective competitor is one who can provide a wide array of products and services. This requires the close collaboration of product specialists, traders, deal makers, and relationship managers. The form most appropriate for that kind of collaboration is what students of organizations call a *matrix:* a project team of specialists who come together to develop a product appropriate to particular client needs. Morgan's team-oriented culture is ideally suited to facilitation of such collaboration. As one investment banker noted, "They have discipline we investment bankers don't have. If Mendoza (the head of Morgan's M&A group) says, `Boys, march!' they don't ask why, they ask how. And then they do it."[29] As the author of the article that quoted this investment banker concludes, "The key seems to be a culture featuring teamwork and communication, [in which] no group competes [with] any other and individual star turns are actively discouraged. Through this culture, the bank has managed to institutionalize creativity and marry it to a formidable delivery system."

Morgan may well be the closest knit of all the large U.S. commercial banks, as a result of its team culture. The culture serves the bank well. Eccles and Crane, in their book on the management of investment banks, describe the importance of developing what they call *lateral linkages* to facilitate needed coordination.[30] Morgan is a model in this regard.

The downside is that the pressure to subordinate individual needs to organizational ones may be stifling to creative people, and the bank has lost such people as a result. One such person explained:

> I came back to corporate headquarters in New York City from my overseas assignment where I was my own boss. After I saw the pressures at headquarters to be such a team player, I realized I didn't want to be in a place like that. The people I seek out and enjoy the most are those who are mavericks, who are original thinkers. I believe the bank does inhibit people who want to engage in true original thought.

Some senior managers at Morgan are aware of this and may be trying to curb the conformist pressures that this culture engenders. One senior manager related, "I once had a headmaster who said he wanted to attract not just the all-around boy but the lopsided boy, the bright, idiosyncratic person who was very creative and had a particular skill. We have to watch out here at Morgan that we don't lose some very able people to our collective, communal culture."

No Screamers Around Here

The team culture is further reinforced by another set of values emphasizing civility and nonconfrontation in relations with colleagues within the bank. "Morgan people have manners," said one long-time staff person. "You won't find any screamers around here," according to another. A third commented, "We have a culture that is very nonconfrontational. We just don't argue. Shouting is the worst thing you could ever do at Morgan." All three people were describing a feature of the culture that may well reflect the bank's patrician, upper-class, British origins. It has much in common in this regard with Chase's culture. Perhaps for some of the same reasons, it reflects a style of understatement that is characteristic of that culture. Some younger officers, particularly those who are new to the bank and accustomed to a different behavioral style, see the Morgan style as cutting off needed discussion and detracting from the quality of decisions. As one said:

> We have a culture that is nonconfrontational. An instructor here who

teaches a lot of senior management courses inside the bank pointed that out to us. At meetings the message is, "OK, now we've made the decision, and let's not have any more discussion." They don't get out all the ideas they might. We don't argue enough. There is pressure to go forward and not dwell on differences. People fear putting good ideas on the table. There is a need at times to confront, and they can't do that.

A colleague commented, "Making waves is not part of the Morgan culture. We are told over and over that four pages of insightful analysis is not nearly as good as two pages that is more general. The culture encourages you to take a more cautious approach."

Again, as with the team culture, civility and nonconfrontation at Morgan are a double-edged sword. People treat one another with much respect and dignity, at least on the surface. At the same time, it takes longer for new ideas to gain expression, because expressing them may seem to be insulting to those who hold a different view. Also, when heads of departments and divisions compete or come into conflict—for example, over their different views about what would be appropriate bank strategy for the future—they often don't express their differences openly, and the differences may fester. "It is a tradition at Morgan that people don't fight," indicated a former Morgan manager. "There are a lot of first-class people at high levels, running their respective divisions, and they are fairly autonomous. Integration of their efforts has been hard."

Chewing Over Decisions

Still another feature of the culture is decision making by consensus, which is associated with Morgan's incremental and gradualist approach to strategic change. This was sometimes annoying to younger Morgan managers, down in the ranks, who were more impatient than senior management to move the bank into new investment banking businesses. "We take forever to make decisions," reported a senior manager. "We keep chewing on the cud, and we love it. We like to try to get it right. This is frustrating to some of our people, but it is our way. We don't like to be a leading-edge firm."

A senior staff person explained:

We agonize a lot over decisions, before we go ahead on things. For example, we are more likely to hold back on getting into new products. We are not the first ones in. We might well be the first to think about it, but we'd rather let Citicorp try it. And if it does work, we will learn from their mistakes. In that sense, we are a conservative institution.

Another commented, "We only get into new things after considerable head scratching. But once in [them], we have an ability to react instantly. So we make less of a rapid leap into new products, but once we move in, we move fast."

The conservatism and caution that have characterized Morgan's culture are driven by many concerns, one of the most significant of which is to maintain continuity with the bank's past. "They often agonize over key decisions," explained a former Morgan staff person. "One reason for that is that they are protective of everything that the bank has built up over the past 100 years. They are very reflective [about] how different new products and businesses will fit into the fabric of the organization."

While this deliberate, consensus-oriented style of decision making has sometimes slowed down Morgan's reactions to changes in its industry, in contrast to Bankers Trust and Citicorp, two more agile and opportunistic competitors, it has protected the bank from some of the mistakes of those faster-moving firms. Again, the parallel between Morgan and Chase is apt, though Chase did not have Morgan's underlying strengths. As a senior manager noted, "Consensus decision making was our style, and it helped us avoid awful mistakes, like buying a brokerage operation in England. We had more caution and conservatism. If being an innovator could be scaled from 1 to 10, we were a comfortable 7, which we always felt was better than a 9 or a 10." Another commented, "We understand that Citicorp and Bankers Trust have a different approach. But that would involve too many mistakes, and that would be unacceptable to us. Citicorp has a style of ready, fire, aim, while ours is sometimes ready, aim, aim. People lower in the ranks do get frustrated [by] the slow pace of decisions here."

The style at Morgan, then, is to do much strategic analysis and planning before moving ahead on some new product or market. This kind of analysis took place throughout the 1980s, and it still continues. A senior manager explained:

> In the late seventies and early eighties, we recognized [that] the industry was changing, and we turned the ship. We concluded that we had to look outside at the market and the world first, particularly at our clients and how they saw us, and then look inward to see whether we were organized and staffed to respond to the new environment. We tried to do it in a building-block way. We spent a lot of time sensitizing our people and the larger bank to the reality of change, to get people accustomed to the fact that things would change and that [the change] would be good and was not to be feared. We tried to get people to accept it emotionally and not just intellectually. So we conditioned people early on, and that made the transition easier.

In contrast to Citicorp or Bankers Trust, Morgan as an institution never acts impulsively but always thinks through beforehand what it will do. This enables the bank to preserve the old values that its senior managers feel will help it to compete effectively in a new situation. It innovates only in the "Morgan way," thereby maintaining a balance between its past and some needed changes for the future. This is, of course, a delicate balance to maintain, particularly in view of the rapid changes that are now taking place in banking; but so far, Morgan remains a high performer. While it is a conservative institution, it is not so conservative as to be out of step with the many changes that are taking place in the industry.

Hiring for Life and Morganizing

Bankers never tire of reporting that their most important resource in the increasingly professionalized financial services industry is people. They put a lot into human resources management: recruitment, training, compensation, performance appraisal, and provision of job rotation and other personal development opportunities. No bank does more of this than Morgan, and there is a distinctive quality to its people management that both reflects its culture and sharply differentiates it from other banks.

While most of its competitors have moved away from traditional, paternalistic practices, Morgan still maintains what is in many respects a Japanese-style, clan-type culture. However, the culture has been changing, as Morgan has become more of a merchant bank. Until very recently, it offered close to lifetime employment to many people, taking great pains in recruiting to screen out those who would not qualify for such a commitment. Its management training may well be one of the most wide-ranging in the world. Continuing education for all staff has become almost a religious tenet. In addition, Morgan has provided extensive, welfarelike services and perks: in-house medical services; a generous health insurance plan; a free lunch; other miscellaneous services, including tailoring; and a vast job rotation program, international in scope, that makes available many growth opportunities for the fast-track employees who are selected to participate. Other U.S. corporations have also maintained such "benefits" cultures—for example, IBM, Cummins Engine, Johnson & Johnson, and People Express (in the early 1980s)—but the scope and scale of Morgan's benefits culture are what make it unique. In the 1985 edition of *The 100 Best Companies to Work for in America,* for example, Morgan got the highest ratings on pay, job security, chance to move up, and ambience. Its human resources program is referred to in that publication as "patrician generosity."

Much of Morgan's attention to these matters starts at recruitment. Lower-level associates and young officers describe, on the basis of their own and their colleagues' experiences, the great pains the bank takes in screening out people who would not fit the culture. The bank sometimes conducts as many as 10 to 15 interviews with a single applicant, and the process may take from 6 to 10 weeks. Interviews are far-ranging and cover such topics as family and educational background, athletic and other leisure-time activities, and social interaction styles. One systems analyst reported:

> I felt like I was pledging for a fraternity. I had 10 job interviews and would have had more, but they were waived. Anybody who will interact with you on the job gets involved in the interviewing. They even take your fingerprints. And if you go in at higher levels, you talk with their staff psychologist and take the Rorshach test. They are not going to take any chances. There is no hiring decision until every piece is in place. "We are hiring you for the rest of your life," is what they tell you. "That's why we go through all this interviewing and later orientation."

Another new officer in systems recalled:

> They wanted to know my SAT and GMAT scores, why I went to the college (non-Ivy League) that I did, where my parents went to school. It went on for 6 weeks. Every question they ask is for a purpose, to develop a personality profile on you. They wanted to know, for example, what sports I participated in. The ones I mentioned—track and tennis—were individual. And they took note of that, because, as I soon learned, it didn't necessarily fit the culture.

The orientation experience is equally intensive. An officer reported:

> They take groups of new hires, and we go to the Arrowwood Conference Center in Westchester for a week. They bring in managers at the senior vice president level from the various divisions and departments. They have to eat at least two meals with us each day, and we are required to get to know all the people in our group. It is like going to camp. There is a guy there who preaches the gospel of Morgan. We are required to participate with groups in sports activities. I remember being in the gym very early one morning, before breakfast, doing Jane Fonda-type aerobics, and there was a guy with a clipboard who came around and checked me off. I was on the floor, and suddenly a guy comes up from behind me and says something to the effect that I was working well at this hour of the morning. You might not believe

it, but my boss spent the better part of 3 days with me on how I should conduct myself during that week, what clothes to wear for dinner, what informal clothes during the day. They actually kept records on how we all performed.

A central part of the orientation program is the sessions on Morgan's history, which further reinforce the culture. The bank has always taken this aspect of orientation seriously, as a way to familiarize new recruits with the bank's beliefs and values. "There is much emphasis put in the orientation experience on Morgan's history," explained a staff person, "on what we are and where we are from. It is like going to Notre Dame and first getting to see the movie *Knute Rockne, All America*."

The perks and other services are also quite extraordinary. A long-term officer reported:

> Lunch is a hidden treasure. Medical benefits are excellent. There is a full-time medical department with all kinds of free services: full physical, blood work, substance abuse help, a psychiatrist, and so on. The change that Morgan and other banks are going through is very stressful, and the medical department is there for us.

Another officer reported, "The benefits remain incredible—health, an entire medical staff. They have the equivalent of a small hospital on the premises." Still another observed, "In addition to the medical facility, they have a company tailor and a photographer. I have seen situations [in which, for example] an officer burst a button on his jacket, and immediately we call the tailor, who comes in and sews it on right away."

The Morgan free lunch is an institution unto itself. Many managers and staff people emphasized that the bank looked upon lunch as a critical opportunity for socializing and "networking" with colleagues, for reinforcing the team culture. New employees reported that they were being urged to take advantage of it for just that reason. One new staff person said, "They will do anything to get you to socialize with colleagues at the bank, and they like you to book lunches as far ahead as possible." Another reported, "There is a lot of time taken to mold people. For example, all officers eat together in a special dining room, and this promotes socialization into the culture."

Two other extraordinary aspects of the Morgan experience are its training and job rotation programs. At one time, there was a general, M.B.A.-type program within the bank that all incoming college graduates went through. "We moved people through our in-house program as cohorts, like the class of 1970 or 1971," reported a retired senior manager. "And it was seen as just like college or graduate school." An old-timer reported:

> It was a general M.B.A.-type education. [The] people in a given class kept in close touch with each other after that, while they went on to different careers within the bank. But that whole process changed, because we began hiring more MBAs, and we didn't need to give such a concentrated, general training for a year. Now it is all much more specialized and fragmented, and [there is] no longer the one year of togetherness. We have separate courses...about new products like swaps, and [they are] more geared to individual needs.

A problem Morgan faced in the past was that it would make a big investment in the general business training of young recruits, only to have some leave for a top business school. One of its reasons for having such an intensive continuing education program was precisely so that it would not lose such people. A senior manager expressed the disappointment:

> Our training program was...equal to an outside M.B.A. Our problem has been that we lose people to business schools after a few years, competing as we do with Harvard and Stanford. We put up to $50,000 into their education and then we lose them. The investment banks do a much better job in that respect. They beat these young people to death and at least get 3 full years out of them. Treating people that way had never been our style.

The rotation experience offers still another growth opportunity, which was developed in conjunction with the changeover to global merchant banking. In its attempt to train generalists, Morgan moves people around every 3 to 5 years. The fast-track people receive foreign assignments that give them a global perspective. According to a senior manager:

> Here, we have a lot more rotation than at other places like Citicorp. There, you may be assigned to a foreign branch, and often you stay for a long time. Here, people have more generalized training and then have the capability to move around. Our people go from corporate finance to bond trading and then off to other things.

Morgan supported its global merchant banking by developing an international senior management cadre. The strategy involved several steps. A human resources staff member described it as follows:

> The first [step] was to have a U.S. manager run a foreign branch. Then we would train a local manager from that country to do it, and our U.S. manager would return to headquarters in New York for another as-

signment. Later, we would have those local foreign managers circulate
around to other countries. And finally we would then promote the best
of them to senior management positions here in New York.

Morgan's pursuit of this strategy—developing talented managers
around the world and then diffusing them through the institution as the
business became more global—gave it a competitive advantage that
other banks would take a long time to acquire. By 1991, Morgan could
boast that three of its top six managers were foreign nationals and that
it had a more internationalized senior manager group than perhaps any
other large bank. A senior manager said, "Sixty percent of our senior
vice presidents are people from outside the United States. And a third
of all people at the vice president level are not Americans."

The other clan-related aspect of the culture was Morgan's strong tendency to rely much more on "home-grown" insiders in its move toward
merchant banking than on bringing in so-called outside gurus to help it
make the transition. As a senior manager explained, "Everything we
did to change has been done with our own people, and not through outside gunslingers." The strategy was to hire, at entry level, the best people it could find; to socialize them to the Morgan culture; and then to
promote them up to middle-level and senior management positions.
This process was commonly referred to as *Morganizing*, and it has as-
sured that the culture would be widely shared and sustained over time.
It was based on the assumption that bright people who had a "generalist" experience within the bank and who supported its culture and style
could be retrained or converted to become specialists in the new and
more esoteric world of merchant banking. They might do at least as
good a job, so the argument continued, as technically trained outsiders
who didn't fit with the Morgan culture.

At the same time, Morgan's senior management did realize that success in merchant banking required some specialists who couldn't be
home-grown, and it recruited outsiders in some fields. "Our outsiders
are traders, systems people, auditors, accountants, lawyers, and professionals in fields like corporate finance," a senior manager explained.
"There are not enough of them to change the basic character of the bank.
And I am amazed at how fast the outsiders assimilate."

Morgan did several things to assure assimilation. First, it kept traditional managers in line positions, overseeing the new specialists.
Second, it recruited as many specialists as it could who already had values that fit the culture. Third, it spent a lot of time on orientation. Some
traders or corporate finance people didn't assimilate, and they invariably left.

Underlying this clan culture was Morgan's history as a small, family firm. It retained this character from its founding in 1860 until the bank went public in 1940, an extraordinarily long time for such an institution to remain privately held. Operating concurrently with the private ownership was the bank's informal, antibureaucratic, partnership ethos, traces of which remain to this day. Many of the strengths of the traditional culture are derived from its history. A senior manager at Morgan explained:

> We had a consultant come in and tell us that he had never seen a big institution that was run as much on "soft systems" as Morgan. All this goes back to our partnership origins. Smallness was our pride, and included in that [were] our old partnership, our team sense, and our short lines of communication. [These qualities were] associated with the fact that we were an 800-man organization in the 1950s. By contrast, Citicorp and Chase, two competitors, were massive organizations, run more like an army, with strict rules, [and] bigness of organization was their pride. Again, ours was smallness, and that made this transition to merchant banking easier.

Morgan, like other institutions, kept reinforcing these traditional values in a variety of ways. Recruitment, annual reports, speeches by senior managers and staff, orientation sessions such as those described above, job rotation, and bonuses and promotions were among the most significant of the techniques used. Even while the bank was changing its strategy rather dramatically in the 1980s, it still emphasized many aspects of the traditional culture.

In fact, much of the traditional culture supports the change. Insofar as merchant banking requires the equivalent of project teams to coordinate the many products and services the bank must provide in complex transactions for clients, the aspects of the culture that have reinforced collegiality have been most helpful. They have included the bonding experience of recruits who went through orientation and training together, the leading of the transition by home-grown people, the rotation experiences, and the short lines of communication within the bank. According to a senior manager:

> When people made decisions on deals, they were expected to touch base with all the experts at Morgan who could help structure the deal. Since we were home-grown, it was very easy to call somebody, say, in Paris, who had a particular expertise. Even though you hadn't seen him for a long time, you still knew him well. You might have gone through a training program in his class, and it was a close-knit community, with [these] kinds of cohesive networks.

At the same time, the traditional culture posed problems in the transition, requiring significant culture changes that the bank has embarked upon in recent years. In the next section, I will discuss the internal stresses and contradictions that these changes were to entail and that Morgan will have to deal with in the 1990s.

No Details Are Too Trivial

Underlying Morgan's emphasis on its culture is a style of meticulous attention to detail. This pervades its operations and is demonstrated dramatically in its style of chewing and agonizing over important strategic decisions and in its conservatism. Until recently, the approach was used in even the most mundane administrative matters, and the cultural emphasis on "getting it right" was also applied. A staff person in systems reported:

> They are very detail-oriented. Things are proceduralized and documented to an extreme. They spent over a year deciding on the size [of], layout [of], and assignment of people to offices in the new building. An associate vice president did it. But [similar procedures] applied to so many things. When I was told that staff from our Belgium office would be visiting, I was [also] told to call the protocol department to find out who should take them to dinner and where we would go. This was the Morgan way of doing things. They are very precise about it.

Again, the continuities with an earlier Morgan culture are striking. Chernow, for example, in his insightful description of the management style of J. P. Morgan, Sr., describes him as a person who could never delegate and who paid "excessive attention to details."[31]

Noblesse Oblige

The last aspect of the Morgan culture to be discussed in this chapter is the concept of community service, which reflects Morgan's patrician, noblesse oblige culture. Though this concept may not be emphasized as profoundly as it was in the past, the bank does still stress the importance of contributing to the wider community, much as Chase did under David Rockefeller. The tradition covers a range of civic activities, from sitting on boards of nonprofit organizations to making financial contributions to and volunteering services within these institutions. Morgan employees at all levels have been encouraged to engage in such activities. As indicated in the *1984 Annual Report*, "The Morgan tradition also includes a direct involvement in community affairs, through philanthropy and volunteer activities—where many of the same skills used in banking can be applied. These efforts are not incompatible with our professional interests. Charitable activities are good business practice."[32] No fewer than 25 pages of the report were devoted to a "pictorial review" of Morgan's philanthropic activities. Moreover, in the *1983 Annual Report*, brief biographies of several senior managers list their civic activities. The positions held by these managers included president of Doctors Hospital in New York City, chairman of the finance committee of the New York Blood Center, board member of the New York Hospital—Cornell Medical Center, and member of the Council of Foreign Relations and the Development Committee of the Central Park Conservancy. One officer reported:

> We [have] always considered ourselves statesmanlike. We feel we should do good. And what better vehicle for people to do good but through the bank? For senior managers to do all these things in the community is the norm. Many of these Morgan people are blue bloods, raised by mothers who were fund raisers and had spent a lifetime in community service. These managers have [each] had a favorite charity since they were kids—opera, hospitals, museums, and so on. This is an exceptional group of people who have a breadth of background, have traveled internationally, have a sense of history, and are caring. They show it in their civic and public service efforts.

A Blue-Blood Past

Implicit in this discussion of Morgan's culture is the notion that it reflects many traditional, upper-class values. The classic stereotype of Morgan held by many observers of banks is that it is still a predominantly "white-shoe" and blue-blood institution. Chernow's description of Morgan partners in the 1920s and 1930s, as being white, male, Republican, Episcopalian, Anglophile, and Ivy League, and as coming from eastern seaboard establishment backgrounds, was not only accurate for that time. It is still true, to a considerable degree, in the present. By 1955, when Henry Clay Alexander, who was sometimes referred to as *the smart hick*, became CEO, the bank was loosening up a bit. Alexander was from Tennessee and was hardly an eastern establishment type.

There is no question but that Morgan has widened the social base of its managers in recent decades, though not to anywhere near the degree

that the other big New York banks have. Chase is the most obvious comparison, and Chapters 6 to 8 have already described the enormous
changes that David Rockefeller himself helped to institute there. The
same could be said for Bankers Trust, a Morgan-founded bank which
was considerably upper-class-oriented in its earlier years. Now, however, it has a highly diversified employee group at all levels. Morgan is
moving in a similar direction, but it has been moving much more slowly
than Bankers Trust did.

The groups at Morgan who represent a new wave are the outsiders
mentioned above: the systems people, auditors and accountants, and
traders. Many of them are not from Ivy League schools and do not fit the
other features of Chernow's profile. After I interviewed several of these
people, I concluded that, while they were accepted into the bank and
while their skills and efforts were rewarded, even the high performers
among them still felt that their opportunities were somewhat limited.
One explained, "There is no question but that it is a caste system. If you
are Ivy League, with a B.A. in liberal arts or an M.B.A. from Wharton,
Harvard, or Stanford, you immediately qualify as a Morgan business
person." Another person from a similar background stated:

> The bank is still very much blue-blood, more so in some departments
> than in others. It is very professional, well-mannered, and well-spoken.
> I didn't go to an Ivy League school, and that hurt me. Several months
> after I arrived, my boss said to me in all seriousness: "Every now and
> then, we find that peoples' educational background is not a reflection
> of their abilities."

Some Morgan staff point to the many foreign nationals now in high
positions in the bank as an example of how it has broadened its social
base considerably from earlier years. While there is some validity in that
argument, it is also true that many of the foreign nationals at Morgan
are from elite, aristocratic backgrounds in their home countries. One
Morgan answer to this objection is that it simply recruits people of the
highest quality and professionalism—and that is of course true.

One of the things that Morgan will probably always hang on to as an
expression of its upper-class and British-oriented past is its emphasis on
taste and elegance. Chase had some of those characteristics as well, but
at Morgan they have always been accentuated. A consultant explained:

> Everything there must be in good taste. They have exquisite taste as
> people, in conduct, in personal appearance, in clothes, in the appear-
> ance of the offices, [in] the artwork, and [in the] decorations. People at
> Morgan are all well-groomed, not like those at IBM or Merrill Lynch,
> where it is a result of deliberateness, but rather by birth. They pride

themselves on not being nouveaux riches like some of their competitors—for example, Bankers Trust. And until recently, and even now, Morgan people were not interested in money, but in elegance of conduct. That is the stamp of the place, and it is much different from others in that respect.

13
The Morgan: Returning to Its Roots

Having described the Morgan strategy briefly in Chapter 12, I will now fill out that description, since it represents such an important, if hard-to-achieve, option for the many wholesale banks that lost their franchises in the 1970s and 1980s. By returning to its roots, Morgan has, since the late 1970s, pursued the strategy of a large and global merchant bank. It might better be called a *hybrid* bank, since it provides both commercial banking (loan) services and a wide variety of fee-based services.[1] To be more specific, it has positioned itself at the high end of a market that includes among its clients major corporations, sovereign states and other nonprofit organizations, financial institutions, and affluent individuals. The particular products Morgan provides are corporate finance services [advisory services, mergers and acquisitions (M&A), leasing, and real estate finance], securities trading (including foreign exchange and various risk-management products), investment management (custodial and trust services), operational services (transactions and information), and private banking.

Since Morgan has no significant pool of demand deposits to finance its many transactions, it is forced to raise funds through "interest rate plays." These involve buying short-term securities in the market at low prices (high yields) and selling them later at higher prices (lower yields), as well as selling its own paper and making money on the spread between the interest that it pays as a wholesale borrower and the interest that it charges as a lender. As a Morgan senior manager explained, "We live by our wits, by raising funds as traders in the market." This so-called liability management strategy may be contrasted with the strategies of such retail banking giants as Bank of America, Citicorp, and Chase. The consumer branches of these banks have attracted enormous deposits.

Morgan's strategy is increasingly that of a full-service bank, providing its clients with a wide variety of advisory, credit, financing, and operations services. It has been referred to in this regard as *a global full-service bank without a retail business* and *a 24-hour supermarket of finance*, so comprehensive are its services.[2] One high-level staff person described the strategy as that of "a wholesale, merchant bank that is global and has a wide range of products for a select group of clients." Professor Roy Smith of the Stern School of Business of New York University has even suggested that Morgan may be moving to become a universal bank, like European banks that provide many services for various institutional clients.

Morgan has become increasingly aggressive and agile in pursuit of its businesses during the past decade, driven both by the highly competitive nature of the industry and by its goal of being a leading player.[3] It has thus become much more opportunistic than it was in the past, which has created internal tension for the bank, since it also wants to preserve much of its traditional culture.

If I were forced to summarize Morgan's strategy in one word, it might well be *balance*. The bank maintains a balance between innovation and continuity—a balance between becoming a more aggressive competitor in emerging investment banking markets and retaining its relationships of trust with clients (which involves Morgan's forgoing short-term profits that might conflict with clients' longer-term needs). There have been increasing debates within the bank about the nature of its balance and how to define it. Such debates will undoubtedly continue for some time, as changes in competitive conditions within the financial services industry force Morgan to constantly reexamine its priorities.

Morgan's past goal of being "the best but not the first" has been one general way of expressing how it pursued that balance. As a Morgan senior manager put it, "The leading edge can easily become the bleeding edge." He was referring to such competitors as Citicorp and Bankers Trust, which have often moved into new markets much more aggressively and with less caution than Morgan has. The style of more evolutionary and incremental change is being challenged increasingly, however, within the bank, and there will undoubtedly be continuing differences among senior managers about how aggressive Morgan should be. One consultant commented:

> The big shift for Morgan, as its people define it, is how far to move to-

ward the style of Citicorp, an exemplar of the more aggressive strategy. It is an issue of how to compete without losing [the bank's] identity and the characteristics [its senior managers] cherish. Morgan staff throughout the bank are clearly of the highest quality—very adaptable and quick learners, so they are capable of change. It's...a question of how fast [to move], how far, and with what impact on traditional values.

Strategic Priorities

One revealing indicator of Morgan's shifting priorities is the relative contributions of interest revenue and noninterest revenue over the past several years. The former represents the traditional loan business, while the latter reflects fee income from new investment banking, investment management, and operations services. In 1980, when Morgan first began its changeover to merchant and investment banking, fee income was only about 12 to 15 percent of gross revenue. By 1988, it was up to 47 percent, and in 1990, it was over 60 percent.[4] This big change is indicative of Morgan's momentum.

The growing noninterest revenue has several components.[5] One is securities trading. Morgan has become a premier global trader in several markets: foreign exchange; swaps; U.S. and foreign government and corporate securities; commodities; and risk-management products other than swaps, including futures and options, and less developed country (LDC) assets. The bank's trading revenue in 1990 was an extraordinary $959 million, or 29 percent of its total. Corporate finance fees constituted another 8 percent (less than one might expect, largely because corporate takeovers and restructurings declined in the late 1980s). Investment management constituted 9 percent and has been increasing in recent years, as trustee services for public, corporate, and union employee benefit funds and for pension trust funds have been in greater demand. Finally, operational service fees constituted another 8 percent. These are remaining stable, in such areas as custody services in connection with securities, corporate and personal trust services, money transfers, and securities lending. These businesses are likely to grow, particularly because Morgan emphasizes them on a global scale and because opportunities in Europe, where they are particularly well positioned, are increasing.

No precise and disaggregated data exist on what proportions of Morgan's revenues come from transactions in different areas of the world. Bank analysts' estimates, however, are that Morgan, as one of the most global banks, does more than half its business outside the United

States, perhaps up to 60 percent. That proportion may well increase in the coming years, as the Europe of 1992 opens up many new financial services opportunities, particularly for Morgan, which has been doing business there for more than a century.

Individual services and product areas in which Morgan is a world leader include interest rate and currency swaps, the private placement of securities, foreign exchange, Eurobond underwriting, gold and bullion trading, the private placement of debt and equity securities, syndicated lending, and M&A fees. In the swaps area, a series of hedging or risk-management services that permit a client to change currencies and interest rates as a protection against volatile shifts, Morgan is one of the leading institutions (Citicorp is another), and it has finished in the top two or three in the industry's so-called league tables since the mid-1980s.[6] Morgan has a strong swaps trading group with offices in Tokyo, London, and New York City, and that group has close linkages with both the corporate finance division and the securities trading division.

In private placements, Morgan overtook both Bankers Trust and Citicorp in 1989. It is now second only to First Boston in this profitable business, because it doesn't utilize capital and offers a service valued by many corporate clients.[7] The service involves selling a debt or equity that does not have to be registered with the Securities and Exchange Commission (SEC) to a limited number of institutional investors. Morgan has the biggest private placement group among commercial banks, and it provides a critical complementary service for clients.

Foreign exchange trading is still another business in which Morgan excels. Citicorp is the leader, but Morgan is very strong. It increased its revenue in that regard from $187 million in 1988 to $309 million in 1990.[8]

The other area of emerging strength for Morgan, in addition to the securities trading businesses, is its M&A services. These services are advisory and financial, and Morgan has come a long way in both since the mid-1980s. Though it had maintained an M&A group for many years, Morgan was an inconsequential player and made little money in the field until 1985. At that time, the bank's senior managers decided it had to have a strong M&A presence if it was to become a global merchant bank, and they appointed a dynamic young banker to head up the group. Roberto Mendoza, who was 39 years old when he was appointed, has since gone on to become vice chairman of the bank, while still running the M&A operation. By 1990, Morgan had become the first commercial bank to crack the top 10, ranking seventh among all financial services institutions in deal value of M&A transactions.[9] Such widely publicized deals as the Hospital Corporation of America

takeover and the SmithKline Beckman merger with the Beecham Group
PLC, which created the world's second-largest pharmaceutical firm,
were engineered under Mendoza's leadership. Much controversy resulted from one deal, in which Morgan counseled Hoffman LaRoche in
its hostile takeover of Sterling Drug, a Morgan client. This incident
raised broad policy questions about how far Morgan planned to go in
reversing its past principles as it moved into investment banking.

Suffice it to say that Morgan has done a remarkable about-face since
the late 1970s, when it became increasingly apparent that the bank could
not survive as a major player in its industry unless it made such a
change. Unlike its major competitors, Morgan was able to reposition itself without having to chase after risky loans in real estate, oil, and
leveraged buyouts (LBOs). To be sure, it did get saddled with nonperforming loans in Latin America, but even there, it was much less burdened than were such money center competitors as Citicorp,
Manufacturers Hanover, Chase, and Chemical.

Was this repositioning a radical one, and did it take place quickly?
The answer to the first question is that it was a significant departure
from the post-Glass Steagall strategy that Morgan had developed when
it was forced out of investment banking, and when Morgan Stanley was
formed as a separate entity to pursue that part of the business. Yet, it
was a return to Morgan's roots, just as Bankers Trust's transformation
was a return to its roots. Moreover, even under the constraints of Glass
Steagall, Morgan had continued to pursue some investment banking-related activities. As one of its senior managers explained:

> For us, it was a much more gradual shift than for Bankers Trust, based
> on some inherited strategic strengths. The small J.P. Morgan before
> 1959 had to live by its wits. It needed capital and was involved as a
> transfer agent and in an advisory capacity. In the early 1950s, it did
> conditional sale financing for the railroads. We are an old investment
> bank for the railroads. Also, we had a statistics department that served
> equity investors, as well as our loan and credit people. It was an ana-
> lytical group for investment business and not just for the credit de-
> partment. And it could convert later to an analysis group for our cor-
> porate finance. So we retained in our bones an element of investment
> banking. A corporation could go to Goldman Sachs for underwriting,
> but we could do the analysis for them. So the bank has always had that
> flavor.

As for how fast the changeover took place, major shifts certainly occurred in the 1980s. However, true to the Morgan style, the process was
gradual and deliberate. One staff person put it very well: "Morgan has

been like a battleship turning in the ocean. Watching it turn, you would never know it was happening, so slowly did that take place. But then, in 1990, you could see that it had become a very different institution from what it had been in 1980."

The rest of the story of Morgan is related to the other changes the bank is making to support its new strategy. Clearly, many aspects of Morgan's infrastructure are undergoing transformation. There are strains and tensions, and some of them are severe, but the changes are going on nevertheless.

Flattening the Pyramid: A New Organization

Not surprisingly, in order to be successful in its new strategy, Morgan had to develop a supporting organization and culture that would enable it to implement the strategy with as few glitches as possible. That its financial performance has been as good as it has indicates that Morgan has done a number of things right in this regard.

One of these things concerns changes in organizational structure. Taking a long-term view, Morgan changed from being very informal and nonbureaucratic throughout most of its history (reflecting its partnership style) to becoming much more hierarchical and bureaucratic after the merger with Guaranty Trust in 1959. At that time, it set up a series of specialized departments, supported by new management control and information systems. It was not possible for a bank of its vastly increased size and scope of operations to continue being organized so informally.

Morgan's strategic change in the 1980s to merchant banking was accompanied by a similarly major change in organization. While it did not move back to the simple, informal structure of its earlier years, it did make several significant changes toward less hierarchy and less bureaucracy. Like Bankers Trust, it became much flatter and more decentralized, giving newly established managing directors and other product division heads more autonomy. There are now more than 500 such directors, and many of the administrative vice presidential levels have been eliminated.

Moreover, the structure is not only flatter and more decentralized; it is also much more fluid and flexible than ever before. It resembles Bankers Trust in that respect, and both resemble investment banks. Some observers have even noted that, as investment banks have taken on more structure and controls following the crash of 1987, and as banks like Bankers Trust and Morgan have loosened their structures, the two branches of the financial services industry are becoming more alike. A top staff person at Morgan summarized the bank's changes in this regard: "There [have been] no...organizational charts for the last few years, largely because we have been reorganizing so much and so fast. They just stopped the presses."

It would be an oversimplification, however, to characterize Morgan as a mainly decentralized organization. At the same time that it was decentralizing the management director level, it was also taking away the decentralized authority of geographic area managers around the world and actually centralizing product directors at headquarters. Morgan managers refer to the result as a *new functional structure,* though it in fact is much like the product divisions of nonfinancial corporations. A headquarters manager reported:

> We have a newly centralized product-driven culture, and that centralization will change the culture. We got rid of area managers, and each geographic area has its own management committee. The chair varies from place to place and is our most recent equivalent of the area manager. Lateral cooperation across businesses is very much encouraged and very important for us, and we do it very informally.

In addition, the bank has established several subsidiaries, often in anticipation of regulatory changes that would allow it to diversify into various securities related businesses. Its senior managers often talk of the "subsidiarization" that Morgan has undergone in recent years, in preparation for increased opportunities that deregulation is expected to provide. A staff person explained, "Morgan set up a lot of subsidiaries, almost as shells, or legal entities, just waiting for the repeal of Glass Steagall. And then we went ahead with capital markets training and global markets seminars. J.P. Morgan Equities was one example."

The many organizational changes Morgan has gone through in the 1980s seem to have followed a pattern established by its strategy. As Morgan became more diversified in its investment banking activities, it established more subsidiaries to manage that diversity. As more of its business came to be in competitive and volatile investment banking markets, its structure became flatter and more flexible, to enable it to respond faster to market changes. As its business became more global, it consolidated some divisions. A retired senior manager explained:

> Our old international and domestic divisions were integrated into one corporate finance division, and this was an after-the-fact structural acknowledgment of a prior strategic change. We now had a global cor-

porate finance business that made that separation of the international and domestic divisions moot.

Finally, Morgan eliminated its former geographic area manager positions, as an unnecessary layer between specialists in particular products and its clients. These specialists now report to the functional division heads at headquarters and do not face the dual authority problem that had existed before, at Morgan and at other banks.

The general approach has been to simplify, consolidate, and flatten, to make the bank more market-responsive and more collegial in its internal relations. According to a senior manager:

> We are very fluid now. The hope is that our collegial culture and flat organization contribute to more collaboration internally. It used to be that headquarters was very flat, like our old partnership. And then the divisions were hierarchical, with several layers of vice presidents. Now, the divisions as well are much flattened and the titles are gone. Instead of [encouraging people to work their] way up to management [positions], we now have as many as five or six hundred managing directors. That has been a big change.

As in all organizations, there are continued transitional problems with this structure. There is, first of all, a need for coordination and control at the geographic market level. Each country now has a management committee, with a chair who is the functional equivalent of the old area manager. Several senior managers indicated that they felt the area manager would return in a more institutionalized way as a necessary position.

A perhaps more serious problem is how to achieve collaboration among the various product divisions. This problem is common to all divisionalized corporations, and there is no reason for Morgan to be exempt. Its team-oriented culture helps, but the divisions foster a degree of loyalty that goes against the culture. Getting them to cooperate will be a major management challenge.

To avoid going into inordinate detail, I will say only that the present structure, as fluid as it is, nevertheless has seven identifiable business groups, which are structured along product lines, and nine support groups, which are structured along functional lines.[10] More specifically, the business groups are (1) securities sales and trading, (2) corporate finance and M&A, (3) operations services, (4) Euroclear (clearing of securities transactions), (5) private banking, (6) investment management, and (7) equity investment. The functional or support groups are (1) human resources, (2) auditing, (3) financial services, (4) credit policy, (5) global support systems, (6) nonbank subsidiaries, (7) research, (8) legal and corporate staff, and (9) other branch and subsidiary staff.

The complexities involved in getting the seven business groups to collaborate and in linking the support functions with the business groups are enormous. Clearly, keeping relations and structures as simple as possible and constantly encouraging collaboration and linkages will challenge the skills and ingenuity of Morgan's managers.

Managing the Transition: Stresses and Strains

Morgan has faced many serious problems in managing the transition to merchant banking, and it will continue to face serious problems for some time. While some of its traditional culture has been helpful in facilitating the transition, particularly its collegiality and its team emphasis, the change has required many other aspects of the culture to undergo significant transformation in order for the strategy to be implemented effectively. New cultural values have begun to pervade the bank, creating much nostalgia among some managers, as well as serious strains and conflicts among different groups within the bank, as the changes get sorted out.

The main cultural changes are as follows:

1. More emphasis on *profits* as a dominant objective of every department

2. A much more *aggressive* and competitive posture in the marketplace

3. More emphasis on *pay for performance*

4. More *outside hiring,* as it became clear that home-grown insiders, even when retrained, might not have all the skills required to pursue the merchant banking strategy

5. A decision style that is *faster* in response time

6. An *abandonment of the lifetime employment commitment* to Morgan staff

7. *Less of the traditional Morgan conservatism regarding cost controls,* as senior management invested in a massive infrastructure of new buildings, technology, and staff as part of an effort to become an aggressive global competitor in merchant banking

Each of these cultural changes made sense from the perspective of the requirements for success in the highly competitive markets into which Morgan was moving. At the same time, each represented a severe wrench away from the traditional culture. There was no guarantee that any of them would lead to success, both because of the many uncertainties of the new markets and because of wider economic and political forces that would affect any firm like Morgan that embarked on such a change. "The jury is still out on us," reported a new staff person at Morgan, "even though our performance to date is ahead of [that of] our commercial banking competitors."

While there is, in the abstract, widespread agreement within the bank about the increased emphasis on profits, there are differing interpretations of how this emphasis should be implemented. The differences focus in large part on the relative amounts of emphasis Morgan should place on short- versus long-term considerations, particularly in relation to how the bank treats clients. The senior managers (some of whom have left) who regard the new opportunism in seeking short-term profits as a mistake are particularly concerned about the bank's beginning to lose its "relationship" focus in the late 1980s and early 1990s. They speak of its having turned against some of the basic principles that made it the great institution that it was. Consider the following from a senior manager:

> We sometimes lose sight of what is important—our strong history and the principles and guidelines [about] how to proceed that are based on that history. Treating clients like clients and not customers, by being very sensitive to their needs, is a big one. Another way of saying this is, "Give the best service in a first-class way." Some of us left because we felt the focus on such basic principles and on the client was lost. Bankers Trust had lost it, and so did we. Both of us became enamored with product instead of relationships, as have the investment banks. And that got reflected in a separate sales force. We started treating clients like customers, and that was a terrible mistake. We lost sight of our history.

This argument, reflecting a generalized disenchantment with the directions Morgan has taken, holds that it is not nearly as solicitous and caring of clients as it had been in the past. In the long term, its proponents maintain, Morgan will lose a lot of credibility and business as a result. One senior manager explained:

> We...started to lose it with our customers. We would ask them, "How much did you buy from me lately?" and based on that, we determined how to deal with them. We began to [make] product-driven, short-

term decisions, and that is the trap Morgan fell into. Without cost accounting systems to measure client profitability, that was foolish. And we had no such systems. So it is increasingly a fiction to say that Morgan is now relationship-oriented. I have talked with lots of CFOs [chief financial officers] from major corporations that had been clients of Morgan. They see this change, and they don't like it. It will take a long time for many to see, because we have had relationship banking so long in our history.

Pay for performance is another change that some Morgan staff see as creating internal tensions that will have to be managed well. In order to become an effective merchant banker, Morgan, like any other institution pursuing this strategy, must attract and retain able traders and other specialists. Providing bonuses somewhat competitive with those on Wall Street and at competitors like Bankers Trust is critical. Morgan, like its competitors, has lost its share of investment bankers who left for jobs with investment banks that paid much more. Interestingly, many returned to Morgan after a short time away, preferring its more civil climate and professionalism to the intense internal competition and conflict on "the Street." A staff person explained:

> We pay less than Wall Street firms and have lost people as a result. This has preyed on management's mind. They try to handle it by saying to these people: "We give you other things here. You don't have to look over your shoulder. There is discouragement of a cult of personality." We have had people who agreed with the message and were pleased to come back for less money than they were making.

While Morgan doesn't quite pay Wall Street-style bonuses, it has increasingly introduced a pay-for-performance culture, which has produced predictable internal strains. "What that does is create the potential to weaken or break down the team culture," said a senior banker. "It has to be managed very carefully." One way of managing it is to include as part of the basis for bonus the extent to which the investment banker is collaborative and collegial. While this assessment must inevitably be based upon subjective judgment, it is reported to help in maintaining the needed collegiality.

However, another retired senior manager is not so sanguine about immediate solutions. He reported that the bonus system did, indeed, contribute to deep-rooted internal tensions. "Given the much flatter structure," he explained, "the only way many people can establish their place in the pecking order is to publicize how big their bonus is. And that has created much chaos inside Morgan. It shatters the team feeling. I saw it a lot."

A related problem may well be the emergence of much more competition and conflict across business groups and of many more so-called stars than had existed before. "Morgan is full of stars now, " explained a manager. "There are 15 to 20 at the very top and lesser ones down below. Sure, it always had some, but there are more now, with the move into merchant banking and the compensation system."

Bringing in more outsiders, many of them midcareer people, is another big change for Morgan. Unlike the other changes, this one seems to have been managed with a minimum of tension. As discussed in Chapter 12, the outsiders tend to be traders, systems people, auditors, accountants, and specialists in areas of corporate finance. Though it is true, as one staff person commented, that "trading is a tough fit with the Morgan culture, since it is not a gentlemanly activity," the traders, systems people, and other outsiders are all managed by home-grown Morganites. Some outsiders have embraced the culture almost on arrival, others have assimilated over time, and many of the rest have left.

One of the biggest cultural problems Morgan has faced relates to the fallout from its infrastructure costs of becoming a global merchant bank. The new strategy requires a huge investment in technology, staff, and physical facilities. Thus, in 1986, Morgan's expenses rose nearly 30 percent, and they were still up 20 percent in 1987. The two biggest components have been (1) personnel costs, as Morgan increased its head count in the 1980s from 10,000 to nearly 16,000 and provided competitive bonuses, and (2) the costs of its new headquarters in New York City and its new facility in London.

Stockholders and bank analysts have been highly critical of Morgan's escalating expenses, and it has responded by moving aggressively to control them. Because of its strong management and its conservative style, the bank probably would have controlled expenses anyway, but the outside push may have speeded up the process. Concretely, that has taken the form of reducing head count and of hiring McKinsey to help it continue to downsize. The bank reduced its workforce from close to 16,000 in 1987 to 12,968 in 1990.[11] As of March 1992 the workforce was up to 13,500, but the general trend of staying lean will continue.

Because of Morgan's "lifetime employment" culture, the downsizing required to manage escalating costs has produced shock waves throughout the bank, even though senior managers have handled the downsizing in humane, "Morganlike" ways. A former senior manager reported:

> It used to be that you had to assassinate people to be fired. I know, because I was a manager, and I would sack people for stealing. But even

then, it was done only in the most mannerly way, because that was the bank's way. Now, we are downsizing, and what we do is what is euphemistically called *job elimination*. And then the person can try to find a job elsewhere in the bank, but there is no more work in the bank for them. We have had much bitterness within the bank, and many people looking over their shoulders like never before. It used to be that we gave employment for life, like in Japan. You had a lifetime probation. Sure, there were people who did not work out [during] the first 1 to 3 years, and they were let go. But they were a rarity.

Some of the downsizing was managed simply by selling off businesses that did not fit the new merchant banking strategy. An example was Morgan's stock transfer business. Morgan had dominated the field for more than 100 years, but in 1989, it sold off the business to First Chicago. This move eliminated 921 employees from Morgan's payroll, though the people continued to work in the same jobs and at the same physical locations. Because people did not lose their jobs, this move was not in conflict with the old culture; rather, it was seen as part of a strategic repositioning of the bank.

Maintaining much confidentiality about terminations is another technique for softening the bankwide impact. People whose divisions are not affected are simply not told about the job losses. A Morgan staff person explained:

> There are more and more layoffs. Morgan does it quietly and generously, there are no sudden pink slips, and people do get good treatment with severance. We may hear, for example, that some people are no longer employed at our Delaware office. But nobody ever says anything, and there is never any notice to that effect, like in the Morgan house organ. It's almost as though these people just disappear. It's hard to handle any other way, since the saying used to be: "You will be employed for life."

There is also a strong belief that the "benefits culture" and Morgan's many perks may soon become a thing of the past or at least be seriously watered down. Not only do Morgan staff talk about who is being "attritted" (given early retirement), but some are increasingly skeptical about whether the bank will maintain anywhere near the level of employee services that it had before. A former senior manager recalled:

> I used to say that Morgan had the most Japanese culture of any American company, but that is gone—not completely, but largely. Morgan couldn't manage its expenses, which grew much too fast for its revenues, and it had to lay off people and cut some personnel services.

> I have told the top management at Morgan that they make a big mistake if they indiscriminately focus on the expense side. That is the wrong battle to be waging, and it can be very demoralizing and debilitating for the bank.

Another former senior manager commented, "The implicit social contract you talk about in relation to our old culture (lifetime employment and many perks) will have to undergo change. We can no longer sustain it, because of the businesses we are in."

Morgan's downsizing became necessary because of its huge investment in people, new facilities, and technology. The cost problems that resulted related, in turn, to the recent cutbacks. Opinions differ about the appropriateness of senior management's judgments on these matters. Many people see the expenses as having been necessary and as having contributed to the bank's successful transformation. They regard the expenses as an investment in the future that will pay off many times over. On the other hand, many of the people who left feel that the bank betrayed its principles and its people. One retired manager, reflecting this view, bemoaned:

> It was just plain silly to go from 10,000 to 16,000 during the 1980s, and most of the new people were in supporting roles and buildings. Increased head count was allowed to creep in until it was just absurd. Downsizing [goes] against our grain, but now we have to [do it]. Trading is the hardest area to manage from that point of view. It is very profitable, but there is no sophisticated cost loan analysis. Every trader or salesman is backed up by several people. We have some terrifying numbers of people in accounting and compliance, for example. We have added...many people at the front end of the ship, [but] when you look down in the engine rooms, there aren't that many.

Morgan's two massive new buildings, one in New York City and one in London, are a focus of much internal discussion. The question is whether the bank was right to invest in this infrastructure to support its new merchant banking strategy, and there are strong advocates both pro and con. Those who favor the infrastructure point to the modular nature of the new facilities, claiming that they allow for much more flexibility in restructuring than would ever have been possible in the old buildings. They also speak of the ease with which the new telecommunications technology for Morgan's large trading business now fits into the new structures, and the ease with which it may be periodically updated with a minimum of expense and upset. They conclude that the buildings were a sound investment that will have tremendous payoffs in the 1990s. One senior manager explained, "The old [New York] building couldn't be wired as easily as this one. Also, in this one we can move whole departments in, given its modular structure. We expect to realize substantial cost savings, and it does fit the businesses we are in." Another New York manager claimed, "It would have been very expensive to modernize our old—50-year-old—building with [the] new technology and wires needed. We had to make the changeover."

The opposing view is that investing in the two new buildings involved questionable judgment. One retired senior manager observed:

> They are huge mausoleums. We will be a long time recovering from that [investment]. Sure, we needed an infrastructure and trading systems, but why did we do it so lavishly? It was done when Morgan was flush, in the mideighties. The real problem is London. We don't need that kind of presence there and will not be able to lease there.

In conclusion, Morgan has made a big strategic change, requiring corresponding changes in structure, human resource practices, and culture that represent major breaks with its past. The cultural changes have been particularly painful and will have to be sorted out over the next several years.

A critical question is: How unified are Morgan's senior managers in their vision of the kind of strategy they want the bank to pursue? It is not easy to probe the senior management of any institution on such matters, and Morgan, with its long tradition of privacy, is particularly difficult to understand in this regard. Based on what I was able to glean, the bank may now face serious differences between at least two visions of its appropriate future directions. One vision is that Morgan should concentrate on corporate finance-related businesses, and the other argues that trading is the big revenue producer and should prevail. Both corporate finance and trading are important. To the extent that the strong conflict between them hampers the bank's effectiveness, it will have to be addressed. Consider the following observation by a senior banker who left Morgan:

> We now have these two schools of thought inside Morgan. one says that it should be a huge trading house that is transaction-oriented and nothing else, and [Kurt] Viermetz takes that position. The other is that Morgan should be a boutique for clients, to serve their many needs, and Mendoza takes that position. [The] debates at times paralyze the institution. There has to be an arbiter to manage [them], and so far, [they have] not been adequately resolved.

The Faceless Collective?

It would be reasonable to expect that the many changes Morgan has experienced in recent years would be driven by strong chief executive officers (CEOs). At each of the other banks I have described, particular leaders either did in fact provide the vision and implementation capability to move ahead or, conversely, did contribute to a failure to do so. Leaders at Morgan are much harder to judge, both because its collectivist culture submerges individual needs to corporate ones and because the bank has such a passion for secrecy.

Ironically, Morgan, more than any other bank, has a history of being almost a one-man operation. As noted in Chapter 12, J. P. Morgan, Sr., ran the bank from 1860 to 1913 as an extension of his own personality. A sign of things to come, however, appeared in the management style of his son, J. P. Morgan, Jr., who was much more delegative and turned the bank into an institution run by a team of independent partners, each of whom was strong in his own right. Decisions were made by consensus at daily partners' meetings. The team culture, with its emphasis on collegiality and consensus decisions, dates from early in this century, when J. P. Morgan, Jr., took over.

The bank has had several distinguished partners since then: Harry Davison, Tom Lamont, Dwight Morrow, Russell Leffingwell, and George Whitney.[12] Few have become household names or been as closely associated with the vision and development of the bank as have George Moore, Walter Wriston, and John Reed at Citicorp; Alfred Brittain and Charles Sanford at Bankers Trust; and Nelson Aldrich, John McCloy, and David Rockefeller at Chase. This is not to say that Morgan has had undistinguished CEOs, but rather that they have not stood out to the same degree as their counterparts elsewhere. One very recent exception may well be Lewis Preston, who held the position of CEO at Morgan from 1980 to 1990 and was largely responsible for leading the bank's transition from commercial to investment banking.

Consider the bank's CEOs since 1960, the year after the merger with Morgan Guaranty. From 1960 to 1969, Morgan was headed by Tom Gates, who had been Secretary of Defense under President Dwight D. Eisenhower and had no banking background. He mainly supported existing Morgan traditions by reemphasizing the collegial, partnership nature of the bank's senior management and strengthening in that regard the office of the CEO. Gates was reported to be responsible for establishing an executive committee of the most senior managers of the bank, any one of whom was empowered to make a decision for the en-

tire bank in an emergency, if all others were away or otherwise un-
available.

Gates was succeeded by John Meyer, who was generally characterized as one of Morgan's most austere CEOs. Meyer carried the bank's
culture of secrecy to new extremes. Some old-time senior managers,
while acknowledging Meyer's characteristics, also suggested that he
was one of the most brilliant of the bank's recent leaders. Others questioned his judgment on critical decisions. "He was too deal-oriented,"
commented a Morgan manager who was at the bank during Meyer's
years. "That style eventually led to one big mistake that was disastrous:
the loan of some $40 million to Penn Central on the eve of its
bankruptcy. We then got caught in a conflict-of-interests situation and
were worried we would get sued by the bondholders."

Meyer's successors included Elmore Patterson, who has been referred
to as "not at all dynamic," and Walter Page, "an establishment person,"
both of whom served in the 1970s.

The contemporary CEO who has made the biggest impact upon the
bank was Lewis Preston.[13] When he took over in 1980, at age 54, Preston
was the youngest Morgan chairman in recent times. He had directed the
bank's London operations, Morgan Guaranty Limited, which concentrated heavily on investment banking businesses, since 1966. He was responsible for transferring his expertise and vision to the United States.
As a consequence, the global investment banking strategy was then implemented, which transformed the bank in the 1980s.

An ex-Marine and a tough-minded manager, Preston was a strong
leader who did not rule without controversy. His style undoubtedly
made Morgan sharper and more aggressive as an institution, because he
did not tolerate mediocrity. He was known as a hard taskmaster who
could make underlings feel very uncomfortable. "There was a lot of turmoil on the board about him in 1980," reported a recently retired senior
banker. "He was seen as much too brash and intimidating, and by 1985,
nobody inside was willing to disagree with him on anything. He had a
whole slew of people in senior management positions who left."
Another remarked, "He is the ultimate Marine. He thinks it is easier to
knock a door down than to open it by turning the knob, and much more
fun."

One may well argue that it takes that kind of strong leader to prod
such a conservative institution as Morgan to change more quickly than
was its wont, in a new banking world that required that kind of transformation. Even people inside Morgan who did not like Preston's management style nevertheless characterized him as a visionary.

At the same time, Preston hardly acted as a "Lone Ranger." A retired senior manager explained, "Instead of being a `leader pull,' Morgan's change has been a `team push.' The changes came from the guys running the businesses, and not from the chairman."

Preston's style in selecting his successor was considered typical of how he had generally managed the bank. Several people were thought to be candidates. In the end Preston chose Dennis Weatherstone, an accomplished foreign exchange trader from England whom he had worked with and mentored for many years. As a senior manager reported:

> We had quite a scramble for succession that was finally resolved in Dennis Weatherstone's appointment. It followed Preston's management style to a T, namely, pick winners. There were several people in line, and in various ways, they were all eliminated [except] Weatherstone. One of my colleagues characterized Preston's management style in handling this as throwing pieces of clay against a wall. Those that fell were out. Those that stuck were in. There was much bitterness among people who had been slapped down unceremoniously. So Preston created a very difficult climate.

Weatherstone, who became CEO of Morgan in 1990, is very different in style and temperament from Preston.[14] British-born, and with only the equivalent of a night school or community college degree, Weatherstone started working at Morgan at the age of 15 and became an outstanding trader. He caught Preston's eye and worked closely with him in the London office before moving with him to New York in the early 1970s. His style is in many respects the antithesis of Preston's. Less austere, aloof, and tough than Preston, he has a consensus approach to decision making.

None of these qualities is necessarily a sign of weakness, though they do reflect a more low-key style than Preston's. It may be, in addition, that just as Preston's style (though perhaps without some of the sharp edges) was appropriate for its time, so is Weatherstone's style particularly relevant for the 1990s.

Morgan may now need fine tuning and orchestrating of internal differences more than it needs significant alterations in its bank's course. Weatherstone is presiding over an organization that needs a CEO with strong conflict management skills. Indeed, the future performance of Morgan will depend very much on the extent to which it can manage an increasingly specialized and diversified organization of multiple business groups in a way that adjudicates their conflicts effectively and encourages them to collaborate and link up to one another on a regular basis. The management and leadership challenge is enormous.

Future Prospects

In attempting to forecast Morgan's future, at least two things should be taken into account. One is the nature of the top management team that Preston put in place in 1990, in terms of what it reflects about the bank more generally. The second is to locate where Morgan is now, in a developmental sense, having made such a big investment in the late 1980s in a new infrastructure of people, technology, facilities, and organization to support its new merchant banking strategy.

In a precedent-shattering move that may well have larger implications, the appointment of the new top management team seems to have purposely skipped generations. With the exception of Weatherstone, the new group in the five-person corporate office is much younger than any of its predecessors. Several slightly older people were passed over. Weatherstone himself is now 60 and might therefore be defined as a transitional, though still important, leader, but the others, one of whom is likely to inherit the mantle of CEO, are in their mid-40s and early 50s.[15]

The only classical commercial banker in the group is Douglas Warner, who is only 45 years old. He is now president and chief operating officer, having moved up in the Morgan hierarchy rapidly and served most recently as head of the new corporate finance group. He is mentioned most prominently as having the best chance of succeeding Weatherstone as CEO.

The two investment banking members are Roberto Mendoza, age 46, and Kurt Viermetz, age 52. Mendoza, whom we described briefly earlier in this chapter, was appointed in 1985 to develop Morgan's global M&A business. He was so effective that Morgan has become a major player. It has passed its recent arch-rival, Bankers Trust, and is now steadily solidifying its position in relation to investment banking competitors. As of June 30, 1991, it had moved into the top 10 among M&A advisers. It was still some distance behind the leading investment banks but was gaining steadily.[16]

Viermetz, by contrast, came up through the treasury department, having developed his skills as a securities trader—for example, in foreign exchange, swaps, Eurocurrency trading, and liabilities management. He and Mendoza together constitute the two biggest segments of Morgan's investment banking thrust.

The last member of Morgan's corporate office is John Ruffle, an accounting and financial control person who is 55 years old. A former CPA at Price Waterhouse, he served as Morgan's chief financial officer (CFO) from 1980 to 1985. He now monitors the businesses that are not under the purview of Mendoza and Viermetz—private banking, financial and administrative functions, and global support services.

Like their predecessors, all five of these senior management people have been at Morgan throughout most of their careers. None has been there less than 20 years, and the three youngest—Warner, Mendoza, and Viermetz—began at Morgan at ages 21, 24, and 25, respectively. In addition, three of the five are foreign-born, reflecting Morgan's global character. They represent, in typical Morgan fashion, a balance between continuity with the best of the bank's past and a new activism and set of skills associated with its push into merchant banking.

In a developmental sense, Morgan's prospects for the 1990s seem quite positive. Since 1980, when Preston took over as CEO, the bank has embarked upon major changes in strategy and infrastructure (as described in this chapter). There were some relatively lean years of high costs and flat earnings, particularly in the late 1980s, even though Morgan had stayed away from the high-risk loans that came back to haunt its commercial banking competitors. Morgan's operating expenses increased by as much as 15 percent annually during the late 1980s, and there has been much concern within the bank about managing costs. Its aggressive downsizing strategy reflects that concern.

In the early 1990s, Morgan's infrastructure is largely in place, and the likelihood is that the bank will become both a trading power and a corporate finance power in the next several years. A recent study by Prudential Securities suggests that it has an earnings potential growth of 10 to 15 percent a year.

Morgan's many competitive strengths reflect a combination of its distinguished history and its more recent initiatives. The most significant of those strengths include its long-time client relationships (with corporations, governments, financial institutions, and individuals); its reputation for quality, professionalism, and integrity; its global presence (in terms of clients, products, people, and general mind-set); its balance sheet; its analytical depth; its consistently high-quality people; its superior technology; its collegial culture, fostering teamwork and reflected in much internal collaboration; its trading expertise and new products; its ability to combine commercial and investment banking skills; and its present triple A debt rating (the highest in the industry).

If one had to place bets on which bank is likely to emerge as a winner in banking by the year 2000, Morgan would likely be near or at the top of the list of good prospects, as it has been throughout much of its history. Because the industry is highly competitive and the external forces that will affect banks' performance are volatile, there are no certainties. Morgan may come as close as any bank can in such an uncertain world to being a player that is likely to manage well.

PART 3

The Context Revisited

PART 3

The Context Revisited

14

What Have We Learned? Winners and Losers

After analyzing the efforts of four big banks to reposition themselves in the face of radical industry changes, I may now ask what it all means. More specifically:

1. Who are the winners and losers? Who are they likely to be in the future, and why?
2. What are the winning and losing strategies and/or businesses within each bank?
3. How do these four banks compare with other money centers and with the superregionals?
4. What more general theory of effectiveness is suggested by the recent experiences both of these four banks and of others that I will discuss?

Winners and Losers

Based on financial performance data since 1980, a fairly clear pattern emerges in comparing these four banks. There are two winners, one loser, and one very mixed bag. The winners, on the basis of a series of financial indicators as well as their reputations, are Morgan and Bankers Trust. Chase is the loser. Citicorp, after an ignominious fall from leadership, may now be more inclined than it was a year or two ago to make the changes that will be needed to restore its financial health.

This is not to say that Morgan and Bankers Trust are without weaknesses, or that Chase and Citicorp lack competitive strengths. Rather, it is to characterize them in broad terms. Citicorp would not have been placed in the mixed-bag category a few years ago, and it should be emphasized that the picture at Citicorp is definitely *mixed*. In 1988, for example, a panel of 15 informed bank observers (transnational banking consultants, regulators, bank stock analysts, and journalists) selected Citicorp, along with Morgan and Bankers Trust, as among the 12 best-managed banks in the world.[1] Its performance in 1990 and 1991, however, and its outlook for the near future merit a much more negative assessment. Indeed, a recent article in *Newsday* highlighted many Citicorp weaknesses that bank analysts and financial journalists have written about quite extensively in recent years.[2] David Cates, for example, a highly regarded bank analyst and consultant, commented, "Citicorp is a weakened competitor. It doesn't have resources to compete. It doesn't have capital. It doesn't have liquidity." Comparative data from Keefe, Bruyette & Woods, a firm specializing in bank research, indicate that among the 50 largest banks, Citicorp ranks forty-first in quality of loans, forty-third in profits, and fiftieth in risk-adjusted capital. As the article concludes, "Overall, no other New York bank fares as poorly."

Turning to particular financial performance indicators, a commonly used one is the Q ratio, which compares a firm's stock price to its book value (assets minus liabilities). As data from Salomon indicate, the average Q ratio for the top 35 U.S. banks in the 1980s, with much yearly fluctuation, was just over 100%.[3] Morgan was the highest of the four over the 11 years since 1980, with 121 percent, followed by Bankers Trust with 98 percent, Citicorp with 89 percent, and Chase bringing up the rear with 64 percent.

Equally important are trends throughout this period. Excluding 1990, for which we don't yet have a full year's record, and comparing the first 5 years (1980–1984) with the last 5 (1985–1989) there is a fairly sharp pattern. While all four improved, as did the 35-bank average, Bankers Trust's and Morgan's improvements far surpassed those of Citicorp and Chase. Both of the former had begun their changeovers to merchant banking in 1980, and by the last 5 years of the decade, their changes were beginning to pay off. Thus, Bankers Trust went from 82 to 114 percent between the first 5-year period and the second and Morgan went from 94 to 116 percent. Compare these figures with Citicorp's improvement from 86 to 102 percent and with Chase's improvement from 64 to 76 percent. Since both Chase and Citicorp had particularly bad years in 1990 and 1991, while Bankers Trust and Morgan continued to do well, the differences between the two pairs will be even sharper when all the data are available.

Asset Quality

As we have indicated throughout, money center banks, in particular, have been plagued with high-risk, defaulted loans since the 1980s. As profitability in traditional wholesale lending diminished, they turned to higher-risk loans and ended up being badly burned. The worst performers were the the so-called less developed countries (LDC) loans, mainly Latin American nations; the loans in commercial real estate; and the highly leveraged transactions (HLTs) associated with mergers and acquisitions (M&A) deals. All the money centers have been hurt, some much more so than others.

Again, the same ranking among the four generally holds, with Morgan far ahead of the pack and followed by Bankers Trust, and with Citicorp and Chase trailing far behind. A commonly used measure is the ratio of nonperforming assets/total assets. In 1990, this ratio was 0.94 for Morgan, 2.53 for Bankers Trust, 3.88 for Citicorp, and 4.46 for Chase, with the latter two climbing. Morgan's conservative credit policies, which made it reluctant to follow the latest loan fads, thus served it well.

In the period 1980–1990, Morgan had by far the lowest ratio of nonperforming/total assets, with an average of 1.17 percent, followed by Bankers Trust with 1.83 percent, Citicorp with 2.36 percent, and Chase with 2.82 percent. Again, what the numbers suggest is that Morgan has always had a conservative credit policy, because it is much more circumspect than its competitors. Chase and Citicorp, meanwhile, have had a huge LDC exposure relative to the others, with Citicorp's still $7.6 billion as of December 1990 and Chase's $3.5 billion. Compare that with $1.3 billion for Morgan and $1.9 billion for Bankers Trust.[4]

The most recent blows have been in commercial real estate and HLTs. Again, the differences among the four banks are marked. In commercial real estate, for example, as of December 31, 1990, Morgan had only $1.2 billion in outstanding loans, as compared to $3.2 for Bankers Trust, $9.2 for Chase, and a whopping $13.26 for Citicorp.[5] John Reed of Citicorp publicly admitted in late 1990 that he had made a big mistake in disregarding warnings that the commercial real estate market was about to collapse. "Now I'm damn embarrassed because the critics were right and we were wrong," Reed said. "We were warned about real estate 2 years ago, we were warned again a year ago, and we pooh-poohed it."[6] While it took considerable courage and honesty (qualities that he showed throughout his career) for Reed to publicly acknowledge such a big mistake, he and his bank had nevertheless made some gross errors in judgment that will likely cost them dearly in the 1990s. For an institution that prided itself so much on its strong credit culture, as Citicorp has always done, this was quite an anomaly if not a major blunder. Morgan, in sharp contrast, had largely bypassed the commercial real estate loan fad, maintaining its asset quality as the benchmark for the money center banks.

Indeed, when we look at the problem assets (i.e., the nonperforming ones) among the banks' real estate loans, Morgan far and away outstrips all the others. Thus, 5 percent of its commercial real estate loans were nonperforming, as compared to 16 percent for Bankers Trust, 26 percent for Chase, and 26.2 percent for Citicorp.[7] These were very big blows for Chase and Citicorp, particularly on top of their LDC and HLT loans.

For Chase, the news was particularly devastating, because it was the second time around. Chase had taken bigger losses in the real estate market declines of the mid-1970s than had any other bank. It was almost as if Chase suffered from institutional amnesia, in that it failed to learn from its past mistakes. It was not alone in that regard; but, as I will discuss in greater detail below, Chase seemed to have taken big losses since the early 1970s in almost every major category of loans in which big banks were hit, which was ironic for such a centralized and bureaucratic organization.

The same patterns hold for HLTs, though with some variations. Bankers Trust suffered most, because it had pursued HLTs much more aggressively than had its competitors. Thus, 16.6 percent of its HLT loans were nonperforming, as compared to 12.8 percent of Citicorp's, 7.1 percent of Morgan's, and only 3.6 percent of Chase's.[8] Morgan still ranked favorably in comparison to the other active HLT originators, and Citicorp still did less well than most. Bankers Trust was a poor performer relative to the other players, in part because of its overzealousness in getting into HLTs. Chase had a better record than the others, contrary to its general pattern, mainly because it was a latecomer.

Rounding out the picture with regard to asset quality is the reserve coverage the banks have provided for their nonperforming assets. Again, Morgan is the runaway leader. For LDC loans, Morgan's reserve coverage is 100 percent, as compared to 78.3 percent for Bankers Trust, 45.1

percent for Chase Manhattan Bank, and only 30.9 percent for Citicorp.

The same general pattern holds for reserves on nonperforming assets other than LDC loans. Morgan had 186.4 percent in reserves and Bankers Trust had 49.9 percent, while Chase had 36.5 percent and Citicorp had 30.1 percent. This is a devastating reflection on Citicorp, though senior management argue that it simply reflects their unwillingness to be too short-term-focused, lest they jeopardize the bank's ability to generate future revenues.

Two other commonly used measures of financial performance are return on equity (ROE) and return on assets (ROA). The first, ROE, is a measure of a company's profitability. It is often used as a benchmark, reflecting the positive working of financial leverage in using debt (i.e., stockholders' equity) to enhance revenue generating. It may vary widely from year to year, depending on such nonrecurring events as the setting aside of massive reserves for nonperforming LDC loans, which took place for all four banks in 1987, or the selling off of particular businesses or facilities.

An 11-year average shows, once again, the same pattern as for most of the other indicators. Morgan and Bankers Trust are the leaders, with Citicorp and Chase falling well behind. Bankers Trust was the highest, with 12.19 percent, followed by Morgan with 11.86 percent, Citicorp with 10.26 percent, and Chase with a dismal 6.69 percent. Chase generally had a lackluster profitability record throughout the 1980s, while at the upper end, Morgan was consistently strong. Bankers Trust had a more volatile income experience, because of its heavy involvement in securities trading and leveraged loans. It had enough outstanding years, however, to come out on top.

In terms of ROA, the ratio of net income/average assets, Morgan scores the highest for the 10-year period, with 0.64 percent, followed by Bankers Trust with 0.49 percent, Citicorp with 0.43 percent, and Chase with 0.36 percent. Again, if 1990 and 1991 were included, the differences would be even greater. Bankers Trust would have gone up a lot, and Citicorp would have been lower.

Why There Are Winners and Losers

What are these numbers telling us? One obvious answer is that the aggressive financial supermarket strategy that Citicorp adopted under Walter Wriston and that Chase also followed in a more reactive way is increasingly untenable in the highly competitive financial services industry of the 1990s. In an admittedly self-serving statement, Charles Sanford, chief executive officer (CEO) at Bankers Trust, nevertheless may have had it right when he observed, "To be in the top ten, every one will have to be a niche player. If we continue to get the right people and maintain our focus, we'll get there. Ours is not a business where conglomerates can work."[9]

One might argue, in defending Citicorp and Chase, that the problem isn't so much the supermarket strategy, since it allows for a diversification of risk, but its implementation. While this position may be defensible, both banks have had many years in which to work out whatever difficulties they faced. They have failed to do so. Consequently, their main strategic priority for the early 1990s will be to determine which businesses they should sell off. The point is that *strategic focus* is critical for survival in the increasingly competitive environment of financial services. There are simply too many specialized competitors, some with extraordinary capabilities, to enable a firm to excel in several fields.

Citicorp and Chase learned this only the hard way, in the late 1980s and early 1990s, and their financial performance indicated how slow they were to catch on. Each pursued the supermarket strategy with its own distinct style. For Citicorp the approach was, as I indicated, an aggressive, entrepreneurial, "cutting-edge" strategy, as a prospector firm. It was epitomized in Walter Wriston's "five I's," in which Citicorp was to be a power in institutional, investment, individual banking, insurance, and information businesses. Variously referred to as *the bank with the boardinghouse reach* and *the pentagon of commercial banks*, it was unable to maintain consistent profitability, largely because it lost so much money on so many ill-timed, poorly managed acquisitions and new ventures. It was one thing to have a high tolerance for mistakes, which Wriston had made a central feature of the Citicorp culture. It was quite another to get into so many new businesses that were such losers and stay with them for so long, for example, Quotron in the information business, AMBAC in insurance, several ailing savings and loans (S&Ls), and Scrimmegour Vickers, the British brokerage house.

The question is, why did it happen? The failures basically reflect the bank's leadership and culture. Both Wriston and Reed allowed it to happen. A combination of pursuit of an aggressive growth strategy (part of Citicorp's entrepreneurial bent) and institutional arrogance (its seeming assumption that it had a God-given ability to turn around and manage many new financial service businesses) undoubtedly contributed. The bank's arrogance took the form of ignoring criticism from numerous bank analysts and consultants, and of refusing to interpret negative feedback from the marketplace as indicative of the need to exit from poorly performing businesses. Instead, it managed some of these businesses by endlessly reorganizing and reshuffling personnel. These measures contributed to even worse results. Citicorp's dramatic success in consumer banking, from which it kept extrapolating, became a model for inappropriate later expansion efforts.

Chase in the 1980s was in many respects a toned-down version of Citicorp, and its results were even more negative. Its performance in 1991, however, suggests more positive prospects for the immediate future. While Citicorp's strategy could be characterized as "Me, first," Chase's was "Me, too." Citicorp was usually a first mover and Chase a follower—not in every respect but in most major ones. The results in Chase's case provide further confirmation of the limits of the supermarket strategy.

Moreover, Chase faced more serious problems of strategic identity than did Citicorp, precisely because it so often seemed to be bringing up the rear and lurching in so many different directions.

The pictures at Morgan and Bankers Trust present a sharp contrast. During a period of about 10 years, some of which was understandably painful, both banks made what management writers call *frame-breaking* changes. Faced with a big drop in the corporate loan business, a jolt common to all the money centers, these two, perhaps more than any of their U.S. competitors, redirected their resources to concentrate heavily on investment banking-related businesses—mainly those associated with corporate finance and securities trading. Both made the move to so-called merchant banking, in which they became financial engineers (advisers) and securities traders for their corporate clients, besides providing them with leveraged loans. They essentially followed their clients to the capital markets in the 1980s and radically transformed themselves as institutions. In addition, they not only changed their strategies—developing new securities-related products and increasing their activities as traders—but also developed an entirely new infrastructure (e.g., culture, organization, people, compensation practices, technology, and dominant coalitions). Both became more focused, concentrating on wholesale banking, and did not presume to compete in consumer banking, insurance, and the information business as Citicorp had done.

Toward a Theory of Bank Effectiveness

Further insights into the dynamics of these four banks and the larger implications of their efforts at repositioning come from an application of Raymond Miles and Charles Snow's models of strategic types, which we discussed briefly in Chapter 2. The four banks analyzed in this book constitute classic cases of Miles and Snow's types. Citicorp and Bankers Trust are clear examples of *prospector* firms, because of the aggressive style in which they develop innovative products and make the first move into various product markets. Morgan, which has a much more conservative approach to strategic and organizational change, has been a prototype of the *analyzer* firm, certainly moving ahead in new products and markets (relative to its past business) but maintaining much continuity as well and preferring to let another bank be first. Finally, Chase epitomizes the *reactor* firm in its lack of strategic identity throughout much of the 1970s and 1980s, in its follower style, and in its tendency to lurch from one set of strategies to another.

In addition to giving these banks labels, the model highlights some of the internal contradictions and weaknesses of the four. Miles and Snow suggest that, although the entrepreneurial, prospector style enhances adaptation to a changing environment, it also runs the risk of low profitability and an overextension of capital. More generally, while organizations that pursue this style are quite flexible, they sacrifice efficiency by misusing resources in their attempt to respond opportunistically to market changes. This was precisely the experience of Citicorp as it bought businesses in new fields that it did not understand well enough to turn around. Citicorp's financial performance suffered as a result, leading one bank analyst to refer to its shares as the *perpetual mañana stock*. Bankers Trust faced the same potential problem, but its agility and willingness to exit quickly from businesses whose spreads had declined put it in a much better capital position than Citicorp.

A critical issue that Morgan faces as an analyzer firm is how to maintain an optimal balance between *continuity* of traditional products and customers and *flexibility* in pursuit of new product and market opportunities. This delicate balance is difficult to maintain. Morgan has historically followed a conservative strategy, innovating only in imitation of demonstrably successful products, and has rarely been a first mover. In recent years, however, it has placed increasing emphasis upon becoming more aggressive, because the product markets it has moved into are so competitive. Some staff members say that Morgan has become more like Citicorp in this regard.

Finally, Chase has suffered from all the problems that Miles and Snow highlight for *reactor* firms, namely, a weakly articulated strategy, a structure improperly linked to strategy, and adherence at times to an outmoded strategy and structure. During much of the 1970s and early 1980s, for example, Chase moved in many different directions without a clear focus. It also maintained a hierarchical, bureaucratic structure and remained internally fragmented, when its new capital markets and corporate finance products needed a much more lateral and integrated organization. In addition, it was generally slower in reacting to market changes than were its competitors.

How is it that organizations like Citicorp and Chase continue on particular trajectories long after they become nonfunctional? Inertia takes many forms. Several management writers argue, however, that despite their differences, all organizations maintain their traditional styles until something earthshaking causes them to change. There is an organizational momentum, a process of evolution that is punctuated by extreme jolts from the outside, forcing organizations to make revolutionary changes. The four banks that are the focus of this book can be analyzed from that perspective.

Citicorp: Aggressive Expansion Run Wild

Danny Miller, a leading management scholar, has coined the term *the Icarus paradox*. He uses it in a remarkable recent book by that name to describe a process that Citicorp personifies. In the parable which is the source of the term, Icarus is the son of the mythic ancient Greek inventor Daedalus. Wearing wings his father had fabricated, he flew so close to the sun that it melted the wax that held the wings on. Icarus plunged to his death in the Aegean Sea.[10] The moral is that great assets and the success that they bring may ultimately lead to failure. Effective strategies may be pushed too far, and this fault may well be a big part of the story of Citicorp.

Citicorp typifies a type of organization that Miller calls the *builder* firm. This type is perhaps best characterized as a diversified megaconglomerate whose strategy of expansion by acquisitions becomes an all-consuming way of life. Miller cites ITT as an example. In financial services, the type would include American Express and Merrill Lynch, both of which Walter Wriston cited as models for Citicorp.

The competitive strength of this type of organization, in Miller's portrait, is the entrepreneurial capabilities of its leaders, who tend to be very aggressive personalities with ambitious goals. As a high-intensity meritocracy attracting talented people, this type of organization has growth and expansion as its principal goal. Sometimes wildly adventuresome, it becomes a leading firm in its industry in moving into new products and markets. This strategy is, in turn, driven by a culture that emphasizes optimism; arrogance; a sense of invulnerability; a neglect of details; a pressure-cooker climate; a sink-or-swim mentality; and either chaos or a bloated, overloaded bureaucracy to maintain bottom-line controls. The consequences are careless expansion, in which the organization bites off more than it can chew. In short, growth becomes a cancer that eventually destroys the organization.

Few institutions better more epitomize this style that Miller so vividly articulates than Citicorp. The initiative came from chief executive officers (CEOs) George Moore and Walter Wriston, who recruited talented bankers and encouraged them to develop new businesses. Citicorp grew from a $16 billion bank in 1967 to a $230 billion financial services conglomerate in 1990. The characteristics that led to meteoric success contributed in the late 1980s and early 1990s to a rapid fall.

For Citicorp to recover in the 1990s, a radical change in its expansionist style and strategy will be required. It will have to sell off nonperforming businesses more rapidly and focus more sharply on a few core businesses. It will have to emphasize, more than ever before, internal collaboration, consolidation, and stronger controls, to regain its position as a leading global bank. Certainly, the consumer bank, which now generates close to 70 percent of Citicorp's total revenues, will be one main focus, as will selected aspects of its wholesale banking: foreign exchange, risk-management products, and syndicated loans. The financial supermarket, conglomerate strategy will have to be abandoned, at least for the present, as an unrealistic goal.

Chase: The Stagnant Bureaucracy Now Awakening

Chase's predicament is explained by a different negative model. Chase pursued the same conglomerate strategy as did Citicorp, though on a smaller scale and in a much more risk-averse manner, largely because of its many past successes and its elite character.

Chase was lulled to sleep by its many successes in the relatively placid, simple, and noncompetitive world of banking of the 1950s, only to awake in fits and starts in more recent years. Indeed, a major report on Chase, published in October 1989 by Salomon, is entitled *Will the Sleeping Giant Arise?* Chase's troubles began when its competitive environment became much more intense and when it was very slow in responding. Organizational change analysts Miller and Friesen describe what they call the *stagnant bureaucracy* as one archetype of the unsuccessful firm. Their description does not correspond in every respect to Chase, but there is enough similarity to make it a relevant model for understanding how and why Chase was so slow in adapting.[11] Miller and

Friesen characterize the stagnant bureaucracy as follows:

1. The firm was well positioned in stable, uncompetitive markets during its early years, often holding a very substantial market share.

2. It was quite centralized and bureaucratic.

3. It wrote off any environmental changes as anomalies that would quickly pass, allowing the firm eventually to succeed once more with its traditional approach.

4. There was much conflict between older, upper-level and younger, lower-level managers about how to interpret market changes and how the firm should adapt to them.

5. The firm consequently had poor information on such changes, a strong bias against innovation, and a lack of up-to-date product mix.

6. It had poorer internal communications than did other types of firms.

A critical point about all these characteristics is how enduring and resistant they were to several senior management initiatives to change them. Thus, in early 1976, after 5 dismal years during which Chase profits plunged significantly, prompting some financial journalists to urge David Rockefeller to resign, he embarked upon a series of reform efforts that dramatically reversed the bank's decline. Contrary to Chase tradition, he brought in three midcareer managers and appointed them to critical senior staff positions—in human resources, strategic planning, and corporate communications—in an effort to shake up the bank. Unfortunately, these appointments, alone, were not a strong enough force to break the old culture.

A further example of the strength of Chase's traditional culture was what happened at a critical potential turning point for the bank: the decision in 1979 about Rockefeller's successor. Some members of the board were said to want an outsider who would reinforce and accelerate the many improvements that Rockefeller had initiated in the late 1970s. These improvements had begun to revitalize Chase as an institution and to increase its financial performance dramatically. Rockefeller's choice was an insider, Willard Butcher, whom he credited with effectively implementing the improvements. He chose continuity, seeing Butcher as most likely to carry on with the reforms that were already well under way.

In sum, Chase, like many organizations, continued to plod along a well-worn and unsuccessful path. Just as Citicorp's inertia revolved around its central theme of aggressive expansion, Chase's was centered on its theme of risk aversion and conservatism. Unlike Citicorp, Chase had tried many times to break out of its old configuration, but to little avail. Its efforts to innovate allowed for only incremental changes, at best.

Management writers argue that only earthshaking events will interrupt this process at Chase and lead to more revolutionary changes. If so, perhaps we are on the verge of such a time in 1991, when U.S. banks have lost their competitive edge globally and when Chase is struggling to just survive.

Bankers Trust: Entrepreneurial Revitalization

Bankers Trust resembles in many respects what Miller and Friesen refer to as the *adaptive organization in a very challenging environment*.[12] It changed from a mediocre, all-purpose commercial bank into a highly focused, global merchant bank, concentrating on fee-based corporate finance and securities trading. It transformed its infrastructure to support this new investment banking strategy. More specifically, it developed a culture that emphasizes transactions, entrepreneurship, and innovation; a reward system that compensates investment bankers with bonuses that are competitive with those given on Wall Street; and a flat, decentralized, and highly flexible and agile organization. All these internal changes fit both the new strategy and the new, volatile investment banking markets into which Bankers Trust had moved.

By the late 1980s and early 1990s, Bankers Trust had not only become one of the highest-performing U.S. banks and gained an increasingly positive reputation, but it had also become more and more like an investment bank. That was certainly the case with regard to its product mix; culture; reward system; and structure, which, as mentioned above, had become very flat, decentralized, antibureaucratic, and collaborative.

Some organizations are able to overcome their inertia and make the revolutionary changes required in times of rapid change and competitive threat. Bankers Trust is one of those and is likely, by dint of its present style, to become one of the high performers of the 1990s. Sanford's controlling and abrasive management style may not be conducive to strong institutional loyalty, but the bank's culture is in most respects compatible with success in global merchant banking.

This alignment presents a classic example of an organization's move to a strategy and structure that will match the newly volatile and competitive industry. As students of organizations have noted, the form that best fits this kind of setting is a highly flexible, adaptive, entrepreneurial firm. It emphasizes opportunism, innovation, and the ability to move in and out of various markets as competition and spreads shift. Bankers Trust epitomizes such an organization.

Morgan: Adaptive in a More Deliberate and Balanced Way

Some institutions seem always to remain at the top of their fields, in terms of quality and professionalism, and Morgan is one of these. It faced the same threatening changes as its competitors—mainly, the decline of the corporate loan business—and it did what one would expect Morgan to do: it adapted. The adaptation wasn't easy, since Morgan had a strong corporate culture. This culture had contributed to its past successes but was incompatible in some respects with a new merchant banking strategy and would have to be changed quite radically. Lifetime employment and slow-paced decision making are cases in point.

Factors that contributed to the success of Morgan's turnaround included:

1. An explicit acknowledgment that banking had changed to such a degree that a transformation had to be made.
2. Extensive analysis and planning, prior to making any changes.
3. An attempt to make the changes while preserving as much as possible of the old culture. The maintenance of long-term relations with corporate customers was included, and home-grown insiders led the way.
4. A tremendous investment in technology and new buildings, both in New York and London, to support the new trading and corporate finance businesses.
5. Corresponding, though gradual, changes in compensation, in organization, and in personnel (i.e., more outsiders were hired), to further support the change in strategy.
6. A strong emphasis on downsizing and expense control, and a reduction of the central bureaucracy, which enabled Morgan to compete with investment banks.

In brief, the bank did make a revolutionary change in strategy and infrastructure, and it made the change in a manner typical of Morgan. At any given time during the 1980s, the change seemed imperceptible, particularly because it was being led by home-grown, long-term, Morgan managers and because some of the most functional aspects of the old culture were being maintained. When the decade was over, however, it was clear that the bank had changed radically.

15

Some Other Winners and Losers

Further insights into bank effectiveness may be obtained by reviewing the records of other banks during the 1980s, and particularly the banks at the extremes: the striking successes and the abysmal failures. I begin with another money center institution, BankAmerica, which was at both ends of the continuum. Its steep decline from 1985 to 1988 was followed by a dramatic turnaround, which culminated in the announcement of a historic merger with Security Pacific in August 1991. Next, I analyze several superregionals that have also been successful, particularly Banc One in the Midwest, Wells Fargo on the West Coast, First Fidelity Bancorp in New Jersey, First Wachovia in the Southeast, and State Street Bank of Boston. I also look at some well-managed mergers in which these banks were involved. I extrapolate from all these cases, including the four New York banks, to develop analytical insights into bank effectiveness. Because of the brisk pace at which mergers are occurring, and because of the importance of mergers in banks' attempts to maneuver for market position in the industry, management of mergers will be a principal determinant of bank effectiveness.

BankAmerica: Up From the Ashes

BankAmerica is a classic case that highlights many lessons from the New York banks' experiences.[1] Its experience in the mid-1980s, particularly under the leadership of Sam Armacost, former head of the World Bank, was one of precipitous decline. The stage was set by Armacost's predecessor, Tom Clausen, whose corporate loan and global expansion decisions were disastrous. From 1985 to 1987, the bank lost $1.8 billion "because of bloated expenses and bad loans to developing nations and to companies in energy, agriculture and real estate,"[2] and it was almost taken over by First Interstate. Citicorp, which had been BankAmerica's East Coast rival for many decades, was also rumored to be casting an acquisitive eye toward it. However, BankAmerica earned more than $1 billion in 1989 and 1990, making it among the nation's healthiest banks. Indeed, this became one of the more celebrated bank turnarounds of the 1980s. It is particularly noteworthy because many money centers fared so poorly in those years.

The contrast in performance between BankAmerica and Citicorp in 1990 is stark. It is also important, since these two banks are now major competitors in the escalating race to create truly national banks. Consider the following: BankAmerica had $1.1 billion in net income in 1990, as compared to $458 million for Citicorp. It fared better in return on assets (ROA) (1.04 percent as compared to 0.20 percent), in return on equity (ROE) (20 percent as compared to 3.75 percent), in equity as a percentage of total assets (5.24 percent as compared to 3.77 percent), in overhead as a percentage of net revenues (62.29 percent as compared to 73.88 percent), and in nonperforming assets as a percentage of total assets (3.04 percent as compared to 4.81 percent).[3]

It can be argued that there is not much to be learned by extrapolating from 1990, a seemingly unrepresentative year for both banks, in which Citicorp suffered unusual losses and BankAmerica reaped spectacular profits. However, I believe that the numbers for that year may well reflect a culmination of a trend for Citicorp and a new strategic initiative for BankAmerica that seems likely to continue.

The strategies that got BankAmerica into its mess in the mid-1980s and that then led to its recovery are by now quite familiar. The poor management that drove the decline involved aggressive international expansion without much strategic analysis, with poor communication back to headquarters from global outposts, and with few credit controls. Meanwhile, the bank was building up enormous overhead costs, and bad loans had proliferated in several depressed industries (energy, agriculture, and real estate) as well as in developing countries. Sam Armacost, BankAmerica's chief executive officer (CEO) from 1981 to 1986, refused to acknowledge to the board that the bank had deep-rooted problems that were not about to go away without major reforms.[4] Armacost was not the source of many of the problems, but his failure to deal aggressively with them led the board to fire him.

The turnaround involved a tremendous retrenchment from the international business, which meant closing down and/or consolidating many branches around the world, as well as developing a strategic focus on and identification with consumer banking in California. For BankAmerica, as for many money center banks, it was not at all clear just where the franchise was, so diversified (in products, customers, and geographic markets) had the bank become.

The consumer banking strategy that became the centerpiece for the turnaround, with strong retail deposits beginning to function as an annuity-style income, had several components and stages. It started with a concentration on the West Coast. The bank developed a retail network in California and Washington and spread it to six other western states. Also involved was much back-office modernization in 20 regional centers, where newly streamlined systems created many economies of scale. Richard Rosenberg was the highly skilled leader of the turnaround. Clausen recruited Rosenberg in 1987 to take over the bank's retail division, with the understanding that he might well become CEO, if he did a good job. Rosenberg had the reputation of being banking's "best mass marketer."[5] He had been in the industry for nearly 30 years at Wells Fargo and at Crocker Bank, and as president of Seafirst in Seattle, Washington. The fit between such a skilled and proven marketer and BankAmerica's huge retail branch system was so good that Rosenberg more than proved his worth and did in fact become CEO in 1990.

His retail banking strategy involved strengthening the bank's position in the West by buying troubled savings and loans (S&Ls) and other banks and by implementing aggressive merchandising initiatives at the branches. These initiatives included calling on customers to ask what they needed, providing a bundle of services at each branch, giving bonuses to branch managers and employees for performance, and developing many other marketing gimmicks (such as free checking accounts or airline tickets for customers who came into a branch on a particular day).

Rosenberg and his colleagues had a larger vision: national banking. Judging from the early results, BankAmerica is moving strongly in that direction. Though it lost out in a bid for Bank of New England, its recent merger with Security Pacific (which results in combined assets of $190 billion), bodes well for its chances of becoming a major force as a national consumer bank. Though just behind Citicorp in total assets, it's ahead in domestic assets. Its consumer bank has been growing rapidly while the big New York banks have been preoccupied with problem real estate loans.[6]

Besides developing this national consumer banking strategy, re-trenching from international operations, and thereby achieving much more focus, Rosenberg has been dealing with many internal tasks, including abandoning the culture of paternalism toward employees, which goes back many decades. Such a culture is obviously incompatible with the aggressive retrenchment from global and corporate banking and the new performance goals. Another task has been to develop a strong emphasis on marketing and merchandising, along with an equally strong emphasis on controls and performance measurement. He has had to instill in the sales force a sense of pride about the company, its leadership, its organization, and its products. After the mid-1980s, many salespeople were "so shell shocked by the bank's problems that they didn't like to admit that they worked there, let alone ask for business."[7] In addition, Rosenberg will need the ability to manage mergers skillfully. He seems to have made a good start in this area by merging with Security Pacific.

In brief, BankAmerica has become another bellwether case, in that it illustrates many larger, generic issues that will face U.S. banks in the 1990s. It serves as a further illustration of my conclusions about the four New York banks. Again, aggressive growth in diverse areas of financial services is no longer viable. There are so many imponderables and so many strong competitors that an aggressive growth strategy is unworkable. Instead, strategic focus is critical. Consumer banking offers a particularly attractive franchise in this regard, with potentially long-lasting sources of funding that could help to bail out some of the big banks. National consumer banking, run on a low-cost basis, with centralized back-office and product and systems development, accompanied by decentralized service delivery in local branches, is one future strategy that may well prove successful.

BankAmerica has already passed through the stage that Citicorp is now in. It has moved ahead with the kinds of difficult retrenchment and divestment decisions that Citicorp has been slower to make. Ironically, as a result of BankAmerica's very bad years in the mid-1980s, it was spared many of the real estate, leveraged buyout (LBO), and junk bond financing binges that beset its eastern money center competitors. It was fortunate in that it didn't have the capital to become involved. In sum, the near-disaster of the 1980s is in large part responsible for BankAmerica's present strength.

There are certainly problems ahead for BankAmerica. The future California economy will probably present difficulties, because personal bankruptcies and mortgage delinquencies are likely to rise. Tax deductions for the years of big losses are now running out. Competition from other money centers and merged superregionals will probably heat up a lot. Nevertheless, a strong senior management group under Rosenberg's leadership should make BankAmerica one of the major players, at least in U.S. banking, for many years to come. In that respect, it may finally realize the most cherished goal of its founder, Amedeo Giannini, who wanted it to become a leading national bank.

Banc One: A New Superstar

The superstars among the money centers include Morgan, Bankers Trust, and perhaps, once again, BankAmerica. The other stars are the superregionals, U.S. banking's new elite, which account for a disproportionate number of winners in the Darwinian winnowing process now under way. Several banks from this group have emerged as leading performers in U.S. banking, and they deserve brief mention. Particularly prominent is Banc One of Columbus, Ohio, which surpassed Citicorp in early 1991 in market capitalization and was itself surpassed only by Morgan and BankAmerica.[8] Pursuing a strategy of growth through careful acquisition, Banc One began expanding at a meteoric rate in the late 1980s under the leadership of CEO John B. McCoy, who succeeded his father in 1984. By 1991, it was six times larger than when the younger McCoy took over. Variously referred to as "the best retail bank in America"[9] and "the best little bank in America,"[10] Banc One had a 1.53 percent return on assets in 1990 that was the highest by far of the country's 50 largest banks. As of July 1991, it was the nation's twenty-second largest bank, with more than $40 billion in assets.

Banc One's strategy is a variation on those of several high-performing superregionals. It more narrowly defines market niches than do the traditionally diversified money centers, focusing on middle-market lending and consumer banking. Avoiding the trendy fields that were so damaging to its money center competitors—loans to less developed countries (LDC), LBOs, and commercial real estate—it has moved instead into new markets in retail banking.

The bank's strategy is a combination of conservative lending, innovative technology, dedicated customer service, and mergers with other banks. Banc One has moved beyond its Ohio base, building up branch networks in Indiana, Illinois, Michigan, Kentucky, Wisconsin, and Texas, all through acquisitions.[11] As of July 1991, it had 858 branches in seven states. Banc One has a formula that has contributed to its extraordinary ability to successfully absorb a steady stream of acquired banks. This formula includes never merging with a peer, not buying a bank more than one-third its size, leaving in place the existing management of any bank it acquires, and allowing each bank to make its own decisions in a decentralized structure. "The power is where the money is made—at the banks, not at headquarters," said John Russell, a corporate vice president.[12] Banc One does impose common products, technology, and monthly report requirements, through consolidated back-office functions. Its management reporting system is regarded as one of the best in the industry and is often used to facilitate comparisons across branches and to improve profitability by sharing tips on what works at different sites. A critical feature of Banc One's success is its incentive compensation program for senior managers as a way to push for earnings growth.

Two other key aspects of the bank's successful strategy are, first, its sophisticated technology and, second, the attractive physical facilities and broad array of products offered at the branches. The technology includes, for example, in addition to the reporting system, a master file on customers that provides information on the products they are most likely to buy, based on age and income. Many of the branches have attractive decors, including glass atria and boutique-style service areas which correspond to particular product offerings and are set off by partitions and glass. The branches are open long hours, seven days a week.

While the money centers are struggling to improve their capitalization, Banc One is cash-rich. It is considering expansion into other regions, perhaps even the East Coast or the West Coast. Wherever it goes, it has a formula, a culture, a structure, systems, and an effective senior management group that bear close examination as a model for success. It is likely to continue along its successful course in the 1990s, solidifying its position as a formidable player in U.S. banking.

Wells Fargo: Another West Coast Success

Wells Fargo has emerged as yet another contender, by implementing its own version of how to succeed in the highly competitive and hostile environment that banks now face. Though it is not without weaknesses, Wells Fargo has nevertheless become another success story in the U.S. banking industry. It is unique in that it has combined a strategy focused on consumer banking with a merger with Crocker Bank (completed in 1986) that almost doubled its size. Under the leadership of Carl Reichardt, a Texan who has been variously described as a "bare knuckled cost cutter"[13] and (by a colleague) "a sort of sawn-off John Wayne,"[14]

Wells Fargo has relentlessly pursued a strategy that includes exercising vigorous expense control, offering basic consumer banking for retail clients and middle-market companies, and building a reputation as the best consumer bank in California. In pursuit of this reputation, it opened a full-service brokerage business in December 1988—the first California bank to do so. It has also offered advice to affluent clients on their investments.

The merger with Crocker is one of the best-managed mergers in the banking industry to date. One consultant characterized it as "the textbook case of how to do a bank acquisition."[15] Not only did the merger nearly double Wells Fargo's size with virtually no additional risk, thus significantly strengthening its presence in California, but also apparently few customers were lost in the process. Heartened by this success, Wells has been looking for more merger partners.

Though many big banks saddled themselves in the 1980s with bad loans, inefficient operations, and unproductive diversification, Wells Fargo limited its exposure on all three counts. The First Manhattan Consulting Group cited it in a statistical study as being among 13 expense control champions.[16]

Reichardt's obsession with cost control has had a lot to do with this record. A financial journalist has noted, "Even among bare-knuckled cost cutters, Wells Fargo's Carl Reichardt is a standout. He bans office plants and Christmas trees, contending [that] their care and feeding [distract] staffers from beating up on competitors like Security Pacific or First Interstate."[17] After the merger with Crocker, Reichardt pruned Crocker's head count from 26,000 to 20,230, having already cut 3000 from Wells Fargo's own staff before then.[18]

Other initiatives that have contributed to the bank's success have been a consolidation of back-office operations to support the increased size resulting from the merger, a risk review methodology that provides close controls over loans, and a generous compensation program. Wells Fargo salaries have tended to average 24 percent higher than those paid by major California banks, and some of its branch managers earn bonuses of $50,000 or more for bringing in new business.

In brief, Wells Fargo maintained its strength and profitability even while continuing to grow at a rapid pace. It did this by staying focused on retail banking and the middle market, by emphasizing productivity and cost cutting, by offering a generous compensation program to attract and retain talented bankers, and by being successful in implementing a major merger with a large competitor. It was left with a strong market position and good prospects for the future.

Wells Fargo experienced a major disappointment when Security Pacific turned down its proposal for a merger but accepted a proposal with BankAmerica. One reported reason for the rejection was the stronger compatibility between CEOs Robert Smith of Security Pacific and Richard Rosenberg of BankAmerica than between Smith and Carl Reichardt of Wells Fargo. Smith reported to the press that he and Rosenberg enjoyed each others' personal styles, noting that they both ran "collegial" operations. "Both of them have a style which is to delegate to subordinates and hold them accountable for their performance, very much a coaching way of management," reported Donald McNees, a financial services consultant at Cresap in New York, who has worked with each.[19] The implication was that Smith didn't want to get involved with Reichardt in a merger because of his more authoritarian and hard-nosed style.

This leaves Wells Fargo with the option of pursuing a merger with First Interstate Bancorp, one of the few remaining big West Coast banks. This merger seems likely to occur in the early 1990s, as the BankAmerica/Security Pacific merger moves forward. Without a union with First Interstate, Wells Fargo might have difficulty in competing with the new West Coast giants.

First Fidelity: Turnaround in New Jersey

A few other success stories that are consistent and show a clear pattern will round out the pattern I am presenting. The story of First Fidelity Bancorp of New Jersey, one of the 25 biggest banks in the country, is that of a remarkably quick recovery by a foundering institution. The key to the recovery was First Fidelity's new CEO, Anthony Terracciano, who took over the job in February 1990. In 18 months he made significant improvements in the bank's profits and stock price. A veteran of more than 20 years at Chase, during which he rose to vice chairman and became a candidate for the CEO slot, Terracciano moved to Mellon Bank in 1987 as president under CEO Frank Cahouet. He helped to engineer a turnaround at Mellon over a 2½-year period, cutting expenses through massive layoffs, consolidation of computer operations, and increases in reserves.[20]

When he was appointed CEO at First Fidelity, Terracciano applied some of the same methods there. He weeded out unnecessary operations, pared costs and payrolls, and developed a strategic focus around a potentially lucrative niche in small-business and consumer lending.[21] Expenses dropped from $248 million in the first quarter of 1990 to $214 million the second quarter of 1991, mostly due to layoffs. The number of full-time employees decreased from 14,176 to 11,860 during that time. This, in turn, boosted profits from $21 million to $52 million and pushed the stock price from $20.375 to $31.75 (the price had dropped, however, to $12.34 during the third quarter of 1990). In addition, the bank brought in Electronic Data Systems Corporation to manage its inefficient computer center.

It is reported that one of Terracciano's ultimate goals is "to be a player when the consolidation of the industry accelerates." If so, he has already made a good beginning. In March 1991, Banco Santander, a large Spanish bank, agreed to acquire 13 percent of First Fidelity for $220 million and took an option to buy 11 percent more. This extraordinary show of confidence boosted First Fidelity's strength at a time when many of its competitors were starving for capital. Most important, the bank has acquired $4 billion in deposits in 116 branches in central and southern New Jersey, adding significantly to its capital base.

In brief, the turnaround strategy that Terracciano used at First Fidelity is one that may well be useful at many other banks around the country. He has quickly reversed the decline of a big bank in a way that may be taken as a model for success. A very intense, impatient man, with a strong sense of urgency, always seemingly concerned about doing things quickly, Terracciano sets very high performance standards for his employees and expects that they will be met as a matter of course. As he explains, "If you worked for me, I'd drive you nuts until you were performing at the level I was convinced you were capable of."

First Wachovia: Solid Superregional

Turning to a region, the Southeast, which has developed several high-performing superregionals, I have chosen to present one of the best of them, First Wachovia of Winston-Salem, North Carolina, as a further model for success. A key to First Wachovia's success has been its exemplary record in avoiding bad loans.[22] When many of its competitors were expanding their commercial real estate lending and their financing of corporate takeovers, First Wachovia refused to become part of the herd. Instead, by pursuing its traditional consumer banking and middle-market loan businesses, it achieved reliable if unspectacular spreads. To supplement these businesses, it invested heavily in cash management products that brought in large corporate customers who might not otherwise have done business with a bank that ranked only twenty-ninth in the country.

First Wachovia's competitive strengths are in the businesses already mentioned and in other fee-producing businesses: the servicing of student loans and credit card fees; enormously diversified consumer products; a computerized, high-tech approach to consumer banking; and an excellent reputation for financial strength. Thus, in late 1990, it had more than twice as much shareholder capital as the minimum set by federal regulators. At present, the bank is considering a big merger with another southeastern bank. Under the circumspect but visionary leadership of its CEO, John Medlin, it has become a leading regional, surpassing in performance such other regionals as North Carolina National Bank (NCNB).

State Street Boston: High Tech in New England

My final success story is that of an often-cited New England bank, State Street Boston Corporation. This institution has prospered at a time of severe economic downturn in its region, when such competitors as Bank of New England, Bank of Boston, and Shawmut Bank were suffering severe losses. A key to its success has been its strategic focus on the technology-driven custodial, trust, and information businesses. It has emerged in recent years as the nation's largest custodian and trustee for mutual funds and pension funds. Thus, fiduciary fees accounted for more than two-thirds of total revenues in 1990, limiting its dependence on the lending business. The bank has been developing a broader array of products in global trust and custody businesses as a top priority, even while much larger banks are also competing for the business.

As a result of this competitive strength, which CEO William S. Edgerly actively developed over a long period of time, State Street Boston was not as vulnerable to local economic declines as were its competitors. It could therefore keep increasing its profits and expanding its businesses when other banks were cutting back. State Street Boston has several big-bank competitors who also seek promising annuitylike incomes in trust and custodial businesses. However, because State Street Boston has focused on these fields while the highly diversified bigger banks have spread themselves thin, it is able to maintain its edge. This is a dramatic illustration of the benefits of maintaining a focus on specific lines of business.

State Street Boston has not completely avoided the loan defaults associated with the New England economy's turndown, but limiting loans to only 18 percent of assets, as compared to 60 percent at other banks, has kept the problem under control.

Because of past legislative constraints on geographic expansion to other regions, banks like State Street Boston and its counterparts in Texas, which had previously faced similar downturns, were very vulnerable. Their decline wasn't inevitable, however, as this case makes clear.

Some Perspectives on Bank Effectiveness

I now return to the central questions of this investigation, which were discussed at the end of Chapter 1: How important is management in determining success? If management is important, what are winning and losing strategies? And how do winning strategies best get implemented?

It is now possible to begin providing some answers. Management really does matter, and State Street Boston is a good case in point. Had Edgerly not developed the bank's expertise in custodial and trust businesses, had he focused instead on lending, and had he concentrated in the late 1980s on commercial real estate and LBOs (as did others in the region, such as Bank of New England) the bank would have been wiped out. Whether by genuine foresight or by luck, State Street Boston did not succumb to the herd instinct and did not follow in the footsteps of so many of its regional competitors. It thereby avoided disaster.

As to whether senior management initiatives or external jolts and pressures count more heavily, it should be clear that there is no categorical answer. Both do count, and both count heavily. Thus, a series of external forces impinging on all banks, particularly the bigger, more globally oriented ones, has significantly affected their opportunities. For the big banks, factors that have had an enormous impact include the decline of the corporate lending business, disintermediation, increasing competition, new electronic communications technology, the volatility of interest rates, regional economic declines, and a restrictive legislative environment which limits banks' opportunities to diversify either geographically or in terms of product. Regardless of differences in the banks' abilities to anticipate these changes—and neither bankers nor forecasting professionals have been very good at anticipating them—all banks have been hurt, to varying degrees.

Followers of the so-called natural selection, Darwinian school of organizational analysis argue that in the long run, say over a period of 50 to 75 years, such environmental shocks as have affected banks in recent decades will result in pervasive market changes that will significantly alter the entire financial services industry, regardless of what particular managers think and do. The Darwinians are right. These impacts will include the creation of new rates of entry and mortality and new market niches for generalist and specialist firms, as well as new opportunities for more bureaucratic or loosely structured firms (tiering into various strategic groups and organizational forms).

More specifically, the natural selection theorists would argue that the dual banking (state and federal) system of the United States coupled with both the restrictive legislation of the 1920s and 1930s (which prevented national banking and product diversification) and the many competitive shocks since the 1960s have created a highly unstable U.S. banking industry. The main elements of that instability are a condition of extreme overcapacity; archaic, dinosaurlike banks relative to new competitive requirements; and a marked decline in global competitiveness. This instability will inevitably be followed, so their argument would continue, by a dramatic shakeout and consolidation in the 1990s. It will be reflected in escalating mergers, which will create megabanks; in increased mortality rates and a sharp drop in the number of banks; and in a new, perhaps more sharply defined tiering among different types of banks.

The contributions of this school are to provide a needed historical macroperspective on how an industry is evolving. Taken to its extreme, however, this view has limits. One is that managerial initiatives play no role in this model, since the macrochanges it looks at are seen as superseding any actions managers may take. Thus, some in this school would argue that success or failure for the firm of any particular CEO or cadre of senior managers is largely a matter of luck, because the macroshocks that the industry faces are not only inevitable but so complex, interrelated, and hard to predict that it is all but impossible for managers to learn enough about them in advance to be able to select an appropriate market niche for survival. From this perspective, taking the model literally, there is no role for the manager. The firm simple reflects larger historical and institutional forces but is never a shaper of them.

The moral of my story is that no perspective or model should be taken literally or pursued to extremes, because doing so would blind us to insights from others. The main models used in this study look at managers not as passive pawns of larger historical forces but rather as important, proactive shapers of their organizations' fates. Thus, not all money centers have declined, nor have all superregionals become rising stars. Much depends on managerial vision and leadership.

Consider again the histories of Citicorp and Chase. It was George Moore's and Walter Wriston's tremendous vision and unflagging persistence that moved Citicorp from a sleepy institution in the 1950s to a high-flying conglomerate in the early 1980s. Wriston's successor, John Reed, carried a good thing too far, failing to understand and adapt to the changing requirements for success in the late 1980s and 1990s. Managerial initiatives, then, made large contributions both to Citicorp's rise and to its decline. In a larger historical perspective, it can be seen that the bank had followed a supermarket strategy in the late nineteenth century and again in the 1920s, providing a receptive setting and precedents for Wriston's later version. Wriston's initiatives as well as those of his sponsor, George Moore, and his protégé and successor, John Reed, counted heavily in driving Citicorp as an institution.

Chase, in losing its leading position in the industry, also reflected its leadership. There was nothing inevitable about Chase's decline, even though both its historical culture and its internal politics tilted it in that direction. In the final analysis, its troubles stemmed directly from a lack of managerial judgment and vision.

Both Bankers Trust and Morgan became leading players because of effective leadership. It wasn't at all inevitable that Bankers Trust would make such a dramatic reversal in its poor performance of the early 1970s and emerge in the 1990s as, in the words of the Salomon Brothers Stock Research Group, "the premier merchant banking organization in the United States, as well as one of the top providers of global finance in the world."[23]

Morgan, by contrast, had a 100-year history of high performance as a global wholesale banker, and so perhaps leadership didn't count for quite as much as at Bankers Trust. However, the major changes the bank has made since the late 1970s are a direct result of the vision and managerial activism of its CEO of the 1980s, Lewis Preston. It could have sat on its laurels and continued trying to coast, as Chase was wont to do, but Preston realized that if Morgan was to keep its position as a leading world bank, it had to make major changes in strategy, culture, and organization—which it did, under his leadership.

Likewise, at the other successful banks described in this chapter, in each instance the CEO played a critical role in setting the culture and strategy that propelled the organization toward high performance. Managers do count, but there is no one best way to achieve success. For some—for example, the superregionals—consumer and middle-market banking seem most appropriate. For others—BankAmerica, Citicorp, and Chase—national and global consumer banking may be the key. For a small group—including Bankers Trust and Morgan—global merchant banking is the way to go. These different approaches will work, however, only with strong CEO leadership. It is correct to say that a macroperspective can tell us a lot about the opportunities and threats confronting an industry, but only a microperspective on how firms react can tell us who will be the winners and losers and why. I have presented both perspectives, to provide a deeper understanding of what is happening to the U.S. banking industry in the 1990s.

16

Bank Reform Strategies

Now that I have analyzed the efforts of four money center banks to adapt to major changes in the industry since the early 1960s (changes that eroded both these banks' competitiveness and that of U.S. commercial banking more generally), I will return in this chapter and in Chapter 17 to the macroindustry perspective of Chapter 1. The central argument of the book is that, while environmental changes (e.g., increased competition, the decline of the corporate loan business, and the rise of mutual and money-market funds as a more attractive alternative to bank deposits) affected the entire banking industry, some banks were much better at adapting than were others. I have indicated which these successful banks were and why they adapted better, placing considerable emphasis on their histories and cultures and, particularly, on their CEOs.

Declining U.S. Banks' Competitiveness: Alternative Explanations

Before the 1960s, such comparisons would have been more difficult, since U.S. banks did not differ markedly from one another, or at least the big ones didn't. Indeed, as a group, they displayed a drab uniformity, even when such presently entrepreneurial banks as Citicorp and Bankers Trust are included. Relative to the past few decades, banks were basically sleepy institutions that marched in place, as their markets and the wider economy around them underwent little basic change, and as they were protected from competition by various banking laws—laws which, for example, prevented other banks from branching into their local markets and imposing interest rate ceilings. As Lowell Bryan, well-known bank analyst at McKinsey, has observed, in the earlier, regulated environment of the immediate post-New Deal years, when U.S. banks were a public utility, they were similar to one another in bottom-line performance. They were probably also similar in management style, given their bureaucratic nature.

Since the early 1970s, in an increasingly competitive and newly deregulated industry, the senior managers of U.S. banks have had more options than before and consequently have developed different management styles, moving their institutions in disparate directions. For example, whereas almost all money center banks in the 1950s pursued the same kinds of wholesale and retail businesses, they no longer function in lockstep to nearly the same degree. Citicorp and Chase are diversified conglomerates, and Bankers Trust and Morgan are much more focused merchant banks.

In brief, the management of U.S. banks today differs across institutions, and the differences play significant roles in the successes and failures of the banks. This book documents the relationship between management approach and performance in each of four New York City money center banks, but the story of these four institutions carries much broader significance for the banking industry in general. I have thus applied my hypothesis about the importance of management to many other banks, which I selected as extreme cases of either effective or ineffective performance. More generally, notwithstanding the greater success of some banks, the entire industry needs rehabilitation. This is true partly because when banks existed as public utilities they traditionally failed to attract "the best and the brightest." As I indicated earlier, public utilities tend not to attract creative people, for obvious reasons. Salaries are often limited, and so are opportunities for creativity.

Laws From the Flapper Age

My consideration of the roles managers have played must, perforce, take into account the effects of federal and state regulations in restricting the activities of commercial banks and undermining their competitiveness. Laws enacted in the 1920s and 1930s, as well as later, have severely constrained the performance of U.S. banks, in this increasingly globalized industry. Foreign banks and domestic nonbank competitors are burdened by fewer constraints. The McFadden Act of 1927 (limiting interstate banking), the Glass Steagall Act of 1933 (limiting U.S. commercial banks from underwriting, distributing, and selling securities), and the Douglas Amendment to the Bank Holding Company Act of 1956 (strengthening the McFadden Act) limited U.S. banks' ability to adapt. At just the time in the industry's history when it had been jolted the most by a series of economic shocks over which it had limited control, antiquated laws prevented it from easily recovering by diversifying geographically or into new products.[1]

Meanwhile, the commercial banks' competitors—giant retailers like Sears, automobile finance companies, investment banks, and foreign banks—have been able to diversify into the banks' turf with depository services, credit cards, and lower-interest loans. While the legal and regulatory system has handcuffed U.S. banks, these other financial institutions have enjoyed wide access to traditional "banking" activities.

As the banks lost their traditional deposit and loan business to other markets and competitors, and as they were prevented from diversifying into new areas of opportunity, they sought to expand their loan business into far riskier markets. The large banks suddenly began to court the very clients that they had turned away in the past: small corporations that could not gain access to capital markets; less developed countries (LDCs); the orchestrators of leveraged buyouts (LBOs) and other highly leveraged transactions associated with corporate restructurings; and shaky real estate, energy, and agriculture ventures. The resulting marriages were consummated more because of the banks' urgency and fear about remaining competitive than because of a desire to capitalize on new opportunities. What was going on was, in part, a desperate search for survival rather than a new formula for success. These new ventures, however, only worsened matters for the banks, as their percentages of nonperforming loans increased substantially.

Native American Populism

The general consensus among bank historians and other knowledgeable observers is that the passage and continued existence of restrictive legislation were driven to a large extent by a widespread populist ideology that was particularly prevalent in the South, the West, and areas other than big cities. The origin of this ideology, according to many, may be traced as far back as the nation's founding—the founding of a country that was in revolt against the centralized power of the king of England. Early in U.S. history, there was strong opposition to a central bank—to anything that would resemble the central banks that existed, for example, in many European countries. Indeed, though there were two U.S. central banks—the first Bank of the United States (1791–1811), under the leadership of Secretary of the Treasury Alexander Hamilton, and the second Bank of the United States (1816–1836)—they were opened amid fervent battles that were fought in both the executive and the legislative branches of government as well as in the Supreme Court. The opposition was composed not only of states' rights proponents and agrarian groups. Large New York City bankers also clamored for the demise of the central banks, both of which were in Philadelphia. Eventually, the opponents of central banking prevailed, and Congress refused to renew the federal charter of the second Bank of the United States.

A dual state and federal banking system developed in the United States. Deep distrust of concentrated economic power was reflected not only in the closing of the central banks but also in the increasing regulation of the *money trusts*—a code name for J. P. Morgan, which was also referred to as the *malefactor of great wealth*. The Pujo Hearings of 1912 and the Pecora Hearings of the early 1930s, which resulted in the enactment of the Glass Steagall Act, were expressions of the deep-rooted American distrust of concentrated economic power and of Wall Street.

Populism and Bank Reform

More recently, distrust fueled the defeat in Congress of a move to expand the powers of commercial banks to include nationwide banking, investment banking, and insurance. The arguments and rhetoric in the congressional hearings on bank reform in the 1980s (e.g., to repeal Glass Steagall) echoed the debates over the establishment of central banks that had been waged earlier in the nation's history. Many legislators, particularly those from the South and the West, proclaimed that permitting big banks to diversify interstate and/or into investment banking and insurance would create giant, monopolistic institutions which would ride roughshod over the interests of consumers, small businesses, and local communities. The outcry, for example, that greeted a proposal by Undersecretary of the Treasury George Gould in the late 1980s to allow what he called *megabanks* was so strong, reflecting the same deeply held ideology, that he was forced to withdraw his proposal and deny that he had ever made it. Even in 1991, the chair of the House Banking Committee, Henry Gonzales of Texas, continued to espouse this populist rhetoric.

Bank reform, then, bucks a powerful American tradition that supports the small bank, the small businessman, the consumer, and the local community in the heartland of America against giant trusts and money centers in the big cities and the East. A coalition of interest groups with disparate agendas has been formed, with the goal of thwarting efforts to empower banks to engage in new activities. Their message is easily understood: "We have always abhorred the consolidation of capital in the hands of a few."

Old traditions and ideologies thus die a slow death, which is one big reason these outdated laws have remained in effect for so long. The proponents of bank reform have failed to refute them with a coherent and compelling message. Moreover, the technical complexities of bank reform have made it of little direct concern thus far to the wider populace. The legislative arena has been composed, as a result, not of citizen groups but of large and monied special interests.

The insurance and investment banking industries, the members of which rightfully fear that permitting banks to diversify would erode their market power, exercise considerable influence upon congressional committees. The Glass Steagall Act segmented financial services into a series of protected, specialized niches and thus gave firms in these industries enormous market power. These firms are understandably committed to the effort to prevent bank reform.

Throughout the 1980s, bank lobbyists, particularly those who represented the biggest and hardest-hit banks, pressed in Washington for the repeal of these laws. They failed to generate the support of enough legislators who were willing to be identified as champions of big banks. Gradually, however, administrative decisions made by state banking departments and legislatures, by the Federal Reserve, and by the U.S. Treasury Department, along with court rulings, gave the banks more powers, even without legislative reforms. In 1989, for example, a few big banks were given the power to underwrite corporate debt, and this was followed a year later by the granting of a similar power to underwrite corporate equities. The Federal Reserve also approved a proposal to allow banks to swap debt and equity in Latin American loans, and their ruling was upheld by the judiciary. Yet, little legislative change had taken place for the industry as a whole, even though it was increasingly clear that U.S. banks were no longer as competitive as they might be.

A classic example of how other agencies have moved much faster than Congress in pushing bank reform appeared in the June 11, 1991, edition of *The Wall Street Journal*. One article reported on a federal appeals court ruling that opened the door for major banks to underwrite and sell insurance nationwide. On the same page (indeed, in the very next column) was another article outlining the strongly negative views of House Energy and Commerce Committee Chairman John Dingell regarding the Bush administration's bank reform bill. He characterized the bill as likely to have "profound negative effects on our economy," going on to state that "though the benefits are slight and hypothetical, the dangers are substantial."[2]

Stalemate on Capitol Hill

In 1991, the Bush administration proposed the most sweeping structural reforms since the 1930s. Several developments influenced the decision to make this proposal. One was the deepening savings and loan (S&L) crisis, which depleted the Federal Savings and Loan Insurance Fund. Bailout costs (estimated to be as high as $500 billion) were to be borne at least in part by the taxpayer. While lobbyists for the large banks clamored for increased powers, their proposals seemed especially unattractive in the wake of the S&L fiasco. A Congress that had reluctantly enacted legislation to pour money into the insurance fund was understandably gun-shy about the prospect of unleashing banks to engage in such speculative activities as securities trading.

Given the large numbers of commercial bank failures in the late 1980s, the Federal Deposit Insurance Corporation (FDIC), the insurance fund for commercial banks, was experiencing a similar depletion, indicating an immediate need for recapitalization and stirring much concern among the general public. A second big hit on the taxpayer seemed in the offing. When the Bank of New England declared bankruptcy in early 1991, raising the possibility that other big banks in that region might do likewise and repeating the earlier experience of several large Texas banks, it became increasingly clear that the nation was indeed facing a severe banking crisis that required aggressive management. Although some economists and bank observers suggested that this crisis was limited to big banks, pointing out that most small and medium-sized banks were continuing to perform well, the big banks account for a disproportionate if diminishing share of the industry.

The recession of 1990–1992 exacerbated the problems, at a time when banks were restricting credit in an attempt to restore their capitalization. This marked the first time since the Great Depression that an economic downturn had been accompanied by bank failures. It meant that the banks might possibly not play the important credit-providing role that would be needed to lift the country out of recession, which caused much concern. Suddenly, the nature of U.S. banks, an otherwise rather specialized and arcane subject, became of great interest to many Americans. Events like the closing of Freedom National Bank in the predominantly black Harlem area of New York City highlighted the political fallout from bank failures.

The failure of the Congress in the fall of 1991 to enact bank reform measures indicated how strong the opposition has been. Treasury Secretary Brady refers to the "yes, but" syndrome in characterizing the politics of the situation. Many groups supported banking reform both in the abstract and in all areas except the ones in which they saw their particular interests as being threatened. "There are a lot of people who want to reform," observed Brooklyn Congressman Charles Schumer, senior member of the House Banking Committee, "but when you get into the detail, it's hard to get agreement."

The politics have been those of narrow constituencies that focused all their efforts on a single point, upon which they sought to maintain the status quo. The likelihood that each will be successful is high. The various sectors focus on winning small battles, with scant concern for the larger issues. As Texas Congressman Henry Gonzalez, chairman of the House Banking Committee, has observed, "I've been on the committee for 30 years, and I think the reason there's paralysis is that every one of these groups thinks it can develop enough muscle to offset the other one."[3]

Diagnosis: What's Wrong with U.S. Banking?

The immediate symptoms of the U.S. banking crisis are quite clear: The banks' financial performance and capital position have declined since the mid-1980s. Consider the following:

1. The number of FDIC-designated "problem banks" has been over 1000 since 1985. The biggest banks (i.e., those with assets over $10 billion) have been the most overrepresented in this category.

2. In the 1980s, more banks failed than in the previous 50 years.[4] An average of 200 banks have gone bankrupt in each year since 1987.[5]

3. Commercial banks' share of total U.S. financial assets held by financial service firms declined from 51.2 percent in 1950 to 30.7 percent in 1989, while mutual funds and private pension funds increased five-fold and money-market mutual funds went from 0 to 4.1 percent.[6]

4. Meanwhile, the composition of bank loan portfolios has shifted markedly since 1980 toward the riskiest borrowers—for example,

nonresidential real estate and highly leveraged transactions (HLTs).

5. This trend, in turn, is reflected in the rise of loan losses as a share of total loans during the past three decades, from under 2 percent in 1950 to over 10 percent and still rising sharply in 1989.[7]

The long-run trends contributing to this decline are well known. On the liabilities side, largely as a result of explosive inflation, depositors turned increasingly to money-market mutual funds, treasury securities, pension funds, and insurance companies, all of which offered higher interest rate returns on their funds than banks could provide. On the assets or loan side, securities markets in the form of commercial paper have gradually replaced banks as a primary source of funds. Whereas corporations once looked to banks for capital to finance new ventures, today they turn to highly liquid capital markets.

Fueling these developments has been the advancement of computer and information technology, which has made possible alternative investments such as mutual funds and has also helped to spawn the movement toward securitization. Securitization became a groundswell development in banking in the 1980s, involving the packaging of loans on mortgages, credit cards, and automobiles and their sale as securities. Though many banks view securitization as a major opportunity, it is actually a double-edged sword. On the benefits side, it allows banks to become liquid and to shrink their asset bases to comply with the Federal Reserve Board's capital standards, and it offers new opportunities for profits. However, securitization also entails costs that undermine traditional banking functions, such as lowering the interest spreads on loans. Though it is advantageous for many banks to diversify away from the loan business, so as to earn more fee-based income, providing credit is still a prime source of income for most banks.[8]

Economists James Barth, Dan Brumbaugh, and Robert Litan describe the vicious cycle in the big banks' decline. As the banks lost their best customers, the blue-chip corporations, they turned to increasingly risky lending. In a further search for a successful strategy, they turned to securitization and thereby lowered spreads. Finally, with such lower spreads, they sought out even riskier borrowers, and the vicious cycle continues.[9]

What are the components of the U.S. banking crisis of 1991? While it is not quite as bad as the S&L crisis, it is threatening to become that bad. The FDIC funds are being severely depleted, and the likelihood is that several big banks may fail, requiring a bailout that would completely exhaust the funds, without emergency intervention from Congress. Meanwhile, the economy has moved into a recession. The so-called credit crunch, which resulted from the banks having become gun-shy, has threatened to make the recession worse, probably pushing more banks over the edge. Under the "too big to fail" doctrine of the FDIC, there has been a threat to the insurance fund and an added burden on the taxpayer. One response has been the bank mergers that have taken place on an increasing scale since the late 1980s.

The other components of the banking crisis are the tremendous *overcapacity* of the industry (too many banks, chasing too few loans and deals) and increasingly severe *capital problems*. Banks now have more *nonperforming loans* than in previous years, and they face a reduced ability to compete globally. Meanwhile, they continue to be constrained by archaic laws applied by multiple regulators (federal and state) with overlapping jurisdictions. Many of these constraints would be either reversed or greatly eased by adoption of the Treasury Department proposal.

Bank Reforms: New Hope or More Proposals to Be Stonewalled?

The U.S. bank reform agenda for the 1990s is clearly being set by the Bush administration's bill and Congress's reactions to it. One reason the initiative came from the executive branch rather than from Congress is that Congress has been paralyzed during the past decade by competing committees which spend more time on turf fights than on policy considerations.

The bill was quite comprehensive, covering such diverse but interrelated issues as (1) nationwide banking, (2) the FDIC fund, (3) new financial powers in investment banking and insurance, (4) commercial ownership of banks, (5) regulatory consolidation, and (6) strengthening bank capital. For each of these components, both the administration and other parties have made proposals, and interest group politics will ultimately determine what gets passed.

Basically, the bill was an attempt to modernize or rationalize U.S. banking. It aimed at making banks more competitive by overriding geographic, product, and ownership constraints; by consolidating the regulatory structure; by requiring higher levels of capital; and by limiting deposit insurance to small depositors rather than providing an ever-increasing subsidy. Again, despite the consensus on these goals when they are discussed in general terms, considerable dispute surfaces when particular proposals are presented.

The Perils of Parochialism:
Nationwide Banking

The disappearing consensus syndrome was particularly dramatic on the issue of whether to permit interstate banking. Princeton economist Alan Blinder, in what he called his "midterm report card" on the Treasury bill, characterized this proposal as one of the most unambiguous, the equivalent of the golfer's "gimme" putt. He stated, "Virtually every economist and banking expert agrees that America's restrictions on inter-state [sic] banking are an absurd anachronism that fosters inefficiency. The only arguments on the other side are thinly disguised excuses for protecting local pockets of monopoly."[10]

The arguments for removing interstate banking constraints were compelling. They related mainly to increasing the efficiency and profitability of banks and, in particular, to reducing their vulnerability to regional economic downturns. A widely cited McKinsey study, for example, suggested that nationwide banking could save the banking industry $10 billion a year in operating, regulatory, and administrative costs.[11] Economies of scale through centralized back-office operations, serving a national network of branches, would be quite substantial. The consensus among economists has been overwhelmingly in support of allowing U.S. banks to diversify loans through national banking. Examples invariably cited to support this argument are the overconcentration by big Texas banks in the mid-1980s on energy loans in that area and by New England banks in the late 1980s on local real estate and construction loans. In both instances, the bank failures and the escalating losses of the banks that survived were largely a result of their high vulnerability to regional shocks. Indeed, studies of U.S. banking in the 1980s have concluded time and again that most failures and losses have been concentrated in such regional pockets. Banks have thus been held hostage to economic downturns in the regions where they operate: as Texas goes, so go the Texas banks. Prevented from pursuing opportunities in other locales, banks must grapple with the harsh realities of their regional economies.

Indeed, an estimated 85 percent of the assets of failed banks during the 1980s were in just four states.[12] Being permitted to diversify geographically, then, would enable U.S. banks to absorb such shocks by balancing them with loans in regions that are not experiencing industry-specific declines. More generally, retail banking through local branches does lend itself to economies of scale and low-cost production. It is very likely that a number of retail megabanks will soon emerge [e.g., Bank of America; Citicorp; Chase; and such superregionals as Banc One, First

Wachovia, FleetNorstar, and North Carolina National Bank (NCNB)]. Small and midsized community banks will continue to exist and will remain competitive, however, particularly since so many of them offer high quality and personal services, and have done so for the same local clients for many generations. Given their fears of future bank failures, consumers may opt to trust the banks they know, even at the expense of lower interest rates on deposit accounts. As economist Henry Kaufman has noted, there is no significant danger in banking concentration if interstate banking becomes a reality.

Since financial markets have long ago become national as well as international, largely because of new technology, repeal of such laws as the McFadden Act would simply acknowledge a reality that has been in existence for some time. In fact, many states already permit banks to branch across state lines.

However, there was tremendous opposition to interstate banking from a group whose members sometimes refer to it as the *Main Street Coalition.* It includes the Independent Bankers Association (an organization for small banks), the American Association of Retired Persons (AARP), and the Consumer Federation of America. These organizations fight against what they call the *Wall Street Coalition* of big banks.[13] Even the American Bankers Association, one of the strongest advocates of the Treasury bill, has not taken a definitive position on interstate banking, largely because 90 percent of its members are small and middle-sized banks.

This small-bank, small-town coalition offered many arguments to support its position. First, they maintain, community banks would be run out of business by the absentee-owned and absentee-managed megabank invaders, which can offer more attractive lending rates and expanded services. Second, the big banks would siphon deposits off local communities, severely weakening community reinvestment and local economic development. Finally, the big banks would remove their assets to tax havens, rather than using them to serve local clients and communities.

Despite the absence of a systematic body of research to buttress these assertions, logic and history provide a compelling case for questioning each of them. Regarding the assertion that community banks would be eliminated, there has been extensive experience with interstate mergers in New England and the Southeast, in the wake of a Supreme Court decision in 1985 which permitted such consolidation. While this consolidation has created superregional banks, vibrant community banks often remain active in these areas.

As for the other arguments, if big banks siphoned deposits off the communities in which they were newly located, they might well be out of business. Any community group could protest, and many small and middle-sized cities are highly organized in this regard. Informed and politically sophisticated local groups would be likely to defend their own interests and to ensure that such "outside" institutions would not exploit their communities. By clamoring about "outsider" institutions raiding their local communities, these citizen lobbyists would offer a persuasive, albeit provincial, case for protecting the "insider" institutions.

Far from leading to balkanization, such internal opposition might simply lead to development of a balance between community and superregional banks. That is, to drive away every superregional bank would be to deprive the local community of needed infusions of capital. Pure parochialism would come at the expense of economic development and job growth.

It is in the big banks' self-interest, then, to promote community development, and a more likely scenario may well be that a money center that opened a branch in such a community would go out of its way to accommodate local concerns, in both its hiring and its loan practices. A likely strategy would be for the money center or superregional bank to hire its loan officer or branch manager from a community bank. Otherwise, it might well lose out to the small local bank, even though it originally had many competitive advantages: more products, more economies of scale. Thus, both sides would need each other. The big banks would offer the local community more services and higher rates of interest, while the local community would provide many of the bankers to staff the big banks' branches, as well as clients to seek loans and make deposits.

How to Fix the FDIC Fund

An even stronger consensus might be expected on replenishing the bank insurance fund, particularly since its substantial depletion in 1990 and 1991 offered an unsettling reminder of the S&L crisis. The immediate issue has been that the fund needs more money to cover expenses and losses incurred in managing the resolution of failed banks. The Treasury plan called for increased borrowing by the FDIC from the Federal Reserve, with the banks paying for it in increased premiums. However, the plan did not propose the bold approach that many economists had urged, namely, restricting the banks' ability to use insured deposits for funding risky ventures by limiting the accounts people could hold in all banks. Instead, it endorsed a watered-down, compromise proposal to limit depositors to two $100,000 accounts at any one bank, allowing depositors of means to hold accounts in many banks. The banks' insurance fund, originally established to protect the small depositor, had over the years become a means of providing easy deposits with which banks can do what they choose. Moreover, depositors have undermined the purpose of insurance by splitting their deposits between different banks, so as to stay beneath the ceiling of $100,000.

The issue on which the Treasury plan had particularly come up short was the "too big to fail" policy, involving the FDIC in the bailout of big banks that were going under. The argument for not abandoning this policy was that allowing a big bank like Bank of New England to fail could trigger a chain reaction in the region, increase the likelihood of other bank failures, and further escalate economic decline. On the other side, the "too big to fail" policy clearly dilutes market discipline and essentially protects poorly managed institutions. In this instance, 8 of the 11 most powerful national lobby groups studied in an *American Banker* survey (published March 1, 1991) said that the Treasury bill did not go far enough.

New Powers in Securities and Insurance

The most contested bank reform issue of the 1980s—giving banks new powers to underwrite and trade securities and to underwrite insurance—has spilled over into the 1990s. At the heart of the debate is a fundamental dispute about whether banks should be permitted to expand their services into markets that have, since the 1930s, been closed to them. The Treasury bill gives such expanded powers to banks, provided they establish separate subsidiaries that would be forbidden to use insured depositors' funds. The underlying goal of the Treasury proposal was to build "fire walls" between the bank in its traditional depository and loan activities and the subsidiary, which would function as a securities or investment firm. Not surprisingly, the Securities Industry Association, a powerful and well-financed trade group representing investment banks, continues to oppose this encroachment of banks into its markets. The Independent Insurance Agents of America has been particularly effective in lobbying against permitting banks into its industry. One outcome of this dispute is that securities firms and insurance brokers—two groups that have often been diametrically opposed—have joined forces. Both are concerned about the competitive advantage of banks, speculating with government-insured funds.

Given the strong vested interests on both sides of the debate, it is unclear what new powers the banks may get. One possible compromise is that only the banks that the regulators judge to be adequately capitalized will be permitted to diversify. Another is that very strong fire walls will ensure a separation between, on the one hand, a bank's core business through its holding company and, on the other hand, its securities transactions through a subsidiary. Many highly regarded economists remain concerned about risks and abuses, however. As Alan Blinder remarked, "We are skeptical that anyone can build a `firewall' [sic] between a bank and its related securities firm that will remain impregnable in a real blaze. Furthermore, neither history nor the current state of Wall Street gives any reason to think that banks will make money in these new lines of business."[14] Henry Kaufman comments:

> Institutions that are both lenders and investors, on the one hand, and underwriters and traders of securities, on the other, have an inherent conflict of interest. How can they possibly propose to do objective due diligence on new offerings for public distribution when concurrently they may have in their portfolios the debt or the equity of the issuer? The government's proposal neglects how such conflicts of interest contributed to the financial excesses of the 1980s.[15]

At the end of 1991, this issue is as stalemated as it has been since the early 1980s, when big banks first started lobbying for expanded powers.

Commercial Ownership of Banks

In an attempt to infuse new capital into U.S. banks, the Treasury plan proposed that commercial, industrial corporations be permitted to own banks. Such arrangements exist in Japan and Germany but have never been permitted in the United States. Indeed, the separation of banking and industry has been viewed as critical in the United States, to prevent the concentration of capital in the hands of a few large institutions. The closest we came to such consolidation occurred in the late nineteenth and early twentieth centuries, when a form of finance capitalism emerged, in which "money trusts" like J.P. Morgan held big ownership shares in major corporations and industries. These trusts played a major role in restructuring economically failing industries and promoting corporate mergers. The interlocking directorates of banks, railroads, and manufacturing companies that resulted were very extensive.

Since the nation was so opposed to concentrated economic power, it moved away from bank-dominated capitalism and toward the stock market capitalism that has existed throughout most of the twentieth century. The concept of bank ownership by industrial companies, then, remains so alien in this country that it has not received groundswell support from either academic economists or interest groups. Henry Kaufman, one of the most outspoken opponents of this concept, argues that it would lead to what he calls a "corporalist state" of "giant banking-industrial combines" that would have "numerous detrimental consequences." These consequences would include creation of a powerful self-perpetuating elite that would become highly protective of the institutions it controlled, retarding economic growth and vitality and subverting shareholder rights. Blinder suggests that allowing industrial companies to own banks "has the potential to create monumental conflicts of interest."[16] Since even the American Bankers Association had not endorsed the idea as of early March 1991, it seems unlikely to remain important in bank reform.

Regulatory Consolidation

Perhaps the most contentious proposal in the entire bill was the proposal to consolidate the regulatory structure. Again, in theory, it makes a lot of sense. U.S. banks are subject to multiple and often conflicting regulations. At the federal level, banks face regulation and supervision by the FDIC, the Federal Reserve, the office of the Comptroller of the Currency, and the Office of Thrift Supervision. In addition, state banking departments enforce their own regulations. This dual regulatory system creates tremendous confusion, and, ideally, the banking system would be regulated more efficiently if it were consolidated. Although the big question is who wins and who loses in such a consolidation, it is likely that no matter what the final decision is, larger political forces will preclude dismantling the present regulatory structure in favor of uniformity. "This is an area that has always been a swamp," noted Edward Yingling, senior lobbyist for the American Bankers Association. "The fact is that when you redraw turf lines in this town," reported Jerome Powell, Assistant Secretary of the Treasury, "it's heavy lifting without regard to merits."

The Treasury bill represented a move in the direction of consolidation, going from the four major federal regulators listed above to two, the Comptroller and the FDIC. In this respect, it was an improvement, but it alienated at least two parties. It relegated the Federal Reserve to a somewhat secondary role, as the regulator of state-chartered banks only, and it established the Office of Depository Institutions Supervision within the Treasury Department to oversee all federally chartered banks. Meanwhile, the FDIC was reduced to the role of book-keeper, while the Federal Reserve lost oversight of the largest federally chartered banks.

Predictably, both FDIC and Federal Reserve officials expressed much dismay at the proposal. Many astute observers, including Alan Greenspan, the head of the Federal Reserve, have argued that severing the FDIC's supervisory relationship with so many of the nation's largest banks might well weaken its implementation of U.S. monetary policy, since these banks are the main conduits. As Henry Kaufman explains:

> I believe that in today's world of complex and highly innovative institutions, the central bank can cope with the task of pursuing an effective monetary policy only if it has intimate knowledge of the working and activities of banking institutions, especially those of the largest ones....This insight into the banking business would be partially obscured under the Treasury proposal.[17]

Some of the same reasoning could be applied to the FDIC. Since it plays such an important oversight role whenever a bank fails and in relation to capital adequacy, it should be a central regulator as well. Yet, it is not given that responsibility in the plan.

One of the strengths of the Treasury plan is that it subjects banks to tighter regulation as their capital declines. Thus, well-capitalized banks would be given more powers to diversify and to lower deposit insurance premiums. By contrast, banks not as well capitalized would be subject to higher premiums and allowed fewer diversification options. These are important innovations that, if passed, might well help to improve the performance of the banking industry.

In addition, a methodology is developed to classify banks into so-called capital zones, according to the extent to which they are meeting minimum capital requirements. Regulators had done this informally in the past, but the Treasury plan provides a more systematic approach. It is coupled, in turn, with an early intervention procedure designed to prevent the kinds of failures that occurred in the past, when regulators, through inattention, sometimes permitted banks to sink into poorly capitalized condition before requiring corrective actions. Other financial service institutions should be subject to the same stringent monitoring.

A Politics of Futility?

Comprehensive banking reform was voted down in 1991, as all its predecessors had been. The reason for the negative vote was the same as it had been throughout the 1980s, namely extreme political fragmentation on the issue. One kind of fragmentation occurs among the interest groups, as discussed above. So many narrow, individual constituencies function as negative veto groups on their particular issues, sometimes even developing larger-based coalitions supporting their position, that each reform proposal seems at times to face almost impossible odds. "Unlike so many issues that Congress takes up," reported a former legislative aide to a member of the House Banking Committee, "banking legislation involves a great many narrowly focused lobby groups." Coalitions constantly shift, so that the banks are fighting the insurance groups on one section of a bill and the next moment they are involved in a dispute against the Securities Industry Association. I have already described many of these groups in reviewing the various provisions of the bill, and it seems unlikely that their resistance, call it *rear guard action* or whatever, will soon diminish. The politics of these multiple players, as they constantly shift coalitions, is in contrast to the politics of many legislative battles (for example, the battle about textile imports), in which opposing groups are easily identified and remain relatively stable over time.

The congressional committee structures provide a second kind of fragmentation. There are two House committees—(1) Banking and (2) Energy and Commerce—each of which presents formidable obstacles and causes turf battles. Many committee members are reported to see substantial political risks in giving commercial banks new powers, lest the banks abuse them as the S&Ls did and cause some of the same results. In addition, the chair of each committee is on shaky ground, having constituency problems of his own. In the case of Democrat Henry Gonzalez of the House Banking Committee, several members of his own party, along with Republicans, tried unsuccessfully to oust him in the early weeks of the 102d Congress. Though he did defeat their revolt, he still has the support of only a minority of the committee. This might seem to bode well for bank reform, since Gonzalez is an avowed populist and very skeptical of the merits of giving banks more powers. On the other hand, there is serious question about the ability of the majority coalition of Republicans and Democrats who opposed him to stick together in endorsing a bank reform proposal.

In addition, the Banking Committee suffers from a constant exodus of members to other, more attractive committees. The many changes disrupt efforts to complete legislation, because institutional memory is lost when members leave.

Then there is House Energy and Commerce Committee Chairman John Dingell. Always identified as wary of giving banks more powers, he indicated in June 1991 that the Bush administration's proposed timetable for the bill was unacceptable in that it allowed only 100 days for review. The son of a New Deal populist legislator who represented the district before he inherited the seat, Dingell has clung to the belief that banks cannot be trusted.

Across the Capitol, the Senate Banking Committee, chaired by Don Riegel, a Michigan Democrat, also has not been overly enthusiastic about bank reform. Moreover, Riegel has been under prolonged investigation for accepting campaign contributions from S&L bankers and pressuring federal regulators to soften their scrutiny of Charles Keating's enterprise, while at the same time considering S&L legislation. He may be wary, on those grounds, about passing a similar bank reform bill.

Contributing to still more political volatility, and thereby further lessening the likelihood that a bill will pass, is a third type of fragmentation: turf struggles among the regulators. William Seidman of the FDIC and Alan Greenspan, chairman of the Federal Reserve, have been quoted frequently in the press as expressing deep displeasure about the diminished role the Treasury plan would give their respective agencies. Each offers compelling points, and the problems involved in attempting to consolidate the regulatory structure for enhanced effectiveness without antagonizing particular agencies to such a degree that they would work to sabotage the plan, are very difficult to manage.

Indeed, it may well require political skills approaching those of a genius to develop a consensus from among all these warring participants. A likely scenario, just beginning to unfold in May and June of 1991, is to divide bank reform problems into two groups, according to their urgency and their ease of management. The first problem to be considered would be the bank insurance fund, which could be depleted by the end of 1991, if not before, and therefore must be attended to right away. Throughout the spring of 1991, the FDIC had been revising upward both its predictions of likely future bank failures and its estimation of the consequent demands that these failures would impose on the bank insurance fund. In May, it told Congress that as many as 440 banks would fail over the next 2 years, an increase over the previous average of about 200 banks per year. Recapitalizing the fund, then, is an immediate priority. Both the urgency of this problem and its being a narrower issue and more of a consensus one than the others in the bill suggest that for Congress to address it in the near future would be prudent. Indeed, there is strong support within Congress for this approach, and it is likely to move forward.

Action on the other parts of the bill is unlikely. Even if the banking crisis were to escalate, there are so many different and conflicting diagnoses of what brought it about that generating a consensus about what to do would continue to be difficult. One set of diagnoses, most prevalent among opponents of bank reform, places the blame on bank management. Proponents of this view see many parallels between the earlier problems of S&Ls and the present problems of commercial banks. Their general argument is that since banks have already piled up so many nonperforming loans, which reflects poor judgment, expanding their powers would simply allow them to dig a still deeper hole for themselves. In a phrase, why reward incompetence? One of the most outspoken proponents of this position is journalist Martin Mayer. He sees the banking crisis as a big one, asserts that the big banks are unwieldy dinosaurs that should not be saved, and implies that bank reform legislation to increase the big banks' powers would simply perpetuate this problem.[18]

The other diagnosis is that, while bad management by the banks is clearly prevalent and has contributed to many of their problems, the entire industry structure, including its regulatory apparatus, has also contributed. From this perspective, some of the bad credit judgments that bankers made, which eventually left them stuck with nonperforming loans, must be interpreted in a wider context as symptomatic of macroweaknesses of the entire industry, which are independent of the "good" or "bad" management of particular bankers. In brief, there will be less likelihood of bank mismanagement in the future, as well as less likelihood that U.S. banks will continue to lose out competitively to foreign banks, if the structure of the industry changes, particularly the regulatory structure.

As in most debates of this nature, both sides have merit, and the most effective public policy would take the best from each. In this context, what is involved is acknowledging the many ways in which mismanagement has contributed to the banks' problems but also acknowledging that this mismanagement is conditioned by the larger institutional and economic setting in which banks exist. Key aspects of that larger setting, therefore, must be changed in order to effectively manage the results of malaise that U.S. banking experienced in the 1970s and 1980s.

It seems likely—given the many divisive political forces discussed above, the 1992 elections, and the interpretation of the S&L crisis as an example of the damage that may result from deregulation of banking—

that no significant bank reform is likely to be passed. There will be attempts to replenish the commercial bank insurance fund, but little else.

Models Implicit in Various Bank Reform Strategies

Implicit in the bank reform strategies now being debated are larger models of what U.S. banks should be like. Two such models that have received increasing attention are the *narrow* or *safe* bank model and the *full-service* or *universal* bank model. The first was developed by such well-known students of U.S. banking as Lowell Bryan, a McKinsey consultant, and economist Robert Litan of the Brookings Institution; it has been supported strongly by the Nobel prize-winning economist James Tobin of Yale. The second is endorsed by advocates of the Treasury plan, who see megabanks as a productive direction for U.S. banking. While the two positions don't necessarily conflict on every point, they do represent vastly different visions of what banks should become.

Lowell Bryan, the main articulator of the narrow bank model, argues that big banks have become unmanageable, largely because they have proliferated product lines without either examining their competitive strengths and weaknesses or developing a management structure to support them.[19] He suggests that banks have been operating with pooled funds and a shared cost structure, in which deficits in one set of businesses are covered by surpluses in others but no systematic assessment is made of how, why, and where the differences in performance took place. His solution would be to break up each bank into a series of self-contained, decentralized businesses, each run by a general manager. There would be no more cross subsidizing of failures, and accountability would be clear. This plan would contribute to each business's becoming more competitive, as the bank could more easily tailor each one to suit critical success factors in its own market. It would make the bank more flexible by enabling it to make multiple bets on the future, rather than one integrated bet. Further, it would help the bank to readily identify the businesses that had positive or negative value so that it could sell off the negative parts more easily.

Such an approach to bank management simply represents good strategic planning, something banks have not done enough of in the past, if they have done any at all. Instead, they have tended to get into too many businesses in which they had little capability, thereby digging a deeper financial hole for themselves.

The relevance of this approach to bank reform is that broader powers, without a major overhaul in management, would not improve bank performance and might in fact make matters worse. Just because banks have such powers does not automatically push them to engage in such strategic planning and make the hard decisions about which businesses to keep and which to sell. Moreover, advocates of the narrow or safe bank argue that the failure of a nonbanking group of businesses could trigger a run by depositors or might stretch the so-called federal safety net of FDIC funds to be used in bailing out the failing businesses. They warn that, even if a bank conducted each of its new businesses, say securities underwriting, in a separate subsidiary, and even if strong "Chinese walls" insulated the subsidiaries from the core bank, the walls might easily break down. Therefore, they contend, regulators and bankers should guard vigorously against this possibility.

The full-service or universal bank model, by contrast, gives legitimacy to comprehensive bank reform along the lines of the Treasury bill. It argues for diversification, highlighting how banks have suffered in the past from legislative constraints that gave them much too limited a set of options, even while their traditional business was going down the drain as a result of macroeconomic forces. Therefore, the way to make banks safe, proponents of this model argue, is to allow them to diversify as they see fit—geographically and in terms of products—just as other financial service institutions and nonbank banks have diversified. Release the handcuffs, they believe, and banks will be able to achieve greater stability and prosperity.

In brief, economists and bank scholars operate with two seemingly opposed models. Yet, the models may be reconciled. The full-service model may incorporate insights from the narrow bank model by requiring that a great deal of strategic planning accompany diversification decisions. It may also require that banks which are given broad powers to diversify insulate the resulting subsidiaries from the core bank holding company and from each other, so as to avoid commingling of funds and conflicts of interest. In short, perhaps both models offer advantages which, to date, have been viewed as mutually exclusive. Rather than seeking to merge the models, both sides have simply pressed harder.

Having highlighted the key regulatory issues that commercial banks face in trying to become more competitive globally, I turn, in conclusion, to some projections about what the future is likely to hold. What will U.S. banking look like in the year 2000? Are U.S. banks likely to become competitive once more? If so, through what types of banks, in terms of organizational forms and product mixes? I will address these questions in Chapter 17.

17
Peering into the Future

The review in Chapter 16 of U.S. banking's most recent history clearly points to trends that will prevail over the next decade. This concluding chapter deals with the future in terms of three broad questions: (1) How will the banking industry change in the 1990s? (2) What forms or types of banks will emerge? (3) What adaptation will be required for survival? Implicit in this question is another: If, as many observers have noted, some banks have become dinosaurs by the early 1990s, what made them obsolete and what is required for success in the future?

Consolidation: Fewer Banks

Because of its costly and debilitating overcapacity, the U.S. banking industry will continue to consolidate in the 1990s, shrinking from 12,500 as of June 1990, to perhaps 8000 or even fewer independent banks by the year 2000. The United States has more independent banks per capita than has any other nation in the world. The consolidation will take place through continued bank failures (at an average of perhaps 200 a year) and through mergers.

U.S. banks are now on the verge of what could well become a groundswell merger movement, accelerating a trend that started in the mid-1980s. At that time, resulting from a U.S. Supreme Court decision permitting banks in adjacent states to merge but denying that opportunity to money centers, there was a wave of regional bank mergers in the Southeast and in New England. Such new superregionals as North Carolina National Bank (NCNB), PNC Financial, First Wachovia,

C&S/Sovran, Fleet/Norstar, and Sun Trust were established. All of them moved into the top 25 bank holding companies in the United States, as of 1990, by total assets.

More regional bank consolidations are likely to occur in the 1990s, along with several other types of mergers. One type will involve money centers merging with one another in the same city or region, as in New York City and on the West Coast—for example, Security Pacific and Wells Fargo. Another will be the merging of a money center with a big bank in another region, similar to the Chemical-Texas Banc merger of 1989. Still others will involve a superregional like Banc One or NCNB merging with a big bank outside its area, or the merging of a regional with small or midsized banks around the country. Though there had been only a small number of these different types of mergers by mid-1991, they are likely to escalate by 1992. The regulators will contribute to the trend by providing various kinds of incentives. As a top staffer at a big New York City bank noted, with regard to the money centers, "The situation now reminds me very much of my first eighth-grade dance, with all the boys on one side and all the girls on the other. As soon as the first couple gets out on the dance floor and breaks the ice, it will be a stampede."

One of the most talked-about impending sites is New York City, where the present climate for big bank mergers is frequently compared to that of the 1950s. A wave of such consolidations took place at that time, creating the diversified money center banks of recent decades. The banks most often mentioned are the poorer performers. The merger of Chemical and Manufacturers Hanover in New York is on its way to consummation, and a union between Chase and Bank of New York is plausible.

There are, to be sure, many obstacles to New York City mergers and to other mergers involving big, poorly managed banks. One is the reluctance of one bank to take on the loan problems of another. A merger between two banks with weak loan portfolios may simply create one huge weak bank. Cynical bank analysts, for example, have characterized the Chemical and Manufacturers Hanover merger as being similar to the Lusitania and the Titanic making an agreement to go down together.

A second problem is that chief executive officers (CEOs) or heirs apparent may be years away from retirement and not ready to give up power in the event of a merger. This is very much the case with the New York City banks and may well have deterred them from merging sooner. Power struggles and problems involved in melding different cultures are common in postmerger integration phases. The prospect of such problems often makes both parties reluctant to go ahead with a merger. Beyond this, if a merger takes place between relative equals, attempts to share power can be disastrous; the new bank may end up with nobody in charge. The classic example of this is shown in the merger of Citizens and Southern (C&S) with Sovran. The managers of C&S/Sovran have followed a consensus management style and have moved too slowly on critical strategic decisions as a result.

Finally, there is the highly charged issue of job elimination. One estimate is that employment in commercial banks could shrink during the 1990s from 2.3 million to 1.5 million as a direct result of mergers.[1] That degree of job loss could have severe consequences, particularly for big cities with high rates of unemployment. New York, already reeling from the loss of 35,000 to 40,000 jobs in the securities industry since the 1987 crash, is a case in point.[2] To lose several thousand more jobs as a result of bank mergers—on top of the big premerger cutbacks in the money center banks, at a time when the city is in a fiscal crisis, and when up to 40 percent of those laid off may be minorities—would create serious dislocations and unrest.

Related to the job issue is a more general concern about the possible impact of mergers on how well localities will be served. In New York City, a merger of Chemical and Manufacturers Hanover is committed to maintaining branches in lower-income neighborhoods. Many community-based groups, as I have said, don't want big outside banks (such as money centers or foreign banks) taking over their local economies. These groups pose the issue as a need to maintain local control and resist the invasion of outsiders. They also see the issue in terms of state control. They want to preserve the regulatory apparatus of each state, to protect both local banks and their clients. The American Association of Retired Persons (AARP), one of many such groups, is opposed to mergers because it feels its members' interests would not be as well served by newly consolidated banks as by existing local banks.[3]

Nonetheless, excess capacity points to a need for further consolidation. The benefits could be substantial, and could include huge cost savings, economies of scale, profit increases, and the pumping of fresh capital into the banking system. The principal problems would involve managing the postmerger integration and making hard decisions about job reductions.

Yet another type of merger may well be that of a money center with a big bank outside its region. BankAmerica, for example, was seemingly in the running to acquire Bank of New England, before Fleet/Norstar finally got the nod from the Federal Deposit Insurance Corporation (FDIC). Earlier, Citicorp had been rumored to be interested in buying

BankAmerica, when that institution was in the doldrums. Other, similar mergers may well be in the offing and may come to fruition in the early or mid-1990s.

The regionals and superregionals have already been quietly assembling empires and are likely to continue to do so on an increasing basis. Superregionals, such as Banc One and NCNB, have been buying up branches and bigger banks in other regions. Banc One was a candidate on the FDIC's short list, along with Bank of America, to buy Bank of New England. As a further illustration, at the time of this writing, Wachovia was involved in preliminary talks about acquiring South Carolina National Corporation, in its first major expansionary move in 6 years. The combination would make Wachovia the biggest bank in South Carolina.[4]

Besides the superregionals, other newcomers have acquired scores of small banks throughout the nation, in a process of steady growth. A prototype in this regard is KeyCorp, of Albany, New York, a midsized community bank that has expanded since 1985 from year-end assets of just under $8 billion to over $19.3 billion and growing, making it the thirty-sixth largest in the country. KeyCorp's status as a small-town community bank is reflected both in its branch locations and in its lending philosophy. Besides the branches in upstate New York, it has main branches in Maine, Oregon, Washington, Idaho, Utah, Wyoming, and Alaska. All these branches house numerous community banks like itself. As indicated in a recent article, KeyCorp "has no foreign loans, no highly leveraged transactions, and a $25 million cap on loans to a single borrower. Small business loans, home mortgages, and consumer lending predominate, while real estate construction loans are just 3.6 percent of the total."[5] It has thus contributed to the industry's consolidation while maintaining the identities and community commitments of the small-town banks it has acquired, establishing a pattern that may be repeated many times in the 1990s.

In brief, U.S. banking is consolidating and will continue to do so on an escalating basis in the 1990s. The number of U.S. banks shrunk by roughly 2000 in the 1980s (from 14,435 to 12,500), and it will likely shrink by at least twice that number over the next decade.[6] Much of the shrinkage will be driven by changed banking laws (some of which are already in effect). Encouragement and incentives from regulators will be another factor, and, of course, the economies of scale of such consolidations will be still a third factor. U.S. banking will thus become much more national, as it follows market developments.

Does this mean that there will be increased economic concentration? Will megabanks take over, and will small and middle-sized banks become relics of the past? The indications are that this won't happen. Community-based banks are expected to continue to exist and to be resilient. They fill an important need, and they have built up such strong personal relationships with local clients that they will continue to be in demand.

Even with consolidation, a sizable segment of the U.S. banking industry, perhaps 75 percent or even more, will consist of smaller community banks. The U.S. banking system will never become like those of Canada, which has only 66 banks; of Japan, which has only 154; or of various European nations, which also have high concentrations.[7] "American-style" consolidation will preserve the dual banking system—state and federal—and the country's preference for small, community-based banks.

Capitalization

Another aspect of the shake-out in U.S. banking that consolidation reflects will be much better capitalization of the banks that remain. Regulators and Congress are increasingly aware of capital inadequacy as a major problem, particularly in the largest banks. This inadequacy has been largely caused by the increasing proportion of high-risk loans that are in default. It is the principal threat to the solvency of the bank insurance fund. Regulatory laxity and accounting practices which have concealed the true condition of the banks have also contributed.

The costs of continuing in a mode of capital inadequacy are widely agreed to be so high that strong regulatory pressures have been developed, both within the Federal Reserve and through the BIS (Bank for International Settlements) on an international level, for minimum capital standards. These pressures should remain high throughout the 1990s and, in fact, should increase.

More Strategic Focus

If there is one basic lesson to be learned from the four case studies and the briefer vignettes of other banks reported in this book, it is that strategic focus is critical for survival, let alone success, in the present environment of U.S. business. The hope of succeeding by being all things to all people, in the Citicorp mode, is delusory. The leading banks of the future will be highly successful niche players which will have to "stick to their knitting."[8] The contrast between, on the one hand, Citicorp's and Chase's lackluster financial performance in the late 1980s, as a result of their diversification strategies, and, on the other hand, Morgan's and Bankers Trust's tremendous successes, accomplished with more focused strategies, contains a larger message. Banks that try to do too many things are doomed to fail in the highly competitive markets of the 1990s or, at best, to give mediocre performances. Bank consultant Stephen Davis pointed this out a few years ago in his book *Managing Change in the Excellent Banks*, and it holds true to an even greater extent now. It also holds true for investment banks that received their rude awakening in the 1987 crash and have been weeding out unsuccessful businesses in great numbers ever since, concentrating instead on what they do well.

The 1980s provided many examples of this lesson. The turnaround of Bank of America, to take one such case, has been closely associated with its exit from overseas wholesale businesses and its increasing focus on consumer banking on the West Coast. Chemical's improvement also was associated with a withdrawal from international markets and more concentration on middle-market, small-business, and consumer banking in the United States.

The experience of U.S. banks with regard to diversification may be taken as a microcosm of American business more generally. Gregg Jarrell and Robert Comment (of the University of Rochester's school of business in Rochester, New York) recently conducted research on 471 large U.S. corporations. They found that an increase in strategic focus among these firms since 1978 has been significantly correlated with substantial gains in stock prices.[9] The percentage of single business segment firms rose from 35.6 in 1978 to 54.3 by 1988. The firms that narrowed their focus outperformed the general market by 2 to 4 percentage points in the year of the change. Conversely, the firms that widened their focus underperformed the market by about 4 percentage points. This pattern replicates on a grand scale what we found for the four banks.

What both my banking study and Jarrell and Comment's larger statistical survey suggest is a sharp questioning of the conventional wisdom of the 1960s and 1970s. The popular growth policy in those years was diversification through conglomerate mergers, and it was followed in Japan and other industrialized nations as well as in the United States. Many benefits were assumed to follow, including a reduction in overall company risk through "earnings smoothing" and the achievement of managerial and financial economies of scale and scope. By 1980, as Jarrell points out, "diversification had become a widely accepted business strategy for risk reduction and profitable growth," even though the poor record of many conglomerates, such as ITT, was a clear but generally ignored contraindication.

Walter Wriston, Citicorp' s CEO during its peak growth period from 1967 to 1984, was the leading advocate in the banking industry of the growth-through-diversification strategy. Citibank's lead was followed by Chase in a fumbling, "me, too" fashion, and by other big banks such as BankAmerica. None of these banks used the strategy effectively, and in their struggles of recent years, all have been moving toward focusing their activities. Of them all, Citicorp has been perhaps the last and most reluctant to move in this direction.

Jarrell concludes, "Today, however, the conventional wisdom on diversification has been completely reversed. Managers now are advised to eschew diversification and restructure the far-flung enterprise that resulted from past diversification strategies: to `focus,' that is, [to] specialize in `core' businesses."[10]

The strategy of growth through diversification did not work for big corporations in many industries, including banking, and it requires reexamination. Neither bigness nor diversification, per se, necessarily leads to success, and both often contribute to poor financial performance. Does this mean that banks should give up their interest in size and diversity? Perhaps they should, to some extent, as the case studies in this book indicate. More to the point, however, banks that are large and diverse will have to develop a management style appropriate for their condition. Neither Citicorp nor other banks that have emulated its strategy have yet developed effective management styles. They will have to learn to be competitive, despite being big and diversified.

The extent to which many big banks are able to accomplish these feats may well define their futures, and may eventually filter down to other banks as well. Much more will be required than simply decentralizing in traditional ways. Some of Lowell Bryan's blueprint for "breaking up the bank" seems particularly appropriate. So does Peter Drucker's suggestion on how to be competitive though big by setting up various product units as separate businesses, or perhaps as separate companies, each with its own CEO and board.[11]

Moreover, senior managers will have to pay increasing attention to the issue of determining the right or optimum size for their bank. Many have pointed to the economies of scale in consumer banking that justify a more nationwide banking system in that set of businesses, and many have also argued for expanding banks' powers to insurance and securities. These businesses, however, are much more problematic than consumer banking, and banks may become competitive in them only if they know how to manage them well. Insurance and securities require a very different management style from the styles required in consumer banking. Bankers Trust and Morgan, the two prototypes of merchant banking, have been able to develop appropriate styles. Citicorp and Chase (as well as other money centers, such as BankAmerica), by contrast, have fared quite poorly outside the consumer banking sector. Citicorp is completely reorganizing its corporate and investment banking groups in Japan, Europe, and North America, after performing dismally in commercial real estate, highly leveraged transactions (HLTs), and loans to less developed countries (LDCs). Chase is closing down many of its wholesale branches in Europe and other industrialized nations for similar reasons. Neither has been able to compete well in these businesses. BankAmerica's dramatic recovery in the late 1980s began with its exit from wholesale banking abroad and its increased focus on the consumer banking business on the West Coast.

Bigness has to be justified both by the economics of a particular business, including its technology, and by a management structure and systems that support its effective implementation. Drucker suggests, in addition, that a dramatic shift "from big to mid-sized enterprise as the economy's center of gravity is a radical reversal of the trend that dominated all developed economies for more than a century."

How might this be worked out in banking? For one thing, it would require the kind of increased attention to strategic planning that Bryan has suggested and that I discussed earlier. Banks will have to look separately at each cluster of businesses; manage them separately; and make the hard decisions about which ones to keep and which to drop, based on their competitive strengths and weaknesses. For another thing, banks will have to develop the particular management structures and systems that will be appropriate for each set of businesses.

Consumer banking, for example, is very different from corporate and investment banking in technology and products, and it therefore requires an appropriately different culture and management. Many bankers are aware of this, but few have acted productively on their knowledge. One of the most visionary—though he is not adept at implementing his vision—is Citicorp CEO John Reed. He astutely contrasts consumer banking, which has a routinized technology and produces uniform and standardized products, with corporate banking, which has a craftlike and research and development (R&D) oriented technology (much as medicine does) and therefore requires a completely different management style. For consumer banking, the appropriate organizational structure is centralized. The products are developed at the top, and a routinized bureaucratic structure prevails in the branches, at the point of delivery. In corporate banking, by contrast, product development and creativity are located at the point of delivery, in interaction with clients, each of whom has unique, specialized service needs. In Reed's words, which sound much like those of a sophisticated organizational sociologist:

> Consumer banking is a little like building cars. Success comes when you routinize things to a point where a group of people at the top build the strategy, drive the creative work, and push new products, while execution takes place relatively effortlessly, through good blocking and tackling....Corporate banking is more like delivering medicine....In the corporate bank, we don't have common products that we design and sell. We have relationships and transactions that are specialized and unique. Moreover, our professional competence sits down low in the corporate bank, with the people on the front lines who deal with customers and devise the transactions. We can't develop new products at the center and push them out. Good corporate bankers are walking product development departments.[12]

Unfortunately, this formulation of the managerial requirements for success in different commercial banking businesses has not been matched by good judgment at Citicorp about what businesses it should be in, nor has it been matched by effective implementation. Banks must engage in the kinds of strategic thinking that Reed and Citicorp have done so well in the abstract, but they must also be adept in implementing their strategic visions. Reed and Citicorp have been less than successful in implementation.

There are other developments that will be associated with banks' increased emphasis on strategic focus. One will be a continuation of the trend toward what is called *outsourcing* (a term taken from auto manufacturing). In outsourcing, banks contract out back-office and other technology functions to data processing firms; they also contract out training. The objective is to avoid performing so many in-house functions. Another development will involve undertaking more joint ventures with outside financial service institutions. Providing some services on their own—services that banks nevertheless want to make available to particular clients—can be too costly. Such joint ventures or collaborations will extend to new patterns of ownership as well, when banks don't have the capital they need to operate in particular product, customer, and geographic markets. Establishing global consortia, in which several international banks share the capital and risk associated with different parts of a business, may be a trend of the 1990s. John Reed, again the visionary, has articulated many creative ideas. He writes:

> We could web the world together. Imagine a scenario in which 10 or 12

international banks—much like the five or six giant oil companies—share the capital and risk associated with different parts of the business. The most effective way for us to become a big corporate bank in Germany might be to own 10% or 15% of one of the big German banks' corporate business. Since it might be hard for that bank to replicate our presence in Asia, we could swap 5% or 10% of that business in return. Somewhere else, we could go to a wholesale bank and say, "How would you like 25% of our consumer business in exchange for a piece of your corporate business[?]"

In brief, instead of pursuing an aggressive growth and diversification strategy, global banks will prune themselves down to what they do best. They will contract out as many of the back-office functions as they can. They will take on products that they don't have the expertise or capital to develop only through joint ventures and consortia. In the language of organization theorists, banks will thus function as *open systems*, with more permeable boundaries than before. They will be able to compensate for portfolio gaps or product limitations without having to either grow or buy their own businesses in a new area. Most important, they will have to learn to think smaller.

More Internal Collaboration: The Seamless Organization

In still another trend that will characterize the 1990s, banks will pursue more internal collaboration and synergies across businesses and product groups. Bankers have talked about this development for a long time, but with the exception of Morgan and perhaps a small number of others, their success in pursuing it has been limited. Thus, it has become all too common for customers of Chase or Citicorp to have service needs that require them to deal with half a dozen or more departments and/or divisions, none of which communicate with each other. Several may be in the corporate bank and several in the consumer bank, and to the extent that the bankers do not communicate, a customer's attempts to deal with all of them can become a nightmare. In the ideally managed bank, a relationship manager or project manager will coordinate all these services to meet the customer's unique needs. The functional equivalent of a project team will be set up, under the direction of the project manager. Tom Labrecque, Chase's CEO, has been one of the most articulate proponents of this organizational form, and it is being increasingly endorsed throughout the industry. It has always existed informally in small and middle-sized banks. Now it must be adopted in the big banks that have reached appropriate levels of specialization (into various functional, product, geographic, and customer groups) but have never effectively integrated or coordinated their various specialties.

Implied in the above discussion about strategic focus are two prescriptions: first, that banks should no longer go on the growth binges of the 1980s that created so much overcapacity in the industry, and second, that they should be sensitive to trying to reach an "appropriate" size. The appropriate size for each bank will be determined by an objective examination of market realities, rather than by wishing or hoping that particular new loans or businesses will turn out all right. At the same time, banks should learn how to play the consolidation or merger game, which will help many of them to survive.

Emerging Types of Banks

Based on developments in the past couple of decades, it seems likely that there will be several different tiers or types of U.S. banks in the future. Their emergence has already begun on a limited basis, and it is likely to continue during the next decade.[13]

One tier will be low-cost, high-volume providers of consumer banking services. The most striking examples now are Citicorp, Bank of America, Chase, Wells Fargo, and some of the superregionals, such as Banc One. These banks will provide profitable consumer banking at a reasonable price and will become national banks as the regulatory barriers to interstate banking break down. For many in this category, consumer banking will be the main set of businesses, after they make the difficult decision to divest themselves of much of their wholesale banking. A model of how to manage such a large consumer bank will be established by Citicorp, the leader in this field. It will be similar to John Reed's vision, which was described above, and it will involve a combination of centralization and decentralization. Products, marketing strategies, and back-office support systems will be developed centrally and exported both around the nation and around the world through what Reed refers to as "success transfer." At the same time, much flexibility will be given to managers of local branches to adapt the products to customer needs.

A second tier will be regional, middle-market banks that will focus on serving midsized corporations in large and middle-sized cities. Chemical is a prime example of this type of bank from the 1980s, as are some of the superregionals. There is a large and growing market for this type of bank, and it will continue to grow at least through the early 1990s.

Contrary to the fears of groups like the Independent Bankers Association, a significant third tier of small banks that provide quality service will also exist. Though the spokespeople of these groups fear a new "too small to save" mentality in Washington and are particularly apprehensive about interstate banking and reduced insurance coverage for small banks, these fears will not materialize.[14] The power of both the states and the small banks is so great that national banks will not be permitted to significantly erode the proportion of small, local community banks in the U.S. banking system.

The last tier will consist of global merchant banks, such as Morgan, Bankers Trust, and their counterparts in Japan and Europe. They will be predominantly wholesale banks, serving corporations, governments, and other financial institutions around the world. Some mixed banks (wholesale and retail) will also persist; the classic example is Citicorp. It is undoubtedly one of the most global banks in the United States, and it has been global, along with Morgan, for much of this century. Whether it can sustain its wholesale business on a large scale after its disastrous performance in the late 1980s and early 1990s remains to be seen. Citicorp, with or without John Reed, is remarkably resilient, and may well pull it off. The odds, however, are strong that the bank will concentrate increasingly on consumer banking worldwide, leaving the corporate, wholesale banking largely to others.

Organizational Forms
Required for Survival

What can be said in conclusion about what it will take to survive in the 1990s? I don't have much to add to what I have already said. The successful banks of the future will be more focused, niche players. They will figure out what they do best and concentrate on their areas of expertise. They will think smaller and will not try to be all things to all people.

Senior managers will pursue this approach through much more strategic thinking than did their predecessors. They will evaluate their performance and capabilities in different businesses more objectively and even ruthlessly. They will be willing to discard or exit from the businesses in which they are not competitive. Peter Drucker has suggested that lack of willingness to exit from unsuccessful businesses is one of the characteristics that distinguishes the public sector from the private. He would probably agree, however, that commercial banks have had the same weakness, in large part as a hangover or residue from the past, when they functioned in protected markets as quasi-public utilities.

Banks will also spend much time in the future on thinking through merger strategies. For many, survival will not be possible without merging, and effective merging will become a major preoccupation. In fact, it already is a major preoccupation for some banks; their planners have already developed numerous scenarios in which the comparative costs and benefits of different mergers are projected. Effective consolidation is critical for bank survival, but it is easier said than done. The relevant skills and technology are not well developed, and banks have little past experience, either their own or that of others, to guide their efforts. The complexities involved in managing the politics and the integration of cultures, strategies, structures, systems, and people are so great that doing it well is going to require a tremendous investment.

Regulators

Since many of the banking industry's problems are increasingly recognized as stemming from faulty regulation, there are likely to be significant changes in the behavior of the regulators. One of their biggest shortcomings has been their slowness in cracking down on unsafe banking practices. A General Accounting Office (GAO) study "on ways to stem the drain on the Bank Deposit Insurance Fund reported continuous delays in moving in on banks that had serious capital problems and/or increases in problem loans." The study concluded, "We have found a history of significant reluctance on the part of bank supervisors to take forceful actions when serious problems are identified during the examination process."[15] The GAO recommended a series of anticipatory interventions that are likely to be adopted in the 1990s. It referred to them as a new "trip-wire" approach to regulation that will require regulators to move much faster than before in forcing bankers to correct unsound management and lending practices. There is much legitimate concern about the likely depletion of the Bank Deposit Insurance Fund and the adequacy of bank regulation, and the GAO's recommendations have received much support in Congress.

If the recommendations are adopted, four trip wires will force regulatory intervention. The first will be triggered by deteriorating internal controls, increasing interest rate risk, or unusually rapid growth; the second by serious asset or earnings deterioration; the third by capital's falling below required levels; and the fourth by capital depletion. In each case, a particular set of interventions is specified, from tightening procedures and slowing loan growth, in response to the first trip wire, to requiring closure or merger of the bank, in response to the fourth. Regardless of how the final reforms differ in specifics from these original recommendations, the general principle that the regulators will be responsible for early intervention has achieved widespread acceptance.

While the GAO's recommendations raise concerns about government interference in the marketplace, there is a recognition that the critical role of commercial banks as a conduit for monetary policy and as the main instrument for credit requires much regulation. One lesson from the savings and loan (S&L) disaster is that it was precisely the lack of intervention and regulation that led to the S&L problems. Congress and the White House have a strong interest in not repeating that pattern.

Another required change will be for the regulators to drop the "too big to fail" doctrine. The main effect of this doctrine has been to shield big banks from the discipline of the market. Not even the Treasury plan faces the issue. Instead, it turns the outmoded doctrine into law by protecting all depositors and paying all losses of big banks that become insolvent, until other banks can take them over. As Prof. James Pierce of the University of California at Berkeley, who is the author of a recent Twentieth Century Fund study of American banking, points out, one major consequence of continuing this policy would be to move major small-bank depositors to larger institutions. By thus protecting the big banks, along with their depositors, this would, says Pierce, "make the nation more vulnerable to major bank failures and vastly increase the chances of massive taxpayer bailouts."[16] He concludes that if the Treasury proposal became law, "big would become downright ugly." As in the case of early intervention, there is so much broad-based support for changing this policy that the change could actually take place during the coming years.

Otherwise, the regulators are likely to encourage mergers, broader powers in insurance and securities, and nationwide banking, as recommended in the Treasury plan. If whatever legislation is passed fails to include these proposals, it is likely that the regulators will continue to press for them through administrative decisions. That was what happened in the 1980s, and it may continue in the 1990s if the political resistance to banking reform remains strong.

The other issue to be fought out will be the particular roles of the regulators. The turf struggles discussed above will continue, and it is not clear how they will be resolved. One critical policy issue is whether the main regulator should be primarily a political entity or an independent entity. Nicholas Brady argues that bank regulation should be in the political realm, for purposes both of accountability and to enable the administration in power to manage the economy more effectively. Alan Greenspan and such senior officials as E. Gerald Corrigan, president of the Federal Reserve Bank of New York and perhaps the most articulate conceptualizer of the Fed's appropriate role, argue that independent control by his agency is "the very essence of central banking."[17] The issue of independent control must be resolved soon. There is broad consensus for regulatory consolidation, but there are big differences about who the prime regulator should be.

Prospects

What, then, are the prospects for the 1990s, based on the diagnosis in this book? The prospects depend largely upon how much the senior managers of U.S. banks have learned from their experiences in the past decades, particularly the 1980s. In many respects, U.S. banking is a declining industry. It is burdened with excess capacity, it has a consequent need for consolidation, and many of the survivors have weak infrastructures. There are exceptions, which I have described: J.P. Morgan, Bankers Trust, Banc One, First Wachovia, First Fidelity, KeyCorp, and State Street Trust. However, many others are poorly managed. I have indicated some of the changes in style and decision making that would be necessary to improve these banks' management.

One of the most recent panaceas, as mentioned above, is mergers. Depending upon how well a merger is managed, it could conceivably result in big cost savings. Unfortunately, banks can bungle mergers, as they bungle other things. Bungling a merger is easy to do, because of the complexities involved in managing postmerger integration problems, regardless of the skills of key players. Some of the biggest problems are related to issues of power and control and of how the cultures of the merging institutions will be blended. Who will run the newly merged bank? Which jobs, products, and functions will be dropped? Which bank's culture will prevail? These questions touch upon incredibly complex problems. No clear blueprint exists for managing these problems, and even if one did exist, the political nature of the problems precludes easy solutions. Mergers seem to go poorly when they take place between banks that are approximately equal in power at the outset, when either or both are still struggling to integrate other institutions acquired prior to the merger, and when each has not closely evaluated the loan portfolio and other weaknesses of the other prior to the merger. A classic case is the merger of C&S with Sovran, but there will undoubtedly be many others in the future.

The larger question remains: How may banks become much better managed? Walter Wriston was once quoted as saying that he went into banking because it was a field that had attracted so many mediocre people, thereby giving him a greater chance of success. As a highly regulated public utility from the 1930s through the 1970s, banking probably did attract disproportionate numbers of relatively unimaginative functionaries. It was a protected business that did not require much initiative or imagination, as I pointed out in Chapter 1. *Business Week*'s money and banking editor, John Meehan, put it very well when he characterized bankers as people who are "good at taking orders and accomplishing well-defined, routine tasks."[18]

The nature of banking has obviously changed a lot since the 1970s. It has been transformed by globalization, electronic communications technology, the increasing volatility of interest rates and currencies, and the emergence of strong new competitors. Bankers can no longer be order takers if they want to survive. They must find new market niches, and they must develop and aggressively market new products. Most important, they must develop expertise in monitoring and forecasting the many complex external forces that impinge upon their industry, and they must maintain the product expertise and organizational flexibility to adapt quickly to significant changes in these forces.

In the banking industry, as in many other industries that are undergoing rapid change, there has been a big lag between the new skills required for success and the people who are now running the banks. Organizations often have an enormous inertia, even in the face of challenges to their very survival. Banks are no exception. Indeed, they may well be a prototype of the principle of inertia. U.S. banks will have to catch up quickly with the new realities they face, or they will be doomed to repeat many of the mistakes of the past. What is discouraging is that so many banks keep repeating past errors. This is, after all, not the first time banks have suffered from the third world and commercial real estate loan losses. One wonders how long it will be before more bankers learn from these experiences. Given the importance of the banking system to the U.S. economy, the stakes are very high. The way banks are managed is of vital national concern. It is to be hoped that the country will respond in a way that will revitalize this critical industry.

The Argument: A Sociological Perspective on Banking

Books on the declining competitiveness of the U.S. banking industry fall into one of two genres, neither of which provides the perspective of this one. The first is books by economists and banking specialists, who usually focus on external macroforces as the source of banking problems. The second is case studies written by financial journalists. While both genres make a contribution to our understanding of how and why U.S. banks have declined, each has limitations that this book was designed to correct.

Economists and banking specialists point to the increased competition from foreign banks and nonbank banks, to the rise of money-market mutual funds which siphon off deposits, and to capital markets products (commercial paper and junk bonds) which are taking away much of the banks' corporate loan business. These forces, they argue, have been the main sources of the decline in U.S. banking.

In addition, so the argument continues, U.S. commercial banks face another set of external pressures. At a time when they need more flexibility than ever to recoup losses in their traditional businesses by being able to diversify geographically and into new products, U.S. banks have been hamstrung by archaic laws that are no longer responsive to the industry's needs. Other financial services institutions have been allowed to encroach upon the banks' turf: Merrill Lynch with cash management and depository accounts, Sears with credit cards, automobile finance companies, and savings and loans (S&Ls) in commercial real estate lending. Banks, the argument continues, have not had similar options. The particular diagnoses and proposed solutions of banking scholars differ, but the discussions all focus on this broad set of external macroforces.

Notwithstanding that much of the variation in the banking industry's performance over the years has been driven by such forces, this book analyzes other factors that are also critical. Instead of dealing with the language of macroeconomics or analyzing the regulatory and legislative structure, it looks for explanations that use concepts from the fields of management and organizational behavior. Writing not as an economist or banking scholar but as a sociologist, I make the assumption that management counts for a great deal in shaping a particular institution or even an entire industry. This book takes, in that respect, a radically different tack from that of most banking scholars. It rests upon the premises that many banks are not well managed and that the nature and adequacy of bank management are critical.

Evidence supporting such a position is not hard to find. Within any single group of banks (money centers, superregionals, regionals, small community banks), all of which face similar competitive and legislative-regulatory environments, there is considerable variation in performance. Industry data as compiled by bank research groups are quite unequivocal. Among the big money centers, as I have indicated, there is wide agreement that Morgan, Bankers Trust, and the BankAmerica of the 1990s (now that it has recovered from its decline of the 1980s), are among the highest performers, while Manufacturers Hanover, Chemical, Mellon, Continental, BankAmerica in the 1980s, and Chase have been among the lowest. A similar consensus exists on the so-called superregionals. Banc One, Wachovia, North Carolina National Bank (NCNB), and Fleet Norstar are among the high performers, while Security Pacific is among the low ones. Even within particular regions that are suffering economic downturns, not all banks are experiencing the same problems. Thus, though the devastating declines in the commercial real estate market hit many New England banks (including Bank of New England, Bank of Boston, and Shawmut) very hard, State Street Boston has continued to do very well. What was peculiar to its management that permitted it to escape relatively unscathed, while its regional competitors suffered so much?

Sociologists are particularly interested in such deviant cases, in which institutions or events run counter to what might be expected. We sometimes learn more from an analysis of the cases that depart from the norm than from the others. In the banking industry, such an analysis requires us to look at how particular banks are managed.

As mentioned above, the second genre of books on banking is made up of clinical case studies written by financial journalists, who get inside banks and through interviews find out how they are managed. Sociologists, including me, find such case studies of much value because they tell the story of how particular banks have fared in the turbulent markets they face. Of course, telling the story is not a simple matter. Journalists, like sociologists, must rely on perceptions of key informants and must put them together in some fashion, taking individual biases into account and matching them with available documents. There are likely to be many such books in the near future, given the present crisis in U.S. banking and the consequent newsworthiness of books about particular banks.

Although sociologists find these books of value, it is important to distinguish what sociologists do from what journalists do. Sociologists, like journalists, are interested in telling a story about institutions based upon case studies, but we are mainly interested in developing generalizations about different types of institutions. We are especially interested in why some types of institutions are more effective than others, and in why some are destroyed by their inertia while others are quite agile and able to adapt to change. Journalists, by contrast, are often more interested in the uniqueness of the particular case and in the personalities of the different players. Sociologists too may be interested in the personalities and behavioral styles of institutions' leaders, but only insofar as this information helps us to generalize about institutions in a broader sense.

In conclusion, I believe that there is a need for the kind of new look at American banking that this book presents. My main argument is that we can better understand the present banking crisis by analyzing the institutions themselves than by looking exclusively at the environment in which they operate. Clearly, the many jolts that the U.S. banking system has faced in recent decades have had devastating impacts. The magnitude of their impacts on particular banks, however, varies considerably, depending upon how the banks have perceived and managed them. To develop better public policy for revitalizing this important industry, we need to know much more about characteristics and patterns of bank management. Only through such an examination can we determine how banks will respond to various market forces and legal changes and ultimately how the industry can be revived. That is the purpose of this book.

Appendix **B**

Getting Inside the Banks

The only way I could do credible interpretive histories of the four banks in this book was to "get inside," so that I could pull together the story by talking either with the people who made that history or with others who were very close to the history makers. Getting inside was not an easy task. There was an understandable wariness among people at all levels toward an unknown outsider who came in and asked questions about how the bank really operated, as opposed to what the public relations departments wanted investors and the business press to believe. Getting inside would have been a problem even in the best of times, and it required years of stubborn persistence.

Auspices, reputation, networks, and luck are always relevant in securing entree into institutions, and that was certainly the case for me. Coming from a well-regarded graduate school of business, with its own institutional and individual faculty ties to these banks, helped a bit to get me in the door. I say "a bit" because it was still a full-time project to acquire the information needed for in-depth analyses of these banks. There was, after all, nothing in it for the people I wanted to interview, as several members of their staffs took pains to remind me. Though I offered to share with them my general findings and insights as an unpaid, informal consultant, they seemed to look upon the exchange as uneven, since they did not anticipate learning much from what I as an outsider might have to say. Furthermore, they saw many risks in letting me in on their "organization secrets."

A common defense that I had somehow to work through was the

comment that the senior managers in these banks simply didn't have the time to talk with an academic about what they were doing. Why didn't I just read their annual reports and other publicly available material?

The result was a very uneven experience. Even after some willingness to cooperate developed—after word went out that it was OK for people to talk with me—much of what some people then told me was more in the nature of what psychologists refer to as "impression management" than information I could use. Even so, getting my foot in the door was a crucial first step. A senior manager at one of the banks indicated:

> I wasn't going to talk to you, and I wouldn't have let you in if you were a journalist. But the fact that you are an academic makes me more comfortable [and makes me feel] that you will do a more objective and searching study. I think that's very important, since the outside world should know how we have managed our way through such stormy and difficult times.

I will not identify the banks in this discussion, since they all did ultimately cooperate with me in varying degrees, for which I am most grateful. Rather, I shall refer to them as A, B, C, and D.

One of my former university colleagues had been a staffer for many years at bank A, the first bank I tried, and he got me an interview with the public affairs chief of a major division. This person sent me on to two senior managers in his division, and both stonewalled me. One suggested that I read some books and articles about his area of banking. This bank has a reputation for institutional arrogance, and my first reaction was that these two managers might be typical of the bank in general. I did in fact then try a few more senior managers there, with similarly negative results. Discouraged about my prospects, I began to pursue the other banks, where I hoped my networks might serve me better.

Happily, however, I didn't write off bank A as a hopeless cause. Several months later, I made contact with a staff member who had collaborated on a project many years before with a couple of my academic colleagues. This bank manager not only gave me a rich interview on the bank's culture, strategy, and politics, with the agreement that it would remain confidential, but referred me to several others inside the bank and outside (people who had left or retired) who did likewise. They were upper-middle-level and senior managers who shared my informant's view that though the bank was an exciting place in which to work (because it had attracted many talented people and developed many innovative products), it had some deep-rooted, systemic problems that should be analyzed by an outsider who had no particular ax to grind. "We need such a sociological examination of our bank," explained one such informant, "because we have some internal problems and if we don't deal with them better, we're going to be in deep trouble down the road."

I was able to reach the people this informant suggested, and in the course of 3 to 4 weeks, I did about fifteen 2- to 3-hour interviews with highly informed senior managers who were also quite open with me, again on condition of anonymity. Now I was beginning to get the kinds of data on the bank's internal workings and style that I needed, so that I could tell the story of how it was in fact being managed. Over time, through a process of referral, sometimes called the *snowball* technique by field researchers, I became able to make my way around quite well.

Thus, after having almost despaired about my prospects of ever getting inside this bank, I stumbled serendipitously into a researcher's gold mine of informants. I had found an "underground" within the institution—biased to be sure, and it was my obligation to take that into account, but still informative about critical developments within the bank that related directly to my research interests. Clearly, however, I had not planned my research that way.

After a while, success began feeding on itself. The more I learned about the bank, the richer my interviews became. As I demonstrated that I knew a lot about how the bank worked, I gained greater credibility. As it became apparent to prospective informants that I had already talked with many high-level people in the bank, they became more expansive and helpful in recommending me to their colleagues. The day I knew I had it made was when a former staff person, who had been at the bank some 25 years and whom I had been trying to reach, called me from Florida to assure me that we would get together as soon as he returned to New York and checked his schedule—and he did follow up.

Later, I was referred to another public affairs officer. Unlike the first one I had contacted, this officer worked hard to arrange my interviews with senior managers. (I later found out that the first public affairs person had lost power by the time I contacted him, because his former boss had left the bank. This probably accounted for the limited assistance he offered me.) This public affairs officer became an informal institutional gatekeeper and provided me with several interviews that I might never have gotten on my own. One constraint was that the officer stayed in the room while the interview was going on, taking notes on the discussion, seemingly to make sure that nothing was said that might be harmful to the bank's interests. Still, I got a lot of useful information on how the bank was coping with changes in the industry.

While I hardly claim to have gained unrestricted access, I was able to reverse an early failure and build momentum. After a while, people I had thought earlier would never speak to me were almost waiting in line to tell me about the bank.

Bank B was an entirely different story. This institution was widely known for being more cautious than many of its competitors. I fully expected some of the same treatment there that I had received in the early stages at bank A, and thus I was truly dumbfounded by my initial encounter. I called a senior manager one morning and, to my amazement, was invited for lunch that day. He turned out to have been a doctoral student at my school, who had taken a course with me. His bank had had many years of lackluster profits, in the early 1970s and again in the early 1980s, punctuated by good years in between. From 1985 through late 1988, it had again experienced improvement, and he wanted very much to get this favorable story out. He seemed particularly interested in overcoming the lag between his bank's negative reputation, based on its bad years, and what he and some bank analysts regarded as its improved recent performance. He not only gave me a broad picture of the bank's changing culture as he saw it but also opened doors to senior managers and staff, who were all highly cooperative. Some interviews with these people were revealing of the bank's culture and style, but much of what they told me contained strong elements of impression management as well. I came away not having a sense of the underlying features of the bank's culture that had contributed to its continued problems and poor financial performance in recent years.

Therefore, I sought out other informants. Through various networks, I was able to find people who gave me a more candid and searching description of the bank—its weaknesses as well as its strengths. Over time, I talked with enough of them to pull together a more balanced and fuller account than I had received from the first group of informants.

My experiences at bank C could also be described as driven largely by luck. Before entering the field, I had heard that the top person in a particular staff function at all four banks might be very helpful. While that was not at all the case in the other banks, that staff person at bank C was tremendously cooperative. He was always loyal to his institution in the ways in which he represented it to me, but he was at the same time somewhat disenchanted with strategic directions which its chief executive officer (CEO) and other senior managers had taken, and he discretely shared some of his doubts with me. We lunched together several times at the bank, and he shared with me many bank analysts' reports and other public documents. He also gave me advice on whom I should try to interview and helped me to develop a strategy for talking with different categories of people. With his help and that of others he had suggested, I was able to "make the rounds" of many senior managers.

Bank D was by far the most difficult to gain access to. Whereas I had been nearly in despair about bank A, at one time I all but wrote off bank D as a lost cause. My first encounter there was a long interview with one of the bank's top staff people. I got to him through a university colleague who had conducted training programs and consulted for his bank. As we were winding down, after 2 hours of significant conversation about the bank's recent history, I asked him how I might gain access to senior management. He essentially said the following:

> You are doing a detailed and searching study, covering a lot of issues: our strategy, our culture, how we are changing. You could only do that by talking with the people here who made many of the big decisions. And that would take a lot of their time, right? Well, the only way you could do that would be to have our top management group and board pass on it. I don't want to sound too pessimistic and prematurely discourage you, but our bank's policies indicate that you're probably not going to get that OK.

Rather than follow up with his board and likely get a formal turndown, I tried other channels. I moved on to the bank's communications officer. He asked me at one point to send him some draft materials, indicating that the way to get the bankers' attention was to give them something in writing. Several weeks later, he sent me back a brief reaction, indicating that he thought the bankers would be interested in my conclusions, when I completed the book. However, he made no mention of how I might get some interviews at his bank and whom I might talk to so that I could in fact finish the book.

I then proceeded on my own to interview several senior managers who had retired or moved elsewhere. I reached them through an old college classmate, who was referred to me by a mutual friend. Collectively, these senior managers provided me with a rich profile of the bank and an informal roster of the key players. They often indicated that I could use their names in my attempts to get interviews with these key players. I then made many calls trying to arrange meetings with the key players. My calls were brought to the attention of the top staffer who had seemingly tried to deflect my efforts when several of the people I had been calling asked him about me and my study. He called me and asked what I was doing. I patiently repeated what I had told him before, that I was writing a book about four New York banks and that his bank was one of them. We finally agreed, at his suggestion, that I would send him a one- or two-page summary of my study (even though the chapter I had sent him many weeks before had already done that). After I sent the summary, I didn't hear from him for a few weeks. When I finally called him, he informed me that he had not had any "takers." "I was unable to persuade them," he reported. Thus I was left to continue my efforts on my own, not knowing how he would characterize my study if people I later called for interviews asked him about me.

I finally did reach many top-level managers at bank D, and several shared some worthwhile insights. It was a slow process, however, which lasted for a period of years, since the two so-called gatekeepers whom I had encountered had not been helpful in getting me into the institution. In mid-1991, however, the communications officer retired, and his replacement was considerably more open and helpful than he had been. This seemed to reflect a general change in bank D's posture toward outsiders. Unfortunately for me, I had already completed my fieldwork by the time this change took place. Even so, I had been able to get much good material.

If I had taken the first staff person too literally, I would most likely have received a turndown from the board and senior management, which would have put me in a weak position, making it difficult for me to pursue further interviews at bank D. Avoiding an institutional rejection was important. Likewise, had I sat back and waited for the communications staff person to pave the way for me, I might still be waiting. I had to proceed on my own, then, in a bank with a culture that didn't encourage the sharing of confidences with outsiders. By persisting, I was eventually able to get some good interviews. At times the process was agonizingly slow, but I got enough information to include the bank in the study. For me, that was a great victory, since bank D's recent history was relevant to the histories of other banks that were undergoing similar changes, and it therefore needed to be told.

Can other researchers who are investigating sensitive issues of institutional culture, strategy, style, and politics learn larger lessons from this experience? I suggest the following:

1. First, it is possible to gain access to institutions, even when one is asking for sensitive information, by being persistent and patient and by making a credible promise of confidentiality. Researchers should not become so discouraged as to drop a project, or to seriously modify it, because of a lack of early access. Such an effort, however, does re-

quire a lot of time. If there are no tight deadlines, it is worth the effort to keep trying, since even the most resistant institutions may become permeable to a researcher who exercises patience and skill. I certainly felt defeated on several occasions, but through a variety of techniques I was able to bounce back, after having been seemingly rebuffed.

2. It is impossible to plan how to succeed in the task of research, since chance seems to play such an important role. However, some researchers are luckier than others, largely because they are not easily discouraged; because they are quick to seize the advantage when even the smallest opening develops; and, finally, because they have the interpersonal skills needed to develop the trust needed to conduct interviews about sensitive issues.

3. Using multiple networks and gatekeepers is indispensable. It lowers the risks of reliance upon any one contact and of losing momentum if that one doesn't work out.

4. Developing a political map of the senior management group and then reaching one or more members of the group early on is also very important, to establish credibility. However, outsiders (for example, people who have retired or moved to another institution, analysts of the particular industry, or consultants) may be easier to reach, may be the best sources, and may be useful as quasi-sponsors, to help open doors.

5. Finding marginal insiders who are critical of the institution and may to varying degrees be disaffected is helpful in providing an important counterbalance to the public relations commentary that is invariably encountered in interviews with high-level people. Managers understandably want to present the best face of the institution to an outsider, and their presentation has to be put into a wider context.

Appendix C

Data Sources

I used two main data sources for this study. One, described in Appendix B, was interviews. The other consisted of many documents, including annual reports, bank analysts' reports, previously published books and studies, articles in the business and financial press, and industry statistics.

I interviewed people outside and inside the four banks. For each bank, I conducted about 50 interviews with insiders at each bank and another 150 with knowledgeable outsiders. The interviews varied in length from 30 minutes to 3 hours, with most averaging about an hour. I conducted these interviews over a 3 1/2-year period starting in early 1988. Each interview covered one or more of the key organizational characteristics discussed in Chapter 2: the bank's culture, strategy, structure, and human resources practices, as well as the visions and management styles of the chief executive officers (CEOs), both past and present. Many of my best insights into the present functioning of these organizations are based upon an understanding of their histories, which I was able to develop from interviews and documents.

I purposely conducted many early interviews with outsiders who were connected with the staffs of the four banks. These early outsider interviews were helpful with the later insider interviews. Many of the outsiders were able to suggest whom I should contact and what issues I should cover with particular inside informants. They also helped to establish my credibility as a knowledgeable person. The outsiders who were most helpful were bank analysts from Wall Street firms, management consultants, staff members of executive search firms, people in the banking associations, regulators, and journalists. These people possess a wealth of knowledge about and insight into the banks and how they work.

The insiders I talked to included senior managers and top staff members, particularly people in corporate planning and human resources but also division and department heads. The central issue in all the interviews was how the bank was repositioning itself or adapting to changes in the industry and how this effort was affected by its culture and CEOs. Needless to say, it took a lot of digging and persistence to get useful information, since, as I indicated above, inside informants often felt bound to present the best face of their organization to an outsider. Not surprisingly, the interviews varied from not very helpful, public relations-type presentations of a party line to searching and candid descriptions of what the bank was really like. To maximize my ability to get candid descriptions, I interviewed people who had left the banks, either for other positions elsewhere or for retirement. The candor of these people has been a source of excellent insights into how the banks evolved and into their cultures and institutional styles.

Certainly there are biases in the reports of many people who left the banks, but that is the case with all informants. In the end, what I did was to put together interpretive histories of the four banks based on my sense of what really happened. As an outside observer with no particular bias, I was able to pool information from many different sources and to look for patterns and areas of consensus upon which I could base my own final judgments. Ultimately, this is the way any researcher proceeds, leaving it to the reader to decide upon the validity of the final version.

Many documents were available on the four banks, and I made use of whatever was available. In addition to books on Citicorp, Chase, and Morgan (which are cited in the chapters on those banks), I used annual reports, bank analysts' studies, speeches by CEOs and other senior managers, and numerous articles in the business and financial press. The U.S. commercial banking industry and many individual banks, including the four presented in this book, have been the subject of voluminous reports and articles. I took as much information as I could from this vast historical record, mainly for the period since the late 1960s. While people who write about these banks as institutions differ in some respects, the consensus among them regarding basic characteristics of the banks is striking. Also striking is the agreement between what has been written and what I gleaned from interviews. This book highlights, in particular, the areas of consensus.

Notes

Chapter 1 The Financial Services Industry Revolution

1. James R. Barth, R. Dan Brumbaugh, Jr., and Robert E. Litan, *The Banking Industry in Turmoil*, presented to the Financial Institutions Subcommittee of the House Committee on Banking, Housing, and Urban Affairs, U.S. House of Representatives, Washington, Dec. 17, 1990, p. 25.

2. David D. Hale, "Global Finance and the Retreat to Managed Trade," *Harvard Business Review*, January-February 1990, pp. 150–162.

3. Fred E. Emery and Eric L. Trist, "The Causal Texture of Organizational Environments," *Human Relations*, vol. 18, 1965, pp. 21–32.

4. Barth, Brumbaugh, and Litan, op. cit., p. 123.

5. Eduard Ballarin, *Commercial Banks Amid the Financial Revolution*, Ballinger, Cambridge, Mass., 1986, pp. 52–59.

6. Harold Van B. Cleveland and Thomas F. Huertas, *Citibank, 1812–1970*, Harvard University Press, Cambridge, Mass., 1985, pp. 183–186. See also Martin Mayer, *The Bankers*, Ballantine Books, New York, 1974, pp. 117–118.

7. Ballarin, op. cit., p. 58; and *Rethinking Glass Steagall*, monograph published by J.P. Morgan, December 1984.

8. *Time*, Dec. 3, 1984, p. 48.

9. Robert G. Eccles and Dwight B. Crane, *Doing Deals*, Harvard Business School Press, Boston, Mass., 1988, pp. 214–221.

10. An excellent treatment of these changes is Arnold W. Sametz, "The `New' Financial Environment of the United States," in Edward Altman and Mary Jane McKinney (eds.), *Handbook of Financial Markets and Institutions*, 6th ed., John Wiley and Sons, New York, 1987, pp. 3–26.

11. Lawrence S. Ritter and William L. Silber, *Principles of Money, Banking, and Financial Markets*, 5th Edition, Basic Books, New York, 1986, pp. 89–92.

12. Ibid., pp. 158–160; and Mayer, op. cit., chap. 17.

13. Ritter and Silber, op. cit., p. 109.

14. This point is articulated well in Bank for International Settlements, *Recent Innovations in International Banking*, April 1986, pp. 1–15.

15. Emery and Trist, op. cit.

16. Federal Reserve Bank of New York, *Recent Trends in Commercial Bank Profitability*, September 1986, p. 15.

17. Barth, Brumbaugh, and Litan, op. cit., p. 24.

18. John Meehan et al., "Banks: Is Big Trouble Brewing?" *Business Week,* July 16, 1990, p. 148.

19. First Manhattan Consulting Group, *Investment Banking for Commercial Bankers*, Feb. 23, 1988.

20. Ibid.

21. The Wall Street Transcript, *Special Report, Financial Services/Money Center Banks*, Mar. 26, 1990, p. 4.

22. A good summary of the arguments on both sides appears in Ingo Walter (ed.), *Commercial Banks' Increasing Presence in the Investment Banking Business*, Salomon Brothers Center, Stern School of Business, New York University, Occasional Papers in Business and Finance, 1989. No. 9.

Chapter 2   Different Banks, Different Models

1. See Richard Daft, *Organization Theory and Design*, 3d ed., West Publishing, Saint Paul, Minn., 1989, chap. 2, for a review of the theories.

2. James R. Barth, R. Dan Brumbaugh, Jr., and Robert E. Litan, *The Banking Industry in Turmoil*, presented to the Financial Institutions Subcommittee of the House Committee on Banking, Housing, and Urban Affairs, U.S. House of Representatives, Washington, Dec. 17, 1990, p. 19.

3. Robert Waterman, Thomas Peters, and Julien Phillips, "Structure Is Not Organization," *Business Horizons*, June 1980, pp. 14–26.

4. Ibid., pp. 18–19.

5. Michael Tushman, William Newman, and Elaine Romanelli, "Convergence and Upheaval: Managing the Unsteady Pace of Organizational Evolution," *California Management Review*, vol. 29, no. 1, 1987, pp. 1–16. See also Donald C. Hambrick and Phyllis A. Mason, "Upper Echelons: The Organization as a Reflection of Its Top Managers," *Academy of Management Review*, 1984, vol. 9, no. 2., pp. 193–206; and Donald C. Hambrick, "Guest Editor's Introduction: Putting Top Managers Back in the Strategy Picture," *Strategic Management Journal*, vol. 10, 1989, pp. 5–15.

6. Frances J. Milliken and Theresa K. Lant, "The Effect of an Organization's Recent Performance History on Strategic Persistence and Change: The Role of Managerial Interpretations," in *Advances in Strategic Management*, vol. 7, JAI Press, Greenwich, Conn., 1991, pp. 129–156.

7. Raymond E. Miles and Charles C. Snow, *Organizational Strategy, Structure, and Process*, McGraw-Hill, New York, 1978.

Chapter 3   Citicorp: From New York Bank to Global Giant

1. Citicorp, *1990 Annual Report.*

2. Roy Smith, *The Global Bankers,* Dutton, New York, 1989, chap. 11.

3. Salomon Brothers, Stock Research, *Citicorp: The Only Clear-Cut American Bank Winner in a Pan-European Environment,* January 1990.

4. Stephen I. Davis, *Excellence in Banking,* St. Martin's Press, New York, 1985. Also Stephen I. Davis, *Managing Change in the Excellent Banks,* St. Martin's Press,. New York, 1988.

5. Salomon Brothers, Stock Research, *A Review of Bank Performance,* 1990, p. 1.

6. *The Wall Street Journal,* May 13, 1992, p. D4.

7. From an interview with a bank analyst.

8. Salomon Brothers, Stock Research, *Citicorp: Problems Persist,* Jan. 16, 1991.

9. Fred R. Bleakley, "Weakened Giant; As Big Rivals Surge, Citicorp's John Reed at a Cross Roads," *The Wall Street Journal,* Aug. 16, 1991, pp. A1-A2.

10. Another very critical article appeared in *Fortune,* on Jan. 14, 1991. It was entitled "Citicorp's World of Troubles" and written by Carol J. Loomis (pp. 90–99).

11. Harold Van B. Cleveland and Thomas Huertas, *Citibank; 1812–1970,* Harvard University Press, Cambridge, Mass.,1985 pp. 259–260.

12. Arthur L. Stinchcombe, "Social Structure and Organizations," in James March, ed., *Handbook of Organizations,* Rand McNally, Chicago, Ill., 1965, pp. 153–191.

13. The history to follow is based on Cleveland and Huertas, op. cit.; George Moore, *The Banker's Life,* Norton, New York, 1987; and John Brooks, "The Money Machine," *The New Yorker,* Jan. 5, 1981, pp. 41–61.

14. It has certainly been in vigorous competition with J.P. Morgan and in the 1960s and 1970s with Chase, both historically aristocratic banks.

15. Cleveland and Huertas, op. cit., chap. 3.

16. Ibid., p. 45.

17. Ibid., chaps. 7, 8.

18. Brooks, op. cit., p. 58.

19. The Salomon research group was later to apply this term to Chase in the 1980s. It was applicable in both instances.

20. A useful source is Moore, op. cit.

21. Cleveland and Huertas, op. cit., p. 261.

22. Brooks, op. cit., p. 59.

23. Cleveland and Huertas, op. cit., pp. 260ff.

24. Moore, op. cit., p. 251.

25. Brooks, op. cit., p. 59.

26. One consultant-academic suggested that this style of decision making by con-
    tention was very much the IBM approach and that perhaps Wriston may have
    been influenced by them.

27. Robert A. Bennett, "Citicorp Is Said to Choose Reed as New Chief," *The New
    York Times*, June 20, 1984, pp. A1, D4; Bennett, "Wriston: A Summing Up,"
    ibid., June 21, 1984, pp. D1, D19.

28. Interview with a senior manager at Citicorp.

29. Reed spent a lot of time with academic social scientists, as former board pres-
    ident of both the Russell Sage Foundation and the New York Blood Center,
    and as a board member of the Behavioral Sciences Center at Palo Alto.

30. Eric N. Berg, "Citicorp Accepts a Big Loss Linked to Foreign Loan," *The New
    York Times*, May 20, 1987, pp. A1, D6; and "Citicorp's Reed Outlines Path on
    Third World Loans," *The Wall Street Journal*, May 28, 1987, p. A6.

Chapter 4   Citicorp: Battlefields
of Diversity

1. Developing nations have no capital markets, and Citicorp pursues traditional
   lending as well as local currency exchange there, along with some investment
   banking. By contrast, it provides many new investment banking products and
   fee-based services in advanced countries.

2. Citicorp, *1990 Annual Report*.

3. See Jeffrey Pfeffer, *Power in Organizations*, Pitman, Boston, Mass., 1981.

4. Salomon Brothers, Stock Research, *Citicorp: An Analysis of Functional Business
   Lines in a Global Context*, January 1988, p. 2.

5. Citicorp Worldwide, *1988 Annual Report*.

6. Citicorp, *1990 Annual Report*, p. 11.

7. See, for example, Salomon Brothers, Stock Research, *Citicorp: The Only Clear-
   Cut American Bank Winner in a Pan-European Environment*, January 1990.

8. Salomon Brothers, January 1988, op. cit., pp. 28–34.

9. Citicorp, *1990 Annual Report*, p. 8.

10. Merrill Lynch, *Citicorp*, June 1, 1989, p. 5.

11. Ibid., p. 9.

12. Citicorp, *1990 Annual Report*, pp. 5–6.

13. Salomon Brothers, January 1990, op. cit., p. 1.

14. Merrill Lynch, op. cit., p. 6.

15. Carol J. Loomis, "Citicorp's World of Troubles," *Fortune*, Jan. 14, 1991, pp.
    90–99.

16. Michael Quint, "Meetings Are Shifted by Chase," *The New York Times*, July 21,
    1990, p. 33.

17. Fred R. Bleakley and George Anders, "Citicorp Is Expected to Name Ruding of The Netherlands to Senior Position," *The Wall Street Journal*, Jan. 13, 1992, p. B10.

18. Michael Quint, "After Losing Luster at Home, Citicorp Risks Future Abroad," *The Wall Street Journal*, Jan. 20, 1992, pp. Al, D3.

19. Citicorp, *1990 Annual Report*, p. 20.

20. Citicorp, *1988 Annual Report* and *1990 Annual Report*.

21. Richard Layne, "Quotron's Troubles Put Damper on Citicorp's Grand Ambitions," *The American Banker*, Nov. 27, 1989, pp. 1, 7.

Chapter 5   Citicorp: Culture Shock

1. Robert L. Daft, *Organization Theory and Design*, 3d ed., West Publishing, Saint Paul, Minn., chap. 12. Also Terrence E. Deal and Allan A. Kennedy, *Corporate Cultures*, Addison-Wesley, Reading, Mass.

2. Noel Tichy and Ram Charan, "Citicorp Faces the World: An Interview with John Reed," *Harvard Business Review*, November-December 1990, p. 140.

3. Ibid.

4. John Brooks, "Profiles," *The New Yorker*, Jan. 25, 1981, p. 47.

5. Paine Webber, *Banknotes*, Feb. 3, 1989, p. 4.

6. Sara Bartlett, "John Reed, Citicorp's Chief, Bumps into Reality," *The New York Times*, Feb. 5, 1989, p. D1.

7. Loomis, op. cit., p. 91.

8. Steven Lipin, "Citicorp's Quotron Became Black Hole Despite High Hopes of Chairman Reed," *The Wall Street Journal*, Oct. 18, 1991, p. A5.

9. Ibid.

10. Paine Webber, op. cit., p. 4.

11. Loomis, op. cit., p. 94.

12. Paine Webber, op. cit., pp. 4, 5.

13. John A. Byrne, "Is Your Company Too Big?" *Business Week*, Mar. 27, 1989, pp. 84–94.

Chapter 6   Chase: A Case of Institutional Lag

1. Chase had $18 billion in total assets in 1967, compared with $17.5 billion for First National City. See Harold Van B. Cleveland and Thomas F. Huertas, *Citibank, 1812–1970*, Harvard University Press, Cambridge, Mass., 1985, fn. 62, p. 439.

2. These measures were computed from Salomon Brothers, Stock Research, *A Review of Bank Performance*, 1985 and 1990.

3. John Donald Wilson, *The Chase*, Harvard Business School Press, Boston, Mass., 1986, p. 9.

4. Ibid., chap. 1.

5. Ibid., p. 56.

6. Ibid., p. 73.

7. Ibid., p. 84.

8. Ibid., p. 97.

9. Nancy Belliveau, "The Analyst vs. The Chase," *Institutional Investor*, July 1976, p. 22.

10. Richard B. Miller, "Chase Manhattan—The Rockefeller Years," *The Bankers Magazine*, April 1980, p. 55.

11. Wilson, op. cit., p. 162.

12. Priscilla S. Meyer, "Burdens of The Past," *Forbes*, July 18, 1983, p. 13.

13. Carol J. Loomis, "The Three-Year Deadline at `David's Bank,'" *Fortune*, July 1977, p. 74.

14. Ibid.

15. Miller, op. cit., p. 55.

16. Wilson, op. cit., p. 217.

17. Loomis, op. cit., p. 74.

18. Gilbert E. Kaplan and Gary Reich, "David Rockefeller," *Institutional Investor*, July 1987, p. 134.

19. Wilson, op. cit., pp. 241, 245.

20. Loomis, op. cit., p. 76.

21. Wilson, op. cit., p. 246.

22. Meyer, op. cit., p. 32.

23. Wilson, op. cit., pp. 253–257.

24. *Fortune*, November 1979.

25. Belliveau, op. cit., p. 21.

26. Loomis, op. cit., p. 80.

27. Wilson, op. cit., pp. 335–336.

28. Ibid.

29. Gary Hector, "Big Banks? How Bad Can It Get?" *Fortune*, Dec. 3, 1990, p. 55.

30. Chase Manhattan Corporation, *1990 Annual Report*, Part Two, pp. 3–7.

Chapter 7 Chase: The Anatomy of a Flawed Culture

1. Salomon Brothers, Stock Research, *The Chase Manhattan Corporation: Will the Sleeping Giant Arise?*, October 1989, p. 4.

2. John Donald Wilson, *The Chase*, Harvard Business School Press, Boston, Mass., 1986, p. 102.

3. Gilbert E. Kaplan and Gary Reich, "David Rockefeller," *Institutional Investor*, July 1987, p. 134.

4. Suzanna Andrews, "Trying to Get Chase Back on Track," *Institutional Investor*, May 1986, p. 78.

5. Ibid.

6. Ibid, p. 75.

7. Richard Daft, *Organization Theory and Design*, West Publishing, Saint Paul, Minn., 3d ed., 1990, chap. 11.

8. Carol J. Loomis, "The Three-Year Deadline at `David's Bank,'" *Fortune*, July 1977, p. 73.

9. Richard B. Miller, "Chase Manhattan—The Rockefeller Years," *The Banker's Magazine*, April 1980, p. 55.

Chapter 8 Chase: Culture, Strategy, and Survival

1. Speech at the Sanford Bernstein Conference, May 31, 1989.

2. Quoted in Steven I. Davis, *Managing Change in the Excellent Banks*, St. Martin's Press, New York, 1988, p. 65.

3. Salomon Brothers, Stock Research, *The Chase Manhattan Corporation: Will the Sleeping Giant Arise?* October 1989, p. 8.

4. Ibid., p. 14.

5. Ibid., p. 17.

6. Chase, *1990 Annual Report*, Part One, p. 18.

7. Salomon Brothers, op. cit., p. 18.

8. Chase, *1990 Annual Report*, p. 8.

9. Salomon Brothers, op. cit., pp. 18–20.

10. Ibid., p. 20.

11. Ibid., pp. 24ff.

12. Associated Press, "Swiss Bank to Acquire Chase Investment Unit," *The New York Times*, Feb. 22, 1991, p. D3.

13. Michael Quint, "Chase to Sell Off Most of Its Leasing Operation," *The New York Times*, Aug. 6, 1991, pp. D1, D4.

14. Associated Press, op. cit.

15. Peter Pae, "Chase Acquires Bank Business in Connecticut," *The Wall Street Journal*, Aug. 12, 1991, p. B4b.

16. Priscilla S. Meyer, "Burdens of The Past," *Forbes*, July 18, 1983, p. 32.

17. Henry Mintzberg, *The Structuring of Organizations*, Prentice Hall, Englewood Cliffs, N.J., 1979, p. 308.

18. Suzanna Andrews, "Trying to Get Chase Back on Track," *Institutional Investor*, May 1986, p. 76.

19. Robert Guenther, "Investment Bankers Lose Out in Chase Reorganization," *The Wall Street Journal*, May 4, 1988, p. 26.

20. Gilbert E. Kaplan and Gary Reich, "The Analyst vs. the Chase," *Institutional Investor*, June 1987, pp. 133–137; John Donald Wilson, *The Chase*, Harvard Business School Press, Boston, Mass. 1986, pp. 117–118; and numerous interviews.

21. Nancy Belliveau, "The Analyst vs. The Chase," *Institutional Investor*, July 1976, p. 22.

22. Wilson, op. cit., pp. 218; and Kaplan and Reich, op. cit., p. 134.

23. Wilson, op. cit., pp. 294–295.

24. Steven Lipin, "Banking Industry Basks in the Glow of Strong Profits," *The Wall Street Journal*, Apr. 30, 1992, p. B4.

25. Chase Manhattan Corporation, *1991 Annual Report*, Part 1, p. 9.

Chapter 9   Bankers Trust: The Great Transformation

1. Peter Lee, "BT Looks to Sanford's Sorcery," *Euromoney*, Jan. 1991, p. 24.

2. The notion of high performance is used here in a relative sense. Some investment bankers insist that Bankers Trust is not yet that high a performer relative to Wall Street firms but only in relation to other commercial banks.

3. Bankers Trust, *1990 Annual Report*, pp. 3–4.

4. Salomon Brothers, Stock Research, *Bankers Trust New York Corporation: The Most Sophisticated U.S. Merchant Bank*, August 1989.

5. Salomon Brothers, Stock Research, *A Review of Bank Performance*, 1989.

6. Bankers Trust, op. cit. p. 3.

7. Montgomery Securities, report on Bankers Trust, Aug. 10, 1989.

8. Soter did an intensive, informal unpublished study of Bankers Trust's transformation and kindly shared many of his insights. Another insightful unpublished study is Felinda Mottino, *Organizational Metamorphosis, A Case Study of Bankers Trust Company*, Spring 1987, Department of Sociology, New York University.

9. Bankers Trust, *The Changing Times of Bankers Trust Company*, 1978, p. 7. The discussion to follow draws heavily on this history, in addition to interviews.

10. Thomas Lamont's biography of Henry P. Davison, *The Record of a Useful Life*, Harper, New York, 1933, chap. VI, is a good source.

11. Bankers Trust, op. cit., p. 35.

12. Ibid., p. 39.

13. Ibid., p. 52.

14. Booz, Allen & Hamilton, Inc., *Bankers Trust: Evolution of a Strategy*, Dec. 14, 1983, chap. 6.

15. Ibid., p. 60.

16. Jeffrey Pfeffer, *Power in Organizations,* Pitman, Boston, Mass. 1982, pp. 142–145.

17. Booz, Allen & Hamilton, op. cit., pp. 112ff.

18. Larry Greiner makes this point in his "Patterns of Organization Change," *Harvard Business Review,* vol. 45, May-June 1967, pp. 119–130.

19. Contrast this clear and straightforward approach to succession with Wriston's approach at Citicorp. Wriston kept the suspense and competition for his job going for more than 2 years by naming three front-runners.

Chapter 10 Bankers Trust: The Benefits of Culture Shock

1. Salomon Brothers Stock Research, *Bankers Trust New York Corporation: The Most Sophisticated U.S. Merchant Bank,* August 1989, pp. 9, 12.

2. Craig Torres, "Wall Street's New Elite Are Global Trading Powers," *The Wall Street Journal,* Nov. 6, 1991, p. C1.

3. Salomon Brothers, op. cit., p. 9.

4. Ibid., p. 11.

5. Tom Burns and G. M. Stalker, *The Management of Innovation,* Tavistock Publications, London, England, 1961.

6. Bankers Trust New York Corporation, *1990 Annual Report,* p. 2.

7. Salomon Brothers, op. cit., p. 6.

8. Ibid., p. 5.

9. Bankers Trust, *1990 Annual Report,* p. 67.

Chapter 11 Bankers Trust: The Future of a Vision

1. Bankers Trust, *The Changing Times of Bankers Trust Company,* 1978, p. 32.

2. Ibid., p. 42.

3. Irving L. Janis, *Victims of Groupthink,* Houghton Mifflin, Boston, Mass., 1972.

4. Thomas Bancroft, "A Headache for Mr. Charlie," *Forbes,* Jan. 21, 1991, pp. 58–60.

5. Robert G. Eccles and Dwight B. Crane, *Doing Deals,* Harvard Business School Press, Boston, Mass., 1988, p. 138.

6. Charles W. Stevens, "Krieger to Work at Soros After Quitting Lucrative Job at Bankers Trust," *The Wall Street Journal*, Apr. 5, 1988, p. 44.

Chapter 12 The Morgan: "Doing First Class Business in First Class Ways"

1. Longstreet Hinton, John Meyer, and Thomas Rodd, *Some Comments about the Morgan Bank*, 2d Printing, Morgan Guaranty Trust, September 1985, pp. 15–16. The best historical sources are Vincent P. Carosso, *The Morgans: Private International Bankers, 1854–1913*, Harvard University Press, Cambridge, Mass., 1987; and Ron Chernow, *The House of Morgan*, Atlantic Monthly Press, New York, 1990.

2. "Bank of the Decade," *International Financial Review*, January 1990. The *Review*'s staff named Morgan "Bank of the Decade."

3. Just since 1975, Morgan's interest revenue has declined from 77 percent of total revenue to 36 percent in the 1990s, as reported in Prudential Securities, *J.P. Morgan & Co.*, Aug. 7, 1991, p. 20.

4. Ibid., p. 15.

5. David Lascelles, "The Noble Hustlers of Wall Street," *Financial Times*, Dec. 1, 1986.

6. "J.P. Morgan: Banking's Class Act," *Business Month*, Dec. 1986.

7. These summary statistics were computed from Salomon Brothers, Stock Research, *A Review of Bank Performance*, 1985 and 1990 editions.

8. Chernow, op. cit., p. 636.

9. Morgan's non-LDC, nonperforming assets (including real estate, highly leveraged transactions, and all other) were only $269 million as of March 31, 1991, compared with $7.8 billion for Citicorp, $3.86 billion for Chase, and $1.49 billion for Bankers Trust. See Prudential Securities, op. cit., p. 100.

10. Hinton, Meyer, and Rodd, op. cit., provide a concise history from which the following was extracted.

11. Chernow, op. cit., chaps. 1–3.

12. Ibid., p. 159.

13. Ibid., chap. 9.

14. Much of the following history of the Morgan partners is summarized in Vincent Carosso, *The Morgan Houses: The Seniors, Their Partners, and Their Aides*. Reprinted from Joseph R. Frese, S. J. Judd, and Jacob Judd (eds.), *American Industrialization, Economic Expansion, and The Law*, Sleepy Hollow Press, Tarrytown, N.Y., 1981.

15. Ibid., pp. 8–9.

16. Ibid., p. 13.

17. Carosso, 1987, op. cit., p. 8.

18. Ibid., p. xi.

19. Ibid., chap. 24; and Hinton, Meyer, and Rodd, op. cit., p. 35.

20. Hinton, Meyer, and Rodd, op. cit., p. 50.

21. Chernow has an insightful discussion of this in *House of Morgan*. Ibid., chaps. 25 and 27.

22. Ibid., chap. 27, for a description of Guaranty Trust.

23. Detailed discussions of the merger appear in Chernow, ibid., chap. 27, and in Hinton, Meyer, and Rodd, op. cit., pp. 1–6.

24. Chernow, op. cit., pp. 532–536.

25. Hinton, Meyer, and Rodd, op. cit., p. 8.

26. An excellent discussion of Morgan's ambience that still holds in its new building appears in Robert Levering et al., *The 100 Best Companies to Work for in America*, Addison-Wesley, Reading, Mass., 1985 edition, pp. 30–32.

27. J.P. Morgan, *1990 Annual Report*, p. 4.

28. Ibid., p. 8.

29. Suzanne Wittebort, "Inside the Morgan Machine," *Institutional Investor*, July 1985, pp. 171–178.

30. Robert G. Eccles and Dwight B. Crane, *Doing Deals*, Harvard Business School Press, Boston, Mass., 1988, chap. 2.

31. Chernow, op. cit., p. 66.

32. J.P. Morgan, *1942 Annual Report*, p. 8.

Chapter 13 The Morgan: Returning to Its Roots

1. See, for example, Prudential Securities, *J.P. Morgan & Co.*, Aug. 7, 1991, pp. 32ff. This report refers to Morgan as "a unique combination of a commercial bank and an investment bank."

2. A statement of this strategy appears in J.P. Morgan, *1990 Annual Report*, pp. 2–8.

3. This change in Morgan's style was highlighted early in David Lascelles, "The Noble Hustlers of Wall Street," *Financial Times*, Dec. 1, 1986.

4. J.P. Morgan, op. cit., p. 9.

5. See Prudential Securities, op. cit., pp. 49–66.

6. Ibid., pp. 58ff.

7. Interview with bank analyst.

8. J.P. Morgan, op. cit., p. 12.

9. Prudential Securities, op. cit., pp. 111ff.

10. J.P. Morgan, op. cit.

11. Ibid., p. 7.

12. Descriptions of Morgan's partners over the years appear in Vincent Carosso, *The Morgan Houses: The Seniors, Their Partners, and Their Aides*; reprinted from Joseph R. Frese, S. J. Judd, and Jacob Judd, eds., *American Industrialization, Economic Expansion, and the Law*, Sleepy Hollow Press, Tarrytown, N.Y., 1981, pp. 5–13; and Ron Chernow, *The House of Morgan*, Atlantic Monthly Press, New York, 1990, pp. 256–262.

13. Articles describing Preston's career and management style include Neil Osborn, "The Ex-Marine Takes over at Morgan," *Institutional Investor*, Jan. 1980, pp. 57, 60; "Banker of The Year, 1983," *Euromoney*, Oct. 1983, pp. 28–32; and Gary Hector, "Morgan Guaranty's Identity Crisis," *Fortune*, Apr. 28, 1986, pp. 64–69.

14. Weatherstone is described in John Meehan, "It's a Jungle Out There for J.P. Morgan," *Business Week*, Jan. 29, 1990; Janet Lewis, "Can a Nice Guy Really Run the Morgan Bank?" *Institutional Investor*, May 1990, pp.82–89; and John Meehan et al., "Mighty Morgan," *Business Week*, Dec. 23, 1991, pp.64–69.

15. A summary description of this senior management group appears in Prudential Securities, op. cit., p. 45–46.

16. Ibid., p. 111.

Chapter 14   What Have We Learned? Winners and Losers

1. Stephen I. Davis, *Managing Change in the Excellent Banks*, St. Martin's Press, New York, 1988, pp. 4–5.

2. Christine Dugas and Greg Steinmetz, "John Reed of Citicorp: Can He Hold On?" *Newsday*, July 7, 1991, pp. 55–57.

3. Salomon Brothers, Stock Research, *A Review of Bank Performance*, 1990, pp. 120–121.

4. Fox-Pitt Kelton, *New York Multinational Bank Holding Companies*, March 1991, table 9.

5. Op. cit., table 7.

6. *Harvard Business Review*, November-December 1990, p. 144.

7. Fox-Pitt Kelton, op. cit., table 7.

8. Ibid., table 7.

9. Davis, op. cit., p. 65.

10. Danny Miller, *The Icarus Paradox*, Harper Business, New York, 1990, p. 3.

11. Danny Miller and Peter H. Friesen, *Organizations*, Prentice Hall, Englewood Cliffs, N.J., 1984, pp. 94–96.

12. Ibid., p. 106.

Chapter 15   Some Other Winners
and Losers

1. Gary Hector, *Breaking the Bank*, Little Brown, Boston, Mass., 1988.

2. Richard Stevenson, "Pressure Growing on Others in California," *The New York Times*, Aug. 13, 1991, p. D6.

3. Gary Hector, "It's Banquet Time for BankAmerica," *Fortune*, June 3, 1991, pp. 69–78.

4. Ibid.

5. Ibid.

6. Floyd Norris, "For Wall Street, A Bigger Bank Is Better," *The New York Times*, Aug. 13, 1991, p. D6.

7. *Hector*, op. cit., p. 72.

8. Kelley Holland, "Banc One Passes Citicorp in Market Capitalization," *American Banker*, Jan. 2, 1991, pp. 1, 12.

9. James S. Hirsch, "Growing Ambition: First-Rising Banc One, Already Big in Texas, Looks at Other Areas," *The Wall Street Journal*, Dec. 26, 1990, pp. 1–2.

10. Steve Lohr, "The Best Little Bank in America," *The New York Times*, July 7, 1991, Sec. 3, pp. 1, 4.

11. Ibid.

12. Ibid., p. 4.

13. Robert Wrubel, "Carl Reichardt," *Financial Weekly*, Apr. 3, 1990, p. 82.

14. George Palmer, "Best in the West," *The Banker*, Feb. 1988, p. 53.

15. Wrubel, op. cit., p. 82.

16. Sanford Rose, "Big Bank Winners of the Expense Derby," *American Banker*, Oct. 30, 1991, p. 4.

17. Wrubel, op. cit., p. 82.

18. Palmer, op. cit., p. 53.

19. R. Michael Lev, "A Key to the Merger: Melding of Personalities," *The New York Times*, Aug. 13, 1991, p. D6.

20. *The Sunday Record*, Aug. 11, 1991, p. A-10.

21. Michael Quint, "First Fidelity Recast for Future," *The New York Times*, Mar. 20, 1991, pp. Dl, D7.

22. Michael Quint, "Four Formulas for Avoiding the Mess in Banking," *The New York Times*, Dec. 23, 1990, Sec. 3, p. 4.

23. Salomon Brothers, Stock Research, *Bankers Trust New York Corporation: A Stellar Stock in a Difficult Environment*, January 1991, p. 1.

Chapter 16   Bank Reform
Strategies

1. See James L. Pierce, *The Future of Banking,* Yale University Press, New Haven, Conn., 1991, for a recent review of U.S. bank regulation.

2. David B. Hilder and Wade Lambert, "Bank Cleared to Underwrite, Sell Insurance," *The Wall Street Journal,* June 11, 1991, p. 3.

3. Kenneth H. Bacon, "White House Bill on Bank Law Reform Faces Hurdles as It Goes to House Panel," *The Wall Street Journal,* May 14, 1991, p. A24.

4. Edwin B. Cox, *Bank Performance Annual, 1989,* Warren, Gorham & Lamont, Boston, Mass., 1989, p. 25.

5. James R. Barth, R. Dan Brumbaugh, Jr., and Robert E. Litan, *The Banking Industry in Turmoil,* presented to the Financial Institutions Subcommittee of the House committee on Banking, Housing, and Urban Affairs, U.S. House of Representatives, Washington, Dec. 17, 1990, p. 24.

6. Ibid., p. 123.

7. Ibid., p. 119.

8. Ibid., pp. 112ff, for an excellent discussion of these points.

9. Ibid., pp. 128–129.

10. Alan S. Blinder, "Treasury's Midterm Report Card: Shows Promise, Needs Improvement," *Business Week,* Mar. 4, 1991, p. 10.

11. Kenneth H. Bacon, "Bank Measure on Branches Clears Panel," *The Wall Street Journal,* May 23, 1991, p. A2.

12. William M. Isaac, "Cop-Out on `Too Big To Fail,'" *American Banker,* Feb. 14, 1991, p. 4.

13. Robert M. Garrison, "Community Bankers Form Coalition to Fight Treasury Plan," *American Banker,* Mar. 25, 1991, p. 10.

14. Blinder, op. cit., p. 10.

15. Henry Kaufman, "The Prospect for Banking: Demise or New Vitality?" speech, delivered before The Bank & Financial Analysts Association, Mar. 27, 1991, pp.11–12.

16. Blinder, op. cit., p. 10.

17. Kaufman, op. cit., p. 15.

18. Martin Mayer, "Too Big Not to Fail," *Forbes,* Apr. 15, 1991, p. 68.

19. Lowell L. Bryan, *Breaking Up the Bank,* Dow Jones-Irwin, Homewood, Ill., 1988.

Chapter 17   Peering into the
Future

1. Phil Roosevelt, "What's Ahead? Fewer Banks, Fewer Bankers, Fatter Profits," *American Banker,* Apr. 16, 1991, pp. 1, 6.

2. As of January 1991, the industry was estimated to have had roughly 69,000 lay-offs since the crash. At least 40,000 are likely to have been in New York.

3. Catherine Yang, Howard Gleckman, et al., "The Future of Banking," *Business Week*, Apr. 22, 1991, pp. 72–76.

4. Martha Brannigan, "Carolina Banks Conduct Talks on a Merger," *The Wall Street Journal*, June 21, 1991, p. A2.

5. John R. Wilke, "Nationwide Banking is Getting a Preview at Growing KeyCorp," *The Wall Street Journal*, May 31, 1991, pp. A1, 5.

6. James R. Barth, R. Dan Brumbaugh, Jr., and Robert E. Litan, *The Banking Industry in Turmoil*, presented to the Financial Institutions Subcommittee of the House Committee of Banking, Housing, and Urban Affairs, U.S. House of Representatives, Washington, Dec. 17, 1990, p. 29.

7. Walter Wriston, former chairman of Citicorp, thinks it would be a mistake not to consolidate more. In an interview with a *Wall Street Journal* reporter in late 1990 on how to restore the U.S. banking system, he said that the U.S. would be far better off if it copied the Canadian model, allowing a few large banks to open branches coast to coast. *The Wall Street Journal*, Nov. 12, 1990.

8. Yang, Gleckman, et al., op. cit.

9. Gregg Jarrell, "For a Higher Share Price, Focus Your Business," *The Wall Street Journal*, May 13, 1991.

10. Ibid.

11. Peter Drucker, "How to Be Competitive Though Big," *The Wall Street Journal*, Feb. 7, 1991, p. A14.

12. Noel Tichy and Ram Charan, "Citicorp Faces The World: An Interview with John Reed," *Harvard Business Review*, Nov.-Dec. 1990, p. 140.

13. Bill Atkinson, "Community Banks Try to Recruit AARP for Treasury," *American Banker*, Apr. 15, 1991, p. 10.

14. Mary Ann Gadziala, "Will Banking Reforms Be Broad Enough to Meet Realistic Needs," *American Banker*, May 30, 1991, pp. 12A, 14A, 15A.

15. Kenneth H. Bacon, "Quicker Regulatory Action to Combat Risky Banking Practices Urged by GAO," *The Wall Street Journal*, Mar. 5, 1991, p. A18.

16. "Congress vs. Brady," *The New York Times*, Mar. 31, 1991, Sec. 3, p. 2.

17. David Rosenbaum, "Fed to Fight Part of Plan on Banks," *The New York Times*, Mar. 5, 1991, pp. D1, D16.

18. John Meehan, "America's Bumbling Bankers Ripe for a New Fiasco," *Business Week*, Mar. 2, 1992, pp. 86–87.

Bibliography

1. Books

Altman, Edward, and Mary Jane McKinney (eds.), *Handbook of Financial Markets and Institutions*, 6th ed., John Wiley & Sons, New York, 1987.

Ballarin, Eduard, *Commercial Banks Amid the Financial Revolution*, Ballinger, Cambridge, Mass., 1986.

Brooks, John, *The Takeover Game*, Dutton, New York, 1987.

Bryan, Lowell L., *Breaking Up the Bank*, Dow Jones-Irwin, Homewood, Ill., 1988.

Burns, Tom, and G. M. Stalker, *The Management of Innovation*. Tavistock Publications, London, England, 1961.

Carosso, Vincent P., *The Morgan Houses: The Seniors, Their Partners, and Their Aides*. Reprinted from Joseph R. Frese, S. J. Judd, and Jacob Judd (eds.), *American Industrialization, Economic Expansion, and the Law*, Sleepy Hollow Press, Tarrytown, N.Y., 1981.

——*The Morgans: Private International Bankers, 1854–1913*, Harvard University Press, Cambridge, Mass., 1987.

Chernow, Ron, *The House of Morgan*, Atlantic Monthly Press, New York, 1990.

Cleveland, Harold Van B., and Thomas E. Huertas, *Citibank: 1812–1970*, Harvard University Press, Cambridge, Mass., 1985.

Cox, Edwin B., *Bank Performance Annual*, Warren, Gorham & Lamont, Boston, Mass., 1987, 1988, and 1989. (Three separate volumes.)

Davis, Stephen I., *Excellence in Banking*, St. Martin's Press, New York, 1985.

——*Managing Change in the Excellent Banks*, St. Martin's Press, New York, 1988.

Dutton, Jane, Ann Huff, and Paul Shrivastava (eds.), *Advances in Strategic Management*, vol. 7, JAI Press, Greenwich, Conn., 1991.

Eccles, Robert G., and Dwight B. Crane, *Doing Deals*, Harvard Business School Press, Boston, Mass., 1988.

Handy, Charles, *Gods of Management*, London, England, Pan Books, 1978.

Hector, Gary, *Breaking the Bank*, Little Brown, Boston, Mass., 1988.

Janis, Irving J., *Victims of Groupthink*, Houghton Mifflin, Boston, Mass., 1972.

Lamont, Thomas, *The Record of a Useful Life*, Harper, New York, 1933.

Litan, Robert, *What Should Banks Do?* The Brookings Institution, Washington, D.C., 1987.

March, James G. (ed.), *Handbook of Organizations*, Rand McNally, Chicago, Ill., 1965.

Mayer, Martin, *The Bankers*, Ballantine Books, New York, 1974.

——*The Money Bazaars*, Mentor Books, New York, 1985.

Miles, Raymond E., and Charles C. Snow, *Organizational Strategy, Structure, and*

Process, McGraw-Hill, New York, 1978.

Miller, Danny, *The Icarus Paradox*, Harper Business, New York, 1990.

Miller, Danny, and Peter H. Friesen, *Organizations*, Prentice Hall, Englewood Cliffs, N.J., 1984.

Mintzberg, Henry, *The Structuring of Organizations*, Prentice Hall, Englewood Cliffs, N.J., 1979.

Moore, George, *The Banker's Life*, Norton, New York, 1987.

Pfeffer, Jeffrey, *Power in Organizations*, Pitman, Boston, Mass., 1981.

Pierce, James L., *The Future of Banking*, Yale University Press, New Haven, Conn., 1991.

Ritter, Lawrence S., and William L. Silber, *Principles of Money, Banking, and Financial Markets*, 5th ed., Basic Books, New York, 1986.

Smith, Roy, *The Global Bankers*, Dutton, New York, 1989.

Sprague, Irvine H., *Bail Out*, Basic Books, New York, 1986.

Wilson, John Donald, *The Chase*, Harvard Business School Press, Boston, Mass., 1986.

2. Monographs

Bank for International Settlements, *Recent Innovations in International Banking*, April 1986.

Bankers Trust, *The Changing Times of Bankers Trust Company*, 1978.

Barth, James R., R. Dan Brumbaugh, Jr., and Robert E. Litan, *The Banking Industry in Turmoil*, presented to the Financial Institutions Subcommittee of the House Committee on Banking, Housing, and Urban Affairs, U.S. House of Representatives, Washington, Dec. 17, 1990.

Council on Financial Competition, *Investment Banking for the Middle Market*, June 1988.

Federal Reserve Bank of New York, *Recent Trends in Commercial Bank Profitability*, September 1986.

First Manhattan Consulting Group, *Investment Banking for Commercial Bankers*, Feb. 23, 1988.

Hinton, Longstreet, John Meyer, and Thomas Rodd, *Some Comments About the Morgan Bank*, 2d printing, September 1985.

J.P. Morgan, *Rethinking Glass Steagall*, December 1984.

Special Report, Financial Services/Money Center Banks, Mar. 26, 1990.

Walter, Ingo, ed., *Commercial Banks' Increasing Presence in the Investment Banking Business*, Occasional Papers in Business and Finance, no. 9, Salomon Brothers Center, Stern School of Business, New York University, 1989.

3. Journals (General Articles)

"Are Banks Obsolete?" *Business Week*, Apr. 6, 1987, pp. 74–89.

Borucki, Chester C., "The Importance of Strategic Staffing as a Component of Human Resource Management," *Human Resource Management*, vol. 22, no.3, fall 1983, pp. 297–312.

Brooks, John, "The Money Machine," *The New Yorker*, Jan. 5, 1981.

Emery, Fred E., and Eric L. Trist, "The Casual Texture of Organizational Environments," *Human Relations*, vol. 18, 1965, pp. 21–32.

"The Giants Retrench," *Business Week*, Apr. 3, 1989, pp. 94–105.

Greiner, Larry, "Patterns of Organization Change," *Harvard Business Review*, vol. 45, May–June, 1967, pp. 119–130.

Hale, David D., "Global Finance and the Retreat to Managed Trade," *Harvard Business Review*, January–February 1990, pp. 150–162.

Hambrick, Donald C., and Phyllis A. Mason, "Upper Echelons: The Organization as a Reflection of Its Top Managers," *Academy of Management Review*, vol. 9, no. 2, 1984, pp. 193–206.

————"Guest Editor's Introduction: Putting Top Managers Back in the Strategy Picture," *Strategic Management Journal*, vol. 10, 1989, pp. 5–15.

Herring, Richard J., and Anthony M. Santomero, *Corporate Structure in a World of Financial Conglomerates*, International Competitiveness in Financial Services Conference Paper, American Enterprise Institute for Public Policy Research, May 31–June 1, 1990.

"International Banking," *The Economist*, Apr. 7, 1990, pp. 5–68.

"A Survey of International Banking," *The Economist*, Mar. 26, 1988, pp. 5–76.

Tichy, Noel, and Ram Charan, "Citicorp Faces the World," *Harvard Business Review*, November–December 1990, pp. 135–144.

Tushman, Michael, William Newman, and Elaine Romanelli, "Convergence and Upheaval: Managing the Unsteady Pace of Organizational Evolution," *California Management Review*, vol. 29, no. 1, 1987, pp. 1–16.

4. Business and Financial Press

The American Banker.
The Banker.
The Bankers Magazine.
Business Week.
Euromoney.
Financial Times.
Financial Weekly.
Financial World.
Forbes.
Fortune.
Institution Investor.
The New York Times.
The Wall Street Journal.
Wall Street Transcript (1980–1990 annual publication on New York money center banks).

5. Annual Reports

Citicorp (1980–1990).
Chase (1980–1990).
Bankers Trust (1980–1990).
J.P. Morgan (1980–1990).

6. Bank Analysts' Reports

Brown Brothers Harriman:
Bankers Trust, 47, Basic Report, Mar. 23, 1987.
Banks in the Bargain Basement, *Banking Outlook,* Sept. 17, 1990.
May You Live in Interesting Times, *Banking Outlook*, Nov. 26, 1990.

Fox-Pitt Kelton:
Bank Holding Companies, March 1991.

PaineWebber:
Citicorp: A Focus on Credit Cards, *BankNotes*, Dec. 13, 1989, pp. 12–15.
Citicorp: It's Always Something, *BankNotes*, Feb. 16, 1990, pp. 4–7.
Citicorp: Momentum Is Low but Potential Is High, *BankNotes*, Nov. 6, 1989, pp. 8–11.

Prudential Securities:
J.P. Morgan & Co., Aug. 7, 1991.

Salomon Brothers, Stock Research:
A Review of Bank Performance, 1980–1990 editions.
Bankers Trust New York Corporation: A Stellar Stock in a Difficult Environment, January 1991.
Bankers Trust New York Corporation: The Most Sophisticated U.S. Merchant Bank, August 1989.
The Chase Manhattan Corporation: Will the Sleeping Giant Arise? October 1989.
Citicorp: An Analysis of Functional Business Lines in a Global Context, January 1988.
Citicorp: Problems Persist, Jan. 16, 1991.
Citicorp: The Only Clear-Cut American Bank Winner in a Pan-European Environment, January 1990.
J.P. Morgan & Co.: Excellence in Merchant Banking, March 1991.
J.P. Morgan & Co.: The Most Profitable U.S. Merchant Bank in Western Europe, February 1990.
U.S. Commercial Banking: Critical Issues in the 1990s, April 1986.

7. U.S. Government Documents

Comprehensive Deposit Insurance Reform and Taxpayer Protection Act of 1991, Report of the Committee on Banking, Housing, and Urban Affairs, U.S. Senate, 102d Congress, 1st Session, Oct. 1, 1991.

Financial Institutions Safety and Consumer Choice Act of 1991, Report from the Committee on Energy and Commerce, 102d Congress, 1st Session, Oct. 4, 1991.

8. Interviews

Approximately 350 interviews during the period from October 1987 through December 1991.

Index

About the Author

David Rogers is Professor of Management and Sociology and Chairperson of the Management Department at New York University's Stern School of Business. He previously taught at Columbia University and Yale University. His prior books include *Can Business Management Save the Cities?* and *110 Livingston Street*. He is one of a select few management analysis scholars who has successfully used in-depth, qualitative interviews with top decision makers and their constituencies to study organizations in crisis. He holds a Ph.D. from Harvard Unversity.